WAR-MAKING AS WORLDMAKING

WAR-MAKING AS WORLDMAKING

Kenya, the United States, and the War on Terror

SAMAR AL-BULUSHI

STANFORD UNIVERSITY PRESS

Stanford, California

STANFORD UNIVERSITY PRESS
Stanford, California

Printed and bound by CPI Group (UK) Ltd, Croydon, CR0 4YY

Library of Congress Cataloging-in-Publication Data
Names: Al-Bulushi, Samar, author.
Title: War-making as worldmaking : Kenya, the United States, and the War on
    Terror / Samar Al-Bulushi.
Description: Stanford, California : Stanford University Press, 2025. |
    Includes bibliographical references and index.
Identifiers: LCCN 2024007543 (print) | LCCN 2024007544 (ebook) |
    ISBN 9781503639744 (cloth) | ISBN 9781503640917 (paperback) |
    ISBN 9781503640924 (ebook)
Subjects: LCSH: Terrorism—Kenya—Prevention. | Internal security—Kenya. |
    Muslims—Kenya. | Kenya—Foreign relations—United States. | United
    States—Foreign relations—Kenya. | Kenya—Politics and government—2002-
Classification: LCC HV6433.K4 A54 2024 (print) | LCC HV6433.K4 (ebook) |
    DDC 363.325096762—dc23/eng/20240317
LC record available at https://lccn.loc.gov/2024007543
LC ebook record available at https://lccn.loc.gov/2024007544

Cover design: Archie Ferguson

Cover art: Pixabay

Typeset by Newgen in Minion Pro 10/15

And so you come and talk to me
About "Peace, Love and Unity"
Expecting me to agree
Parroting your parody
In my poetry:
Decorating your tyranny
With bouquets of perfumed words and imagery
To drive away the stench of your treachery
And hoodwink humanity.
I refuse!

—Abdilatif Abdalla, "Peace, Love and Unity: For Whom?" 1988

CONTENTS

Preface   ix

Introduction   1

1   Kenya to the Rescue? Race, Gender, and the Cultural
    Politics of Security   29

2   Securing Paradise: Race, Capital, and Suspect
    Citizenship on the Coast   57

3   Phantom Epistemologies: Navigating the Urban
    Gray Zone   83

4   Home as Thoroughfare   108

5   On Friendship and Freedom Dreams   134

    Conclusion   157

    Acknowledgments   163
    Notes   167
    Bibliography   203
    Index   233

PREFACE

When violence erupted in the wake of Kenya's December 2007 presidential elections, I was working with a nongovernmental organization (NGO) called the International Center for Transitional Justice (ICTJ) in New York. In the weeks and months after the elections, the ICTJ closely followed discussions in Kenya about accountability for the postelection violence. When Kenyans took to the streets in response to allegations that the presidential elections had been rigged, the police launched a large-scale crackdown, deploying live ammunition against the protestors. The tensions triggered older grievances over land and the unequal distribution of wealth, which political leaders framed in the language of tribe rather than class. As the violence became more organized and coordinated with the help of politicians and business leaders, reprisal killings unfolded, with the Kalenjin, Luo, Luhya, and Kikuyu populations in the Rift Valley most affected.[1] The violence was devastating: in the two months following the election, more than 1,100 people were killed and 700,000 displaced.[2]

Like other international human rights groups, the ICTJ was particularly concerned about the use of excessive force by police against the protestors. Alongside discussions about a possible case for the International Criminal Court, my colleagues stressed the importance of police reform. Euro-American donor governments and rights organizations jointly insisted on the importance of capacity-building trainings in human rights in order to rebuild public trust in the security apparatus as a key component of broader efforts to restore democracy and the rule of law.

As the ICTJ became more involved in promoting police reform efforts in Kenya, I wondered about the implications of the growing US military presence on the continent for the pursuit of these seemingly abstract ideals. President George W. Bush had announced the creation of the US Africa Command

(AFRICOM) in 2007, roughly coinciding with the US-backed Ethiopian invasion of Somalia in late 2006. But even before this, in the aftermath of the 1998 Al-Qaeda bombings of the US embassies in Nairobi and Dar es Salaam, the US State Department, through its Anti-Terror Assistance Program, had begun to channel substantial amounts of security-related foreign aid to the region. The massive influx of funds enabled the Kenyan government to create numerous domestic security bodies, including the Anti-Terrorism Police Unit (ATPU), the Joint Anti-Terrorism Task Force, and the National Counter-Terrorism Centre.[3] In the lead-up to the 2007 elections, an issue of particular concern to Kenya's Muslim minority population was the role of these new bodies in the arbitrary arrest and disappearance of Kenyan Muslims.[4]

Yet these developments exceeded the frame through which most of my colleagues approached the issues at hand. Their project was a prescriptive one driven by a commitment to accountability, whereas I sought to understand the broad political dynamics fueling and enabling police abuse. Like other human rights organizations, the ICTJ located the problem squarely within the boundaries of "the African state"—so often interpreted as a problem to be managed, and as a seemingly discrete unit disconnected from wider geographies and histories.[5] Given the political and economic pressure placed on the Kenyan government to embrace the US counter-terrorism agenda, I raised questions about how American interests and funding might be shaping the priorities of the Kenyan state, and how this could be reconciled with prescriptive calls for the rule of law. What happens when Kenyan citizens are deemed to be a security threat, and what if the US government holds more power than the Kenyan government in defining this threat? I asked. What should we make of the fact that—often under the guise of professionalization and "security sector reform"—the United States trains Kenyan police in human rights on one day, and in counter-insurgency tactics on the next?

While some of my colleagues acknowledged that this indeed presented a conundrum, most were reluctant to engage further. This hesitation, I believe, reflects a number of phenomena that have since been the focus of scholarly critique in relation to the spheres of human rights and transitional justice: first is the emphasis on technical solutions rather than political ones; second is the narrow focus on individual crimes at the expense of confronting the structural and systemic abuses born of colonialism, imperialism, and racial capitalism. By suggesting that the actions and interests of the US government should be factored in—and that police abuse would likely persist unless the US role was addressed—I was disrupting what Gregory Feldman refers to as the "agreed upon set of lenses" through which my colleagues looked at the situation on the ground.[6]

This book seeks to bring Kenya and the United States into a single analytic frame in order to shed light on political-military relationships and associations that "are often denied, covered up, or ignored," with dire consequences for the populations of East Africa.[7] While I am interested in capturing the outsized political and economic influence of the US government in Kenya today, I do not approach dynamics in Kenya as merely responsive to US directives and interests. Against theorizations of post-9/11 imperial warfare that emphasize a unidirectional imposition of power, I aim to shed light on the lived realities, histories, and politics of the populations that have become entangled in its working—demonstrating how a range of Kenyan actors, too, are making and remaking the world in the age of militarism and endless war. My goal is neither to romanticize this as a form of worldmaking "from the South," nor to pathologize it as an example of illiberal governance and democratic "backsliding." Instead, I emphasize the relationalities and interdependencies that co-constitute the contemporary world.

Partly inspired by anthropological discussions about the importance of studying "up," and by nascent scholarship on the Kenyan middle class, I gravitated toward actors and institutions in the murky "middle": rights activists, politicians, journalists, and other middle-class actors whose class position compels us to reflect critically about how power operates not simply through strategies of violence and exclusion but equally through liberal modes of inclusion and consent.[8] While policymakers emphasize political inclusion as a corrective to the historical marginalization of Kenya's Muslim minority population, one cannot talk about inclusion without confronting the ways in which the project of "security" (one that implicates liberal internationalists as much as it does security practitioners themselves) frames understandings of citizenship in relation to the imperatives of surveillance and policing. It is in this context that we can appreciate why many urban middle-class Kenyan professionals (Christian and Muslim alike) have objected to the rights *abuses* of the so-called "war on terror," but generally have *not* questioned the war on terror itself.

* * *

When I began my research, I had no idea that my father had been deported from Kenya in the mid-1970s. At the time, my father (whose birth name coincidentally was Msafiri, Swahili for "traveler") was employed as a pilot for East African Airways, based in Nairobi. It wasn't so much his Tanzanian passport that irritated the Kenyan immigration official (after all, Tanzania, like Kenya, was a member of the East African Community). Rather, it was his Arabic name. As my father recounted the story to me, the official grunted something along the lines that he was a foreigner and not an African. That he did not belong. There was no room for negotiation, as the official quickly stamped "persona non-grata" on the passport and escorted him away. He was placed on a flight back to Dar es Salaam, and from there he contacted his employers to explain what had happened, and to strategize about how he could reenter Kenya, where he and my mother were living at the time.

It was not until 2015, when my parents were planning a trip to visit me in Kenya, that I learned this story. While my father was excited about the prospect of returning to Kenya after nearly forty years away, I also sensed that he felt some trepidation. When he eventually shared what had happened, I realized that he was anxious about the possibility that he would be subjected to similar treatment this time upon arrival. Though my parents entered the country without hassle, I have since thought about how my father's encounter with the immigration official speaks to the less perceptible traces of imperial rule that, as Ann Stoler describes, settle "into the social and material ecologies in which people live."[9] To speak of debris and ruination is to capture "the degraded personhoods, the soils turned toxic, and the relations severed between people."[10] Although historians of East Africa often attribute the introduction of racial thought to British colonial rule, there is a risk here of bypassing the significance of the Omani empire in laying the groundwork for racial and ethnic division, in part through its sponsorship of Arab planters and Indian financiers, and through its role in the slave trade.[11]

In many ways, this project is informed by my own entanglement in this complicated history. While on the one hand I am inspired by my own family's biography of transregional connections across the Indian Ocean, there is a risk of feeding into myths of ethnic fluidity and racial harmony unless we situate these connections in relation to economic, political, and legal infra-structures of power and inequality.[12] My positionality as an upper-middle-class woman with ties to vastly different geopolitical locations (Tanzania, Oman, the United States) has contributed to my own shifting identifica-tions and experiences of distance and proximity. While I conducted most of my research in Kenya, I locate Kenya in relation to other people and places that extend beyond the boundaries of the nation-state in an effort to foreground—rather than silence—histories of interrelation.[13] In this sense, the book departs from traditional area studies scholarship that elides his-torical routes of interconnectivity and that dislocates Africa from the wider world.[14] It is precisely histories of mobility, encounter, and exchange that have engendered transregional solidarities that pose a threat to empire.[15] British colonial officials could not handle such mobile cosmopolitans as they could national independence fighters, "for their geographic mobility often meant crossing imperial and departmental jurisdictions, stretching the capacity of empire for political intelligence."[16]

Today, the fact that intelligence and policing bodies increasingly cooper-ate across borders has implications for the ability of scholars (particularly those of us who do not fit the traditional mold of the white male researcher) to study and shed light on these very security partnerships.[17] For example, I considered traveling to Uganda with hopes of interviewing Kenyans who were held on suspicion of their involvement in the twin bombings targeting crowds who had gathered to watch the 2010 World Cup Final. But I was discouraged by the knowledge that others before me had been arrested, had been prevented from entering Uganda, or had subsequently been banned from reentering Kenya.[18] As I conducted my research, I reflected on the fractured information that my interlocutors relayed about these and many other incidents: no one knew for certain which governing body had made the decision to arrest, to deport, or to ban from entry. The idea that foreign powers increasingly shaped the security landscape—but in ways that were dif-ficult if not impossible to track—was the source of tremendous unease. This visceral domain of paranoia and uncertainty offers critical insights into the lived experiences of imperial power in East Africa today. I myself regularly made strategic decisions about whom *not* to interact with, and where *not* to travel, based on my embodied awareness that my actions were likely monitored by multiple governments. At the same time, I was compelled to critically assess the potential consequences of my research for my interlocutors, who themselves experienced far more insidious forms of surveillance and policing. This has inevitably shaped the story that I tell in the coming pages, including my decision to rely primarily on the use of pseudonyms. What some have referred to as an "ethics of obfuscation" may necessarily entail making decisions *not* to write about particular people or topics, or to consciously omit certain details.[19]

The book is the product of fifteen months of ethnographic research in Kenya (with the bulk of research conducted between 2014 and 2015) and two decades of studying ongoing political dynamics in the region. Although I draw from interviews and participant-observation primarily with Kenyan Muslims living in Nairobi and Mombasa, this is not a conventional ethnography. I am indebted to work in political anthropology, Black studies, African studies, transnational feminism, decolonizing international relations, critical geopolitics, critical security studies, American studies, and postcolonial and subaltern studies. As an interdisciplinary work, the book foregrounds race, gender, and the geopolitical imagination, attending to the power of spectacle and representation in making and remaking worlds. As an ethnography, it explores how differently situated Kenyan Muslims make sense of their experiences of surveillance and criminalization in the context of the war on terror. While the counter-terror apparatus strives to pacify and contain, this book sheds light on strategies of safety and solidarity that gesture to new modes of worldmaking and belonging.

WAR-MAKING AS WORLDMAKING

INTRODUCTION

IN JANUARY 2007, Abdul and Zaina were stopped at the Kenya–Somalia border as they attempted to cross back into Kenya.[1] Like hundreds of others, they were fleeing the violence that ensued in the wake of the US–backed Ethiopian invasion of Somalia the month before. Although they could not have known it at the time, they stumbled directly into a transnational border operation in which Ethiopian and Somali ground troops, with American air support, were channeling all those fleeing the war zone toward an area of the border where many would then be captured.[2]

Zaina, a Tanzanian citizen from the town of Moshi, had moved to the Kenyan coastal city of Mombasa a few years earlier to be with Abdul after they married. Abdul ran a mobile phone repair shop in Mombasa, but his business was struggling. The pair decided to relocate to Mogadishu in 2006 with hopes of finding a more stable source of income. At the time, the Islamic Courts Union (ICU) had brought a degree of stability to Somalia when it took control of large parts of the country. But everything changed at the end of the year when foreign powers invaded, dislodged the ICU, and imposed a new government.

At the border, the two were separated and interrogated about Abdul's alleged connections to Al-Qaeda. Kenyan authorities seized Abdul's Kenyan passport and ID card, claiming he was on a "most wanted" list of terror suspects, and transported him to Nairobi where he was detained for weeks without charge or trial. Zaina was held at the border for ten days along with other women and children before she was taken to Nairobi. As Abdul was shuffled between different police stations, he was interrogated, tortured, and denied the opportunity to communicate with family members or a lawyer. Kenyan authorities doubted his documented ties to his homeland, arguing that the lack of public outcry about his arrest suggested that he was not in fact a Kenyan citizen.

At least 150 men, women, and children from nineteen countries were arrested at the Kenya–Somalia border that month. Abdul and Zaina were among the roughly eighty-five people who were eventually transported from Kenya to Somalia and Ethiopia in the first publicly documented instances of mass "renditions" (or government-sponsored abductions) in Africa.[3]

Among friends and family members of each of the detainees, the stories that circulated made painfully clear the dangers of being a traveling Muslim in the world today, even in a region characterized by longstanding kinship ties and trade practices defined by cross-border mobility. Abducted from their police cells in the middle of the night, the detainees were flown, blindfolded and handcuffed, on three different privately chartered flights to Baidoa and Mogadishu, and then transferred to prisons in Addis Ababa where officials from the FBI awaited them.[4] Upon her release, Zaina recounted the details of their transfer from Nairobi to a local human rights organization:

> It was so chilly and drizzling. We were bundled into pickups and driven to the runway. I saw very many people, including women kneeling. The lady called [Tuweil] Kamilya (UAE) was sitting down crying. The men were blindfolded and had their hands handcuffed behind their backs. Their feet were chained. I was led to the group of women and ordered to kneel there too. An armed man came to me and pulled down my headscarf to cover my eyes as had been done [to] the other women. There were many children. Some were crying loudly. The men had black hoods covering their heads. We stayed kneeling there for quite some time, until our knees ached. We were then taken up to the plane, still blindfolded. I could however see through my headscarf as it was of a light material . . . It was very scaring, cold, and wet.[5]

Once she reached Ethiopia, Zaina was held in a prison cell with approximately twenty women and children, including a Swede, a Sudanese, and a Yemeni.[6] Doctors soon discovered that Zaina was pregnant, and she was released in April. Pressure from human rights groups eventually compelled the Kenyan government to repatriate Abdul and other Kenyan nationals back home. Despite the fact that a military court in Ethiopia had cleared Abdul and his compatriots of any wrongdoing, the Kenyan government maintained an aura of suspicion around the returning men, declaring that they would remain under government surveillance. National newspapers reproduced the government's rhetoric of suspicion, referring to the men as "Osama agents" whose return "stirs painful memories" of the 1998 Al-Qaeda attacks in Nairobi and Dar es Salaam.[7]

The story of Abdul and Zaina—like those of the other detainees—remains largely overlooked by those who have sought to document the costs of the so-called "war on terror."[8] Yet the events of early 2007 point to the rise of "entangled pacifications," wherein seemingly marginal Global South states play increasingly critical roles in the shape-shifting topography of global policing, counter-insurgency, and war.[9]

In the wake of the toppling of the Islamic Courts Union and the rise of the Somali militant group Al-Shabaab, the Kenyan state increasingly conducted militarized operations in partnership with foreign powers. Kenyan Muslims took note of this shift: 2007 was an election year, and the country's Muslim minority population united around shared concerns about their safety in the face of invasive, often deadly police tactics. Surveillance, arbitrary arrests, and disappearances had become common practice despite the efforts of activists to forestall the enactment of new laws that would grant the police discretionary powers to fight "terror." Of growing concern was the US–trained Anti-Terror Police Unit (ATPU), a special branch of the Kenyan police that has since become notorious for its plain-clothes death squads that operate with impunity.[10] By 2012, accounts of the ATPU's phantom-like power circulated in homes, schools, mosques, and community spaces, raising alarms about the spread of elusive policing practices that disappeared their relatives and neighbors. These terrifying practices persist today: on good days, missing relatives or neighbors eventually appear in court. On bad days, their bodies are found in un-marked graves outside of town.

War-Making as Worldmaking chronicles how life is lived in a place that is not understood to be a site of war, yet is often experienced as such by its targets. In the past twenty years, the very notion of a "war zone" has become porous, as the US military has sought to avoid full-scale invasions (e.g. Iraq and Afghanistan) in favor of discrete, targeted actions in places where the United States has not of-ficially declared war (e.g. Somalia).[11] The US military often refers euphemistically to these more recent sites of engagement as "gray zones," claiming that they do not easily map onto traditional conceptualizations of war or peace. In a strik-ing parallel to colonial-era framings of Africa as the 'dark continent,' American military officials conceive of Africa *in its entirety* as a "gray zone" characterized by complex, volatile political environments in need of "stabilization."[12]

This book challenges the tendency among policymakers to normalize such obfuscating language, and instead aims to shed light on the very real human impact of the so-called war on terror in East Africa. As we shall see, this region has become an experimental ground for temporally open-ended and spatially dispersed military operations, and for the redistribution of risk from US forces to US–trained African forces.[13] This has had the effect of expanding both the geographies and technologies through which life is regu-lated and policed. While we have some knowledge of the destructive effects of drone strikes in Somalia, the growing role of specially trained "counter-terrorism" police forces in places like Kenya demands that we adopt a wider geographical lens when reflecting on the lived realities of the war on terror in the region. From surveillance, disappearances, and extra-judicial killings to the infiltration of social and family life, the reliance on counter-insurgency strategies means that the war on terror is as much a form of police action as it is military engagement.[14] Against theorizations of war as an exceptional event that is distinguishable from "peace" time, I approach the war on terror as a multilayered, protracted assault on the dignity and safety of its targets. My focus is *not* on spectacular instances of violent destruction, but on how people learn to live through the structural, incremental, and less visible forms of violence that have their own devastating effects.[15]

* * *

Kenya has long been a key ally of the United States in the war on terror. Considered a frontline state against terrorism, it hosts the largest US embassy in Africa and is among the top recipients of US security assistance on the continent.[16] Between 2010 and 2020, the US Department of Defense provided $400 million in counter-terrorism "train and equip" support, enabling Kenya to vastly expand its security architecture.[17] This has emboldened the Kenyan state to perform and enact its power in new ways. In October 2011, for example, the Kenyan military dispatched 2,000 troops across the border into Somalia in the name of quelling the threat posed by Al-Shabaab. The invasion came at a time when the International Criminal Court (ICC) investigations into crimes related to the 2007 postelection violence risked jeopardizing Kenya's image abroad, and risked reigniting ethnic tensions within the country. War became a distraction from both issues—uniting the country against a common enemy, and shifting international attention away from its problems at home by declaring itself a leader on matters of peace and security abroad.

I situate my analysis of Kenya within a broader geopolitical landscape that has embraced military solutions to political problems. While the war on terror serves as a driving force for this shift, a wider lens enables us to account for the ways in which security orientations permeate the realm of transnational governance, from democracy promotion to humanitarianism and development assistance, displacing critique of militarism and military power.[18] Indeed, the rise of what scholars refer to as "liberal," "feel-good militarism" is made possible by invocations of law and legality, and by a rhetoric of nonwar (e.g., "peace enforcement," "stabilization," "human security") that simultaneously authorizes more war even as it obscures war's brutal realities.[19]

This new military "normal" enables African states to expand their policing, military, and surveillance capabilities and to crack down on dissent, all in the name of security.[20] In 2021, for example, (then) President Uhuru Kenyatta proudly boasted that Kenya's police-to-population ratio had jumped by nearly 40 percent since he assumed office in 2013, reaching the highest level in Kenyan history.[21] Meanwhile, covert paramilitary units armed and trained by the US Central Intelligence Agency have been granted the license to engage in offensive operations including renditions, disappearances, and alleged summary executions.[22] But because Kenya is understood to be a "democracy" in the formal sense of the word, these developments prompt minimal scrutiny, particularly among its Euro-American donor-partners. It is the seeming normality and naturalization of the state of affairs in Kenya that guides my interest in the entanglement of militarism, imperialism, and liberal-democratic governance in East Africa today. At a time when political analysts are attempting to understand the wave of military coups that have swept the continent in recent years, we have been presented with theories of democratic "backsliding," wherein the democratic underpinnings of those countries that have experienced a coup are understood to be in crisis. With a primary focus on the idea of a crisis, the liberal-democratic project itself is overlooked and presumed to be an inherent good. While analysis of the coups is important, one effect of the sudden flurry of media coverage is a concomitant glossing over and naturalization of the purportedly good/stable/ functioning democracies—like Kenya—against which the coup-ridden states are being measured and evaluated. The fixation with the seeming exception risks depoliticizing the norm—reducing "democracy" to civilian rule and the practice of holding regular elections.[23]

This book invites us to reexamine the norm by grappling with the increasingly blurred boundaries between civilian and military power in a democratic state that is often upheld as a model for neighboring states. It is only by turning away from the seeming exception that the tensions inherent to the liberal-democratic project become clear: in 2010, Kenya adopted a new constitution that was widely celebrated for its commitment to human rights and political inclusion—seen as a positive step for the country's historically marginalized Muslim minority population. At the same time, the government was becoming more deeply ensconced in a war against a purported enemy in the figure of the Muslim "terrorist," prompting discriminatory and abusive practices against Muslims in the name of security. These two seemingly conflicting dynamics are in fact closely related: it is precisely Kenya's professed commitment to democracy that simultaneously works to legitimate and obscure its embrace of militarism and war.

Having ascertained that political leadership and recognition on the global stage are increasingly associated with a readiness to act in the name of "security," the ruling elite in Kenya has harnessed the country's participation in the war on terror to produce new fantasies, emotions, and subjectivities about its place in the world. Specifically, I consider how performance, ritual, and public relations strategies work to distinguish Kenya as a leader on matters of peace and security, and to cultivate popular support domestically for militarized responses to "terror." War-making and race-making are intricately entangled, as Kenya's rise as a self-appointed leader is predicated on its seeming exceptionalism—on its standing *apart* from the "typical" African country plagued by violence and instability.[24] So too is it predicated on an articulation of difference in the form of the suspected terrorist.

While Kenya has emerged as a regional power with growing international visibility, left largely unexamined are the simmering low-intensity assaults on the dignity and safety of its Muslim minority population at home. As Kenyan Muslims increasingly link their own experiences of policing and criminalization to the subjugation of Muslims elsewhere in the world, some characterize the war on terror as a war on Islam and Muslims. Rather than pathologize these articulations as evidence of "extremism," this book asks how they give meaning to histories of interrelation that transcend national and regional boundaries, constituting a worldmaking practice. My interest is therefore not in religious or cultural enmity, but in modes of political consciousness and solidarity that form contingently in relation to power.[25] By tracing how Kenyan Muslims learn to live through the blurred boundaries between war and peace, the political and the criminal, citizen and suspect, I tell a story not simply of abject oppression, but of solidarity and survival as differently situated people remake a world made and unmade by militarism and endless war.

Moving the Center

For East African Muslims, memories and experiences of the so-called war on terror date back not to September 2001, but to August 1998 when Al-Qaeda militants attacked the US embassies in Nairobi and Dar es Salaam. What transpired in the weeks and months following these attacks closely resembled what unfolded after 9/11: government officials declared "radical" Islam to be a threat and authorized mass arrests and interrogations of Muslims. Hundreds of FBI agents landed in the region, triggering the largest investigation that the FBI had ever conducted outside of US borders.[26]

Soon thereafter, the Clinton administration sought to strengthen its relationship with the Kenyan state as a security partner, negotiating access to Kenyan military facilities on the coast and to air bases across central Kenya. Already a regional hub for multinational corporations and the United Nations, Kenya's position on the Indian Ocean afforded the US unhindered access to South Asia and the Middle East. In the wake of the withdrawal of US forces from Somalia in 1993, Kenya's shared border with Somalia was of equal interest. The Kenyan government was quick to capitalize on this interest: in 2005 the Bush administration awarded Kenya the largest slice of security assistance from the East African Counter-Terrorism Initiative (EACTI). At $88 million, Kenya's share represented nearly 90 percent of the total for the region.[27]

Because of the power imbalances that characterize Kenya-US relations, Kenya is often dismissed as a proxy or mercenary force in what many conceive of as an American-led theater of operations. There is no question that the Kenyan state has been on the receiving end of considerable political and economic pressure to embrace the counter-terrorism agenda.[28] Yet the consequence of a US-centric frame is that Kenyans are rendered to the background, understood only as victims, perpetrators, or unthinking proxies for US interests. This book questions traditional conceptualizations of empire as a unidirectional imposition of power and instead weaves together multiple scales of analysis to demonstrate the ways in which seemingly marginal "peripheries" are bound up in, and constitutive of, our geopolitical present.[29] In asking how a different vantage point might generate new thinking about contemporary imperial formations, I aim to read empire otherwise, as "a story of multiple plots in small places."[30]

To this end, *War-Making as Worldmaking* engages calls to decolonize the study of world politics by pluralizing our subjects of inquiry.[31] Even as I recognize the vast power discrepancies at play, political dynamics in the region are hardly reducible to the needs and interests of US empire. As Tanzanian President Julius Nyerere observed of dominant geopolitical analysis in the 1960s, "Every possible attempt is made to squeeze African events into the framework of the Cold War or other big power conflicts." This implies, he says, "that Africa has no ideas of its own and no interests of its own."[32]

Indeed we have a growing understanding of the ways that political leaders in Asia and Africa—in the postindependence period of the 1960s—were "asserting their right to define themselves and their relationship to the universe from their own centers" across the Global South.[33] In his book *Moving the Centre*, Ngũgĩ wa Thiong'o foregrounds the ways that novelists and literary critics like himself sought to claim their own space and "to name the world for ourselves."[34] In the political realm, as Adom Getachew documents, figures like Kwame Nkrumah, Nnamdi Azikiwe, and Julius Nyerere were not just anticolonial nation builders, but *worldmakers* who strove to radically reconstitute the racialized, asymmetrical global order.[35]

Yet scholars have also come to appreciate the need for a more sober accounting and assessment of worldmaking from the South. As Ella Shohat observes, "the 'wretched of the earth' are not unanimously revolutionary, nor necessarily allies to one another."[36] The lingering tendency to romanticize subaltern populations in their encounters with imperial power comes with the risk of obscuring ambiguity, contradiction, and competing visions of the future. I am interested in grappling with Kenya's contradictory positioning in relation to South–South solidarities: it is a place that once symbolized a threat to empire in the bold figure of the Mau Mau freedom fighter, but that—since obtaining independence—has been a counter-revolutionary force rather than a revolutionary one.[37] As Kenyan political elites are increasingly complicit in the normalization of militarism and endless war, we are witnessing the rise of a contradictory genre of Pan-Africanism that celebrates symbolic affirmations of Africa even as it reproduces racialized global power formations that differentially expose Africans to violence, exploitation, and premature death.[38] There is perhaps no better recent illustration of this than the Kenyan government's announcement in August 2023 that it would lead a multinational armed intervention in Haiti, the world's first independent Black nation born of organized slave rebellion. That Kenyan officials frame their decision to intervene in the language of Pan-Africanism serves as an important reminder that what were once utopian visions of unity and liberation are today entangled in imperial war-making and the reproduction of racial hierarchies.

With these contradictions in mind, this book emphasizes worldmaking's simultaneous productive and destructive potential—at times charting emancipatory futures, while at times exclusionary and violent.[39] Embracing multiplicity and heterogeneity, I conceive of worldmaking as a situated practice that maps and remaps relations of power at different scales and localities.[40] This necessarily *pluriversal* framing includes but extends beyond the largely masculinist domain of the political elite to encompass variously positioned actors whose day-to-day practices, desires, and imaginings co-constitute ongoing processes of making and remaking the world.

War-Making as Worldmaking

Launched in the aftermath of the 9/11 attacks in New York and Washington, the US-led war on terror violently inaugurated a new global order. War-making became a form of worldmaking, as the theater of operations gradually expanded to encompass and transform the lives of people in Afghanistan, Iraq, Syria, Yemen, East Africa, and the Sahel. In Africa, the defense department's establishment of a dedicated regional combatant command (AFRICOM) has been integral to establishing new spaces of control, characterized by a diffuse, networked model of empire that facilitates access to markets and resources through the threat (and in many cases the full-fledged deployment) of violence.[41] Djibouti is host to AFRICOM's largest presence on the continent, with roughly 4,000 US and allied personnel. Kenya hosts four US bases, including an airfield in Wajir, a contingency location in Laikipia, and cooperative security locations in Mombasa and Manda Bay, the latter of which serves as a launch pad for US drone strikes in Somalia and Yemen.[42]

In the past two decades, investigative journalists have worked tirelessly to collect and circulate information on the workings of the US military on the continent, focusing especially on AFRICOM.[43] Thanks to their efforts, we have learned about the network of military bases and detention sites that constitute the infrastructural backbone of counter-terror operations in Africa. From Mali and Niger to Kenya and Djibouti, we now have maps of logistics hubs, forward operating sites, cooperative security locations, and contingency locations—all of which help us conceptualize AFRICOM as a geopolitical assemblage whose everyday functioning across time and space facilitates imperial power.[44]

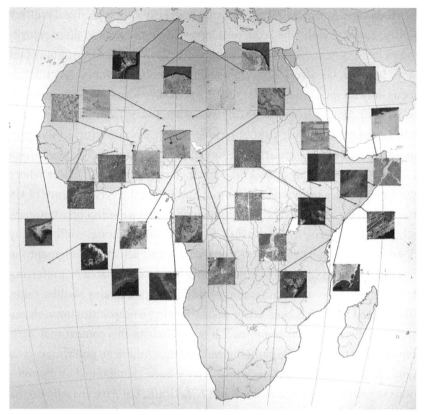

FIGURE 1. Satellite image artistic map of US military presence in Africa.
Source: Tricontinental Institute for Social Research.

Yet such maps privilege a god's-eye view of a monolithic war machine seemingly detached from history, and from the lived realities of populations on the ground.[45] In many ways, the establishment of AFRICOM merely formalized a longstanding practice on the part of the US government of building infrastructures of terror in the form of specially trained militarized forces that were designed to protect US interests on the continent. During the Cold War, as Mahmood Mamdani documents, the United States supported armed groups around the world, "from RENAMO in Mozambique to UNITA in Angola, and from contras in Nicaragua to the mujahideen in Afghanistan—through third and fourth parties." Framed in the language of "low-intensity conflict," this was, as Mamdani argues, terrorism by another name.[46]

Today, the American left's fascination with US technological and military power, coupled with "the seduction of revealing the hidden politics lurking in large systems," leads many critics to believe that the most important story lies with US actors.[47] Yet the tendency among anti-imperial critics to focus only on the United States constitutes its own form of US exceptionalism.[48] *War-Making as Worldmaking* asks what a view from East Africa can tell us about the shifting configurations of imperial warfare, as more and more operations are conducted by so-called partner forces.[49] Across Africa today, the United States relies on African security forces in places where the United States is not officially at war, and where the very presence of US troops is likely to raise eyebrows. This demands that we reflect on what some scholars characterize as *diffuse, distributed,* or *elastic* empire—differentially distributed, opaque networks of technologies and actors that augment the reach of the war on terror to govern more bodies and spaces.[50] "Preferring to frame its interventions as temporary and limited," explains Madiha Tahir, "the United States has been adept at distributing its capacities for violence among networks of collaborators."[51] It is precisely in this context that African security forces—once pathologized by Euro-American policymakers as symbols of violence and state failure— have been championed as the solutions to instability. In Somalia, it is not Americans, but Africans who do the bulk of the fighting. In addition to providing funding for a "peacekeeping" operation composed (at its height) of 22,000 troops from across East Africa, the United States has trained specialized police units in Somalia to engage in counter-terror operations against Al-Shabaab.[52] The idea underpinning US strategy, to borrow the words of Adekeye Adebajo, is that "Africans do *most* of the dying, while the US does *some* of the spending to avoid being drawn into politically risky interventions."[53]

As it has with other countries across the Global South, the United States has adeptly exploited African states' reliance on foreign credit to ensure their cooperation on security matters.[54] The fact that Kenya's national debt has multiplied fivefold since 2013 means that its decision-making has inevitably been shaped by concerns about access to credit.[55] The growing investment in militarism across the continent must therefore be situated within an understanding of the continued significance of finance imperialism.[56]

Despite the economic meltdown brought about by the COVID-19 pandemic, African governments expanded their military spending in 2021 to almost $40 billion, with Algeria, Egypt, Morocco, Tunisia, Libya, Nigeria, Kenya, South Africa, Angola, and Uganda featured among the top ten spenders.[57] Yet there remains a tendency to privilege political economy as *the* primary frame of analysis, obscuring the fact that war-making is as much a cultural field of representation and meaning as it is a violent project.[58] Africans are not simply "cannon fodder" in an externally driven war, but in some cases seek meaningful participation in the war on terror as a universal endeavor.

In *The Universal Enemy*, Darryl Li offers a broad analytical framework that can help us reflect on the ways in which populations worldwide are *culturally* conscripted into the contemporary project of "good" vs. "evil." "In this world order," he writes, "there have been two primary ways of characterizing armed conflicts: localized ethnic wars and a globally threatening militant Islam. The former, marked by the 'post-Cold War' is presented as peripheral, regionally confined, and destabilizing in only a distant sense, producing hordes of hapless victims in need of mercy and management . . . The latter, framed as 'post-9/11' produces the figure of the terrorist as the one the world must band together to defeat."[59] In short, the war on terror is a civilizational project undergirded by carefully constructed distinctions between those who purportedly belong to civilized humanity, and those who do not. [60]

With this backdrop in mind, Kenya's growing assertiveness on matters of security is not merely a political-economic calculation, but equally a universalist claim and aspiration of belonging to the "civilized" world.[61] As mentioned earlier, Kenya is one of only a few African nations to have attained relative prominence in Western media and scholarly circles, often constituting the standard against which observers measure the so-called successes and failures of other African states.[62] The country's seeming exceptionality was apparent in global reactions to the 2007 postelection violence: when former UN secretary general Kofi Annan traveled to Nairobi to mediate peace talks, he lamented the possibility that Kenya could become yet another "failed" state: "We can't let this happen to Kenya! We'd seen a lot of destruction in the region—Rwanda, Somalia, Sudan, Darfur—and Kenya had been the safe haven for refugees. And suddenly Kenya itself was going!"[63] So invested was the Kenyan ruling class in maintaining an image of the country as exceptional that at this political juncture they established Brand Kenya and hired US lobbying and public relations firms for damage control.[64]

As the figure of the Muslim "terrorist" now threatens the carefully crafted image of the country as a beacon of stability, Kenyan politicians have sought to demonstrate leadership in the domain of security. By cultivating a popular common sense about security-as-responsibility, Uhuru Kenyatta and William Ruto have positioned themselves as moral actors in the crusade against "evil," reframing the war on terror as "*our* war"—one that Africans have a responsibility to fight. Kenya is not alone in this regard: Uganda's President Yoweri Museveni was the first African leader to visit the World Trade Center site after 9/11, offering $150,000 to the victims of the attacks.[65] Uganda was also the first to send troops for the African Union peacekeeping mission in Somalia (AMISOM).[66] More recently, Rwanda has gained international visibility for its "proactive" approach to security since it unilaterally deployed troops to Mozambique.[67] Yet the ongoing tendency to confine African states to the periphery of global affairs means that we have few analytical tools to grasp the increasingly central role these states play in shaping the norms and politics of post-9/11 militarized interventionism.[68] Theories of the post-colonial "predicament," combined with methodological nationalism and lingering Eurocentrism, have led scholars to cede analysis to mainstream international relations (IR) theory.[69] My objective is neither to celebrate nor condemn, but to create an analytical opening: rather than confine the actions of the Kenyan state to the more limited domain of "African politics," I wrestle with imperial entanglements.

War-Making as Worldmaking contends that only by writing Kenya into the story of post-9/11 imperial warfare can we trace the extension of militarized interventionism into ever-expanding domains. Historically, Kenya has been a key contributor to UN peacekeeping missions, but has been reluctant to dispatch troops to operations with an enforcement component. The decision to invade Somalia in 2011 therefore signaled an unprecedented shift toward a more aggressive foreign policy—one that was shaped as much by national and regional political considerations as by wider forces.[70] Prior to the invasion, for example, the Kenyan military had been the object of ridicule as an "untested," largely ceremonial army. Several of my interlocutors made note of this, describing jokes exchanged among political leaders and military officials from neighboring states that indirectly questioned the masculinity of the Kenyan military on the grounds that it had yet to engage in "real" combat. Hardly unique to Africa, and inevitably inflected by colonial-era practices that questioned the masculinity of the colonized, Kenya's nascent assertions of militarized masculinity are unfolding in a broader geopolitical context that equates political leadership with experience on the battlefield.[71]

As we shall see, the war on terror has become a site for geopolitical performances and contestations of manhood as Kenyan leaders work to project an image of strength and virility at home and abroad. Alongside a dramatic surge in military spending (in 2016, Kenya's military budget of $993 million stood at more than double the spending of neighboring Uganda and Ethiopia *combined*),[72] the Kenyan state has displayed a missionary zeal as it presents itself as a moral force ordained with special responsibilities on questions related to security.[73] As Kenyan officials reframe the war on terror as one that Kenyans have a duty to fight, we become attuned to the emergence of paternalistic assertions of authority and superiority over purportedly uncivilized others both near and far. This compels us to consider the significance of rhetoric, symbols, and meaning—and more specifically, the centrality of gender alongside race in shaping the symbolic bases of power on the global stage. Rather than maintaining a more limited focus on political economy, this book pushes us to expand our conceptualization of the geopolitical to encompass the realms of imagination, emotion, and popular culture.[74] Indeed, affect and emotion (be it fear of the enemy, or desire for security) are constitutive of—rather than epiphenomenal to—our increasingly militarized world.[75] The performative dimensions of geopolitics are not simply a façade, but are themselves part of the making and unmaking of the world through war.

Africa, Islam, and the Geopolitics of Race

The rise of violent attacks by Al-Shabaab is an uncontested reality, one that has had a devastating impact on the lives of people in the region.[76] Euro-American policymakers generally interpret this violence as the product of local forces, and in doing so mobilize racialized ideas about Africa as a violent place. The effect of such interpretations is to disassociate the United States and Europe from any clear relationship to the violence. In problematizing the very notion of the "local," and of bounded, territorial units, this book approaches Kenya, Somalia, and East Africa more broadly *not* as discrete geographies, but as relational constellations, meaning that any expression of violence in a particular place is necessarily imbricated in wider dynamics.

"Africa" as idea and geopolitical space has long been racialized as the quintessential other in the global order of nation-states.[77] The concept of the "failed" or "fragile" state, on the one hand, and the need for "good governance," on the other, constitute two strands of a conceptual vocabulary that international policymakers regularly employ in relation to Africa, often to warn about conflict, instability, and the threat of terrorism.[78] While on the surface such terms may appear to be free of racial tropes, scholars have demonstrated the ways in which they are both informed by and *produce* racialized ideas about place and space.[79] As Siba Grovogui documents, the history of colonialism requires that we scrutinize the racialization of international knowledge, wherein the so-called international community is generally portrayed as white, male, Christian, and guided by morality and neutrality.[80] Indeed, the discursive production or "cultural coding" of certain peoples and places is deeply informed by racialized notions of governance, rationality, and civilization.[81]

We have a rich understanding of the significance of race and racism in legitimating imperial exploitation and intervention. But we must look beyond the mere functionality of race to empire.[82] Approaching race as a dynamic and contingent field of power, we become attuned to the ways in which political and cultural identities emerge in dialogue with the legacies of colonialism, racial capitalism, and the enduring myth of white supremacy. Given that colonial rule was as much a cultural project as a system of economic exploitation and dispossession, postcolonial African societies continue to be haunted by racialized notions of hierarchy that view whiteness "as the standard for all that is good, true, and valuable."[83] In Kenya, writes Christine Mungai, "whiteness remains an organizing philosophy, an epistemological tool, and a way of being in the world, normalized so thoroughly as not to need white bodies to enact it." To grapple with this reality, as Jemima Pierre observes, is "not to deny or diminish the significance of other processes of identification such as ethnicity, nationality, religion, gender, and class."[84] Rather, it is to recognize "how even in independent Africa, race is the modality through which many of these identifications continue to be structured."[85]

The war on terror offers fertile terrain to explore continuities and transformations in processes of racial formation, attending to the cross-cutting and multiscalar dimensions of race and racialization in Africa today. While racialized constructions of threat represent one side of the war on terror, less explored are the ways in which race is refashioned and reproduced through warfare. With the rise of the post–Cold War security framework of "African solutions to African problems," racialized evaluations of African capacity to govern have been extended to the domains of war and policing. Militarism in the name of "global peace and security" has thus become a vehicle to symbolically overcome the degradations of colonialism, racism, and white supremacy. In many ways, the Kenyan state's growing visibility as a leader in the war on terror is suggestive of a new, more equal global order in which African states can overcome their racial and categorical subordination on the world stage.

Here, the mobilization of the *idea* of equality is imbricated in the reinforcement of lingering racialized distinctions and structural *in*equalities—a hallmark of racial liberalism. [86] Indeed, Kenya's rise as an exceptional Black nation is predicated on rewriting racism as a question of bias and prejudice rather than as a systemic problem rooted in political economy. It is also predicated on distancing itself from fellow Africans, including the figure of the purportedly foreign Muslim terrorist. This offers an opportunity to deepen our understanding of the historically specific ways in which race is imbricated with religion, as information economies about "unstable" Africa intersect with those focused on "violent" Islam.[87] There is growing scholarly interest in tracing the legacies of colonial-era mappings of alterity about Blackness and Islam, and about Africa and the Arab world—racial, religious, and geographic categories that are often simplistically portrayed as distinct from one another.[88] These artificial divides are reinforced in university settings by area studies frameworks that fail to account for geographies of interrelation. Despite the close conceptual association between Islam and the Arab world, there are in fact far more Muslims in Africa: the continent's population is, by conservative estimates, well over 40 percent Muslim.[89] Yet the tendency in both policy and scholarly circles to speak of "Islam in Africa" has the effect of positioning Islam as an alien, external force on the continent, and of reifying colonial geographic imaginaries that are fundamentally out of step with reality.[90]

This book thus attends to the ways in which race and religion emerge as geographic conceptualizations of difference, signifying not only "status in a hierarchy from superior to inferior but also a spatial positioning as *in-* or *out-of-place.*"[91] Informed by scholars of transregionalism and Indian Ocean studies, I employ a relational approach in order to foreground cross-border connections and circulations, as well as to consider the co-constitution of ideas about difference across multiple, overlapping geographies and histories.[92] Indeed, careful consideration of Kenyan history reveals the need for critical analysis of Africa's racial others beyond the Black/white binary. During the colonial era, British officials employed a racial system that constituted Asians and Arabs as "immigrant" races. These populations (and, for a brief period, Isaaq and Harti Somalis) were generally classified as nonnative citizens alongside Europeans, thereby blurring the boundaries between the colonizer and a minority *among* the colonized.[93] These "subject races," as Mamdani refers to them, do not fit neatly into conventional histories.[94] While on the one hand they enjoyed legal protections not afforded to their "native" counterparts, they also point to the presence of an internal "other."

The war on terror has repoliticized notions of foreignness and belonging, leading Kenyans to question those "who racially might be seen as the same," but who are "associated with some 'morally suspect' past (colonial), space (borders), or activity (political party or social movement)."[95] These incongruous, conflicting conceptions of Africanness and Blackness are in tension with the monolithic constructions that dominate discussions of Africa in the US academy, reminding us of the instability of Blackness/Africanness as categories of social organization.[96] Inattentiveness to this complexity has the effect of overdetermining homogeneity, obscuring the myriad historical, political, and cultural influences *within* the continent, and *between* Africa and the wider world.[97] In Kenya, Muslims of different racial and ethnic backgrounds (e.g., the Giriama, the Swahili, the Somali) have long negotiated racism, ethnocentrism and questions of hierarchy, status, and power.[98] Yet racial identities and meanings have always been fluid in practice, shifting according to context. Today, Kenyan politicians and national media outlets actively shape public fears by fostering a Christian majority sensibility that associates the country's Muslim minority population *as a whole* with suspicion and violence.[99] What it means to be Muslim in Kenya today is therefore increasingly shaped by a shared subjection to surveillance and criminalization that links otherwise divergent experiences of racialization. Indeed, as government officials warn of a network of suspicious actors emanating from a seemingly unified Muslim "community," racialized distinctions *within* Kenya's Muslim minority population collapse to produce the global figure of the threatening Muslim.[100] The racialized figure of the person who "looks Muslim" has appeared on "wanted" posters across Kenya, from billboards to national newspapers. While security experts speak in abstract terms about the need to stabilize "volatile" environments, this book aims to shed light on the visceral, embodied dimensions of the war on terror. As suspicion and surveillance increasingly structure daily life for Kenyan Muslims, social interactions and routine movements are shaped by the perception—and sensation—of being watched, or what Ronak Kapadia refers to as the "sensorial life of empire."[101]

Colonialism and the Long War on "Terror"

In April 2014, seven months after a devastating Al-Shabaab attack at Nairobi's Westgate Mall, the Kenyan state launched a large-scale security crackdown. Roughly 6,000 security personnel descended on the Somali-dominated Nairobi neighborhood of Eastleigh with the declared objective of identifying individuals with potential links to Al-Shabaab. Nearly 4,000 people were arrested as security forces raided homes and businesses, harassing and extorting residents. In a move that elicited harsh condemnation from international human rights organizations, the government converted a sports stadium into a detention center where more than 1,000 people—mostly Somali—who lacked "proper" documentation were detained for questioning.

Kenyans were quick to draw parallels between "Operation Usalama Watch" and colonial-era tactics of collective punishment against the anticolonial Land and Freedom Army (popularly referred to as "Mau Mau"). Former prime minister and opposition figure Raila Odinga disparaged the state's collective punishment tactics, arguing that they reminded him of "the Mau Mau days, when the British handled the Kenyans in the most brutal and inhumane manner imaginable."[102] Writer and political analyst Nanjala Nyabola decried what she characterized as the state's "failure to exorcise the demons of colonialism and its rapacious desire to create categories and assign benefits of belonging."[103] Meanwhile, poet and activist Shailja Patel was one among many who employed the hashtag #kasaraniconcentrationcamp, invoking memories of the British government's confinement and captivity of Mau Mau "terrorists" in the 1950s and 1960s.

Kenya is haunted not only by the enduring scars and memories of British imperial violence, but also by postcolonial practices of state terror against Kenyans of Somali descent whose loyalties were questioned in the early days of independence. Confronting a separatist movement with Pan-Somali aspirations, Kenya's first president, Jomo Kenyatta, launched a counter-insurgency campaign to quell the movement, erecting detention camps for suspicious persons. The government's framing of what became known as the Shifta War (1963–67) as a fight against "rebels," "bandits," and "terrorists" allowed it to justify the collective punishment of ethnic Somalis. Paramilitary units originally formed by the British were permitted to arrest, detain, and shoot suspected rebels, as well as to confiscate livestock and property.[104]

Despite a negotiated end to the conflict in 1967, the state of emergency remained in place until 1991, meaning that northern Kenya fell within a separate legal regime for nearly thirty years. During this time, the military's attempts to disarm locals took the form of state terror, with the massacre of at least 2,000 ethnic Somalis by the Kenyan military near Wagalla in 1984 as the most prominent example.[105] The Kenyan state was therefore not only born of violence, but specifically born of anti-Somali violence.[106] "In holding whole communities responsible for acts of lawbreaking," observes Keren

Weitzberg, "the state not only criminalized Somali populations writ large, but also obscured the forces that generated insecurity in the north, many of which were tied to regional and geopolitical dynamics."[107] Today, Kenyans racialized as Somalis—much like those racialized as Arab or Swahili (mixed-race, or Afro-Arabs)—continue to be singled out from their fellow citizens as they struggle to acquire national ID cards and are subject to police terror.

A view from East Africa therefore offers a productive opening to deepen our understanding of "national security" as a racializing project grounded in coloniality.[108] This book interrogates the seeming newness of contemporary security regimes by foregrounding the ways in which colonial logics and hierarchies of humanity are implicated in what some refer to as *the long war on terror*.[109] To come to terms with these entangled histories is to wrestle with British imperial strategies of containment and their postcolonial afterlives.

Living With Surveillance and Criminalization

Lost in the sensationalized, pathologizing rhetoric about "violent extremism" are the daily realities of Kenyan Muslims whose lifeworlds have been transformed by regimes of surveillance and repression. Drawing on ethnographic research in Nairobi and Mombasa, I look beyond the spectacle and performance of "security" to shed light on how life is lived by those caught in the crosshairs of the war on terror. I approach these urban landscapes not as exceptional spaces singularly defined by police violence and oppression, but as lively terrains where differently situated actors learn to live with—and at times contest—criminalization and surveillance.

During my extended period of research (2014–15) I was based in Mombasa, a predominantly Muslim coastal city. There, I spent the bulk of my time with civil society and rights activists, as well as politicians, journalists, and university students. While my middle-class interlocutors are by no means the most vulnerable, their class position renders them relatively well positioned to challenge counter-terror policies and to mobilize support from politicians and international organizations when needed. They are pious liberals, in the sense that they regularly articulate their commitment to equality and human rights.[110] But the war on terror is reconfiguring understandings of these ideals: first, by reframing conceptualizations of citizenship in relation to the imperatives of policing and security, and second, by bringing to the fore tensions between legal equality and majority sensibility that have long been at the heart of states that profess to be secular and democratic.[111]

While Kenya is formally a secular state, Kenyan political culture is imbued with Christian language, imagery, and sensibilities.[112] Since independence, political leadership has been dominated by Christians, with Muslims obtaining a few high-level appointments for the first time under Moi's presidency.[113] In the 1990s, church leaders stood at the forefront of antigovernment protests and demands for social justice, often working alongside Muslim leaders and activists. In the past twenty years, however, American Pentecostal and evangelical organizations have exerted more influence on national politics.[114] This has had a marked impact on public life: church leaders have narrowed their interests to evangelical concerns rather than broader social, political, and economic issues, and Kenyan political culture—particularly in the wake of Al-Shabaab attacks—has become more overtly hostile to Islam and Muslims.

It is with dynamics such as these in mind that scholars like Saba Mahmood insist that the discourse on religious liberty and national minorities must be reexamined beyond the limiting lens of human rights.[115] As Kenyan leaders invoke the frame of national security to defend the country against Muslim "terrorists," popular conceptions of law and order come to be infused with racialized forms of suspicion, rendering human rights—at best—an abstract ideal, if not a secondary concern. Here, the central question is not about equal citizenship, but about how understandings of "good" or "bad" citizenship are configured in dialogue with the purported imperative of security. By actively questioning the criminalization of their fellow Muslims, many of my interlocutors disrupted the image of the compliant subject privileged by the security state, rendering themselves suspect citizens.

In the days and weeks immediately following the 2007 border operation, for example, rights activists from the Nairobi-based Muslim Human Rights Forum (MHRF) went from one prison to another in Nairobi to inquire about the whereabouts of those being held as suspects. Where possible, they met with affected family members. In 2012, I spoke with Al-Amin Kimathi, one of the activists, who explained that it was in this context that he and his colleagues developed an understanding of who was making what decisions, who was released, and who remained behind bars. Eventually, they managed

African Express Airways

PASSENGER MANIFEST
(I.C.A.O. ANNEX 9 APPENDIX 2)

Aircraft _5Y—AND_
(Registration Marks and nationality)

Flight No. _XU527_   Date _20/1/07_

Point of Lading _NAIROBI_
(Place and Country)

Port of Unlading _MOGADISHU_
(Place and Country)

SURNAME AND INITIALS	SEX				FOR USE BY OWNER OR OPERATOR ONLY	PCS	WT	FOR OFFICIAL USE ONLY
	M	F	C	I				
1 Hussein Ali	✓							
2 Sakataa Enam	✓							
3 Said Shifa	✓							
4 Nur Gurare	✓							
5 Sharff Jamal	✓							
6 Suma Soliman	✓							
7 Abdi Abdullah	✓							
Sesfalct Sima		F						
7 Osman Moh'd	✓							
8 Salam Idris		F						
10 Salsang Ngana	✓							
11 Jamal Abdal	✓							
12 Ahmed Hassan	✓							
13 Moh Mavllani	✓							
14 Rashid Moh'd	✓							
15 Tafa Balssta	✓							
16 Lamr Talal	✓							
17 Pabab Lami	✓							
18 Elli-eta Tasin	✓							
19 Aclement Cana	✓							
20 Ibrum Othmanu	✓							
21 Nur Moh'd 'ali	✓							
22 Ali Abdi	✓							
23 Abukaa Hure	✓							
24 Al Husein Ahmed	✓							
25 Osman Abdi	✓							
26 Moh'd Hassan	✓							
27 Salama Abdur	✓							
28 Abdulahi Moh'd	✓							
29 Albasan Sulmen	✓							
30 Moh'd Lable	✓							
31 Dahir Sugaru	✓							
32 Mohamed Adan	✓							
33 Abdirizak Adan	✓							

FIGURE 2. African Express Airways passenger manifest, January 2007.
Source: Al-Amin Kimathi. Reprinted with permission.

to obtain a copy of the flight manifest that contained not only the names of the passengers but also the name of the private carrier that transported them from Nairobi to Mogadishu. This was a critical step in the effort to update families about the whereabouts of missing loved ones, and to trace the opaque web of actors that constitute the counter-terror apparatus in East Africa.

But Al-Amin's inquiries had come at a heavy price: his activism had garnered scrutiny by the police, and his movements and interactions were closely monitored. In 2010, he was detained when he traveled to Uganda to observe the court hearing of Kenyans who were being held as terror suspects in the aftermath of an Al-Shabaab attack in Uganda's capital city of Kampala. Al-Amin was imprisoned for one year in Uganda, during which time the Ugandan government never presented his lawyers with evidence against him. While the role of the US government in the decision to detain him was never proven officially, Al-Amin was certain of their involvement. He lives with a noticeable unease about his continued subjection to surveillance and remains troubled by the opacity of power that governs his daily life. Here, the body and the senses become guides, as Al-Amin experiences this seemingly phantom power with a materiality that leaves little doubt about its existence, and he learns, instinctively, to anticipate new risks.[116] In chronicling these kinds of experiences, this book foregoes authoritative big-picture assessments in favor of micro-histories, turning to the daily realities of those who navigate the disorienting effects of the war on terror. What emerges is an enlivened geography, a contested sphere, and real places with real people—compelling us to think more critically about imagined geographies of empire that remain limited to abstract metaphors of "black sites" and "everywhere war." Recognizing the wide-ranging constraints under which my interlocutors live their lives, I focus less on explicit forms of resistance, instead privileging the more subtle, everyday negotiations that make and remake the world in an era of hypermilitarism and endless war.

Book Overview

War-Making as Worldmaking aims to bring into dialogue people and places otherwise thought of as independent of one another, arguing that Kenya offers unique insights into the making of our geopolitical present. Drawing on recent theorizations of contemporary imperial formations, I emphasize collaboration and complicity rather than a single, unidirectional imposition of power.[117] The story I tell is one that attends to the ways that colonial pasts bear on the contemporary period, one that privileges multiple and layered histories rather than linear trajectories. So too is it attentive to a shifting geopolitical landscape and the potential waning of US hegemony.[118] At a time when the African continent is once again interpreted by analysts in the Global North through the lens of great power rivalry, there is a risk of overlooking Africans themselves, for whom the geopolitical is not merely an analytical backdrop but an everyday reality animated by embodied knowledge formations and practical calculations about safety and survival in an increasingly militarized world. It is through insights into day-to-day experiences and imaginations that we become privy to the multiple, heterogeneous processes by which worlds are made and remade.

Chapter 1 explores the growing symbolism attached to the Kenyan military in the context of its role in the war on terror. It foregrounds the significance of the Shifta War (1963–67) and the inheritance of colonial-era counterinsurgency practices for the rise of the Kenyan security state. Returning to the present day, I situate Kenya's invasion of Somalia within a broader geopolitical landscape that privileges militarized interventionism in the name of security. I focus specifically on the cultural politics of security—namely, the systems of signification and meaning that cultivate popular support for the war on terror. I consider how race is refashioned through warfare, as African security bodies that were once the subject of critique are increasingly embraced as the solutions to insecurity. Militarism and intervention are also gendered phenomena: whereas the mobilization of militarized masculinity in Kenya has traditionally been limited to national politics, the war against Al-Shabaab has become a site for geopolitical performances and contestations of manhood. The country's highly-trained special operations forces, as dramatized in the Kenyan blockbuster political thriller *Mission to Rescue*, are increasingly central to the government's efforts to project an image of strength and virility at home and abroad. Yet tensions and contradictions abound between the symbolism attributed to the military and its actual operations, as ordinary Kenyans contend with the myriad effects of militarism in their daily lives.

Chapter 2 traces the processes by which worlds are made and remade on the Kenyan coast, arguing that the coast is central to the making of Kenya as place-in-the-world. The significance of race should not be understated, and yet is defined by a paradox. On the one hand, the war on terror has repoliticized longstanding debates about race and indigeneity, as coastal Muslims racialized as Arab and Swahili have long been viewed as question-ably indigenous and out-of-place. Yet it is precisely these notions of difference that produce the coast as an Oriental wonderland and exotic space, making it an integral part of the national tourism industry. I therefore highlight the Kenyan state's growing preoccupation with branding as a strategy to market Kenya as exceptional, unlike the "typical" African country plagued by vio-lence. Branding is entangled in colonial nostalgia and the (re-)production of colonial whiteness as it works to project an image of tranquility and stability in which Europeans are at home in a foreign land. My goal is to wrestle with the continuity of colonial dynamics in a context where formal colonial rule has long been abolished. While the war on terror has reinscribed colonial-era ideas about Arab, Swahili, and Somali "foreigners" in Kenya, these racial dynamics must be situated within a consideration of enduring structures of white supremacy both in and beyond this former settler colony.

The subsequent chapters offer ethnographic insights into the lived expe-riences of the war on terror in the cities of Nairobi and Mombasa. Against imaginative geographies that delineate between Somalia as a space of war and Kenya as a space of peace, I tell the story of differently situated Ke-nyan Muslim middle-class men and women who have been caught in the crosshairs of the war on terror. Everyday life for these populations entails a series of negotiations, wherein the spaces they inhabit, the friendships they forge, or the questions they ask become the source of suspicion and scrutiny, prompting new modes of surveillance and policing. This serves as a critical reminder that AFRICOM's network of military bases is only one aspect of a much wider set of power formations that intimately shape the lifeworlds of people across the continent. Indeed, the fixation with the overtly militaristic in the form of the US military base comes with the risk of obscuring far more expansive and enduring forms of intervention whose reverberations in daily life are more subtle but not necessarily less destructive.[119]

As US–trained Kenyan police employ military tactics of tracking and targeting potential terror suspects in quotidian urban spaces, chapter 3 sheds light on the doubt and uncertainty that haunt Kenyan Muslim activists as they contend with the expansive and illegible forms of police power authorized by the war on terror. While the Kenyan police have long been agents of abuse and objects of public speculation, the phantom-like power of supranational actors has contributed to the spectral quality of police violence, as deaths and disappearances become entangled in rumors and conspiracy theories about the geopolitical actors and interests at play. In this context, activists are compelled to weigh long-term calculations (documentation and account-ability) against short-term ones (safety), drawing on their own everyday geopolitical knowledge to navigate shape-shifting urban landscapes. If the Kenyan state and its partners collect information to anticipate risk and guide decision-making, so too must the subjects of surveillance and policing make calculations about their own security as they grapple with what it would mean to remake a world unmade by war.

Chapter 4 illustrates how surveillance and militarized incursions into the homes of Muslim families rupture the sense of place that constitutes home.[120] My interest in the homeplace is informed by postcolonial, Black, and transnational feminist scholars who have foregrounded the political stakes in what is defined as public or private, and relatedly, what kinds of sites are relevant for our understandings of war, empire, and geopolitics. As counter-insurgency doctrine embraces a population-centered approach to policing, bodies and spaces previously coded as private or feminine are increasingly targeted—whether coercively through police raids of the home, or socially through calls to monitor children for signs of "extremism." The focus on family and domesticity is not a new phenomenon, but recalls colonial-era tactics of gendered and racialized modes of social engineering and control. Drawing on ethnographic research with a Nairobi family, I illustrate how the purportedly apolitical sphere of the home has become a site in which to make sense of the war on terror, and is itself a target *of* the war on terror, intimately entangled in relations of power and violence. But the war on ter-ror does not wholly define life inside the home: centering the everyday, we become attuned to new modes of worldmaking and belonging.

Chapter 5 tells the story of two young men whose friendship is integral to their ability to make sense of the world they inhabit, and to find humor and solace in the context of racialized surveillance and criminalization. The chapter situates the micro-interactions of daily life against the backdrop of the war on terror's portrayals of young Muslim men as one-dimensional characters whose "manipulated minds" are purportedly in need of monitoring and reform. In doing so, I demonstrate how the war against Al-Shabaab is waged on highly gendered terrain: contemporary calls to rehabilitate (primarily male) "violent extremists" present decontextualized figures stripped bare of the social and political histories that animate their lived realities. The lens of friendship offers insights into the struggle to redefine and remake the self, as young Muslim men draw on reciprocal relations of care and trust in order to process their experiences, and to survive in the midst of paranoia and uncertainty. For young men like Fahad and Mohideen, friendship has become a practice of freedom, an imaginative place in which to process shared experiences, and to chart new possibilities for the future.

As Kenya prepares to lead a multinational intervention in Haiti, I conclude by suggesting that the government's decision to lead such a mission further illustrates that militarized interventionism has become a key terrain in which African states negotiate their relationship to the wider world. Again, we are compelled to attend both to political economy and to the art of politics—namely, the significance of rhetoric and performance in producing particular ideas and meanings about Kenya as place-in-the-world. That Kenyan officials invoke the language of Pan-Africanism to legitimate foreign intervention points to shifting significations with regard to race and Blackness, wherein the affirmation of some is inextricably entangled in the policing of others. While some critics have accused Kenya of choosing imperialist servitude over Pan-African solidarity, I reiterate my assertion that we must examine Kenya and the United States *together* in a highly interactive, albeit unequal, political field. The Kenyan state's embrace of militarized interventionism in the name of Pan-Africanist solidarity, and the US government's championing of "African solutions" cannot be interpreted independently of one another. Each has become a part of the other's remaking.

KENYA TO THE RESCUE?

Race, Gender, and the Cultural Politics of Security

ON SEPTEMBER 21, 2013, Al-Shabaab's assault on Nairobi's up-scale Westgate Mall captured the world's attention. The four-day standoff between the attackers and Kenyan security forces was widely covered by global media outlets, many of which offered minute-by-minute accounts of the siege. Witnesses to the attack were quoted stating that the suspects "looked like Somalis" and that they "chanted 'Allahu Akbar' as they entered the building." The spectral and racialized image of the terrifying Muslim quickly came to the fore, while the Kenyan security apparatus emerged as a paternal figure as armed men in uniform ushered women and children out of the building to safety.

As citizens rushed to blood donation centers to support the victims, Kenyans invoked the notion of shared blood, constituting the nation as a biopolitical collective.[1] In a televised address to the nation, President Uhuru Kenyatta declared that the overwhelming response to the appeal for blood donations showed that "deep inside, where it counts, we are one indivisible national family."[2] Kenyatta's use of the metaphor of family stirred up feelings of paternal care and protection, which were then replicated by commentators in national newspapers and on social media. In the words of an editor at one of the country's main news outlets, *The Standard,*

> Unknown to the cowardly attackers, the whole incident brought out the
> real picture of who we are; a country full of valiant patriots ready to do

anything to safeguard the "glory of Kenya, the fruit of our labour." I saw it every time a plainclothes police officer emerged from the scary cavern, proudly carrying a toddler in his one hand as eyes darted this way and that, while the other hand firmly clutched a pistol. The defiance I saw in those eyes, unmoved by the staccato hail of bullets from the attackers, was for me the true image of Kenya. And just when I thought the cop would walk out after ensuring the child was out of harm's way, he would break into a run back to what seemed like a scene from a bloody movie, later to emerge triumphantly holding aloft a lady—and all this armed with just a pistol! Comrades, the valour of those gallant heroes was a summation of who we are; a people unbowed.[3]

Both the state and national media sought to shape Kenyan interpretations of the tragedy. While many people were perplexed by the ineptitude that characterized the initial response, and incensed by reports that the police and military were caught looting during the siege, official rhetoric extolled the bravery and heroism of the security forces. The subtext of much of the state's discourse was that an explicitly Christian morality guided the country's defense against what it characterized (in relation to Al-Shabaab) as "the very epitome of evil."[4] The power to name and classify the violence of Al-Shabaab in this way, while framing its own violence as a force for good, worked to police the boundaries not only of legitimate/illegitimate violence, but also of permissible politics. As some wondered whether Kenya had opened itself to attack because of its decision to deploy troops to Somalia, questions began to surface from opposition figures like Raila Odinga about whether the military should withdraw from Somalia. The government was quick to push back, conflating opposition to the war with support for Al-Shabaab.[5]

In the decade since the Westgate attack, the state has devoted considerable time, money, and effort to shape understandings of Kenya's role in the war on terror. This chapter traces the growing symbolism attached to the Kenyan military in public life, exploring the role of rhetoric and performance, and the politics of race and gender. I focus especially on Uhuru Kenyatta's administration (2013–22), during which time retaliatory attacks by Al-Shabaab were on the rise and popular debate came to be shaped by concerns about (in)security. Given that wars are fought not only on the battlefield but equally on the home front in the realm of memory and popular sentiment, my interest is in the ways that Kenyans have been culturally conscripted to support "the Kenyan military in its war on terror."[6] As scholars have documented, the cultivation of pride and innocence around the military is sustained through careful censorship of the tragedies and brutalities of actual war.[7] Alongside imposing censorship, states often work to suppress public memory of such tragedies—either with alternative narratives or by vacating (effectively silencing) discussion of the tragedy from public speech. Noteworthy here is that the reopening of Westgate Mall in 2015 was not accompanied by a public commemoration or memorial, meaning that the 2013 tragedy joined a long list of silenced pasts in what Yvonne Adhiambo Owuor refers to as a "national propensity to amnesia for 'bad things.' "[8]

Indeed, the 2013 attack was a dramatic blow to the image of the Kenyan military, once considered "a beacon of professionalism and honor in an otherwise seamy and degenerate sea."[9] As Patrick Gathara observes, Westgate "cruelly exposed the rot in the military and completely exploded the myth of discipline, competence and integrity."[10] Since that time, the state has actively worked to replace narratives of corruption and incompetence with narratives of bravery and heroism. It is increasingly apparent that the war on terror is not simply about defeating Al-Shabaab, but equally about summoning a new national consciousness that is united around the figure of the soldier-hero.

Kenyans have been invited to attend the now-annual Kenya Defence Forces Day, where they have the opportunity to publicly show their support for soldiers fighting on the front line. The Kenyan military parade has become a highlight of the annual Jamhuri Day celebrations at Nyayo Stadium, where thousands gather to celebrate Kenya's independence. These celebratory and commemorative "security rituals" are integral not only to the production of nationalist sentiment, but also to constructing a felt relationship to the war on terror as "*our* war."[11] Meanwhile, national newspapers regale their readers with stories of the valor of the Kenyan military replete with images that provide a "front seat view of the battles our gallant soldiers have fought and the sacrifices they have made."[12] Betraying the news media's close ties to the government, some of these publications promote state-produced accounts of the war. In a two-page spread published in a Christmas weekend edition of the *Daily Nation* in 2019, for example, readers learned of the heroic story of a team of elite soldiers who quelled a group of Al-Shabaab militants on the "most dangerous beach on earth." The paper's dramatic rendering of this operation was a plug for a newly released book, *The Soldier's Legacy*—the second to be published by the military detailing the valiant role of its forces in the war against Al-Shabaab.[13]

Scholars and analysts have observed that political and military leaders across the world have appropriated the logics of the post-9/11 war on terror to consolidate their power and pursue their own strategic interests.[14] In Kenya, the state has increasingly deployed the military within the country for security operations in what many characterize as a breach of the 2010 Constitution.[15] In this context, troops have assumed law enforcement roles ranging from the installation of roadblocks; securing critical infrastructure such as the Likoni ferry in Mombasa; employing stop-and-search operations in Mombasa, Wajir, and Garissa; and arresting and detaining individuals identified as terror suspects.[16]

But we have yet to adequately explore the cultural politics of security— namely, the systems of signification and meaning that cultivate popular support for war. During the course of my research, I was continually struck by how few Kenyans questioned the war against Al-Shabaab. In the words of one of my interlocutors, "war is simply in the background." But, he elaborated, "when it does come to the foreground, few people question it because it is seen as a war of necessity." Coming to terms with how this came to be requires that we attend both to the significance of Kenyan history, and to more recent attempts by the Kenyan military to capture the imagination and loyalties of the Kenyan public.

The Home Front

Writing about the US context, Catherine Lutz has shed important light on how the war terrain extends beyond the battlefield to include the home-front.[17] The ability of political elites to justify war, she writes, depends on "cultural deployments, affective munitions, and mental recruitments" that address the general public's anxieties about violence and intervention.[18]

A key element of this process is to "build a sense of responsibility toward the war." The goal is "to create a sense of collective project, to convince the public that a war is 'our war,' these young people 'our soldiers,' better yet 'our' boys and girls."[19] Equally important in the context of the war on terror, as Talal Asad observes, is that the public comes to believe that "there is an essential difference between war (civilized violence) and terrorism (barbaric violence)."[20] Asad emphasizes the construction not only of certain forms of violence as legitimate, but equally of the everyday sensibilities and dispositions that accompany and sustain these constructions.

What we learn from Lutz, Asad, and others is that militarized societies need not involve direct or overt dominance by the armed forces.[21] This is not to dismiss the clear significance of coercive power, but rather to point to the more subtle and diffuse ways that militarism permeates and shapes society, contributing to what Lutz refers to as "military normal."[22] It requires that we look beyond the more obvious domains of security institutions themselves to examine militarism's cultural and ideological dimensions, from the glorification of military action in popular culture to the belief that a militarized approach is fundamental to security.[23] Alongside the political economy of militarism are the attitudes and values that support war, and that come to structure social relationships in ways that are informed by hierarchies of race, class, gender, and sexuality. As Amina Mama and Margo Okazawa-Rey observe, these more enduring features often "precede the explicit emergence of military regimes and conflicts, and persist long after 'peace' has officially been declared."[24]

Kenya has long been in search of a national hero.[25] Despite the centrality of the Land and Freedom Army (often referred to as "Mau Mau") to the struggle for independence, it continues to elicit contradictory sentiments among Kenyans. When Jomo Kenyatta assumed power in 1963, he upheld the ban on the movement and sought to bury memories of the resistance, despite the fact that he himself had been imprisoned by the British for his purported role in the struggle.[26] Even among those who take pride in the history of the Mau Mau revolt, they have wrestled with the uncomfortable reality that there were as many Kikuyu who fought alongside the colonial government as there were who fought against it.[27]

Since Kenya embarked on its war against Al-Shabaab, the military has become increasingly visible in public life, and the state has sought to cultivate popular nationalist sentiment around the figure of the soldier-hero. State-produced documents recognize the importance of nurturing and sustaining public support for the military and its operations in Somalia—demonstrating a clear understanding of the connection between popular consent and the state's ability to continue to make war.[28] In fact, there is a correlation between *declining* support for the war and the government's growing *investment* in strategic communication initiatives to promote a more positive perception of the Kenya Defence Forces (KDF) and their role in Somalia. Opinion polls conducted by Afrobarometer in 2016 indicate that while a majority of Kenyans believed the KDF operations in Somalia were necessary, this figure decreased between 2014 (66 percent) and 2016 (57 percent). "At the same time," according to the report, "fully half of Kenyans support KDF withdrawal from Somalia—a paradoxical finding that may suggest the population's mixed feelings about the operation."[29] The timing of the Afrobarometer survey is significant, as interviews were conducted in September–October 2016, roughly nine months after a deadly Al-Shabaab attack on a Kenyan military base in El Adde, Somalia, that claimed the lives of roughly 150 Kenyan soldiers.

The El Adde assault was (and remains) the deadliest attack on the KDF since it invaded Somalia, and represents the largest military defeat since Kenya gained independence in 1963. In the immediate aftermath of the attack, Kenyans were troubled and perplexed by the government's failure to disclose information about what had occurred. On social media, they coalesced around the hashtags #IStandWithKDF and #KDFOurHeroes to demand that a public memorial be held in honor of the troops who died. In Uhuru Park in Nairobi, they congregated and paid their respects to the fallen soldiers. In many ways, the attack in El Adde and the public's response to it was a critical event, prompting new and difficult questions about the violent realities of war.[30] Since that time, the state has actively worked to shape public perceptions of the military and to maintain a sense of responsibility toward defeating Al-Shabaab. This compels us to wrestle with the amount of cultural and imaginative labor required to socialize populations into accepting the logic and necessity of war.

In what follows, I situate the rise of Kenya's "military normal" within a longer history of governing strategies that have blurred the boundaries between civilian and military power. Just as British colonial authorities employed counter-insurgency strategies against the anticolonial Land and Freedom Army, the newly independent Kenyan state relied on emergency powers to quell a secessionist movement along the border with Somalia. The government's framing of what became known as the Shifta War (1963–67) as one between the purportedly lawful, rational state, on the one hand, and "irrational," "lawless" rebels on the other allowed it to justify the collective punishment of Kenyans of Somali descent. Violence was at the heart of the performance of Kenya's newfound sovereignty, and this history is integral to our ability to appreciate how Somalis have long been racialized as threatening—making them a natural enemy against which the Kenyan state, decades later, defines and constitutes itself once again.

Yet the political context in which Kenya is today embracing militarized intervention is notably different from the era of the Shifta War. In the early days of independence, African leaders were generally wary of intervening in the affairs of other states. As I outline later in the chapter, this changed in the early 2000s when the African Union abandoned the principle of noninterference long upheld by its predecessor, the Organization of African Unity. With the rise of the UN doctrine of the "responsibility to protect," intervention was explicitly depoliticized and reframed as a moral and ethical obligation. In this context, the very African security bodies that were once the subject of critique by Western policymakers for contributing to violence and instability have been championed as the solution to insecurity. This offers an opening to reflect on the ways in which race is resignified in the context of war, as African soldiering has acquired symbolic and political value since the onset of the war on terror. It is therefore critical that we situate Kenya's intervention in relation to a wider set of actors and histories, and in doing so, deepen our understanding of Africa's relationship to race-making and the construction of modern Blackness.[31]

Militarism and war are also gendered phenomena, contributing to particular understandings of masculinity and femininity.[32] Whereas the mobilization of militarized masculinity in Kenya has traditionally been limited to national politics, the war against Al-Shabaab has become a site for geopolitical performances and contestations of manhood, making gender and sexuality central to the cultural politics of security. Before its invasion of Somalia, Kenya had been derided and even mocked for "punching below its weight" in regional politics.[33] Today, the readiness of the Kenyan military to deploy to the front lines of the war on terror has been central to the government's efforts to project an image of strength and virility at home and abroad. In the Kenyan blockbuster film *Mission to Rescue*, for example, viewers are invited to dwell on the valor and hardship of an elite all-male squad who prevail in their mission to rescue hostages from the hands of Al-Shabaab.

Ultimately, as we shall see, the cultivation of pride and support for the military is in tension with the material realities of war, and with the relations of inequality that continue to structure the global order. Kenya's embrace of "African solutions" has the effect of reinforcing existing racial hierarchies, as the deployment of African troops to the front lines of war reproduces racially differentiated vulnerability to premature death. As soldiers are sent home in body bags, or return burdened with lasting injuries and war-related trauma, the questions and contestations of ordinary Kenyans reveal cracks in the official war story. Thus the government's attempts to make and unmake new worlds through war is itself productive of other worlds. It is by accounting for these dialectical dynamics that we become attuned to the pluriversal processes by which worlds are made and remade.

Colonial and Postcolonial Inheritances

If we are to adequately grasp the rise of militarism in Kenya today, we must study its historical antecedents. As Amina Mama reminds us, "colonial rule was in its essence military rule":

> The military might of imperial and colonial armies was buttressed by a far-reaching array of technologies of power. These ranged from brutal forced labour and taxation systems to sophisticated psychological and cultural strategies, including abduction, eviction and land seizure, hostage-taking, incarceration, rape and torture, to which women and men were variously subjected. These strategies worked together to create complex tapestries of consent and coercion, terrorizing local populations and orchestrating com-

plicity, and provoking anti-colonial resistance. The examples of Algeria dur-ing French colonialism . . ., British colonialism in Kenya . . ., the Belgian occupation of the Congo . . . and Rwanda . . . illustrate how colonial regimes relied on military force and modern weaponry, deployed along with a for-midable array of political, economic, and social technologies, to militarize the societies they conquered and governed. These extended far beyond the barracks, into the very fabric of peoples' lives.[34]

Colonial military structures served the broader purpose of conquest and extraction, protecting classed, gendered, and raced interests. Militarism was not simply an instrument of violence and repression; it was, as Patricia Mc-Fadden observes, "central to the deployment of the state as a site of accumu-lation of various ruling classes." [35] Militarism was infused with paternalistic discourse, which presented colonial rule as a benevolent, guiding authority often articulated in the metaphor of a father's protection of his children. Across Africa, countries emerging from colonial rule inherited regimes that were infused with a patriarchal militaristic logic that was both authoritarian and antidemocratic.[36] The analysis of Mama and McFadden resists linger-ing tendencies to parochialize and peculiarize the modern African state as "somehow pathologically flawed and deficient."[37] Instead, it reveals that force has been central not only to the making (and underdevelopment) of modern Africa, but also to the making of the global order more broadly.[38]

The area constituting present-day Kenya was declared a protectorate of British East Africa in 1895, and the King's African Rifles (KAR) was born in 1902. The primary function of the KAR was to secure critical infrastructure, such as railways and port facilities, in order to protect the extraction of re-sources. Colonial officials sought to establish control over a large swathe of territory without needing to deploy a large number of troops. To accomplish this, they employed tactics of divide and rule, turning to populations that the British believed to be both loyal and possessing martial traits. By 1959, as Ma-sumbayi Katumanga outlines, "the Kalenjin, Kamba, Samburu, and Somali—all pastoralist communities with an age-mate system that emphasized the role of young men as 'warriors'—supplied approximately 77 percent of the total strength of the KAR battalions."[39] Military service became the most highly paid and highly respected form of wage labor, but this came at a price: a willingness, when needed, to use force against the civilian population.[40]

In the face of anticolonial resistance by the Land and Freedom Army (Mau Mau), British authorities granted extensive powers to the police and military. This meant that militarized violence was at the foundation of the security apparatus of the newly independent state.[41] As David Anderson explains, Kenya came to independence already fighting an internal insurgency in the northeastern part of the country, where the region's ethnic Somali inhabitants, fearing that they would be marginalized in a predominantly Christian state, launched a secessionist movement.[42] Calls for decolonization had precipitated heated debates about identity, citizenship, and belonging—both on the coast (see chapter 2), and in northeastern Kenya, where residents' conceptualizations of belonging exceeded the contours of the nation-state. In this regard, decolonization was a process "not simply of building nations from colonies but also of subordinating competing nationalisms into their fold."[43] As Keren Weitzberg elucidates, "Northern Kenya became one of the major sites on which Western and African leaders displaced broader anxieties about national independence."[44]

The residents of what became northeastern Kenya constituted just one percent of a population of roughly 8 million at the time of independence, yet they inhabited an area that amounted to one-fifth of Kenya's total territory.[45] Kenyan leaders were therefore determined not to surrender this territory to the Somali state, despite the findings of a 1962 referendum demonstrating the overwhelming desire of the region's inhabitants to join the newly formed Somali Republic.[46] It was in this context that Kenya launched what became a four-year counter-insurgency campaign known as the Shifta War. Jomo Kenyatta, the country's first president, sought to depoliticize the secessionist demands by characterizing the Somali population as hooligans or *shifta,* and worked to consolidate control over territories that belonged to the nation-state in name only.[47] Paramilitary units formed by the British during the colonial state of emergency employed tactics of collective punishment against the population, arresting, detaining, and shooting suspected rebels, and confiscating livestock and property.[48] Nearly 2,000 people labeled by the state as *shifta* were killed.[49]

Despite a negotiated end to the war in 1967 and state-led promises of development, political and economic marginalization persisted. The ability of the government to launch and maintain a state of emergency in this region for nearly thirty years (1963–91) was closely tied to the fact that the British had long approached the north as a distinct geography requiring a separate system of military administration.[50] Hannah Whitaker explains:

> This region is the epitome of what Richard Reid calls a "militarized margin": peripheral areas that can be found all across the globe with long histories of economic distress, political marginalization and oppression, social dislocation and violent conflict . . . This was regarded as a volatile "backward" territory, whose inhabitants gained a reputation as violent and unruly. When Kenya gained independence, the existence of a Somali separatist movement in NEP simply confirmed the image of it as a dangerous and unstable place, and reinforced an idea that the people living within the region had dubious loyalties to the state. Counterinsurgency, collective punishment, and the use of state violence have all therefore been seen as "necessary" against a population that is believed to be "hostile" to the interests of the state.[51]

In February 1984, the government launched a large-scale security operation in the northern town of Wajir. In what the state characterized as an effort to bring an end to cross-border raiding and arms smuggling, Kenyan soldiers surrounded the town and ordered all residents to leave their homes, setting fire to the homes as a strategy to forcibly evacuate them. Approximately 5,000 men were rounded up and detained at the nearby Wagalla airfield, where they were subject to "screening" exercises, violence, and torture. Over a period of four days, at least 2,000 were killed.[52] While the scale of the killing at Wagalla distinguishes it as the deadliest state crime in the country's history, Anderson notes that its character and manifestation reflected strong continuities in governing strategy toward the north. It is this history (from the vilification of Somalis, to the normalization of militarized rule in the name of security) that made it possible for Kenya to invade Somalia in October 2011 with minimal public outcry.

The Moralization of Intervention

On 16 October 2011, the Kenyan military dispatched approximately 2,000 troops across the border into Somalia. Citing a spate of kidnappings by Al-Shabaab in northern Kenya, government officials invoked Article 51 of the UN Charter, arguing that its territorial integrity had been threatened. In the ensuing days and weeks, political and military leaders asserted their authority in the language of paternalism and national security, declaring that Operation *Linda Nchi* (Protect the Nation) would safeguard Kenya from the threat of Al-Shabaab. The government quickly garnered diplomatic support for its actions: in a meeting between then President Mwai Kibaki, Yoweri Museveni of Uganda, and Sheikh Sharif Ahmed of Somalia, the three leaders jointly characterized the Kenyan incursion as a "historic opportunity" to defeat Al-Shabaab.

Together these men embodied the Africanization of the war on terror: their declarations and assertions of control worked to reframe the war as "*our* war." This resignification of the war on terror as one that Africans have a responsibility to fight is at the heart of the cultural politics of security in the region. It is sustained through daily repetitions and invocations in the media, contributing to the emergence of a populist common sense about "security as responsibility" that normalizes paternalistic assertions of authority and superiority over seemingly uncivilized or suspect others, both near and far. The ubiquity of high-level meetings in the region, widely covered in the press, that are dedicated to addressing the threat posed by Al-Shabaab further contributes to the normalization of militarized approaches. In February 2023, for example, Somali president Hassan Sheikh Mohamud hosted leaders from Kenya, Ethiopia, and Djibouti in Mogadishu for a "Somalia Front-line States Summit" to discuss a coordinated military offensive in what Mohamud has characterized as an "all-out war" against Al-Shabaab.[53] These gatherings are key sites for African leaders to project an image of themselves as leaders on questions of global concern, and to present militarized intervention as moral, and as necessary for the attainment of peace and security.

Historically, African leaders have been wary of interfering in the affairs of neighboring states. In an explicit reference to the principle of respecting the sovereignty and territorial integrity of member states, the Charter of the

Organization of African Unity (ratified in 1963) maintained a commitment to noninterference. Despite formal declarations of independence across the continent at the time, leaders like Kwame Nkrumah of Ghana were mindful of the potential for new forms of colonialism to compromise African sovereignty, contributing to the rise of client states. For Nkrumah, political independence was merely a prelude to economic and military integration, all of which were integral to the effort to defend the continent against neocolonialist designs.[54] His vision of an African federation (modeled on the United States) included the creation of an African Military High Command to protect African states in the face of interference from global powers.[55] "If Africa was united," he wrote, "no major power bloc would attempt to subdue it."[56]

One year after Nkrumah penned those words, he was deposed in a military coup orchestrated by the CIA. According to the US State Department at the time, Nkrumah's "overpowering desire to export his brand of nationalism unquestionably made Ghana one of the foremost practitioners of subversion in Africa."[57] These events sent a clear message to other African leaders, many of whom had assumed power just a few years earlier. It was not until the late 1990s that Libyan President Muammar Gaddafi returned to Nkrumah's proposal when he called for the creation of a "United States of Africa" with a single army and currency, at a September 1999 summit of the OAU.[58]

Ultimately, neither Nkrumah's vision, nor Gaddafi's came to fruition. In the early 2000s, the African Union (which replaced the OAU) *did* establish its own security architecture, including a Peace and Security Council and a Continental Early Warning System. It also proposed the creation of an African Standby Force that would be capable of deployment in times of crisis.[59] But in doing so, it abandoned the principle of noninterference long upheld by its predecessor, the OAU.[60] This shift came in the midst of collective guilt about the genocide in Rwanda, which prompted a reevaluation of the sanctity previously accorded to the notion of territorial sovereignty, and which culminated, at the United Nations, in the introduction of the concept of the "responsibility to protect." In today's liberal internationalist order, intervention has become a moral and ethical obligation rather than a political act.

Tracing the rise of this new, liberal militarism in Africa, Rita Abrahamsen observes that whereas the militarism of the Cold War era was domestically oriented, today's militarism is oriented toward foreign intervention. Since 9/11 and the rise of AFRICOM, new alliances have emerged between political leaders and militaries in key partner states like Kenya, Ethiopia, and Uganda in the name of fighting terrorism and violent extremism. "Political order, statebuilding and containment of local conflicts remain key objectives," she writes, "but contemporary assistance is also centrally focused on defeating violent extremist groups that are perceived as threats to domestic and international stability. This requires African militaries to be combat ready and prepared to fight, in defense of development, both within and beyond their own borders."[61]

Ethiopia was the first African state to intervene in Somalia, in December 2006, sending 8,000 troops across the border. Ethiopian leaders were motivated by their own geopolitical interests, namely, a concern that then-rival Eritrea was working closely with Somalia's ruling Islamic Courts Union (ICU) to train militants that could infiltrate and destabilize Ethiopia.[62] At the time, the ICU had presided over six months of relative stability in Somalia. Contrary to mainstream media coverage that claimed it had ties to Al-Qaeda, the ICU was an indigenous response to CIA-backed warlords, whose drug and weapons trafficking had subjected Somalis to years of violence and uncertainty. The group's popularity grew not because of a unified Islamist ideology, but because of a shared desire to counteract the warlords. As the International Crisis Group observed in 2005, "The courts' promise of order and security appeals to Somalis across the religious spectrum. Their heterogeneous membership and diversity of their supporters mean that attempts to label the Sharia system 'extremist,' 'moderate' or any other single orientation are futile."[63] Nevertheless, US officials were convinced that the ICU was controlled by Al-Qaeda.[64] With American-supplied aerial reconnaissance and satellite surveillance, Ethiopian forces drove the ICU into exile "with astonishing speed, force and cruelty."[65] In their place emerged more militant factions with an explicit anti-imperial and anti-occupation agenda. In short, as scholars and analysts have shown, the invasion and subsequent occupation planted the seeds for the growth of what is now known as Al-Shabaab.[66]

In the immediate aftermath of the invasion, the United States and its allies blocked two attempts at the UN Security Council that called for an

immediate Ethiopian withdrawal.[67] The United Nations effectively legitimized the invasion when it amended a 1992 arms embargo and authorized
an African Union–led peacekeeping mission known as AMISOM to protect
the UN-backed Transitional Federal Government. Scholars and policymakers alike touted AMISOM as a key opportunity for the African Union (AU)
"to fulfill one of its core missions by asserting ownership over an African
conflict."[68] It is in this context that Kenya's invasion of Somalia in 2011 was
largely interpreted in policy circles as being in line with the values of peace
and security.[69] In some ways Kenya's decision to act unilaterally offered precisely the flexibility that security analysts suggest is needed to respond to
the world's "new" security challenge of combating extremist groups that
operate through diffuse, formless networks.[70] But within a few months of
the invasion, Kenyan officials were forced to contend with the price of their
operations: observers estimated that the deployment had already cost the
government $180 million.[71] When the AU Peace and Security Council agreed
to incorporate Kenyan troops into AMISOM, it both conferred legitimacy
for maintaining a military presence in Somalia and deflected the costs of
deployment onto the AU's international donors.[72]

While AMISOM's mandate was initially for six months, it gradually
morphed into a military occupation that has lasted more than fifteen years.[73]
What began as a small operation of 1,650 troops eventually grew to a force of
22,000 from at least five African states (Burundi, Djibouti, Kenya, Uganda,
Ethiopia). It is important to emphasize here how the rhetoric of peacekeeping
conceals the militarized dimensions of AMISOM, masking what is in fact a
war-making apparatus. While AMISOM's initial rules of engagement permitted
the use of force only when necessary, it soon began to assume an increasingly
offensive role, engaging in counter-insurgency and counter-terror operations.[74]
This occurred in the midst of a broader transformation in peace operations
around the world, which have come to assume war-fighting mandates.[75] But
as the United Nations itself has acknowledged, approximately one-third to
one-half of all weapons and ammunition delivered to AMISOM by the United
States have ended up in the hands of Al-Shabaab.[76] Meanwhile, the territorial
displacement of Al-Shabaab from major urban centers had the paradoxical
effect of enhancing its spread across the broader Horn of Africa region.[77]

Over the years, AMISOM's relationship with the Somali population has deteriorated, leading to further displacements and to rising injuries and death tolls of civilians and soldiers alike.[78] By 2016, the cost of AMISOM's operations exceeded $900 million per year, with the United States having spent approximately $1 billion since 2007, and the EU spending $2.5 billion over the same time period.[79] Cognizant of critiques about endless wars, policymakers have engaged in a delicate dance between illustrating progress made toward "stability," all the while insisting that the threat posed by Al-Shabaab persists, and that more work therefore remains to be done, primarily in the form of "advise and assist" trainings provided by the US military.[80] It is in this context that the African Union announced in early 2022 that AMISOM would be converted into ATMIS (the African Union Transition Mission in Somalia), whose purpose would be to gradually transfer control of security operations to the Somali National Armed Forces by December 2024. The question remains, however, whether the incentives to withdraw are sufficient: African states' readiness to deploy their own troops to the front lines has been critical to their continued ability to access foreign aid in a global economy dominated by logics of security. Many of these leaders know that aid is dependent not on their ability to deter terrorism, but on the continued perceived *risk* of terrorism.[81] In effect, the African Union's embrace of intervention in the name of security has entailed a growing intimacy with empire, and the vast array of actors involved has generated political and economic entanglements that extend well beyond the territory of Somalia itself.

Meanwhile, the troops themselves are regularly reminded of the precariousness of their own position in this warscape: while they are promised higher salaries than they receive back home, their injuries, deaths, and in many cases their struggle to get paid are of little concern to the political elite who authorize their deployment. While he was deployed to Somalia, Christopher Katitu spent two years manning a mounted machine gun from a trench in the port city of Kismayo. In April 2015, following the Al-Shabaab attack at Garissa University in northeastern Kenya, he was sent to Garissa where he was tasked with manning a military checkpoint. But after ten years in the army, while he was on a short leave back home at his family's farm, he suffered a mental breakdown. Rather than offer him treatment for post-traumatic stress disorder, the government charged him with desertion and sent him to prison.[82]

Christopher is just one of the approximately 4,000 Kenyan troops that have been serving in Somalia, roughly twice the number that were initially deployed in October 2011. As mainstream accounts of this war paint a picture of the US military, on the one hand, and Al-Shabaab, on the other, people like Christopher remain entirely imperceptible as actors entangled in this landscape. Lured by the promise of a good salary, and by the potential to be recognized as heroes for their service, Kenyan troops find themselves caught in a racialized military supply chain that is designed to transfer the risks that come with direct combat onto *their* bodies and minds. Hundreds have died while deployed in Somalia, and hundreds have reported that they suffer from symptoms related to post-traumatic stress disorder (PTSD). Those who have sought psychological help have, like Christopher, been demoted or discharged, and swept out of public view.

War as Viagra: Racializing, Gendering, and Sexualizing Intervention

Historically, Kenya has been a key contributor to UN peacekeeping efforts, but has been reluctant to dispatch troops to operations with an enforcement component. It was with this history in mind that President Yoweri Museveni of neighboring Uganda, one month before Kenya's decision to invade, mocked the KDF as a "career army" that was unable to venture into "real" war.[83] Museveni's words serve as an important reminder of the need to expand our conceptualization of the geopolitical to consider the significance of rhetoric, symbols, and meaning—and more specifically, to explore the centrality of gender alongside race in shaping the symbolic basis of power on the global stage. It also pushes us to reflect on the question of how *regional* dynamics shape and reshape imperial warfare, including forms of cooperation, competition, or coercion between Global South states.

In the face of ridicule by Museveni, Kenyan commentators began to wonder aloud about what a failure to participate in the war against Al-Shabaab would mean for Kenyan masculinity, demonstrating just how integral gender and sexuality politics are to the cultural politics of security. One journalist derided what he characterized as "the seeming impotence of our security apparatus," arguing that the call to war "is a demonstration that a sleeping lion will only take so much provocation, and no doubt it will be a source of pride that Kenya can hit back at a bunch of extremist crazies."[84] Another declared, "There is no man like one who has taken up arms in defense of his farm, his village, and its right to chart its own destiny."[85] Highlighting the significance of gendered anxieties for what he refers to as "Kenyan Politics as Male Spectacle," Keguro Macharia observed that war would function like Viagra. "Our boys will prove they are MEN. No. Longer. Impotent."[86]

Within a matter of weeks following the invasion, the narrative began to shift. Ugandan journalist Charles Onyango-Obbo published an article in the *East African* entitled "How War Boosts Kenya's Regional, Global Clout." He wrote:

> While Kenya's entry into the Somalia fray has its critics, it has kicked off a wave of nationalist sabre-rattling on the Internet. Not surprising, because though Kenya is the EAC's leading economy, it was largely viewed as a wimpish nation, with an untested military led by pampered generals growing potbellied in luxury and never having to worry about firing a shot in anger. . . . In a few weeks, all that has changed. Writing in Uganda's main independent daily, the *Daily Monitor* (a sister publication of the *East African*), Member of Parliament Capt Michael Mukula noted, "Kenya has displayed that it is not a mere careerist. Its military hardware display inside Somalia has certainly raised eyebrows among regional military strategists. . . . Meanwhile, in the past few weeks Kenyans have seen more photographs of soldiers and weaponry, and heard army chiefs and spokesmen speak, than they have for all of the past 15 years—including the period of post-election violence in 2008. A national aversion to a high-profile role for the military could just disappear in the process."[87]

Soon thereafter, President Uhuru Kenyatta began to weave references to the military into his daily appearances, normalizing the presence of the military in public life. In September 2014, photos emerged of the president walking the corridors of State House (Kenya's equivalent to the White House) clad in military attire. He appeared in military uniform on numerous occasions, arguing that he wanted to build unity and support for Kenyan soldiers who have sacrificed on behalf of the nation. Kenyatta's actions represent a marked shift from his predecessors: following two failed coup attempts in the 1970s and 1980s, prior heads of state maintained an uneasy, if not paranoid relationship to the armed forces.[88]

FIGURE 3. President Uhuru Kenyatta in military uniform, 2014.
Source: Nation Media Group.

These developments suggest that the war against Al-Shabaab has created an opening for symbolic shifts in the meanings attached to the military. As Kenyatta's performances illustrate, the legitimation of war-making depends on new articulations of idealized masculinity—namely, on the figure of the strong, virile man *who fights wars*.[89] While Kenyatta's predecessors rarely associated themselves so directly with the military,[90] state power in Kenya has nonetheless long been constructed as a male affair. Grace Musila traces distinct forms of hegemonic masculinity over the course of Kenyan history, pointing to the continued significance of the phallus for the performance of power.[91] Emphasizing that gender is a social construct with multiple iterations, she highlights the interconnected figures of "(i) the patriarch/father of the homestead, (ii) the heroic-warrior figure of nationalist liberation struggles, and (iii) the 'husband of the nation,' each of which manifest themselves in different, often contradictory shades."[92] In dialogue with Ann McClintock, Musila observes that the privileging of the phallus in Kenya "traces its roots further back to the colonial mapping of the imperial conquest through grammars of phallic penetration of feminized territories."[93] While the intersection between masculinity and power in the postcolonial era has generally been limited to national politics, the emergence of Al-Shabaab has triggered gendered, sexualized, and racialized anxieties about Kenya's readiness and ability to "act" on the world stage, while also prompting new articulations of militarized masculinity and power, as evidenced by Kenyatta's embrace of military regalia. In short, today's hegemonic masculinity—itself sustained through a constructed opposition to various subordinate and devalued masculinities and femininities—is becoming hypermasculine, with gendered stereotypes and expectations taken to the extreme.[94]

The rise of the new ideal type of hypermilitarized masculinity must be situated within a broader frame, as gendered and racialized evaluations of African capacity to govern have now been extended to the domain of war, wherein partner states in the war on terror are evaluated for their readiness to engage militarily. Indeed, President Museveni of Uganda was not the only public figure to question Kenyan manliness when he doubted Kenya's capacity to wage "real" war. In a conversation hosted by the Center for Strategic and International Studies in Washington, DC, in March 2022, the moderator asked then Deputy President William Ruto about Kenyan foreign policy, characterizing Kenya as a regional power that had previously been "timid and reluctant," but suggesting that this had changed when it intervened in Somalia. Ruto concurred with this assessment of Kenya's newly assertive foreign policy, highlighting the sacrifices that Kenya has made to maintain peace and stability in the region as it assumes its "rightful place" on the global stage.

Alongside new iterations of militarized masculinity, these exchanges and articulations also push us to consider how race is (re-)fashioned through warfare.[95] Militarism in Africa has historically been construed as deviant and as the opposite of idealized notions of "modern" (in other words, white/Western) armies and political order. Today, however, militarized interventionism—in the form of participation in the war on terror—has become a vehicle to symbolically overcome the emasculating dimensions of racialized, hierarchical world order. Dominant imaginaries of the so-called "international community" do not typically include Africans, who are more often conceived as victims than as saviors. Today, however, the African Union peace "enforcement" mission in Somalia affirms Africanness as a symbol of liberal modernity, and troop-contributing countries emerge as adult nations that are now in a position to help others rather than simply being on the receiving end of white saviorism.

This suggests that we must explore how the championing of "African solutions" reconfigures racialized conceptualizations of Africa as idea and geopolitical space.[96] In *Race and America's Long War*, Nikhil Pal Singh considers the ways in which racial difference both persists and reconstitutes itself in contexts of political change. Examining the relationship between post-9/11 warfare and the changing contours of race and racism in the United States, Singh observes that war-making and race-making are deeply inter-twined. From the election of President Barack Obama to Secretary of State Condoleeza Rice's claim that the civil rights movement helped the United States to "find its voice" as an armed champion of democracy overseas, the incorporation and celebration of Black figures and histories into the fabric of empire makes race *appear* to recede in significance.[97] Building on Singh's work, Erica Edwards observes how figures like Obama and Rice came to symbolize the dawn of a new racial order wherein the struggle for equality can confidently be declared complete. For both scholars, racial liberalism—in the form of inclusion and incorporation—provides cover for ongoing forms

FIGURE 4. Cover of AMISOM Magazine, 2013. Source: AMISOM.

of war and state-sponsored terror, even as it reinforces or articulates new racial hierarchies. The rise of figures like Obama and Rice is predicated on their exceptionalism, which effectively functions as a mode of divide and rule, distinguishing the good Black citizen from the bad. As Edwards explains, "the

FIGURE 5. Cover of AMISOM Magazine, 2015. Source: AMISOM.

culture of empire returned obsessively to narratives of Black exceptionalism even as it posited racial Blackness as, still, the exceptional . . . threat to order."[98]

This offers a useful entry point to study the emergence of equally divisive narratives of exceptionalism in Africa today. In June 2019, Kenya launched its campaign for a UN Security Council seat when it hosted a high-level UN counter-terrorism conference in Nairobi.[99] In an interview on national television, Cabinet Secretary for Foreign Affairs Monica Juma declared that Kenya had the right "pedigree" to join the Security Council, pointing to the country's long history of contributing peacekeepers to UN missions. "Our story has been one of searching for peace throughout the world," she continued. Explaining that regional and international stability was integral for the well-being of everyday Kenyans, Juma stated that joining the Security Council would have great benefit not just to the *wananchi* (citizens), but also in terms of "responding to a growing demand for our leadership globally."[100]

In her statements to the press, Juma positions Kenya as exceptional, as standing apart from its purportedly violent or uncivilized neighbors. Her emphasis on "pedigree" and the "demand" for leadership shapes the meanings that Kenyans attach to their country's role in world affairs. This manifests in part through calls (whether on social media or in daily conversations) for Somalis to show gratitude for the sacrifices Kenya has made to provide shelter for Somali refugees, and to restore stability to Somalia. Paternalism and militarism work together to cohere into a new nationalist sensibility, one that sees intervention as a moral imperative. In the wake of an Al-Shabaab attack in Mogadishu in late 2019, for example, law professor Makau Mutua (a prominent scholar of Third World approaches to international law) suggested in a widely circulated tweet that external powers like Kenya should dismember Somalia. "For God's sake," he declared, "Somalia is beyond reclamation. Post-colonial's Humpty Dumpty has reached its nadir. Let's face facts—neighboring states need to dismember so-called Somalia and take all of its parts for the sake of the world."[101] Here we can piece together the structures of feeling that animate Kenya's newfound missionary zeal, or what Sherene Razack refers to as the "deeply held belief in the need and right to dominate others for their own good."[102]

In early 2021, a Kenyan visual production company called Foxton Media released its first full-length feature film, a military action thriller called *Mission to Rescue*. In line with the company's mission to promote "positive awareness of the masses towards our security bodies" the film extols the bravery and sacrifice of Kenyan Special Operations Forces in this fictionalized account of a mission to rescue a group of hostages from the hands of Al-Shabaab. Garnering millions of online viewers in Kenya and beyond, the film won the ZIFF (Zanzibar International Film Festival) award as the best feature film in East Africa and was Kenya's submission to the Academy Awards in 2022.

Mission to Rescue is a poignant example of the power of cultural production in shaping the meanings that Kenyans attach to militarized masculinity in the context of the war on terror. More broadly, it is an illustration of what we gain analytically by expanding our conceptualization of the geopolitical to encompass the domains of performance and ideology. What is arguably most significant about the film is its framing of the war against Al-Shabaab as one that is led by Kenyan soldiers only—despite the involvement of a wide array of geopolitical actors and interests in the war. In this limited frame of "us" versus "them," the film juxtaposes the violence of Al-Shabaab and that of the Kenyan military, reinforcing racialized depictions of Somalis as threatening outsiders, and distinguishing "what *they* do" from "what *we* do."[103] Focused almost exclusively on the members of the Special Forces, the main characters are disciplined professionals who act with integrity. Thus the film participates in the imaginative construction of new "enforcement masculinities"—troops whose discipline, training, and operational flexibility makes them uniquely positioned to address the world's new security challenges.[104] Counter-insurgency and war emerge as necessary evils undertaken by highly trained professionals in the name of "peace."

The construction of this particular brand of militarized masculinity is dependent not only on differentiating itself from other (often devalued) masculinities, but equally on the construction of particular femininities in order to reaffirm perceived differences between men and women. As Cynthia Enloe observes, militarized masculinity "cannot succeed without making women also play specifically feminine parts in the militarizing process."[105] Enloe's analysis is instructive in the context of recent calls by Kenyan leaders for gender integration and equitable participation in the Kenyan military.[106] With the introduction of so-called "female engagement teams," we observe how policies and strategies of inclusion and gender equity in fact reproduce gender essentialisms, such as women's seemingly unique ability to provide care.[107] National news outlets, for example, have documented the efforts of the military's female engagement teams who work closely with the "most vulnerable" members of Somali society: its women. Popularly referred to as "the KDF Queens," these troops have been tasked with performative care work among the civilian population in Somalia by distributing milk "ATM" machines, where mothers can procure milk easily from milk dispensers. Echoing a strategy deployed by the US military in Iraq and Afghanistan, the Kenyan military has discerned the value of women's gendered labor for counter-insurgency.[108] Through these engagement teams, the KDF illustrates its compassion while ensuring that gender roles are maintained, as women help other women with the purportedly feminine task of acquiring milk for their infants.

As a collective, the men and women who constitute the Kenya Defence Forces emerge as a force for good, and as partners in the project of war.[109] The cosmopolitan militarism they embody (disciplined men and caring women) stands in contrast to that of the Al-Shabaab militant, who is depicted as aggressive, irrational, and violent, and to that of the Somali woman who requires the feminized paternalistic care of the KDF Queens.[110] While I am interested in how these newly militarized masculinities and femininities lend weight to the performance of sovereign power on the world stage, it is imperative that we situate their emergence within a wider landscape of power characterized by longstanding racialized assessments that infantilize African men and women, from the colonial era to the present day. Raymond Suttner and Pumla Dineo Gqola urge us to consider the contexts in which assertions of masculinity are taking place, noting that they can be expressions of *both* freedom and patriarchal power, and as such, compel us to reflect on the layered and contradictory meanings attributed to manhood.[111] While we have a growing understanding of the gendered mappings of power at the national level, expanding our lens beyond the boundaries of the nation-state offers new analytical openings to study the production of gendered symbolic orders *among* and *between* states, across multiple scales.

Dicey Entanglements

In January 2020, Al-Shabaab fighters attacked a military base in northeastern Kenya that houses Kenyan and American troops, and that serves as a launch pad for drone strikes in Somalia and Yemen. Three Americans were killed when the fighters launched a rocket-propelled grenade on a plane piloted by contractors from L-3 Technologies, an American company hired by the Pentagon to carry out surveillance missions in Somalia. Due to Kenyan government secrecy about the loss of its own troops, it remains unclear how many Kenyans lives were lost.

In the subsequent days and weeks, Kenyans struggled to come to terms with the claim made by the US military that Kenyan troops assigned to defend the base fled and hid in the grass while American troops were left with little protection. At stake, once again, was the question of Kenyan manliness and Kenya's capacity to wage "real" war. While a Kenyan military spokesperson sought to deflect attention from the potentially embarrassing actions of their troops by claiming that the base was an American facility, and therefore the responsibility of the Americans to protect, Kenyans on Twitter debated how to make sense of the events. Some expressed shame and frustration about the seeming cowardice of the troops, while others echoed the narrative offered by their government, declaring, "So our soldiers hid in the grass. Good for them, it was not even their war."

As we have seen in this chapter, the cultural, ideological, and performative dimensions of war-making are integral to the practice of war. I have focused on the cultural politics of security, namely the systems of signification and meaning that mobilize popular support for war. Celebratory and commemorative rituals like the now-annual Kenya Defence Forces Day and the film *Mission to Rescue* not only contribute to the production of nationalist sentiment, but also work to cultivate a felt relationship to the war on terror as *our* war. But as scholars have observed, even as cultural production and spectacle produce political power, they simultaneously invite transgressions.[112] Underlying the reactions to the Manda Bay attack was a troubling question: *whose war was this, after all?*

Indeed, it is through sustained ethnographic attention to social interactions and everyday commentary that we can observe cracks in the carefully constructed image of itself that the Kenyan state has attempted to curate. For one, the idea that the Kenyan military is single-handedly taking on Al-Shabaab—as implied in *Mission to Rescue*—is dispelled in moments like the January 2020 attack, when Kenya's subordinate relationship to, and dicey entanglement with, the US military comes to the fore. Given the US military's concerted effort to operate in the region with minimal visibility and scrutiny, the extent to which Kenyan officials can effectively recalibrate public attention *away* from these entanglements has worldmaking implications. In short, the US ability to sustain war-making in Somalia depends not only on the presence of US military bases in the region, or solely on the Kenyan military's role as practitioners of violent labor, but equally on the popular consent of the Kenyan population. Many of the figures I have highlighted— whether cabinet secretary Monica Juma, law professor Makau Mutua, soldier Christopher Katitu, the staff of Foxton Media, and of course, President Uhuru Kenyatta himself—have actively *co-constituted* the project of remaking the world through war. To speak of co-constitution and interdependence is not to dismiss asymmetrical relations of power, but to acknowledge the ways that empire is sustained by and through relations with subaltern populations.

The effects of Kenya's embrace of war have been painfully felt in the wake of Al-Shabaab attacks. As we saw in relation to the Westgate Mall tragedy, it is often in the aftermath of such attacks that the government and media rush to shape popular responses to the incident. While racialized ideas about Somalis contribute to dispositions of disregard about the ongoing and devastating effects of war in Somalia, it is the rising physical and psychological toll on Kenyans themselves that prompts doubt, grief, and, at times, anger.[113] It is in these moments that we find hints of other worlds. As the brother of a soldier killed by a roadside bomb asked, "How many other young men are we going to lose before our boys are brought back home? How many more families should bear the pain of this war fought in distant lands?"[114]

2 SECURING PARADISE

Race, Capital, and Suspect Citizenship on the Coast

ON A WARM EVENING IN MARCH 2015, Jamal was out in the Mombasa neighborhood of Floringi watching a pickup game of football. As a young twenty-something employee of a local nonprofit organization, he was hoping to unwind after a long day's work. But at 8:30 p.m., roughly half an hour after he had arrived, police stormed the neighborhood. Thirteen youths were arrested that night, one of them just nine years old. Some were dragged from inside a local barbershop and thrust into the back of police trucks. Others took off running instinctively and managed to escape the police's grasp, but Jamal stood his ground.

I did nothing wrong, he recounted to me. *Why should I run?*

One officer approached Jamal and asked what he was doing outside that night. He was perplexed by the question. "*Why shouldn't I be outside?*" he retorted.

Jamal was asked to produce his ID. He made sure to provide every form of ID he had in his possession, including his work badge. In the end, Jamal was lucky, and he thinks that it may have been his work ID that saved him that night. The police told him to return home and stay out of trouble.

As a mixed-race (Afro-Arab, or Swahili) Muslim, Jamal was accustomed to harassment by the police. He was also familiar with the demand to produce identification—a tactic regularly employed by the Kenyan security apparatus to establish whether the person in question is in fact a Kenyan citizen. More often than not, as I learned over the course of similar conversations with many others like Jamal, the default assumption of government officials when it comes to Muslims on the coast (many of whom identify as, or are racialized as, Arab or Swahili) is that they are foreigners. In part, this can be traced to the fact that these populations did not fit neatly into the racial classifications formulated by colonial administrators, due to the longstanding cross-regional ties that extend across the Indian Ocean to the Middle East and South Asia. The association of Arab and Swahili Muslims with foreignness attained new meaning in the latter days of colonial rule when they campaigned for coastal autonomy, fearing that they would be treated as second-class citizens in newly declared nation-states.

Bitter memories of what was ultimately a failed struggle for autonomy continue to inform perceptions of this region of the country. In the aftermath of the 1998 Al-Qaeda bombings of the US Embassy in Nairobi, for example, Kenyans clung to rumors that the perpetrators were specifically Arab Muslims from the coast who had been radicalized by other "foreign" Muslims. In response, Kenyan security forces, accompanied by the FBI, conducted raids across Mombasa, focusing particularly on the majority-Muslim Old Town where residents were subjected to sweeping arrests and interrogations. With the rise of Al-Shabaab in the mid- to late 2000s, policymakers zeroed in on the coast as a likely site of recruitment, thereby licensing expansive modes of surveillance and policing in the name of security and countering "violent extremism." Alongside a rise in disappearances and extrajudicial killings, the daily challenges faced by coastal Muslims in obtaining ID cards, passports, and other legal documents, such as title deeds, serve as a constant reminder that they are viewed as questionably indigenous, if not as suspect. Meanwhile, the growing influx of *Wabara*, or "up-country" (predominantly Christian) people—along with shifts in land ownership tied to the national tourism industry—has fueled concerns among coastal inhabitants about unequal land distribution, and about external domination of the coast more broadly.[1] During my extended period of research in Mombasa, my interlocutors were keen to draw connections between the multiple, interlinked modes of power that shape coastal Muslims' lived realities of inequality and suspect citizenship.

This chapter traces the processes by which worlds are made and remade on the Kenyan coast, arguing that the coast is central to the making of Kenya as place-in-the-world. The significance of race cannot be overstated, and yet is defined by a paradox, demanding a relational analysis. On the one hand, the war on terror has repoliticized longstanding debates about race and indigeneity, as coastal Muslims racialized as Arab and Swahili have long been viewed as questionably indigenous and out-of-place. Yet it is precisely these notions of difference that produce the coast as an Oriental wonderland and exotic space, making it an integral part of the national tourism industry. I therefore highlight the Kenyan state's growing preoccupation with branding—a project that is imbricated in colonial nostalgia and the (re-)production of colonial whiteness. My goal is to illustrate that colonial logics continue to scaffold the imaginaries and actions of the ostensibly postcolonial state. While the specific context of the so-called war on terror has reinscribed colonial-era ideas about Arab, Swahili, and Somali "foreigners" in Kenya, racial dynamics in Kenya must be situated within a consideration of wider processes and histories of race and racialization—including structures of white supremacy—in this former settler colony.[2]

The first part of the chapter explores the intersection of race and space, wherein certain spaces and their inhabitants are marked as having distinct characteristics.[3] Conceptualizations of difference were accentuated in the early days of independence when Jomo Kenyatta's government implemented policies of "Africanization" that fueled ideas about coastal Muslims as less Kenyan. Despite the diversity of social, cultural, religious, and political life on the coast, the Kiswahili term *wapwani* (coastal people) gradually emerged as a cohesive unit in the national imaginary, one that is associated with a specifically "foreign," "Arab" Islam. Thus we see how political discourse becomes infused with geographic claims and assumptions, producing what Edward Said refers to as "imaginative geographies," which map difference onto place and space.[4] Today, spatial taxonomies (such as "hot spots") employed by policymakers and security experts alike construct popular understandings of neighborhoods like Mombasa's Old Town as prone to violence.

Paradoxically, even as the state has imaginatively constructed the coast as a site of threat and Arab foreignness, it has simultaneously promoted this region as an Oriental wonderland for tourists and investors. As one tourism guide states, "The coast has its own fascination. Towns such as Mombasa, Malindi, and Lamu have a unique and special magic. Their Arabian Nights ambience that forever holds one's imagination is simply unforgettable."[5] But in the wake of violent attacks by Al-Qaeda and Al-Shabaab, images of this once serene "paradise" were shattered.[6] In response, the Euro-American governments have issued travel advisories discouraging their citizens from travel to the coast. The political elite in Kenya are painfully aware that these advisories constitute a mode of valuation and risk that racialize certain geographies and their inhabitants as threatening, thereby hindering much-needed foreign investments in the country. The second part of the chapter therefore turns to the state's growing preoccupation with nation-branding, wherein state officials (often in dialogue with the corporate sector) work to produce favorable and distinctive representations of the nation-state in the public realm. I argue that nation-branding operates as an affective technique for Kenya to geopolitically refashion itself in a global economy structured by racial logics, including fear of so-called terrorists. Yet branding is entangled in colonial nostalgia and the (re-)production of colonial whiteness as it works to project an image of tranquility and stability in which Europeans are at home in a foreign land. As the coastal elite embraces the project of security in the name of protecting the tourist economy, we observe the continuity of colonial dynamics in a purportedly postcolonial state.

The final part of the chapter aims to shed light on how Mombasa residents grapple with the shrinking space for public deliberation and debate, and with the role of the ruling class in maintaining colonial relations of power. Mombasa has become a key site of governance on issues related to violent extremism, as local leaders of nongovernmental organizations (NGOs) with the right contacts have sought to tap into foreign aid funding for civic educational programming on this theme.[7] The rise of "countering violent extremism," or CVE, as a form of soft power has coincided with the rhetorical championing of pluralism and inclusion, with the goal of discouraging coastal Muslims from joining Al-Shabaab. And yet it is precisely in this context that the domain of civil society has become a space of heightened surveillance and exclusion, as equal citizenship is now conditioned on a willingness to participate in the project of security.

As coastal Muslims link their own experiences of policing and criminalization to the subjugation of Muslims elsewhere in the world, some
characterize the war on terror as a war on Islam and Muslims.[8] While it is
important to recognize that a range of perspectives exists within this broad
claim, I am interested in how it gives meaning to histories and imaginaries
of interrelation that transcend the borders of the nation-state, constituting
a worldmaking practice.[9] My focus is not on religious or cultural enmity,
but on the experiences of alienation and modes of political consciousness
and solidarity that form contingently in relation to power.[10] In dialogue
with Michel Rolph Trouillot, who observes that the experiences of people
outside of the West are often pathologized and trivialized when they challenge normative understandings of a given order, I reject the mainstream
tendency to pathologize and suggest instead that coastal Muslims are not
merely describing their world, but *analyzing* it, offering important signposts
that link seemingly distant global power formations to daily life.[11] Indeed, the
experiences of people like Jamal reveal that everyday life on the coast entails
a series of negotiations, wherein even seemingly mundane activities like a
neighborhood football game become a source of suspicion and scrutiny. I
have often reflected on the story Jamal shared with me of his harassment
by the police, realizing that in many ways his response was informed by an
awareness of the broader structures of power that were at play. *I did nothing
wrong,* he said to me. *Why should I run?* The tone of his voice was not defiant
but matter-of-fact. Yet the words themselves gesture to a politics of standing
one's ground in the face of intimidation, of assaults on his dignity, and of the
wide-ranging injustices that circumscribe his life chances.[12] While security
analysts either dismiss young men like Jamal or pathologize them by associating their observations and analysis with "extremism," I ask what it would
mean to take these modes of subjugated knowledge seriously, recognizing
that knowledge-making itself is a form of worldmaking.[13]

Race and the Construction of Suspect Citizenship

My approach to race and racialization is informed by scholars who emphasize that race is best understood as an "unstable and decentered complex of
social meanings" rather than as a biological or phenotypical descriptor.[14] If
we think of race as a social construct, we can attend to the ways in which

ideas about difference and hierarchy are historically and geographically specific, constituted in different ways across varying contexts. Omi and Winant's emphasis on fluidity and instability problematizes conceptualizations of race as fixed, while the field of Indian Ocean studies pushes us to think beyond the templates of area studies and the nation-state. Against the cartographic and epistemic regimes that have divided the world into seemingly distinct and bounded regions, I aim to think about relationality across difference. This allows us to be attuned to cross-regional histories and relationalities that have contributed to layered and at times fractured forms of place-making and belonging.[15]

I employ a relational approach to race in order to foreground connection, circulation, and multiplicity, as well as to consider the co-constitution of ideas about difference across multiple, overlapping geographies and histories. In short, I question the tendency to flatten difference *within* seemingly homogeneous conceptualizations of Blackness, brownness, and so on, and suggest that we must attend to the coexistence of multiple orders of racialization and domination. Even as populations within Kenya are differently positioned in relation to each other, everyday interactions are shaped by situated understandings of the continent's ongoing relationship to global racialized hierarchies. By necessity, therefore, my analysis extends beyond the borders of the nation-state to wrestle with global racial and political-economic configurations, and with the various transnational significations associated with Africanness, Arabness, and Islam. A relational approach allows us to explore the racialization of subordinate groups in relation to one another, *and* to shed light on the shared logics that undergird broader racial capitalist formations.

Scholars have traced the efforts by colonial officials to assign African subjects distinct ethnic and racial identities, and to link these identities to territory.[16] These processes of differentiation legitimated the introduction of separate laws that governed the lives of "natives" and "nonnatives." As Mahmood Mamdani documents in *Citizen and Subject*, Africans were racialized as "natives" and subject to customary law, whereas Europeans, Asians, and Arabs were racialized as "nonnatives" and governed by civil law. In practice, these categories were subject to debate and often in tension with local conceptualizations of race, culture, and geographic origin. Mixed-race populations posed a challenge to colonial officials' desire to clearly delineate between native and nonnative, making it impossible to reach a conclusive, universally applicable definition.[17] Nonetheless, colonial categories had consequential material effects, creating a minority *among* the colonized who enjoyed political and economic privileges that their "native" counterparts did not. In Kenya, populations racialized as Asian, Arab, and Somali therefore have complicated if not complicit histories, as they became both the source of collaboration with the colonial enterprise *and* nationalists who agitated against it.

While Mamdani and others attribute the introduction of racial thought on the continent to European colonizers, a growing number of scholars have pushed us to expand our frame of analysis to consider the multiple, overlapping processes of racialization beyond the traditional lens of white/ Black, colonizer/colonized.[18] Some of this scholarship has also decentered the colonial period, drawing attention to pre- and postcolonial histories in order to wrestle with the interlocking of pasts, presents, and futures, and their significance for our ability to consider layered processes of racialization.

In the precolonial era, the Kenyan coast was under the control of the Omani Al-Busaid dynasty. Omani rulers laid the groundwork for racial and ethnic division along the East African coast, in part through their sponsorship of Arab planters and Indian financiers, and through their importation of African slaves.[19] As Jonathan Glassman writes, "Omani governors consolidated their political control over the towns of the mainland coast, using force to marginalize indigenous rulers who proved refractory and patronage to co-opt the rest. Such patronage proved especially flattering to elites who were already proud of their own Arab or 'Shirazi' ancestry, and even when it produced tensions, Omani rule only further strengthened local concepts of Arabocentrism."[20] Glassman continues:

> In many ways, the sultanate was a colonial state that had been built on conquest, its political authority derived from the status of belonging to a foreign and supposedly superior racial caste. Early in the twentieth century before the ascendance of anticolonial sentiment, intellectuals with ties to

the sultanate's ruling families were unapologetic about the colonial nature of Omani rule. Like their British mentors, however, they often papered over the violence inherent in Omani colonialism, a violence that was central to the governing practices by which the Busaid state sought to define and divide its subjects.[21]

Glassman's work offers vital insights into the role played by Zanzibari intellectuals, including those who later emerged at the forefront of nationalist struggles, in the circulation of discourses of racial difference, including ideas about Arab supremacy.[22] When the British established political control in the region (1890–1920), their strategy of indirect rule had the effect of magnifying difference along the lines of race and class, partly through economic policies designed to preserve Omani Arabs as landlords, and through administrative and educational policies that protected Arab access to political and cultural capital. As Hassan Ndzovu observes, the appointment and incorporation of Arabs in the nascent system of colonial administration was informed by British assumptions about Arab enlightenment and superiority.[23] At the same time, the British introduced laws and classificatory systems that heightened awareness of social difference. This created the context for bitter and violent antagonisms in the late colonial period, as race increasingly became the basis for establishing legal status, taxation, and land ownership.[24]

The formal end of colonial rule posed a dilemma for coastal populations: whereas anticolonial rhetoric championed the reclamation of indigenous rights in relation to continental geography, coastal inhabitants self-identified in relation to overlapping continental, diasporic, and maritime imaginaries.[25] In Kenya, the movement for "*mwambao*," or coastal autonomy, campaigned for autonomy from what would soon be independent Kenya, with some adherents calling for Zanzibar, Pemba, and the Protectorate of Kenya (a narrow strip of Indian Ocean coastline that was once under the control of the Sultan of Zanzibar) to be united as a single nation.[26] Sheikh Abdillahi Nasir, an elected member of Kenya's pre-independence Legislative Council from 1961 to 1963, recounted to me in an interview in 2013 that people on the coast were divided at the time between those who wanted full-fledged autonomy, those who wanted to be a part of Kenya, and those who wanted to unite with Zanzibar. Like their Somali counterparts in northeastern Kenya, many feared what minority status in a Christian-majority state would mean, whether in relation to education, jobs, or land ownership.

The overlap of race and space strongly shaped political dynamics, as well as how the movement was understood: critics denounced the call for secession as an attempt by British imperialists and Arab supremacists to maintain racial privilege and to deprive Kenya from continued access to the port in Mombasa.[27] In this context, differently situated actors invoked competing notions of belonging, with some viewing Arabs, Swahilis, and Asians as indigenous to the land, and others viewing Black Africans as the sole "natives" of the coast region. As Ngala Chome observes, racial thought has constituted a frame of reference through which inhabitants of the coast identify themselves in relation to others; it has historically been connected to broader concerns about status, rights, and resources; and it has contributed to the emergence of mutually exclusive racial identities within a shared geographic space.[28] Those who identified as Arabs, for example, embraced colonial classifications and used them to their advantage, emphasizing ideas about origin and descent to distinguish themselves from others. Often, this overlapped with geographic distinctions, wherein "up-country" or mainlander Africans (*Wabara*) have come to represent a seemingly distinct group of economically and politically powerful Christians whose growing presence on the coast is perceived as threatening to their interests.[29]

Today, Muslims constitute roughly 20 percent of Kenya's predominantly Christian population, with the majority living in Mombasa and along the coast.[30] Race, ethnicity, class, gender, and doctrinal difference push against homogeneous representations: no individual or institution has ever succeeded in monopolizing claims to represent Kenyan Muslims as a united entity. Drawing lessons from their colonial predecessors, successive governments have manipulated class interests by working to incorporate middle- and upper-class Muslim citizens into the folds of state power. The state has also sought to maintain divisions along the lines of race and ethnicity.[31]

In the context of the war on terror, policymakers have accentuated these divisions, naturalizing constructed distinctions between "African" and "Arab" Islam. In doing so, they build upon the work of scholars who remain wedded to colonial racial geographies that conceived of Islam as an alien, external force on the continent.[32] The language deployed works to differentiate presumed innocent "locals" from the polluting ideas of "radical" "foreigners," thereby mapping "putative doctrinal differences . . . onto geographical ones."[33] Darryl Li illustrates how this discourse extends far beyond the East African context:

> From Bosnia-Herzegovina to Somalia to the Philippines, to say nothing of Afghanistan and Iraq, the United States and its allies have repeatedly invoked the need to separate foreign Muslim fighters—typically portrayed as Arab, rootless, fanatical, and brutal—from local Muslims, whose potential for moderation must be nourished whenever possible.[34]

At stake is what Li characterizes as the racialization of Muslim *mobility* as threatening, with the effect of reifying the construct of the nation-state.[35] Here, the category of the "foreign" functions as a discursive strategy designed to arbitrate difference, and to separate "good" from "bad" Muslims. For Mamdani, judgments of good/bad Muslims in the context of the war on terror refer to *political* identities rather than to cultural or religious ones. The "culture talk" employed by self-appointed experts on Islam like Samuel Huntington, he argues, dehistoricizes the construction of political identity and frames culture as having a tangible essence, explaining politics "as a consequence of that essence."[36] Moreover, through what Simon Springer describes as the fetishism of place, culture talk works to mobilize popular geographic prejudices, and to dissociate certain actors from their own violent entanglement in those spaces.[37] The particular categorizations of Islam in East Africa must therefore be understood as the product of discursive processes that overlook historical specificity and complexity. A 2007 report by the Combating Terrorism Center's Harmony Project at West Point, for example, located prospects for radicalism within the "small but significant Arab, Arab-Swahili and Somali minorities concentrated in coastal Kenya, Nairobi and several other urban centers."[38] It pointed to Indian Ocean histories of trade, study, and intermarriage as indicative of the coastal population's nonnative roots, and as the source of their so-called radicalism. Thus we see how a historically indigenous "African" Islam is constructed in contradistinction to a "foreign" Islam that is said to disturb the previously stable religious and political fabric of the continent.

As mass-mediated ideas about the transnational Muslim militant have gained hold in the Kenyan public sphere, they are informed by this constructed dichotomy of local/foreign, African/Arab, occluding longstanding histories of connection and interrelation. Yet it is precisely these geo-racial categorizations of difference that produce the coast as an exotic space, making it an integral part of the national tourism industry.[39] Here, we see that tourism is not incidental to war-making but in fact constitutes an overlapping mode of power, shaped as it is by racialized and gendered ideas of security. In the aftermath of the 2002 bombing of the Israeli-owned Paradise Hotel in Mombasa, for example, hundreds of coastal residents were swept up in police operations, with local journalists characterizing Mombasa as a city under siege. Meanwhile, Euro-American tourists and aid workers disparaged what they referred to as "trouble in paradise," as the coastal landscape that once evoked images of palm-lined beaches and wafting sea breezes increasingly elicited anxieties about violence and instability.[40]

The Kenyan government has since sought to restore the image of the coast as a serene getaway for tourists and investors. The next section therefore turns to the marketing and commodification of Kenya, demonstrating that the state's prioritization of branding and tourism serves as the condition of possibility for the (re-)production of colonial whiteness. I suggest that the branding of the coast as an Oriental paradise compels us to grapple with logics of racial capitalism that extend beyond Black/white binaries, attending to the ways in which multiple racial formations (Africanness, Arabness, Muslimness, Blackness, whiteness) are linked and mutually reinforcing. Yet the ruling class project of cultivating an image of paradise seemingly untouched by histories of colonial and racial violence remains an aspirational one, as Kenyans increasingly challenge the logics underlying it.

White Man's Paradise

In *The Predicament of Blackness*, Jemima Pierre productively builds upon Mamdani's discussion of the colonial configuration of racial and ethnic identities, and the resulting classificatory distinctions between "natives" (subjects) and "nonnatives" (citizens).[41] As Pierre observes, this citizen/ subject binary was only *one* side of the racializing colonial process, the other side being "the homogenization of European groupings and the making of colonial Whiteness."[42] In Kenya, the making of colonial white-ness is an important entry point to explore the construction of Kenya as a white man's paradise.[43] From the recruitment of white settlers in the 1890s to contemporary branding campaigns that feature idyllic sandy beaches along the coast, the idea of Kenya as a paradise evokes racialized and gen-dered notions of passivity and penetrability, of a landscape ripe for exploi-tation and discovery. Approaching "paradise"—and the broader notion of uninhabited landscape—as a fiction that has been conjured,[44] I reflect on the co-construction of whiteness as a claim to civilization and modernity.

In a 1953 essay on the rise of the Kenyan Land and Freedom Army, George Padmore characterized colonial Kenya as a "white man's paradise" where British settlers lived like royalty on expropriated land.[45] Settlers first arrived in the 1890s and grew in number in the early 1900s as the British colonial government initiated a series of land-grabbing ordinances to facilitate white settlement. The 1902 Crown Lands Ordinance became the precursor for large-scale dispossession, followed by subsequent laws that privileged individual ownership and dismissed longstanding practices of communal land use.[46] The establishment of native reserves—allegedly intended to "protect" African rights to land—sanctioned the displacement of Africans from areas that set-tlers desired, even as it expanded colonial control over the spaces in which the African population lived. In 1908, East African Estates Ltd., one of the largest colonial companies operating in Kenya at the time, acquired 260,000 acres of land south of Mombasa on the coast.[47]

The colonial government's power to control ownership of prime land was legitimized by white supremacist discourses about "proper" land use.[48] As Musila observes, the process of land alienation "was discursively medi-ated by the vacuation of the land as large expanses of empty space without owners, inadvertent or feigned ignorance of local land use and owner-ship cultures, which gave the impression of 'unoccupied land.'"[49] African landscapes were constructed, she writes, "as Edenic wildernesses endowed with a certain savage innocence and beauty for which the fast-modernizing West yearned as a rejuvenating breath of primordial purity and tranquility."[50] Guided by narratives that equated English common law concepts of property with civilized life, colonial officials and settlers alike *believed* that Kenya demanded white settlers.[51] At the same time, British farmers and ranchers could reinvent themselves, benefiting from their white skin to become "somebody."[52] Ngugi wa Thiong'o vividly captures the nature of this transformation in *Wrestling with the Devil*, reminding us that whiteness is an identity that is *constructed*, with "all too real consequences for the distribution of wealth, prestige, and opportunity."[53]

> Coming ashore into Kenya meant literally riding on the backs of black workers into a white tropical paradise, and this was true for the titled and untitled alike. By setting foot on Kenyan soil in Mombasa, every European, even those soldiers resettled on stolen lands after the First World War, was instantly transformed into a blue-blooded aristocrat. An attractive welcome: before him, stretching beyond the ken of his eyes, lay a vast valley garden of endless physical leisure and pleasure that he must have once read about in the *Arabian Nights* stories. The dream in fairy tales was now his in practice. No work, no winter, no physical or mental exertion. Here he would set up his own fiefdom.[54]

White rule—and the attendant privileges that had come to be associated with whiteness—came under threat with the rise of the Land and Freedom Army in the early 1950s. Colonial officials concluded that the insurgency was the product of witchcraft, a psycho-pathological phenomenon rather than a political response to the violence and dispossession that characterized colonial rule.[55] In doing so, they maintained their claim to normativity against which nonwhites were measured.[56] The British refered to the resistance as "Mau Mau," a neologism that quickly came to be associated with violence and barbarism. As Caroline Elkins documents, "the historical record is littered with lengthy descriptions from settlers and colonial officials of Mau Mau 'vermin,' 'animals,' and 'barbarians'. . . . like other predatory animals, they were 'cunning,' 'vicious' and 'bloodthirsty.'" In short, Elkins explains, the insurgency "ushered in a critical change in the settlers' already racist hierarchical segregation of humanity. There was a shift in language and belief, from simple white supremacy to one that was overtly eliminationist."[57] British officials instituted a state of emergency in 1952, launching a campaign of forced removals and detaining up to 1.5 million Kikuyu in purported "rehabilitation" camps. It was, in Ngũgĩ's words, a "calculated act of psychological terror against the struggling millions."[58]

Despite the eventual demise of colonial rule, this psychological terror left a durable mark.[59] In the debris of what Ngũgĩ refers to as the "cultural bomb," the colonized lost "belief in their names, their languages, in their environment, in their heritage of struggle, in their unity, in their capacities and ultimately in themselves."[60] The protracted quality of this decimation, writes Ngũgĩ, "makes them see their past as one wasteland of non-achievement and it makes them want to distance themselves from that wasteland. It makes them want to identify with that which is furthest removed from themselves; for instance, with other peoples' languages rather than their own. It makes them identify with that which is decadent and reactionary, all those forces which would stop their own springs of life."[61]

Ngũgĩ wa Thiong'o's observations push us to reflect on colonialism's enduring presence in the so-called postcolonial world, as an independent Black nation like Kenya looks outside of itself for validation and rejects the value of its own history, language, and culture. Even as the ruling elite that assumed power spoke in the language of rights and recognition, whiteness lingered as aspirational ideal and symbol of modernity. As Wandiya Njoya elucidates, drawing on the work of Gideon Mutiso, appointments to key leadership positions were made largely on the basis of Western education. Because the educated elite deemed themselves superior to their uneducated counterparts, the language of "qualifications" functioned to mask what in effect was an investment in whiteness. British nationals remained civil servants in major positions even a decade into independence, under the pretext that they were more qualified. Here it is just as important to look beyond actual racialized white bodies to contend with whiteness as ideology, as whiteness in Kenya has been normalized so thoroughly "as not to need white bodies to enact it."[62]

When he assumed power in 1963, Jomo Kenyatta ruled out the national-
ization of foreign-owned assets, including European-owned land. In addition
to rejecting calls for land distribution, he introduced new settlement schemes
and granted select parties (primarily Kikuyu) the right to acquire plots near
or on the beach, appropriating land that villagers on the coast had used for
centuries.[63] As Alamin Mazrui and Ibrahim Noor Shariff observe, "Bent on
protecting its own kleptocratic interests by refusing to reform Kenya's land
policy, and incapable of creating new economic opportunities, the Kenyatta
regime was caught in a vicious circle of dispossessing one group of Kenyans in
order to fulfill the more assertive demands of another."[64] Meanwhile, Kenyatta
embarked on an expansive global marketing campaign to promote an idea
of Kenya that would entice Euro-American tourists. The goal was to "make
Kenya a knowable and familiar space to Western audiences, corresponding
to a specific gendered and racial order, and one not so distant from the colonial past."[65] As officials set out to "refashion the cultures of work and even
daily life in Kenya to help promote tourism," schools incorporated tourism
studies into their curriculums, and the state launched a national campaign
to educate Kenyans about the role of citizens "in helping the advancement
of the industry."[66] White men and women featured prominently in Kenyan
travel brochures, naturalizing their presence in the country.[67]

Scholars have productively traced the ways in which the tourism industry
in East Africa produces whiteness through frames of colonial nostalgia.[68]
Mayers Ranch, for example, a private tourist attraction in the Rift Valley
launched by a white settler family in 1968, invited European visitors to in-
dulge their fascination with "tribal peoples" through enactments of Maasai
"dancing in their warrior compound, chanting and carrying spears, proud
and aloof."[69] As Bruner and Kirshenblatt-Gimblett observe, sites like Mayers Ranch give colonialism a second life, playing on Western fantasies about
the savage, and "re-enacting an image of the stability of the colonial order
in which Europeans like themselves are in charge."[70] The industry has been
integral to sustaining the myth of Kenya as "a place of loyal servants and
resplendent views, of sundowners in the evenings, and journeys down roads
that were dusty in the dry season and oceans of mud in the rains."[71] The function of the myth, as Will Jackson articulates, is to sidestep the political. It is

"to make what was in fact structured by relations of political and economic power appear to be something naturally or divinely ordained."[72] The myth of "paradise" relies on the complete effacement of colonial violence, and of African resistance to that violence.[73]

The state was eventually compelled to close Mayers Ranch in the 1980s in response to protests from the Kenyan public, and this action is instructive, as it points to the ways in which logics of white supremacy underlying the tourism sector become the source of contestation and debate. In more recent years, the rise of nation-branding has similarly generated pushback. In the immediate aftermath of the 2007 election violence, the ruling elite scrambled to maintain an image of Kenya as peaceful, turning to US lobbying and public relations firms for "damage control."[74] Njoya observed that the priority of the country's leaders could have been to heal the nation, pursue justice and reparations, and work to address the structural inequalities that were at the heart of the political crisis. "But in the midst of such trauma and need for healing and reconciliation," she writes, "what did President Mwai Kibaki do? He set up Brand Kenya." As she elaborates, the primary preoccupation of the ruling elite

> was that Kenya remained a country in which foreigners could invest or relax. The government's target audience was not the people of Kenya but foreigners . . . Every time Kenyans are in distress, the main worry of the government is whether the investors will notice anything, and how soon we can cover up our human weaknesses so as not to scare them away.[75]

Njoya reflects on the psychological effects of this fixation, echoing Frantz Fanon's (1963) observations about the violence with which the supremacy of whiteness is affirmed:

> The focus of Kenya's consciousness on foreign affirmation would explain why Kenyans experience daily life and institutional and collective processes as a form of physical, moral, emotional and intellectual violence. . . . the colonial rationale is repeatedly and deliberately reinforced in the present day. Decade after decade, regime after regime, government institutions have

wired themselves, built themselves, and reproduced policy documents to remain focused on the West, and to wipe Kenyans out of the picture. . . . Kenyans will have to go through a national mental re-engineering that heals us of our inferiority complex and deals with our historical wounds, and then write an affirmation of dignity as human beings.[76]

Njoya's contribution is especially poignant for our analysis of the forms of policing that are increasingly rationalized in the name of security. As Muslim "terrorists" threaten the image of Kenya as an oasis of stability, and concomitantly threaten the tourism sector itself, the ruling class has frantically worked to assure tourists that it is still safe to visit the country. Alongside police crackdowns, mass roundups, extrajudicial killings, and disappearances, this has entailed a refashioning of racial significations, such that images of African men and women in military fatigues (at airports, malls, hotels, and so on) have come to signify—for white visitors—modernity and *safety*. This refashioning is predicated on the construction of an external enemy. As shown in the last section, policymakers have accentuated colonial-era distinctions between natives and nonnatives to locate "violent extremism" among populations with supranational, transregional ties. Attention to these overlapping processes of racialization (the refashioning of "native" Blackness, on the one hand, and the demonization of the "foreign," on the other) is integral to our understanding of emergent modes of world-making, and of the various modes of labor it entails.

In 2015, the government announced a $1 million partnership with CNN International with the objective of connecting CNN's "premium international audience with Kenya's appeal to tourists." In part, this initiative was a rational economic response to Euro-American travel advisories that discouraged citizens of Europe and North America from nonessential travel to the region. But President Kenyatta's language at the time revealed that it was equally informed by frustration about the inequalities that continue to shape Kenya's location in the global economy, gesturing to the emotional, or affective dimensions of geopolitics at the interstate level: "We are fed up with these threats that we keep getting in travel advisories," he declared. "Kenya is as safe as any other country in the world." Armed with a supplemental budget of KSH 5 billion (approximately $50 million) the Ministry of Tourism recommitted itself to promote Kenya as an ideal tourist destination and to "counter the negative publicity occasioned by restricted travel advisories in our key source markets [Western countries]." Promotional video clips tailored to the uncertain political context featured "white bodies in the Kenyan landscape looking to assure other (white) westerners that it is 'safe' to come to Kenya."[77]

Crucially, these images are conjured through the imaginative labor of the tourism industry, and sustained by the racialized hierarchies that it engenders. Branding in the age of "terror" is thus the condition of possibility for the reattribution of value to whiteness, and for the erasure of settler colonial violence. But again, the state's efforts to disentangle the idea of Kenya from the ruins of colonial rule remain aspirational rather than a *fait accompli,* as Kenyans are quick to disrupt the narrative and to unsettle the tailored scenery. Some of the country's most influential online commentators have been at the forefront of these critiques: in a Twitter post from June 2020, Patrick Gathara chastised the Kenyan ruling class for its imbrication in neocolonial tourism strategies that displace Africans from their own land and sanitize histories of colonial violence. In reference to the country's first president, Jomo Kenyatta, Gathara wrote: "This is what happens when a Kenyatta cuts a deal to become one of the *wakoloni* (colonists) and then goes to Nakuru and promises to forgive and forget. It is what happens when we cannot hear the crying out of the blood of the *miros* (Blacks) who died so the place could exist." Ecologist Mordecai Ogada is one of many who have protested the ways in which Kenya's tourism sector is entangled in the reproduction of white supremacy. In response to an image of white tourists on safari posted by the Kenya Tourism Board, Ogada chastised the Kenyan government on Twitter for "shaming Black Africans since 1865." Directing his message to the cabinet secretary for tourism, Ogada tweeted, "Those of us who are Black are simply sick of this nonsense. Staff your ministry with people who can see Black. This white supremacy is so *pass[é]* in August 2021. *Fedhehe kubwa* (A great disgrace)!"[78]

Meanwhile, Njoya argued that decolonization requires abolishing the Ministry of Tourism altogether: "They are the ones who keep the colonial narrative alive. Its colonial fantasy captures all other ministries and places them at the foot of white supremacy."[79] Each of these observations (Gathara, Ogada, Njoya) is informed by a situated understanding of Africa's relationship to global racialized hierarchies. They are shaped by an awareness that the *outcome* of these hierarchies, or of racial capitalism at work, is, as Christine Mungai describes it, "land grabs, lynchings, genocide, and cultural extermination, all done with a thin smile in the name of civilization and progress."[80] What we learn from their analysis—and by attending to the continued significance of whiteness for tourism and the national economy—is that the historical specificity of racial politics in Kenya necessarily extends beyond the boundaries of the nation-state. Not only are local realities structured by global racial capitalist configurations, but Kenyans themselves are implicated in these worldmaking processes.[81] In what follows, I shift away from the tourism sector to consider the civil society sphere in Mombasa, where Muslim residents increasingly feel there is little room for public deliberation and critique, lest it invite suspicion and scrutiny.

Divide and Rule

In March 2015, I attended a *baraza* (public assembly) in Old Town Mombasa. Hundreds of people packed into the town square to hear from elected officials and religious leaders in the wake of a spike in violent incidents in Old Town that prompted concerns about rising cases of "radicalization" and attendant risks for the coast, which relies heavily on income from tourism. At the gathering, which was flanked by security officers, the governor of Mombasa announced that local leaders would no longer turn a blind eye to crime and radicalization. "Enough is enough," he declared. "We are putting the parents of those youths on notice. If they do not stop terrorizing people, we will move from house to house with the police and arrest them. We will even hire lawyers to make sure they are properly prosecuted and jailed."

While the crowd included many people who I knew were critical of state discourse about crime and "radicalization," few dared to publicly question the leaders' interpretation of recent developments, knowing that this could mean subjecting themselves to the very police powers that the governor was prepared to unleash. The timing of my research coincided with a rise in violent incidents in Mombasa. Very soon after I arrived in June 2014, a Russian tourist was shot dead steps from Fort Jesus, a UNESCO World Heritage site. Weeks later, a German tourist was shot and killed, also in Old Town. In response, the British, French, Australian, and American governments all issued travel advisories discouraging their citizens from travel to the coast. Travel advisories had become a common enough practice in recent years that the number of Euro-American tourists had already dropped by almost 28 percent between 2011 and 2014. The effects were devastating for the local economy: Mombasa's Moi airport had received forty chartered flights per week from Europe in 2011, but by July 2015 that number had dropped to three.[82] Hotels were operating at minimal occupancy and many simply shut down, leaving thousands of people without work. Many of my interlocutors were understandably anxious about the impact that travel advisories were having on the coastal economy and the concomitant loss of jobs.

At the same time, they grappled with the reality that the state's efforts to reassure tourists came with the introduction of police and military checkpoints, arbitrary arrests, killings, and disappearances. The indiscriminate targeting and harassment of Kenyan Muslims by the police gained considerable attention during this period, whether from international human rights organizations or media outlets like *Al Jazeera*.[83] Rights activists and policymakers decried what they feared as the potential for these heavy-handed practices to backfire, leading Muslims into the hands of Al-Shabaab. In this context, the question of belonging and inclusion came to dominate policy discussions, with donors and policymakers emphasizing the need to win "hearts and minds." Here we can observe a shift from an initial reliance on coercion to a strategy of coercion *and* consent. At public events I attended in Mombasa, civil society leaders eagerly gestured to Kenya's revised Constitution of 2010, which recognizes the diversity of the population and stresses the importance of political inclusion.[84] Much like the British embrace of indirect rule during the colonial era, the focus shifts from exclusion to inclusion with the goal of understanding and managing difference—what Mamdani refers to as *define* and rule.[85]

In practice, the framing of "good" citizenship in relation to the imperatives of security simultaneously has brought to the fore tensions between abstract *principles* of legal equality, on the one hand, and *everyday sensibilities,* on the other, wherein Kenyans continued to view certain segments of the population with suspicion.[86] As violent extremism is increasingly identified as a threat to national security, the emphasis placed on how citizens can "make a difference" assumes a sinister component, contributing to sensibilities of doubt and suspicion. The object of concern shifts from state-sanctioned violence to one's inner social circles, a classic divide-and-rule strategy of population-centered counter-insurgency.[87] *The person next to you could be a terrorist,* proclaimed Mary the facilitator at one civil society workshop on "countering violent extremism" (CVE) that I attended in Mombasa in 2015. *Security starts with you and me!*

I observed the effects of this form of divide and rule when I spent time with the staff of the Kenya Muslim Youth Alliance (KMYA), a national non-profit youth network that is staffed by Muslims and Christians alike. One day, I was chatting with a young man whom I will call Abdi, a Kenyan of Somali descent in his early twenties. What began as a conversation about the Kenyan military's role in Somalia quickly became a debate about suspect citizenship when his colleague Henry spoke up, accusing Abdi of being "biased" because of his "roots in Somalia." When Abdi pushed back, insisting he was a Kenyan, Henry claimed that "as a Somali Kenyan," Abdi was "Somali first." *That's the bottom line,* he continued, *you come from there.* Further positioning Abdi as an outsider, Henry drew a connection between Somaliness and violence and criminality. *You people,* he said, pointing to Abdi, *protect and hide criminals. If they are terrorists and thugs, they should face the law.* As this exchange reveals, the championing of liberal inclusion in civil society spaces like KMYA has occurred *alongside* a rearticulation of difference, wherein certain populations are positioned as suspicious, and as racialized outsiders.

I attended a number of civil society workshops focused on CVE and observed that these gatherings became sites for the naturalization and cir-culation of ideas about policing one's colleagues, friends, family members, and neighbors. Human rights organizations that once documented and chal-lenged police abuse began to encourage coastal residents to work closely with law enforcement actors and to build relationships with actors they once viewed with antagonism. *You see the police as part of the problem rather than the solution,* said a police commissioner at a workshop organized by the rights

FIGURE 6. Polisi Ni Rafiki campaign poster, 2012. Source: Boniface Mwangi.

organization Muslims for Human Rights (MUHURI). *But there has been a paradigm shift. We are working to cut off the levers of patronage. Look, we have an institution now that we can work with. Don't throw stones at the conference room—walk in!* Here, the police commissioner worked to re-instill faith in the police as the primary source and most legitimate form of protection from violence. Some groups went further, working to cultivate sympathy for the police as human beings whose sacrifices "keep us safe." In 2012, activist Boniface Mwangi launched a campaign entitled *"Polisi Ni Rafiki"* (the police are our friends) featuring images that appeal to Kenyans for engagement and empathy with the security sector.

Such appeals contribute to the cultivation of race- and class-inflected sensibilities that police the boundaries of legitimate and illegitimate violence, and of permissible politics.[88] Any invocation of injustice is read as suspect, and as a potential call to violence.[89] At the workshop I attended in 2015, for example, the facilitator Mary acknowledged historical marginalization as a potential contributing factor to political frustration, but reduced injustice to a "feeling" or a "perception" that was at risk of manipulation. The implication was that feelings and perceptions of injustice were not in fact grounded in lived reality: *Marginalization, real or perceived, by governments of Muslims is often considered marginalization of the entire community,* she said. *This feeling has been harbored by Muslims, so it becomes very easy to convince a Muslim youth to "stand up and defend your rights."* Here, Mary explicitly questions the political analysis of coastal Muslims, dismissing it as naïve. As I observed in other, similar gatherings, the facilitators of CVE workshops not only normalize expansive modes of policing but *pathologize* those who question them, contributing to a form of political gaslighting. At a time when coastal residents desperately needed a space to process their anxieties about surveillance and policing, donor-backed civil society programming actively worked to dismiss their grounded knowledge formations.

Conclusion

Focusing on the Kenyan coast, this chapter has wrestled with the continuity of colonial dynamics in a context where formal colonial rule has long been abolished. I have shed light on geographically based, racially informed regimes of subordination and exploitation that Mombasan scholar Ali Mazrui once characterized as a form of internal colonialism.[90] Marginalized and pathologized by the Christian-majority government, yet simultaneously central to the Kenyan tourism industry, the coast constitutes an integral site through which a relation of coloniality and war is sustained and reproduced. While the intent of the state and its counter-terror partners is to contain coastal populations, this is not a simple story of suffering and exploitation. Coastal residents' experiences and interpretations of their relationship to multiscalar power formations challenge prevailing state-centered conceptualizations of "security" and point to alternative modes of knowing and making the world.

During my interviews and informal exchanges with Muslims in Mombasa, many raised critical questions about the political and economic interests motivating the war on terror. Rumors circulated about it serving as a cover for large-scale land dispossession, as families desperate for income began to accept outside offers on their properties. Others went further, pointing to what they saw as the unchecked power of the United States, and characterized the war on terror as a war on Muslims. Indeed, many linked their own experiences to the oppression of Muslims across the world. With this in mind we can begin to unpack why Osama bin Laden became an icon for young people in the region after 9/11, and why calls for secession resurfaced in the run-up to the 2013 national elections.[91] Soon after the 9/11 attacks, bin Laden iconography appeared on posters, tee shirts, and the walls of shops and buildings across Mombasa. As Jeremy Prestholdt observes, "What propelled him to 'superpower' status among some young people was that he not only symbolized irreverence for America and a general critique of global injustice, but he also appealed to Kenyan Muslims' sense of marginalization and common struggle with other Muslims around the world."[92] Bin Laden's popularity, Prestholdt writes, "offers insights into the way that young people have evoked symbolic aspects of an icon without reference to the ideology of the political figure."[93] Yet as Prestholdt notes, the Kenyan state and its counter-terror partners have conflated political *frustration* with political *violence*, a superficial interpretation that associates popular support for certain figures with a belief in, and readiness to employ violence for, political ends.[94] The effect of such a misreading has been to further alienate coastal Muslims by pathologizing them as "radicals," foreclosing discussion about the claim itself: namely, that Muslims on the coast (and elsewhere) are the targets of an unjust war.

What would it mean to take this claim seriously? Michel Rolph Trouillot insists that the language and categories employed by everyday people *matter*, and offer signposts about the relationships and institutions of power that shape daily life.[95] In Nairobi, Wangui Kimari observes that the use of what she calls "war-talk" among youth in poor urban settlements indexes the siege that those who live within the margins of the city experience every day.[96] I found, like Kimari, that the actions of Kenya's Anti-Terror Police Unit (ATPU) in Mombasa were "visceral catalysts for embodied feelings of siege."[97] When a mother in the Floringi neighborhood of the city awoke early one morning to loud bangs of the police knocking down her front door, she entered her living room to find heavily armed officers dressed in military fatigues. "There were so many of them. They looked as if they were going to war," she recounted of the ATPU's killing of her son minutes after they raided her home.[98] The spike in extrajudicial killings attributed to the ATPU (more than eighty cases between 2012 and 2016) left a palpable mark on coastal residents, and the fact that some of the cases were later revealed to be instances of mistaken identity further accentuated people's anxieties.[99] As one young man in his twenties observed to me of the ATPU, *We live in fear every day. We cannot have a normal life. Our brothers have been kidnapped and tortured. When they arrest us, they tell us openly that they will kill us.* Connecting the ATPU to its foreign backers, another young man in Old Town asked, *How am I supposed to think of the UK and US governments when they fund and train a killer squad that kidnaps and tortures people in Mombasa? But* we *are supposed to be the "terrorists"?* And in the words of Ali, who lives in the neighborhood of Majengo: *All of us know that we are at war. If they [the government] see you coming to a certain mosque, they decide that you are among the youth that should be tracked down to be killed. We as youth want to be free. We want to be safe. We cannot be chased, tortured, killed by the government. If we are killed, we have to take revenge. But the government is the one with the weapons.*

These articulations of siege gesture to what Lisa Bhungalia refers to as "asphyxiatory violence," a slow debilitating process that progressively erodes conditions of livability.[100] As we have seen, the ability to engage in mundane daily activities—commuting to work or school, visiting one's friends and neighbors, and even sleeping in one's own home—entails a series of negotiations and calculations that are fraught with risk. These experiences are the foundations for an embodied form of political analysis that offers critical insights into the operations of power in Kenya today. Recognizing that empire sustains itself through the active *exclusion* of these forms of subaltern knowledge, we have an opportunity to reflect on the ways in which new modes of political consciousness unfold in dialogue with one's everyday encounters with power. Whether in the form of donor-backed civil society workshops that actively question one's grounded knowledge, or in the form of explicit harassment or abuse by the police, these overlapping cultural and material assaults on the dignity of coastal Muslims have cumulative effects that warrant being seen and heard on their own terms. It is by centering these forms of subjugated knowledge that we become privy not only to circumscribed life chances, but equally to new modes of inhabiting and remaking the world, as young people like Jamal—the young man harassed by the police for simply attending a pick-up football game— insist on standing their ground.

3 PHANTOM EPISTEMOLOGIES

Navigating the Urban Gray Zone

IN AUGUST 2010, Hamisi was kidnapped in broad daylight outside a Nairobi shopping center. Kenyan police transported him by car, hooded and handcuffed, across the border to Uganda. Along the way, he learned that he was suspected of involvement in the bombings that had occurred the previous month in Uganda's capital city of Kampala, claiming more than seventy lives.[1] After twelve hours on the road, he was ushered inside the headquarters of Uganda's Rapid Response Unit, where British and American interrogators awaited him. The interrogators accused Hamisi of having ties to militants in the region and pressured him to work as an informant. When his answers proved to be unsatisfying, he was subjected to psychological and physical abuse, and threatened with rendition to Guantanamo.

Back home in Nairobi, Hamisi's wife Maryam frantically sought information on his whereabouts. Witnesses to the abduction noted that the apprehending men were dressed in plain clothes and used an unmarked vehicle. This was consistent with the modus operandi of the Anti-Terror Police Unit (ATPU), a special branch of the Kenyan police formed in 2003 with funding and training from the United States and United Kingdom. The ATPU has since become notorious in Kenya for its plainclothes death squads, which operate with impunity. Families and rights activists in search of answers are often told by Kenyan officials that the ATPU is simply following instructions provided by outside powers.

In August 2014, I learned about another family's search for answers. At a press conference hosted by Haki Africa, a Mombasa-based human rights organization, I listened as Mohamed recounted the kidnapping of his brother, Abdul, by the police the previous day. The brothers, who lived in the Majengo neighborhood of Mombasa, had been on their way home from Friday prayers. As the young men approached home, eight officers jumped out of two unmarked vehicles and apprehended Abdul. The officers then pointed a gun at Mohamed, who was watching in shock, rendering him powerless to intervene. With the help of eyewitnesses who recorded the license plate of one of the vehicles, he immediately reported the incident at Makupa police station nearby. Still clinging to the possibility that Abdul could be found, he requested that the police erect a roadblock along the Mombasa–Nairobi highway, where he believed the cars were headed. But as Mohamed shared despondently with the press the next morning, the police instructed him to file the requisite paperwork, and to leave the premises. This seemingly indifferent bureaucratic response compounded the family's distress, and contributed to their suspicion that the kidnapping had been authorized by the ATPU.

Following Mohamed's testimony, a member of Parliament spoke to the press. "The man who was taken yesterday," he proclaimed, "is not only a constituent of mine, he is also someone whom I went to school with. 'Ninamjua—I know him.'" He went on to ask, "What is his sin? Being a young person from Mombasa? Until answers are forthcoming, let us agree on this point: When you wake up in the morning and don't know whether you will go back home alive or dead, and your family must continuously call you to see if you have been picked by a poacher, then there is no need for us to pay taxes."

The MP's fiery statement reflected the anger and frustration that permeated the air among Mombasa residents at the time, as disappearances of friends and family members had come to haunt daily life. Abdul was one of at least twenty people who had disappeared in the previous eight months in Mombasa alone. Haki Africa's office was cluttered with posters of missing persons, with several focused on the case of Hemed, who had disappeared in the wake of the police raid of Masjid Musa earlier that year. While most of the one hundred youth arrested in February eventually appeared in court, Hemed was never seen again. The Haki Africa staff, whom I worked with closely during my extended period of research, worried about the likelihood that Abdul's fate would be no different. In the months that followed, we began to compile a report that tracked each of these cases. We met with ATPU officers and officials from the British and American governments hoping to learn what laws and political bodies had authorized police action in each case. But information was hard to come by, and the search for it was often met with suspicion and scrutiny.

Disappearances and extrajudicial killings at the hands of the police predate the onset of the war on terror. In 1998 the Kenyan Human Rights Commission observed that the police killed an average of three people per week, and that they justified their actions by referring to their victims as thieves or wanted criminals.[2] At the height of police repression of the vigilante group known as Mungiki, approximately five hundred people disappeared in a five-month period in 2007.[3] Kenyan activists are therefore prone to suspect the police in cases of unclaimed acts of killings and disappearances. They have also been at the forefront of demands for accountability. In the aftermath of the 2007 postelection violence, these demands mounted, as the police were found to be directly responsible for a sizable percentage of the 1,100 election-related deaths.[4] Yet calls for accountability were occurring alongside the state's growing entanglement in the war on terror and the concomitant emergence of supranational forms of police power.[5] This has fundamentally altered the landscape of human rights activism, as activists are forced to contend with the secrecy that shrouds these coordinated, entangled, modes of police power.

This chapter captures the doubt and uncertainty that haunt Kenyan Muslim activists as they contend with the expansive and illegible forms of police power that are authorized by the war on terror. While the Kenyan police have long been agents of abuse and objects of public speculation, the phantom-like power of supranational actors has contributed to the spectral quality of police violence, as deaths and disappearances are productive of rumors and conspiracy theories about the geopolitical actors and interests at play. It has now become common sense that "the Americans" are involved in counter-terror operations; yet the dispersal of violent authority to Kenyan security bodies makes US participation less visible and thereby less traceable, rendering it a phantom power.[6] When Kenyans confront the actual workings of power in specific contexts, this everyday common sense is haunted by empirical elusiveness. Activists wrestle with the fear and paranoia that come with their own subjection to surveillance and suspicion, as well as with the knowledge that is needed to navigate unpredictable urban landscapes. I employ Kristin Peterson's conceptualization of "phantom epistemologies," to capture the tentative, often unverifiable forms of knowledge that circulate about the opaque forms of policing that are at work.[7] I approach phantom epistemologies as embodied forms of everyday geopolitical knowledge that are steeped in fear and uncertainty, but that nonetheless serve a practical function for people confronting life-and-death predicaments in Kenya today: because knowledge "gained in fear or discomfort is especially well learned"; even the smallest kernel of information sharpens the senses and circulates with a certain urgency.[8]

In what follows, I trace the shape-shifting nature of contemporary imperial formations, foregrounding the networked assemblages of police power operating in specifically urban theaters of the war on terror.[9] US military strategists increasingly apply counter-insurgency thinking to non–war spaces, working closely with partner forces—here, in the form of specially trained Kenyan police squads. As security operatives identify everyday urban spaces as sites of concern, the people who inhabit them are ascribed risk categories based on their potential connection to resistance movements or violent groups. This has fundamentally transformed the daily lifeworlds of urban residents, reminding us that cities are "both critical sites in which to inquire into worlding projects, as well as the ongoing result and target of specific worldings."[10] I briefly explore the legacies of colonial rule in order to situate contemporary Kenya in a landscape steeped in longer histories of counter-insurgent policing. Having inherited the British colonial fetishization of "order" (evidenced most poignantly in response to the anticolonial Land and Freedom Army), the Kenyan ruling class has participated in the creation of ever-present enemies in an effort to sort the obedient from the dissident, citizen from suspect. Longstanding experiences and memories of the criminalization of dissent inform the thinking of many of my activist interlocutors in Kenya today. But the simultaneous professionalization of activism has contributed to the importance of verifiable knowledge, making the search for information all the more pressing. In this context, activists are compelled to weigh long-term calculations (documentation and accountability) against short-term ones (their own safety, as well as the needs of affected family members). In doing so, they draw on their own everyday geopolitical knowledge to navigate the shape-shifting geographies of the war on terror. War-making is therefore productive not simply of violence and destruction, but equally of creativity and collaboration: if the Kenyan state and its partners collect information to anticipate risk and guide decision-making, so too must the subjects of surveillance and policing think anew and make calculations about their own well-being and security.

Empire's Laboratory: The Urban "Gray Zone"

In a 2021 report entitled "Overkill," the International Crisis Group observes that the expansion of the war on terror's African fronts has occurred quietly behind the scenes, propelled not by political leadership at the White House, but by special operations forces on the ground in the region.[11] Indeed, the African continent has in many ways become a laboratory for the US military to deploy more flexible and diffuse maneuvers that are designed to match the seeming amorphousness of the so-called enemy.[12] While critics rightly decry the escalation of drone strikes in Somalia, a singular focus on drone warfare is to miss the wider matrix of violence that is at work, wherein US-trained African police forces increasingly employ military tactics of tracking and targeting potential suspects in quotidian urban spaces.

The discretionary authority afforded to the US Africa Command (AFRICOM) has effectively empowered it to approach the entire continent as a "gray zone," a terrain that military strategists conceptualize as falling within the ambiguous spectrum between war and peace. As Danny Hoffman explains, this concept gained traction in the 2010s and circulates primarily among US special operations forces to characterize a "range of activities designed to achieve the traditional objectives of warfare 'without the overt use of military force.'"[13] In practice, gray-zone operations are conducted not by US troops, but by partner forces presumed to be more "naturally capable" of functioning in Global South cities—urban geographies that the US military racializes as unknowable and threatening.[14]

Lisa Bhungalia's conceptualization of "elastic empire" is productive here in helping us contend with the mutability and shape-shifting character of US empire.[15] At a time when the US government is wary of the costs associated with its own direct intervention—whether in dollars, lives, or legal and political blowback—the US Africa Command (AFRICOM) increasingly relies on a growing number of African security forces to assume the burden of counter-terrorism missions on the continent. Here, the very security bodies that were once the subject of critique by Euro-American governments for contributing to instability (particularly in the wake of the 2007–8 post-election violence) have now been championed—via capacity building and security sector reform initiatives—as the solution to "insecurity." Human rights concerns aside, partnerships with elite African police and military units make it politically possible for the United States to rely on surrogate forces in cases where the United States is not officially at war, and where the very presence of US troops is likely to raise eyebrows.[16] Such creative realignments and reformulations, writes Bhungalia, "proliferate the sites and means" through which life is regulated.[17] Along similar lines, and writing about Pakistan's relationship to the war on terror, Madiha Tahir employs the term "distributed empire" to characterize the differentially distributed, opaque networks of actors and technologies that augment the reach of the war on terror to govern more bodies and spaces.[18] Tahir's emphasis on the dispersal of power unsettles the seeming singularity and homogeneity of US empire by emphasizing relations of interdependence across time and space.

The readiness of African states to deploy their own security forces to the front lines of the war on terror has been critical to their continued ability to access foreign aid. While scholars often point to the material ruination of African cities in the wake of structural adjustment and state withdrawal, these dynamics are unfolding alongside a hyperinvestment in new forms of policing and social control.[19] Nairobi and Mombasa are now marked by a preponderance of permanent security-related infrastructures—from CCTV cameras to privately guarded compounds, as well as the police itself, which

Wangui Kimari astutely refers to as a de facto form of urban infrastructure and spatial management.[20] These cities are also witnessing a rise in mobile, flexible police maneuvers designed to match the amorphousness of the so-called enemy. Believing that terror suspects operate through diffuse, formless networks embedded in urban centers, security actors increasingly rely on "pop-up" police tactics (checkpoints, house raids, abductions, killings) that are producing new uncertainties and insecurities.[21]

While the public's focus in Kenya has almost exclusively been on the ATPU, an August 2020 investigative report revealed that a secretive Kenyan police unit known as the Rapid Response Team or RRT (housed within the paramilitary General Service Unit, or GSU), had in fact been the primary force behind many of the "high value" or "high risk" targeted operations in the country.[22] Composed of roughly sixty highly trained commandos, the RRT is trained, equipped, and financed by the CIA, allowing the US government to circumvent human rights restrictions imposed by the Leahy Law.[23] In addition to the CIA, the RRT has partnered with Britain's MI6 as well as Israel's Mossad and is believed to be responsible for an unknown number of "kill or capture" raids, summary executions, and enforced disappearances, including raids and killings that were found to be based on mistaken identities.[24]

The most striking manifestation of Kenya's expansive police powers unfolded in April 2014, when 6,000 security personnel descended on the Nairobi suburb of Eastleigh, raiding homes in the dead of night. While the declared objective was to "weed out" Somali refugees—whom the Kenyan state has increasingly blamed for recent attacks—the national media's construction of Eastleigh as a "terrorist haven" shaped public sentiments about anyone and anything connected to this section of the city. Indeed, the subsequent internment of more than a thousand people in a Nairobi sports stadium revealed that Kenyan citizens, too, were among those targeted.

Kenyan security officials increasingly cite the state's inability to effectively prosecute transnational crime alone in order to legitimate cooperation with supranational bodies.[25] In 2014, Kenya signed an agreement with an Israeli firm to develop a biodata system for national identity cards.[26] Five years later, it unveiled the controversial biometric initiative Huduma

Namba (or "Service Number"), designed to provide a "single source of truth" about each and every Kenyan.[27] Meanwhile, national media outlets reported that the US National Security Agency has been secretly monitoring telecommunications systems in Kenya through a program called MYSTIC. These coordinated forms of police power have had deadly consequences: communications surveillance in Kenya is conducted without legislative oversight, and intercepted content is shared and abused to spy on, profile, and track so-called terror suspects, often leading to their arrest, torture, and disappearance.[28]

Dangerous Knowledge

Many of these counter-terror–related human rights abuses have now been widely documented, largely thanks to the efforts of Kenyan human rights organizations.[29] The very process of documenting and verifying information related to counter-terror abuses constitutes an integral element of what it means to be a respected human rights professional today. As Winifred Tate observes in connection with her research in Colombia, the professionalization of human rights knowledge (which began roughly in the 1990s) has fundamentally altered the nature of activism. With this shift came a focus on credibility, and on making quantifiable and verifiable claims. "The veracity of specific claims—including dates, time lines, places, and responsibility—was critical."[30] More broadly, the emphasis on reliable information "centered on objective reporting that depoliticized human rights knowledge, adhering to legal standards, and uses dispassionate tone rather than express explicit alliance with leftist programs."[31]

While my interlocutors identify as rights activists, they are all too aware of the limitations of a depoliticized human rights framework. Legal and rights-based claims, for example, do not address context-specific political questions (e.g., Why have I been banned from travel, and by whom?). Very few cases against terror suspects in Kenya make it to court, and those that do typically do not result in convictions. Moreover, the reality on the ground makes it impossible to be dispassionate, as family members plead for help in tracking down the fate of their loved ones. Many so-called "terror suspects" identified by the state are familiar names and faces, and social and kinship ties work against simplistic binaries of innocence and guilt. I understand activism in this context to mean the concerted effort to make legible the amorphous assemblages that characterize imperial policing. As activists learn how to navigate uncertainty, they confront the war on terror as a practical challenge that requires "their own form of lived subjective research."[32] Importantly, collecting information *about* the forms of power that are at work should not necessarily be conflated with resistance to them; to do so would risk obscuring the circumscribed agency of these activists, many of whom rely on donor funds from the very governments that fund and train the ATPU. Their actions nevertheless open a space of what Jacques Rancière theorizes as dissensus—in this case, of disidentification with dominant imaginaries of "security." If policing as defined by Rancière refers to an ordering of subjects that allocates ways of doing, being, and saying in particular places, then the activists' readiness to raise questions about killings and disappearances represents a break, an undoing of "the perceptible divisions of police order."[33]

But any effort to learn about the security actors, evidence, and decision-making underlying such cases is deemed suspicious. To ask questions, as Ngũgĩ wa Thiong'o reminds us, is a "dangerous exercise."[34] It is to destabilize the notion that violence and secrecy are the prerogatives of the state and its security partners. In practice, much of human rights work is about revealing what is *already* widely known. For activists who are immersed in and surrounded by stories of police abductions and killings, the goal is to "make public what was known but cannot be said, transforming the public secret into the public transcript."[35] Anthropologist Michael Taussig invoked the notion of public secrets to capture the circulation of particular forms of knowledge in the context of counter-insurgency campaigns in Colombia in the early 1980s, when "people dared not state the obvious." As he observed,

> We all "knew" this [collusion between death squads and the military], and they "knew" we "knew" but there was no way it could be easily articulated, certainly not on the ground, face to face. Such "smoke screens" are surely long known to mankind, but this "long knowness" is itself an intrinsic part of knowing what not to know . . . Such is the labor of the negative, as when

it is pointed out that something may be obvious, but needs stating in order to be obvious. For example, the public secret. Knowing it is essential to its power, equal to its denial.[36]

In the context of the war on terror, the security state's preoccupation with secrecy produces a world in which "knowledge is always rendered suspect."[37] For activists (as well as researchers), this has implications for where one can go, what questions can be asked, and what can be shared publicly. It has implications for how one manages the possession of information that they are not supposed to know.[38] When the actors from whom you seek to obtain information *themselves* do not know (as in cases where the Kenyan police execute an arrest without necessarily knowing whether the order was issued by authorities in Nairobi or Washington, DC), the landscape is murkier still.

One morning in April 2015, I experienced this firsthand. That day, I went to the offices of Haki Africa in Mombasa to meet Adam, the organization's rapid response officer. Adam and I planned to visit the ATPU headquarters in Mombasa to inquire about the list of people who had disappeared or been found dead in recent months. When I arrived, Adam was already halfway out the door. *Let's go to court, client is waiting, haraka haraka, twende* (quickly, quickly, let's go). As we ran down the stairs to the front door, I asked what was happening in court. *Remember the boy who went missing and was found in Mandera?* he asked. *Yes,* I said, *isn't that the cousin of Rashid?* (a colleague who works with the county government). *Ndiyo, ndiyo* (yes, yes).

Hailing a *tuk tuki* (rickshaw), Adam implored the driver to hurry: *fanya haraka, tunaenda kotini; we are "rapid response"!* Outside the law courts, the security officers could hardly be bothered to search Adam, as he is known for his frequent comings and goings; once I caught up, Adam had learned that the case was adjourned until a later date—a common enough occurrence that neither one of us was surprised. *Twende ATPU,* he said, *let's go to the ATPU.*

The guards outside police headquarters were similarly uninterested in our arrival. Each of them knows Adam, and we had visited the police compound together before. We walked past the collection of impounded cars rusting in the parking lot, and a group of men came into view. Adam, recognizing them as ATPU officers, greeted them and explained why we had come. The officers glared at us in disgust and soon began hurling accusations: *You people, you like bloodshed! Where were your condemnations of the killings in Garissa?*

Neither Adam nor I had thought about the timing of our visit. The Al-Shabaab attack on Garissa University in northeastern Kenya had occurred just days before, and emotions ran high. Adam acknowledged the horror of the previous week's attacks and then tried, slowly, to bring them back to the topic at hand: we were hoping to obtain an official response from ATPU on the list of killings and disappearances. The men remained bitter and disdainful of our very presence. It is likely that our questions were sensitive, not because the police did not want to provide answers, but because they could not—and neither could their superiors, who in theory possess the authority to do so. We were in the thick of uncertainty produced by phantom power, what Greg Beckett defines as "the strategic use of political armies . . . by a power that is removed from or beyond the reach of the national sovereign."[39]

The US government did come up as a topic of conversation, albeit indirectly. At one point in our exchange, when the police were inquiring about my relationship to Haki Africa (having deduced that I was a foreigner), I offered that I was a researcher from the United States. One of the officers seized upon this information to launch an indirect critique of the US government: *The US is worse, they drone people!* he said, defiantly. As I processed the (potentially legitimate?) attempt to deflect blame as well as the question of whether and how I should respond, there was a sudden shift in tone—*but we need you human rights people, the rule of law is important*, the officer said. *You must advise us on how to arrest these terrorists!* I don't entirely remember how Adam engaged them in his response, but I do recall an earlier observation he had made that the police were fickle: on some days they were friendly, on other days, not at all. On at least one recent occasion, he said, an officer had threatened him: *One day we will come for you.* As the conversation came to an end, we agreed to leave the draft copy of our report with one of the officials inside, and were instructed to await a formal response.

Later that day, as I walked the streets of downtown Mombasa, I was conscious of the fact that I was wearing a bright red shirt, one that would make me easily identifiable among the crowds. However irrational the thought of being singled out was, it spoke to my own paranoia in the wake of making myself known to the police as someone who was searching for answers. This paranoia and fear were something that my colleagues at Haki Africa experienced nearly every day, as each encounter with the police was the source of new trepidation. As I observed simultaneous excitement and nervousness in the search for information, I reflected on the question of dangerous knowledge and its embodiment, wherein power is experienced "close to the skin."[40] Begona Aretxaga's work on the phantasmic quality of stories and conspiracy theories about the police offers a productive lens through which to analyze Kenyan activists' efforts to make sense of phantom-like entities like the ATPU. Drawing on Walter Benjamin, she illustrates how the elusiveness of police power makes it the object of constant speculation and fear.[41] The rumors and conspiracy theories that emerge in these contexts become a means through which to engage with uncertainty and to process the simultaneous display and disavowal of imperial power.[42]

As the project of national security "renders all behavior into signs," activists navigate their daily lives knowing that any one of their fellow citizens could report "suspicious behavior" to the authorities.[43] They know that they are marked by a contingent ability to become suspects without awareness or intent.[44] Thus, they wrestle both with the fear and paranoia that come with their ambiguous positionality *and* with the knowledge that is needed to navigate uncertain landscapes. They are often compelled to weigh long-term calculations like documentation and accountability against short-term ones, whether in relation to their own safety, or to the needs and priorities of affected family members. Take the extrajudicial killing of Sheikh Aboud Rogo, a high-profile and known sympathizer of Al-Shabaab, in Monday-morning traffic along the Mombasa–Malindi highway in August 2012.[45] Believing that the ATPU was responsible for killing her husband, Rogo's wife called the staff at Muslims for Human Rights (MUHURI) to the scene and told the police, "It is you policemen who have killed him, we don't want a postmortem or any help from you."[46] The riposte to the police was both defiant and in keeping with Islamic law, which requires the immediate burial of the body. As protests broke out across Mombasa, MUHURI condemned the murder. In this case, as in others, it strategized about whether and how to arrange for a postmortem. While autopsies can be useful in mounting a legal challenge, they also require forgoing the ritual of burying the dead as soon as possible.

The decision by MUHURI staff to play *any* role in identifying next steps in these scenarios is a risky one, as it opens the door to claims of guilt by association. As Hassan Mwakimako observes, the association of nearly any form of Muslim activism with terrorism has effectively criminalized Muslim moral economies of care.[47] Even for groups that are not religiously oriented or motivated, the fact that Muslims seek assistance or support on issues that specifically concern Muslims (difficulty obtaining national ID cards or, more recently, counter-terror abuses) has meant that their activities acquire religious connotations.[48] One month after Hamisi was kidnapped by the police in August 2010, for example, Ugandan authorities arrested activist Al-Amin Kimathi when he traveled from Nairobi to Kampala to arrange legal representation for each of the Kenyan citizens who had been illegally rendered to Uganda on suspicion of involvement in the bombings that took place during the 2010 FIFA World Cup. Suddenly, Al-Amin stood accused of the same crimes as the men he was trying to help. He was detained at Kampala's Luzira prison in solitary confinement for twelve months before the charges against him were dropped.[49]

When I first met Al-Amin in July 2012—one year after his release and return to Kenya—he described the rapidly shrinking space for discussion and debate on the lived realities of the war on terror. While Kenya's Muslim minority population had at one point been vocal in their critiques of counter-terror abuses, Al-Amin explained that many feared the consequences of speaking out. He was aware that his arrest and year-long detention were directly tied to his own activism. For at least three years, Hamisi and Al-Amin had been tracking the cases of Kenyans who had been arrested or disappeared—including Kenyan citizens who were illegally renditioned to prisons in Somalia and Ethiopia in 2007. The two visited prisons to inquire about individuals who were being held as terror suspects; where possible, they met with affected family members. In this context, they developed an understanding of who was making what decisions, who was released, and who remained behind bars. They began to map the opaque web of the counter-terror apparatus in East Africa, conducting the groundwork for subsequent investigations by international human rights groups. In effect, they were counter-mapping the very apparatus that sought to monitor and control them.[50] *The government was not happy,* Al-Amin said to me with a mischievous smile. *By 2009, I knew I was marked.*

Al-Amin's efforts to trace the assemblage of actors and institutions that police "terror" in East Africa had garnered the scrutiny of those very actors—making him the subject of a diplomatic cable made public by Wikileaks. Despite his release from detention, he continued to confront the reality of life under suspicion. When we reconnected in 2013 at his office in Nairobi, Al-Amin was in the midst of processing his mail. Opening and momentarily holding the contents of an envelope in his hands, he looked up at me and relayed that he had been invited to attend the upcoming July 4 celebrations at the US embassy in Nairobi. *What am I to make of this,* he asked uneasily, *knowing that the US government likely played a role in my arrest and detention? What do they want from me?* The complicity of the US government in Al-Amin's detention was never proven officially. But as he held the invitation in his hands, he seemed to be reliving the fear and confusion he experienced at the time of his arrest. The unease was palpable as Al-Amin sought to reconcile in his mind the idea that a government that once treated him as a criminal now sought out his company at a cocktail party.

Histories and Ideologies of Law and Order

This section foregrounds the legacies of colonial law-and-order policing, approaching contemporary Kenya as a landscape steeped in longer histories of imperial violence.[51] While we have growing knowledge of the infrastructural apparatus that makes the war on terror possible today, the histories of Global South partner states are often overlooked in these analyses. Yet grasping the enduring presence of colonial logics is critical to our understanding of how a past that is imagined to be over "persists, reactivates, and recurs in transfigured forms."[52] In the postcolonial period, I focus especially on the criminalization of the Islamic Party of Kenya (IPK), an entity whose rise and fall constitutes a vital reference point for Kenyan Muslims. The state's response to the IPK is an example of a longstanding pattern of the criminalization of dissent, wherein efforts by Muslims to mobilize politically around their shared oppression *as Muslims* have been deemed suspicious, illegitimate, and subject to pacification. This history of criminalization informed activists' responses to antiterrorism legislation when it was first introduced in the early 2000s.

The body now known as the Kenyan Police Force was established in 1920 when Kenya became a British colony. Recruitment efforts were heavily shaped by the idea that some ethnic communities were more receptive to the colonial project than others. Because police officers were prevented from serving in their own towns or cities, residents increasingly viewed the police as an oppressive, alien force.[53] Policing was concentrated in Mombasa and Nairobi, which constituted the heart of the settler economy. Surveillance was a key technology of social control, with the *kipande* as the most obvious early example.[54] Introduced by the British after World War I, the kipande was a special ID card that contained the holder's name, fingerprints, ethnicity, employment history, and signature of their employer, as well as prescribed limitations on their movement in urban areas. It was designed to monitor, track, and confine the African population, marking them as inherently suspect.[55]

In a 1987 essay, Kenyan historian E. S. Atieno Odhiambo coined the term "ideology of order" to describe the political elite's fetishization of order—a preoccupation, he argued, that they acquired from colonial administrators. In urban areas under British rule, the police were tasked with serving white settlers who viewed unemployed Africans as a source of criminality.[56] The British fixation with law and order intensified as its colonial subjects increasingly questioned the legitimacy of colonial rule. In addition to the growing militancy of African trade unions, the activities of newly formed political parties threatened the colonial endeavor, leading the police to operate primarily as instruments of containment and pacification.[57]

In the face of mounting opposition from the Land and Freedom Army, British officials declared a breakdown of law and order. Referring to members of the resistance as terrorists, the British launched a campaign of forced removals, displacing Kikuyu from their land and into detention camps. If the kipande represented the banal institutionalization of suspicion, then the state of emergency instituted in 1952 represented its more spectacular iteration. While the emergency was conceived as a police rather than a military action, the police provided the justifying framework "on which the action of military forces could be superimposed." Intelligence gathering was crucial to the counter-insurgency and operated beyond the purview of legislative and judicial scrutiny.[58]

Much like the British before them, Kenyan leaders often interpret challenges to their rule through the lens of criminality. Facing ongoing threats to its authority, the ruling class has actively cultivated moral panics and popular preoccupations with law and order through the introduction of new "criminal types" in need of policing.[59] The Mombasan poet Abdilatif Abdalla was Kenya's earliest political prisoner, arrested and charged with sedition in 1969 for publishing a pamphlet that challenged the state's intolerance of critique.[60] His writings, like those of fellow political prisoner Ngũgĩ wa Thiong'o, inspired generations of activists who dared to ask questions of their leaders. This compounded the anxiety of figures like President Daniel Arap Moi, who authorized the creation of special police units like the Flying Squad and Rhino Squad to monitor and suppress dissent; during Moi's rule (1978–2002), the arbitrary arrest, detention, and torture of students, journalists, lawyers, and politicians contributed to a climate of crippling fear.[61]

It was in this context that the IPK first emerged on the coast. The introduction of multiparty politics in the 1990s ushered in a period of dramatic political changes, and religious organizations were at the forefront of efforts to push for political reform, publicly challenging the Moi regime.[62] But the limits of support for multipartyism came to the fore when Muslims sought to create a political party in 1992. While other Muslim organizations, such as the Supreme Council of Kenyan Muslims (SUPKEM), had been active for some time, SUPKEM was known for its close ties to the Moi government, and for this reason had lost legitimacy.[63] The IPK's founders sought recognition as a formal political party with hopes of unseating the repressive system upheld by President Moi and his allies. The group's nonsectarian approach (working alongside churches and other political parties), along with its calls for social justice, made it a substantial threat to the ruling party. As Bakari observes, "This was the era of ethnic, ideological, and religious alliances. For the first time Muslims worked side by side with the Christian clergy in posing a real challenge to Moi."[64]

The organization was spearheaded by a young generation of leaders who were disillusioned by the state of affairs within the ruling Kenya African National Union (KANU) party, as well as within Muslim leadership circles. The IPK's emergence as an organized constituency coincided with the period that ushered in the politics of Islamism elsewhere in the world, and more generally with the heightened presence of Islam in politics.[65] Highlighting political and economic grievances that had been neglected by national leaders over the years, the party sought to mobilize Muslims to vote en bloc—both to increase the representation of Muslims in Parliament, and to widen the bargaining power of Muslims as a group. It found a strong base of support in urban areas like Mombasa, Malindi, and Lamu.[66] The IPK invigorated a cross-section of young Muslims by fusing Pan-Islamist currents with demands for greater rights within the Kenyan state: thus, it offers an apt illustration of how pious sensibilities, national allegiances, and transnational imaginaries have coalesced into new, hybrid forms of political self-identification. Its founders were inspired by Muslim political movements elsewhere in the world, from Sudan to Afghanistan to the United Kingdom. In short, the group was internationalist in orientation, even if the focus of its energies was national politics.

Ultimately, the government refused to recognize the IPK as a political party on the grounds that it was religious in nature: the Moi regime argued that the word "Islamic" in the name implied that the party was motivated by religion and that it would be restricted to Muslims. The ultimate banning of the IPK triggered a wave of protests along the coast, with residents decrying their perceived position as second-class citizens.[67] The party's leaders organized large-scale acts of civil disobedience, including a one-day civil strike that paralyzed the city as schools and offices remained closed and businesses and transport companies withheld their services, in what was heralded as the most successful strike since Kenya had obtained independence.[68] In response, the government instigated a mass police crackdown, killing a number of youths and arresting several of the group's leaders, including Sheikh Khalid Balala, against whom it leveled charges of treason. As Prestholdt observes, this "stoked rising flames of discontent, not only drawing more young people to the IPK cause but also driving thousands onto the streets."[69] Buses were set ablaze, and police stations became the target of petrol-bomb attacks. Fearing rising discontent, the government banned a lecture by Mombasa's most prominent academic, Ali Mazrui, who had been scheduled to speak at the Islamic Center of Mombasa in June 1992. Mazrui ultimately delivered his lecture in Nairobi, warning of the potential for a Black Intifada on the coast.[70]

In an attempt to divide and rule, Moi sponsored a rival organization, United Muslims of Africa (UMA), which accused the IPK of being an Arab-dominated organization.[71] Led by KANU youth leader Omar Masumbuko, the UMA was composed primarily of Mijikenda youth who organized counter-demonstrations in order to draw IPK supporters into divisive clashes.[72] Further, Moi charged the IPK with promoting Islamic fundamentalism, and with obtaining funds from the governments of Iran and Sudan.[73] National media outlets similarly fixated on the idea of external influence by focusing on the charismatic cult of Sheikh Khalid Balala, who had spent time in Saudi Arabia.[74] With the help of the media, Moi framed Muslim politics in Kenya as an extension of developments elsewhere in the Muslim world, rather than as grounded in Kenyan political history.[75]

The refusal to recognize the IPK led to the rise of other groups that sought to address the needs and concerns of Kenyan Muslims, including the Council of Imams and Preachers of Kenya, the Muslim Consultative Council, and Muslims for Human Rights (MUHURI).[76] But memories of the state's crackdown and attempts to discredit the IPK lived on, and made coastal activists especially wary of proposed antiterrorism legislation in the early 2000s. Introduced in the wake of the November 2002 bombing of the Paradise Hotel in Mombasa, this legislation was partly a response to pressure from the US government, which had passed its own antiterrorism law in the form of the Patriot Act after 9/11. The proposed legislative measures sanctioned the arrest of suspects without evidence of involvement in terrorist acts, holding detainees incommunicado, and indefinite detention without trial. In contrast to neighboring states like Uganda and Tanzania, where antiterror laws came into effect with minimal resistance, Kenyan rights activists were staunchly vocal in their opposition, with many groups decrying the potential criminalization of the country's Muslim minority.[77] Kenya's Prevention of Terrorism Act eventually passed in 2012, and two years later, in the wake of mounting attacks inside the country (including Westgate), the Security Laws Amendment Act of 2014 passed with comparatively minimal public outcry. This, despite the fact that the act (which expanded upon the existing Public Order Act of 1950) broadened the powers of security officials to arrest and detain people, and augmented the powers of the National Intelligence Service (NIS) to monitor communications without a warrant. By this point, the political landscape had changed dramatically, as government officials increasingly accused critics of attempting to "derail Kenya's efforts to fight terrorism."[78] During his Independence Day address that year, President Kenyatta singled out the bill's critics, saying, "No freedoms are being curtailed, unless of course you are a terrorist yourself."[79] It is against this backdrop that activists have sought to trace and respond to rising cases of disappearances and extrajudicial killings in the country.

Instinctive Cartographies

At 3:00 a.m. on a Monday in November 2014, in the immediate aftermath of an Al-Shabaab attack in the northeastern town of Mandera, roughly six hundred Kenyan police and General Service Unit (GSU) officers descended on the Mombasa neighborhood of Majengo, stopping first at two mosques. After collecting roughly twenty people from the mosques, they moved from house to house in search of "armed militants." As the hours passed, youth who fit the profile of young, male, and Muslim were pulled from their beds, from the streets, and from speeding *matatus* (minibuses), and thrust into the back of police trucks. At least 250 youths were arrested, and one was killed. Phone calls and texts quickly streamed in to local politicians and human rights groups. My colleagues at Haki Africa reported over WhatsApp that they were heading to Majengo to learn more.

Later that day, after a trip to police headquarters to demand information about the basis for the mass arrests, we exchanged theories about what prompted the raid. Ziad surmised that the national government was under pressure to demonstrate control of the security situation. In the year following the debacle of the 2013 Westgate attack, the rise of Al-Shabaab attacks inside Kenya compounded doubts about the effectiveness of the Kenyan security apparatus. Thirty-six people had been killed in Mandera, and emotions ran high. The Mombasa police claimed that the directive for the raid had come from Nairobi. *They want to impress the British and the Americans,* said Ziad. Mombasa—despite its location more than 500 miles away from Mandera—was a convenient site for police action, as Kenyans had come to view it as a "hotbed" of Al-Shabaab sympathizers. As with the operation in Eastleigh six months earlier, the fact that the security apparatus often lacks sufficient information to pursue concrete leads is rendered inconsequential, as the affective infrastructure of the security state does its work—stoking fear against a racialized threat.[80] It was partly with this in mind that we made sense of the raid. By detaining dozens of young men, security officials simultaneously engaged in a spectacular demonstration of their power *and* gained easy access to potential sources of information. Meanwhile, the families of those detained wondered anxiously about the fate of the young men. Following a court hearing later that week, they gathered under the shade of a tree outside the Mombasa courthouse for a report back from activists and local politicians, who pleaded for patience as they promised to push for the young men's release. But patience was hard to come by; what began as murmurs and whispers soon became loud expressions of frustration and despair. The crowd began to disperse, people making their way home filled with the same anxiety that they had come with.

Families often turn to each other for support, and in their search for answers, become activists themselves. As Hamisi's wife, Maryam, sought clarity on her husband's case, she began to reach out to the relatives of the Kenyan suspects being held in Kampala in connection with the 2010 attack there. She and other wives and mothers spent their spare time talking to lawyers, journalists, and prison guards as they attempted to piece together information. Like their counterparts during the anticolonial struggle and later during the days of Moi's repression, they have defied gendered notions of respectable citizenship that confine women to the home, where they are tasked with domestic duties—which today include monitoring and guiding their children away from "violent extremism."[81] In addition to visiting Nairobi prisons in search of missing persons, Maryam anonymously ran a Facebook page where she posted updates about other cases of arrests and disappearances. When an American investigative journalist uncovered details about a secret CIA-run prison in Mogadishu, for example, she finally learned what had happened to

Ahmed, a twenty-six-year-old from the Nairobi suburb of Eastleigh who had disappeared in 2009. The police had crashed through the front door of his home and whisked Ahmed away. Since that time, his parents had anxiously sought information about his whereabouts. Maryam relayed to them what she learned from the investigative report: Ahmed had first been taken to a secret location in Nairobi and then transported to the underground prison in Mogadishu.[82] His family could begin to connect a few dots.

If the Kenyan state and its partners collect information to anticipate risk and guide decision-making, so too must the subjects of surveillance make calculations about their own security. In some cases, this entails relying on their own geopolitical knowledge about prior security operations in order to be prepared for potential confrontations or barriers to their movement. As Mohamad Junaid observes of everyday life under military occupation in Kashmir, "bodies become barometers of fear and anxiety, sensing trouble in some places and normality in others."[83] With every fresh Al-Shabaab attack, Maryam retreats to her home out of fear of incrimination. On the day of the Garissa University attack in northeastern Kenya, she had just arrived in Mombasa for a family wedding. I met her for lunch hours before the news broke. Upon hearing what had occurred, Maryam's instincts kicked in. Anticipating a police crackdown in Mombasa, she rushed back to Nairobi the following morning. In the past, we had discussed why Mombasa was the site of such trepidation for her; if anything, her daily routine in Nairobi would make it easier for the state to monitor her movements. But in order to attend the wedding, she would need to travel along the same road where at least two high-profile suspects—including Aboud Rogo—had been assassinated at the hands of the ATPU. She had come to internalize and anticipate the unpredictability of state terror through her knowledge of the urban geographies where the police had wielded its power before.[84]

A friend at the Kenyan National Human Rights Commission described to me the strategies he has employed, some planned and others not. Just before Munir and a colleague departed on a research trip to Lamu, the colleague's relative who worked in intelligence called to warn them about potential threats to their life. *Please travel at a different time, when it is light,* the relative appealed, and so they did. Before another research mission, Munir had a concrete plan in place. *I was in Northeastern for a case. When it came time to leave town, we had a strategy: send a decoy vehicle in one direction (Wajir), and send the other in the direction of Nairobi. I was traveling in that car. We were pulled over by the military. As we were descending from the vehicle, I managed to get a photo of the military vehicle. But then I lost network. They had us lie down on the ground, heads facing down, put guns to our heads, and I thought, this is it. But suddenly the police appeared and demanded that they let us go.* Munir never learned who was behind the decision to stop the car, or the decision to let them go, but he suspected that the ultimate decision to release them had something to do with upholding the Kenyan government's image in the eyes of its donor partners.

Elastic Empire

By 2014, the ATPU and its plainclothes officers who policed and occasionally gunned down urban residents from their signature white—unmarked—Toyota Probox vehicles had become code for "British and American." When Al Jazeera released an investigative film in December 2014 that included interviews with ATPU officers who confirmed that they received instructions from foreign powers, any lingering questions that such claims were mere rumors quickly faded away. By the following year, however, it became increasingly clear that to focus exclusively on the ATPU was to misrecognize the flexible and mutable arrangements that sustain imperial power today.

In a meeting with a US embassy official, we learned of the US government's frustration with the Kenyan security apparatus in the wake of a recent police crackdown by the ATPU that had garnered public scrutiny. *It makes it harder to get the job done,* said the official, whom I will call Andrew. It was clear that the embassy was bracing itself for a barrage of questions about why the US State Department continued to fund and train this unit. Andrew insisted that the ATPU constituted a small percentage of the wider set of security partners in Kenya. In the ensuing months, we began to hear stories about other organs of the Kenyan security apparatus, from the KDF to the GSU to the Kenyan Wildlife Service—that were implicated in arbitrary arrests, killings, and disappearances.

Eventually, we were compelled to look beyond the institution of the police itself. In April 2015, the Kenyan government released a list containing the names of eighty-six individuals and organizations with suspected ties to Al-Shabaab. The groups I had worked closely with, Haki Africa and MUHURI, were on the list. At this point, the consequence of asking questions was made painfully clear: my colleagues had been rendered suspect *because* they had dared to inquire about the underpinnings of imperial policing. Within twenty-four hours, the organizations' bank accounts were frozen, and the NGO Coordination Board took steps to cancel their operating licenses.

In the ensuing weeks, the organizations' directors shuttled back and forth between Mombasa and Nairobi to meet with their European and American donors and with any Kenyan state official who would grant them a meeting. The inability of their donor partners to clearly answer questions about the criminalization of their work suggested that the decision to place these groups on the government list had been endorsed by Kenya's Euro-American partners. It prompted Abdul to reflect on the mixed messages he so often received from Euro-American diplomats who publicly professed support for democracy and accountability but who privately exhibited signs that they were threatened by him and what he represented, from their security details to subtle nudges about what his activism *should* look like (e.g., work *with* the police rather than against them). Abdul recounted to me a conversation he had had with a Scandinavian donor official who suggested that Abdul was too closely linked to Al-Shabaab by virtue of his organization's willingness to take on legal cases of individuals who had been accused of ties to the group. In retrospect, Abdul wondered if this had in fact been a veiled threat.

Confusion emerged when we learned that a foreign-run, Nairobi-based think tank might have played a role in the decision to include the organizations on the list. Both groups had previously engaged with this think tank, believing it to be a benign entity "dedicated to promoting peace, security, and development." We had met with members of its staff just weeks before in Mombasa. Stories quickly began to circulate about the actors behind the think tank, including rumors that one of the group's top officials at one point had worked for the British intelligence agency, MI6, and that another employee was in regular contact with the US Department of Defense. The potential role of this think tank was disorienting. The fact that we had interacted with some of its employees concretized the organization as material fact, but its elusive ties to foreign intelligence bodies made it the subject of paranoid and whispered conversations: What had we possibly said or shared with the organization that led to this situation?

These embodied exchanges, situated at the border of the tangible and the opaque, contribute to phantom epistemologies about the amorphous character of policing in the urban "gray zone": it is everywhere and nowhere at once, as its fluid, ad hoc character is constantly subject to reorganization. The very "unknowability" of this elastic mode of empire, writes Lisa Bhungalia, is precisely the point:[85] the ever-shifting distribution of authority to various entities enables the United States to offset the public scrutiny and liability that comes with its own direct involvement. "It is no wonder that U.S. power is the subject of such outrageous conspiracy theories," writes Sean T. Mitchell. "The corollary of the United States' often invisible and frequently disavowed power is suspicion of omnipresence; if something is visible nowhere then it might be everywhere."[86] Just as American policymakers embrace speculations about "master terrorists," so too did we speculate about certain actors in our midst as James Bond–like master spies.[87] While the information that circulated among my colleagues did not offer a conclusive account of how imperialism works in East Africa today, it *did* provide pause for reflection about its shifting configurations. Their embodied, everyday geopolitical knowledge invites us to think otherwise about the kind of analysis currently on offer about the war on terror in Africa. While purported expert-critics present authoritative, "big picture" assessments, Kenyan activists are accustomed to uncertainty, recognizing that their knowledge remains incomplete.

Conclusion

The war on terror is actively reshaping the contours of Kenya's largest cities, as well as the ways their inhabitants navigate through them. As military ideas of tracking, identifying, and targeting potential terror suspects permeate everyday urban spaces, daily life for these populations is haunted by the anticipation of violence at the hands of a seemingly illegible power. For Kenyan Muslims, this is a war enacted not through the spectacular violence of bombs or foreign military occupation, but through more subtle, seemingly conventional practices of policing that have their own debilitating effects. Ethnographic attention to how people live and make sense of this emergent reality helps concretize geographies of urban warfare not simply in negative terms as sites of loss and despair but equally as lived, material landscapes linking imperial power formations to the rhythms and calculations of everyday life. Activists in Nairobi and Mombasa grapple not simply with fear and paranoia, but with the information they need to navigate the shape-shifting geographies of the war on terror. Congregating in police stations, courthouses, living rooms, and street corners, they disrupt the prevailing political order in which secrecy and imperial meddling reign. What emerges is an enlivened geography, a contested sphere, and real places with real people who continuously recreate new life-worlds in the face of violence and uncertainty.

4 HOME AS THOROUGHFARE

AS SHE OPENED AN ELABORATE Eid gift basket from her friend Njeri, an employee at Nairobi's upscale Villa Rosa Kempinski hotel, Maryam chimed in to the conversation about President Obama's impending visit to Kenya. *I texted Njeri to ask her if Obama will stay at the Kempinski. Have you seen the rooms there? Ah! Kweli, they are so nice!*

My eyes widened as I processed what it meant for Maryam to be inquiring about the movements of the US president in Kenya. Noting my expression, she laughed, adding, *I'm just curious! We are all curious.*

At some point, the conversation shifted. Maryam's maternal uncle, visiting from the coastal town of Lamu, made an observation about a group of Somali men he had encountered at the mosque earlier in the day. According to Jamal, these young men were so attached to their mobile phones that he observed them scrolling through Facebook and Twitter *while* they were praying. *After prayers they were posting photos of themselves,* Jamal remarked, clearly perplexed by the idea that prayer required this form of recognition.

We Muslims have so many double standards, Maryam expounded. *Now that Ramadhan is over, you'll find all the buibuis dancing in Mercury Lounge. Hawana dini!* (They don't have religion!), she said, chuckling.[1]

The conversation offered everyone a respite from the heavier topic weighing on our minds. The holy month of Ramadan had just ended, and the Eid holiday served as a reminder of one more year spent apart from an important member of this family. Five years earlier, Maryam's husband Hamisi was apprehended by the antiterror police outside a Nairobi shopping center. While it was several days before she pieced together what had occurred, she later learned that Hamisi was one of at least a dozen suspects who had been apprehended on suspicion of their involvement in the twin bombings that had occurred the previous month in Uganda's capital city of Kampala targeting crowds who had gathered to watch the 2010 FIFA World Cup.

In the immediate aftermath of Hamisi's arrest, Kenyan police descended on the family's home, claiming to look for evidence. Panicking and unsure about what was happening, Maryam tried to inquire about her husband's whereabouts. Rather than offer an explanation, the police accused *her* of being uncooperative. The police, it seems, did not anticipate her readiness to confront them, and quite possibly were nervous about her potential to expose the limits of their own authority, given the likelihood that they were following instructions from Euro-American powers.

During my visits with Maryam in her home, I learned about her continued efforts to obtain a semblance of clarity on the opaque inner workings of the counter-terror apparatus. Whether the police who abducted Hamisi were uniformed or plain-clothed, for example, constituted important information as she attempted to piece together lines of authority. Meanwhile, Maryam discovered that she too was the object of suspicion. As an accomplished professional in the information technology industry, she traveled regularly for work. But after she was barred from entering South Africa and placed on a plane back to Kenya, she learned that she was the target of an inexplicable travel ban—a restriction that prevented Maryam from traveling to Uganda to visit Hamisi in prison. For years, she sought out meetings with various Kenyan political officials in an attempt to address the problem, but to no avail. It remained unclear which law or political body (Kenyan or non-Kenyan) had authorized her travel restrictions. Had the Kenyan government passed information to the Americans, or was the US government issuing instructions to the Kenyans? While claims that the US government interfered in Kenyan affairs permeated everyday conversations among Kenyan Muslims, it was another thing entirely for people like Maryam to navigate the *bureaucratic* implications of the opaque arrangements that sustain Kenyan–US security cooperation.

Over the course of my extended period of research in Kenya (2014–15), when I lived in Mombasa, I stayed with Maryam in her home during my short trips to Nairobi. On weekdays, we would each be out of the house—she for work, and I for interviews or meetings related to my research. But in the evenings or on weekends we could gather in her living room together with her two young boys, where we would exchange stories about our day and, more often than not, catch up on the latest developments related to Hamisi's case. Maryam devoted whatever spare time she had to learning what she could about the laws and evidence related to the case, and to discerning what steps she needed to take to address her travel restrictions. Occasionally, visitors would stop by to check in on Maryam and the boys, or to relay information that they believed was relevant to the case, including suggestions about whom she might speak to for assistance. Maryam's living room is a space where geopolitical knowledge circulates with a certain urgency, as family members and visitors relay the latest information they have come across about the inner workings of the war on terror.

At the same time, however, the number of visitors had dwindled, as paranoia circulated about the possibility that anyone with ties to this family could soon become the next victim of the counter-terror apparatus. The paranoia was not without reason. While the trial for the Kampala attack was finally under way in the summer of 2015, Ugandan police arrested Hamisi's brother as he left the courthouse. Soon thereafter, Hamisi's mother approached the police to inquire about her second child to have been whisked away, and she too was arrested. When Maryam shared these developments with me, it had been two weeks without any word from either of them.

The news of these arrests served as a chilling reminder to family members that they should keep their distance. Some conveyed to Maryam directly that they were not prepared to risk the same fate. Soon after her mother-in-law was arrested, one of Hamisi's older brothers, who lives and works in Saudi Arabia, traveled to Kampala to inquire about his relatives and to look after the children who had been in his mother's care. But he stayed in his mother's home for just two days before concluding that he too could be at risk, and so he decided to leave. *Anaogopa* (he is afraid), Maryam said to me.

Militarized incursions into the home are a growing feature of everyday life for Muslims in East Africa. In April 2014, 6,000 security personnel were deployed in door-to-door operations in the Nairobi suburbs of Eastleigh and South C, leading to the arrests of more than 4,000 people.[2] While the Kenyan state characterized Operation Usalama Watch as a strategy to distinguish citizens from noncitizens (contending that noncitizen refugees from Somalia were potential terrorists), residents' experiences of the police raids confirmed that even citizens were viewed with suspicion.[3] In September of the same year, armed police stormed a home in Mombasa in search of a "wanted terrorist," killing a young man inside. As his mother later recounted, "They broke our doors while we were still asleep. They ordered everyone to lie down before they ransacked my bedroom and those of my children, turning mattresses and beddings upside down. After what seemed to be hours, I heard my son saying 'I have surrendered, I have surrendered.' Then I heard three gunshots and all was quiet."[4]

This mother's narration of her son's death inside her home is just one of many instances in which the homes of Muslim families have been targeted in the context of the war on terror. While we have a growing understanding of the devastating impact of drone strikes, police raids constitute a terrifying, albeit subtler instantiation of war on the homeplace. And as we shall see, the post-9/11 embrace of "soft power" strategies also implicates home and family life, as security experts identify mothers as integral to broader efforts to monitor children and youth for signs of "extremism." As counterinsurgency doctrine embraces a population-centered approach to policing, bodies and spaces previously coded as private or feminine are increasingly targeted—whether coercively through police raids of the home, or socially through calls for mothers to monitor their children for signs of potentially criminal behavior.

This chapter illustrates how these multifaceted, multiscalar intrusions of the war on terror into the homeplace expand the geographies and technologies through which life is regulated and policed. In doing so, I challenge normative ideas about the homeplace by illustrating that it is equally caught up in relations of power and violence. As military officials increasingly believe that the war on terror cannot be won singularly through military means, they have turned to the civilian realm where they hope to shape attitudes and alliances within the population at large.[5] This "re-strategization of war through the civilian realm," writes Lisa Bhungalia, points to "the evolving character, spatialities, and modalities of war, its realignments and reformulations, and its increasingly concealed and shadowy forms."[6] The effect, as Laleh Khalili observes, has been to fold "bodies and spaces previously coded as 'private' or 'feminine'—women, non-combatant men, and the spaces of the 'home'—into the battlefield."[7]

What happens in the homeplace is not a distraction from, nor adjacent to, the "real" of post-9/11 imperial warfare, but in fact central to it, demanding that we consider the entanglement of the intimate and the geopolitical.[8] My interest in the home is inspired by postcolonial, Black, and transnational feminist scholars who have foregrounded the political stakes in what is defined as public or private, and relatedly, what kinds of sites are relevant for our understandings of war, empire, and geopolitics. These scholars emphasize the significance of the intimate and the everyday as relevant sites for the study of international politics, offering insights into how multiscalar power relations intersect and play out.[9] As Katherine Brickell argues, the homeplace offers a productive site to reflect on "the interactive and entangled nature of domestic life and geopolitics, collapsing together the dualism often set up between small 'p' non-state politics (read: home) and big 'P' politics (read: geopolitics)."[10] Rather than the more mainstream examination of the impact of a seemingly disembodied, state-centered geopolitics *on* home life (which continues to privilege big "P" politics), we have an opportunity to consider how the geopolitical is itself shaped by the realm of the intimate.

The notion that insurgents are "hidden" within civilian infrastructures circulates widely among political, military, and intelligence operatives within Kenya and beyond.[11] In the aftermath of an Al-Shabaab attack at Garissa University in April 2015, for example, President Uhuru Kenyatta declared that "the radicalisation that breeds terrorism. . . . occurs in madrassas, in homes and in mosques with rogue Imams." Asserting that the planners and financiers are "deeply embedded in our communities," he asked: "Where are the parents and the families of those who are radicalized, where is the community leadership, where is the political leadership? Where is the religious leadership?"[12] In this context, spaces that are not conventionally associated with war (e.g., homes, schools, hospitals) are seen by military strategists as potential battlegrounds.[13] The physical destruction of a home comes with a range of devastating effects for its inhabitants, but contemporary counter-insurgency tactics are designed in such a way as to transform *without necessarily destroying* civilian infrastructure.[14]

Police operations have different, lingering consequences for one's continued habitation within the home, and push us to consider what it means to conceive of the home not as a private space, but as a *thoroughfare*. As we know from the US-led hunt for Osama bin Laden, the architectural layout of the home has implications for intelligence and counter-insurgency strategists as they contemplate how to gain visual, audio, and physical access *inside* the walls of the suspect's home.[15] Thermal imaging enables security actors to see and shoot through walls, "making solid architecture effectively evaporate."[16] Meanwhile, drone operators—who increasingly constitute another dimension of the spatiality of power in the region—develop an "eerie intimacy" with their targets, as they monitor who enters and exits, as well as what happens inside the walls of a home.[17]

Like ongoing forms of surveillance, police incursions into living rooms and bedrooms are not singular events: they have enduring effects and are productive of environments steeped in fear and uncertainty. Indeed, police infiltrations fundamentally destabilize the homeplace—not simply as a safe physical haven, but also as the place "where all that truly mattered in life took place—the warmth and comfort of shelter, the feeding of our bodies, the nurturing of our souls."[18] As bell hooks writes, it is "there we learned dignity, integrity of being; there we learned to have faith."[19] And as Nadera Shalhoub-Kevorkian observes, in the context of Palestinian experiences of life and death under Israeli settler colonialism, "it is that space of membership that defines the meanings and practices of belonging. It is a place about which to make claims and tell the stories and memories of belonging despite uprooting, demolition and the politics of erasure."[20]

Much like colonial-era counter-insurgency tactics, state-sanctioned surveillance and policing of homes works to fragment families and communities. As Frantz Fanon observed in *A Dying Colonialism*, we must "look more
closely . . . walk step by step along the great wound inflicted on the Algerian
soil and Algerian people . . . and measure the fragmentation of the Algerian
family, the degree to which it finds itself scattered . . . a woman led away by
soldiers . . . a husband taken away by the enemy . . . children scattered to the
winds . . . it is not possible to imagine that the Algerian family can have remained intact and that hatred of colonialism has not swelled immeasurably."[21]

In Kenya today, Muslim families and their homes have come under assault. Police incursions and the concomitant apprehension or killing of family
members have lingering repercussions, haunting the homeplace long after
the police have left. Haunting, writes Avery Gordon, is "an animated state
in which a repressed or unresolved social violence is making itself known,
sometimes very directly, sometimes more obliquely." Gordon uses haunting
to capture the "singularly yet repetitive instances when home becomes unfamiliar, when your bearings in the world lose direction, when the over and
done with come alive."[22] These "ghostly matters" have ongoing reverberations
as militarized incursions rupture the sense of place that constitutes home.[23]
In occupied East Jerusalem, the afterlife of home invasions by the police extends well beyond the geography of any single home, as neighbors inevitably
worry about "whose house would be invaded next, whose son or husband
arrested or shot."[24] Meanwhile in Indian-occupied Kashmir, the door to the
home has attained symbolic significance as families are in a constant state
of waiting for the disappeared to return.[25]

But militarized incursions do not wholly define everyday life inside the
home. I do not dwell on violence and victimization, which comes with the
risk of objectifying certain populations in ways that render them intelligible
only through the lens of violence. Even as state-sponsored violence shapes
the lives of my interlocutors, it does not continuously or exclusively define
their lives. When we look beyond the violence, as Munira Khayyat articulates,
we begin to see "more historicized, nuanced, grounded, complex (and relat-
able!) living landscapes."[26] We may also observe instances "when haunting
inspires, pushes, nurtures, and cultivates hope."[27] Indeed, the homeplace is

also a productive site for the reconstitution of social bonds, as those most directly affected gather and exchange knowledge about the war on terror— about its places and spaces, its actors and institutions, and its forms of power. Centering the everyday, we become attuned to the *will to life*, and to new modes of worldmaking and belonging.[28]

In what follows, I explore how social relations in urban Kenya are increasingly shaped by a politics of warning, as Kenyan Muslims contend with the possibility of guilt by association, and thereby make regular calculations about whom they can associate with, and in what spaces.[29] I situate my ethnographic findings within a broader political landscape that has identified Muslim homes as sites of geopolitical concern, as the counter-terror apparatus conceives of the Muslim "community" as a network of suspicious persons linked together by social relationships. In doing so, I illustrate how the intimate sphere of the home is a site in which to make sense of the war on terror, and is itself a target *of* the war on terror, intricately entangled in relations of power and violence.

Through an analysis of the political thriller *Eye in the Sky* (focused on the decision by Euro-American military officials to launch a drone strike on a home in Nairobi), we again see that the war on terror encompasses not only the traditional battlefields of desert terrain, but equally civilian spaces like the homeplace. Racialized by the counter-terror apparatus as a space of suspicion, the homes of Kenyan Muslims are transferred directly onto the battlefield, subject to police raids on the ground and drone warfare from above.

I then shift to a discussion of more subtle entanglements of gender and geopolitics, wherein women are championed by development and military actors alike as key actors in the realm of soft power. As Jennifer Greenburg observes, "Military literature from the mid to late 2000s understands the household as the link to the central counterinsurgency category of 'the population,' whose loyalties determine military success."[30] Women in particular became a focus: the influential counter-insurgency theorist David Kilcullen, for example, declared in the *Marine Corp Gazette*: "Win the women, and you own the family unit. Own the family, and you take a big step forward in mobilizing the population."[31] With this in mind, I explore how seemingly benign gendered policy language and frameworks (e.g., "The Role of Mothers in Countering

Violent Extremism") are leveraged to fulfill military agendas. What interests me about the "countering violent extremism" (CVE) discourse is how gendered constructs (in particular, women *as* mothers) are integral to the war on terror. The focus on family and domesticity is not a new phenomenon, but recalls colonial-era tactics of gendered and racialized modes of social engineering and control. Finally, I return to a discussion of everyday life inside Maryam's home. Much like women elsewhere who have been forced to contend with the realities of state-sanctioned violence and terror, Maryam has actively worked to restore and reclaim her home as a site of dignity, critical consciousness, care, and community. Her story points not only to the contingency and contradictions of counter-insurgent warfare, but equally to underexplored modes of worldmaking in contexts of social and political uncertainty.

Surveillance, Suspicion, and the Politics of Warning

When I first communicated with Maryam by phone in 2012, she invited me to her home in the upper-middle-class neighborhood of Kilimani for dinner. Although the home itself is quite small, Maryam lives on a serene tree-lined block not far from where many international NGO offices are located. While Maryam's class position enables her to send her children to private school and to live alongside and socialize with the Kenyan elite in cafes and restaurants like Java and Art Caffe, the transnational make-up of her family contributes to their racialization as out-of-place Muslims. Maryam is from the coastal town of Lamu, and one of her grandfathers was British. Hamisi was raised in Nairobi by his Kenyan father of Yemeni origin, and by his Ugandan-Rwandan mother. Due in part to the continuation of longstanding Indian Ocean mobilities, and in part to the demands of the global economy, their relatives are scattered in different parts of the world, from Dubai and Kampala, to London and Seattle. Kinship networks have meant that their home has long been open to visitors from across Africa, the Middle East, and beyond. In this sense, their home can already be understood as a thoroughfare. It is precisely the fluid and transnational nature of certain homes that makes them a site of interest.[32]

The counter-terror apparatus constructs such mobile and interconnected Muslim cosmopolitans as suspicious actors.[33] Among policymakers and in the media, for example, Hamisi came to be mythologized as a key figure in *both* Al-Shabaab and Al-Qaeda in the Islamic Maghreb (AQIM). In 2014, the Ugandan press reported that security agencies had foiled a pending attack led by AQIM on Luzira Prison that was intended to release Hamisi and "other al-Shabaab terrorists." The media's construction of Hamisi as a James Bond–like superhuman with ties to "terrorist cells" across the world blurs the distinctions between fiction and reality, endowing him with a phantom-like quality.[34]

While the Kenyan government never produced evidence tying either Hamisi or Maryam to Al-Shabaab, surveillance and spectacle worked to incriminate them in the public imagination. Early on, I was advised to be cautious about associating with Maryam. Other interlocutors, including international human rights activists who had direct experience of surveillance and policing, discouraged me from spending too much time with Maryam, and especially from staying in her home. Social relationships have come to be shaped by paranoia and a politics of warning, whereby individuals caution one another from being seen with certain actors. Friends and family members keep their distance, having given in to the uncertainty and fear of guilt by association. When Maryam's son Kareem, then thirteen years old, presented me in 2014 with a "Certificate of Appreciation" for "staying with the family with ease," I was reminded of the extent to which Maryam and her children have been forced to contend with the *un*ease that many people in their social network now feel about their home.

I therefore want to think about the ways in which the war on terror runs through Maryam's home. I take seriously the work of historians, feminist scholars, and geographers who point to continuities between colonial and postcolonial modes of governance, who push us to think beyond public/private dichotomies, and who insist that we look not simply up, down, and across, but *through*.[35] In this sense, Maryam's home is not a separate "private" sphere, but rather a space deeply bound up in the war on terror.

Eye in the Sky

This section situates my ethnographic findings within a broader cultural and political landscape that has identified the homeplace as a material and ideological entity of geopolitical concern. I offer a brief analysis of the 2015 feature film, *Eye in the Sky* (directed by Gavin Hood), in order to demonstrate how the war on terror cultivates doubt about the homeplace—when it is inhabited by Muslims. My objective is to demonstrate the political work that films like this one do.[36] With the onset of the war on terror, racialized visual economies about "unstable" Africa now intersect with those focused on "violent" Islam. *Eye in the Sky* reinforces "skepticism about Africa's ability to function" as it sets in motion Orientalist imaginative geographies of threat.[37] It is ripe for analysis about visuality and white supremacy, and about the alienation of drone optics from the people and places under surveillance and assault.[38] As a film that is almost entirely focused on the imperial war room, it is in some ways a dramatized version of the widely circulated White House situation room photo that centers high-level US officials as they follow live feeds of the hunt for, and assassination of, Osama bin Laden in 2011. Whether in the form of the situation room image or of the film *Eye in the Sky*, visual frames play an instrumental role in legitimating empire's right to extraterritorial killing.

My focus here is on how the homeplace is variously entangled in the war on terror. In the film, political and military officials in the United States and United Kingdom debate whether to launch a drone strike against suspected militants in the Nairobi suburb of Eastleigh, a neighborhood inhabited primarily by Kenyans of Somali origin. In this British-led operation, intelligence actors on the ground in Kenya claim to have information about a terrorist cell that will converge inside a specific home in Nairobi. As the film unfolds, British and American officials rely on satellite imagery to trace the movements of the suspected militants (led by a British female convert to Islam) from the Nairobi airport to the home in Eastleigh where the plan to conduct a "terrorist" attack, we learn, is under way.[39]

Eye in the Sky features multiple war rooms: Creech Air Force Base in Las Vegas, an Image Analysis Unit in Pearl Harbor, the British Cabinet Offices Briefing Room (COBRA) in Whitehall, and a military base in Sussex led by Colonel Katherine Powell (played by Helen Mirren). But there are additional war rooms that also feature prominently: the "terrorist" headquarters inside two Nairobi homes, as well as the home office of Colonel Katherine Powell.[40]

In the beginning of the film, the drone transmits images of the movement of suspected militants in Nairobi. With the help of a remotely controlled "bird" operated by a local informant (played by Barkhat Abdi, famous for his role as a Somali pirate in *Captain Phillips*), a mobile surveillance camera flutters on the outside of one home. The military officials in London are determined to gain visual entry through the windows, with the help of this "bird." Yet each of the windows is covered with blinds or curtains. What would otherwise be construed as an everyday act of privacy renders the homeplace into a sign, as viewers are led to believe that the occupants of this home have something to hide.[41]

When the suspects move unexpectedly to a different home in a neighborhood that has been overrun by the militant group Al-Shabaab, the local informant manages to deploy a mobile "fly" *inside* this home. Viewers are now privy to the assembly of suspected militants in the living room, where they sit drinking coffee. Then, the flying camera moves to the bedroom, where a man is in the process of assembling suicide vests. *Shit,* murmurs Colonel Powell as she processes the image before her. *This changes everything,* says Lieutenant General Frank Benson (played by Alan Rickman). *Get legal in here right now*! Powell commands. *We need to put a hellfire through that roof*!

FIGURE 7. Colonel Katherine Powell (Helen Mirren) processes the images before her from a military base in the United Kingdom: to the left is an image of the living room inside the terror suspects' home; to the right is the satellite image of the home from above. Source: Eye in the Sky/Bleecker Street Media.

Keith Feldman aptly refers to the use of aerial surveillance as "racialization from above," which recalibrates Orientalist imagined geographies of threat and transmutes the temporality of warfare through notions of preemption and precision targeting.[42] The bulk of the film is devoted to the anxious dispositions of British and American military figures who fix their gaze on a collage of video screens. The eye functions as a weapon, as a visual register of racialization, through which Muslims in the homeplace are deemed to be threatening.[43] Upon discovery of the suicide vests, Colonel Powell and her colleagues assume the white (wo)man's burden of preventing a seemingly imminent threat to human life in an African state that is rendered incapable of managing its own affairs.[44]

This racialization from above is also gendered. The ability to launch a drone strike on the home is troubled by the presence of a young girl named Alia, who comes from a family of "good" Muslims. In contrast to the Al-Shabaab militants in her neighborhood, Alia's father permits her to study *and* to play: early on in the film, we are privy to Alia twirling a hula hoop, placing her firmly in Western minds as both a familiar and empathetic figure. When she unknowingly places herself in the line of fire just outside the cement wall bordering the home, the drone operators panic.

The remainder of the film is then dedicated to averting the risk to Alia's life, with Powell in an endless state of anxiety about the effort to spare her life at the expense of dozens more who could soon be victims of a suicide bombing. Alia, whose name and face are known to us as viewers, evokes compassion and empathy in a way that positions her in the category of grievable life; those around her on the bustling streets, however, are not accorded the same compassion.[45] Meanwhile, Powell's resoluteness about the need to proceed irrespective of the ultimate outcome for Alia renders her a reliable security feminist—sufficiently attentive to humanitarian concerns, but without allowing these concerns to cloud her judgment when military action is required. As such, she represents the rise of what Laleh Khalili characterizes as the (primarily white middle-class) "female security-wonk" who has "made it" in the previously closed domain of military masculinity.[46]

In contrast to the extended deliberations in London and Washington that eventually lead to the decision to adjust the coordinates of the strike, the film does not grant viewers access to similar conversations that may be taking place inside the Nairobi home. Without "ears" to accompany the "eyes" of the electronic fly, we are therefore unable to hear the discussions and debates among the suspected militants about what constitutes a legitimate target, or how civilian casualties might be avoided or minimized. The very fact that the occupants are Muslims who have weapons inside the home is all that is necessary in order for the viewers to draw conclusions about intent.[47] Whereas the more technologically sophisticated war rooms inhabited by Colonel Powell and Lieutenant General Benson enable the collection of every conceivable detail needed to deliberate what would constitute a legal (and hence "humanitarian") drone strike, the "terrorists" in question are not bogged down by such details, as humanity is evidently not their concern.[48]

Importantly, the film destabilizes gendered binaries of civilian/combatant and public/private: as a security feminist, Powell has transformed one of the rooms in her own house into a war room, where she reviews data that guide her decision-making on the battlefield. The image of Mirren as Powell in her bathrobe, much like the scene in which Rickman as Benson is preoccupied with buying a doll for his granddaughter as a birthday present, evokes Laura Wexler's conceptualization of "tender violence," whereby ideas about domesticity and family work to soften the violently brutal occupation of imperial warfare.[49]

Between Colonel Powell's home office and the suspects inside the Nairobi homes, viewers learn that the war on terror encompasses not only the traditional battlefields of desert terrain, but equally domestic spaces (albeit in different ways). The fact that the first home to trigger suspicion on the part of Powell and her colleagues is located in the serene middle-class suburb of Parklands works to remind viewers that suspects may be lurking in spaces other than the expected "ungoverned" territories dominated by Al-Shabaab. Racialized by the counter-terror apparatus as a space of suspicion, Muslim homes in purportedly peaceful urban Kenya are transferred directly onto the battlefield, subject to police raids on the ground and drone warfare from above. The construction of doubt and threat in relation to these homes works to differentiate and exclude them from the norm, marking them as unfamiliar spaces.

FIGURE 8. Colonel Katherine Powell (Helen Mirren) processes the images before her from her home office. Source: Eye in the Sky/Bleecker Street Media.

Gendering Counter-insurgency

In Kenya, public critique of counter-terror abuses led the state and its partners to deploy new tactics in order to cultivate support for the project of security. Conceived as complementary to "hard" security measures, "soft power" increasingly drives policymaking and development assistance in the region, with the goal of developing a deeper understanding of "the cultural and social predispositions of East African Muslims."[50] In the lead-up to a 2015 regional summit in Nairobi on CVE, "countering violent extremism" became the new catch-phrase for NGOs seeking to regularize and secure funding, with the leaders of these organizations scrambling to market their work as contributing to "peace and security."

In the burgeoning literature on violent "extremism," scholars and policymakers have turned their attention to family life and parenting. Among other factors, they have identified the disintegration of "traditional family and social structures"[51] as precipitating a rise in the number of young people traveling to Somalia to join Al-Shabaab.[52] In this context, mothers are singled out for the potential role they can play in discouraging their children from joining extremist groups. Cloaked in the language of gender equality and empowerment, women *as mothers* have been identified as valuable contributors to the project of security.

In this section, I consider the gendered character of counter-insurgency strategies, exploring how seemingly benign gendered policy language and frameworks (e.g., "The Role of Mothers in Countering Violent Extremism") are leveraged to fulfill military agendas.[53] The emphasis on inclusion and empowerment draws women into the project of war, even as it reinforces essentialist understandings of femininity—framed through the lens of emotion, motherhood, and domesticity.[54] As Laleh Khalili explains of counter-insurgency doctrine more broadly, it maps civilians onto particular gendered grids, assigning men and women to different categories of utility for combat and pacification:

> Because counterinsurgency requires the categorization of population into combatants and non-combatants, and because the easiest way to quickly identify and categorise populations as high-risk combatants or low-risk civilians is by gender, the combatant/non-combatant distinction becomes fully gendered, where the all-encompassing suspicion against men is operationalized into specific actions, while women are afforded the status of being "naïve" objects of protection, pacification, and humanitarian salvage. . . . what counterinsurgency does is to transform the [undifferentiated] "womenandchildren" into either actors considered by the counterinsurgent to be complicit with the combatants, a terrain upon whom the counterinsurgency's social engineering experiments can be performed, or increasingly, as hostages and literal or symbolic message-bearers for the work of counterinsurgency.[55]

What interests me about the CVE discourse is how gendered constructs (in particular, women *as* mothers) are integral to the war on terror. As Inderpal Grewal writes, the mother "defines the proper gendered female subject within the home, community, civil society and nation."[56] Because the work of security is increasingly devolved and defined as "everyone's job," parental concerns about family security are now sutured to government concerns.[57]

Equally striking is the instrumentalization of gendered labor, wherein the affective labor of mothers becomes a tool of counter-insurgency.[58] In the words of one report on the role of women in CVE:

> Mothers are often well-placed both in their emotional relationship to their children, as well as in their strategic location within the home, to be key sources of information about the social and psychological landscape of the current generation of adolescents and young adults. As a group—regardless of their social background—mothers contain valuable data on what renders individuals vulnerable to radical influences, holding economic, political, and socio-ecological factors constant. In particular, mothers of radicalized youth can make sense of their children's journeys of coming-of-age, navigating the uncertainties of the inevitable "identity crises" that occur throughout adolescence and young adulthood. As a result, they can shed light on the behavior and decisions that are incomprehensible to those on the outside.
>
> Furthermore, not only are mothers a point of unique access and deep knowledge of already radicalized youth, but they are also strategically placed to serve as a buffer between radical influences and those who are next to be targeted. They are the starting point of building resiliency within their children's early years of development and often the first to recognize and address signs of distress including anger, anxiety, and withdrawal. This dual capacity to both pre-empt and respond to radical influences makes mothers essential participants in an effective security paradigm.[59]

The instrumentalization of gendered, affective labor is not entirely new: empire has long been entangled with questions of domesticity, and women played an integral role in late colonial strategies of social engineering.[60] In colonial Kenya, state encroachment into the sphere of home and family life was legitimized in the name of fostering "good" or "civilized" subjects. As Luise White observes, British colonial officials were preoccupied with creating a respectable urban working class, believing that "single men bred crime and dissent." Families, the officials believed, would make the working class respectable, "keeping men from congregating with other men in overcrowded rooms and beer halls.[61] Specifically, they believed that wives would offer "partnership, support, someone to talk to."[62]

Ultimately, however, this strategy backfired. In the context of the anti-colonial uprisings, "not only did wives not tranquilize their husbands, they seemed to have made them more rebellious."[63] To the frustration of British authorities, women constituted a high proportion of the anticolonial Land and Freedom Army membership. British official Tom Askwith, who was tasked with "rehabilitating" the Land and Freedom Army members, was convinced that mothers were responsible for brainwashing their children; it was on this basis that he advocated for women, too, to be placed in detention camps.[64] The insurrection therefore provided colonial officials with a new basis to refashion gender roles, and to police women's political activities.[65] As part of a broader "stabilization" effort, mothers were instructed to abstain from political involvement and to concentrate on domestic duties within the nuclear family.

We learn from this history that the fashioning of gender (specifically, constructing particular roles for men and women) has been central to se-curing and maintaining the imperial enterprise.[66] Empire has long operated at multiple scales, including the seemingly private space of the home. In the donor-funded civil society workshops I attended in Nairobi and Mom-basa that highlighted the significance of gender for countering "extremism," women were engaged almost exclusively as mothers whose task was to moni-tor their children; the discourse of empowerment has been transferred to parenting, as mothers are trained to look for "early warning signs" in their children, and to trust the police in order to report suspicious behavior.

The appeal to mothers to join forces with the war on terror demonstrates that empire *needs* women as mothers just as much as it needs access to mili-tary bases, whether to address military intelligence deficits or to cultivate young citizen-subjects who consent to policing and war. This demands, as Jennifer Greenburg observes, that "we move beyond binary military language of 'kinetic' (violent) and 'nonkinetic' (nonviolent) activities."[67] The reliance on women's affective labor, she reminds us, is integral to the actual violence of war.

In practice, however, the everyday functioning of this mode of counter-insurgency is not without tension and contradiction. The outsized focus of the aid industrial complex on CVE has shifted funding away from other sources of insecurity, whether gender-based violence or poverty and socioeconomic marginalization.[68] Many of the Muslim women I spoke to were painfully aware of the ways in which the law "sees" criminals in certain bodies and not in others. They questioned the language of violent extremism and terrorism, observing that it is used only in relation to nonstate armed groups like Al-Shabaab. Other researchers noted similar observations: a gender expert at a peacebuilding organization in Nairobi reported that "when asked about violent extremism, people were telling us that according to them, the police were the violent extremists. Why? Because it was them who came to their homes in the middle of the night, ransacked their houses and took their children away."[69] In addition to the one-sided approach to the question of violence, these observations serve as an important reminder that the embrace of civilian-focused preventative strategies has occurred alongside the continued deployment of state terror.[70] In February 2021, residents of the Likoni neighborhood of Mombasa were subjected to a series of nighttime police raids in which young Muslim men were dragged from inside their respective homes, in many cases never to be seen or heard from again. Because local police denied any knowledge of these incidents, residents concluded that this was the work of Kenya's Rapid Response Team, a clandestine police force trained by the CIA.

What should also be clear from these tensions is that women are not simply instrumentalized by powerful forces. While scholars rightly critique attempts to conscript women into the project of war and counter-insurgency, Elizabeth Mesok reminds us that there is a risk of reinforcing other gendered and racialized essentialisms—namely, that women in the Global South and Muslim women in particular are "duped by security actors and agendas."[71] These assumptions "assign such women false consciousness, rendering agentive capacity as only ever knowable through a liberal feminist conceptualization of resistance." The effect, she observes, is to foreclose "a deeper understanding of the affective, relational world of gendered agency within securitized spaces."[72] Indeed, my research reveals that the framework of CVE—however much it may instill doubt and uncertainty about one's friends, family, and neighbors—fails to account for the fact that families directly affected by the war on terror are in need of collective thinking and support. As Maryam sought clarity on Hamisi's case, for example, she began to reach out to the relatives of the other Kenyan suspects being held in Kampala. She and other wives and mothers spent their spare time talking to lawyers, journalists, and prison guards as they attempted to piece together information. Like their counterparts during the anticolonial struggle, and more recently the Mothers of Victims and Survivors Network, which has mobilized in response to mounting cases of police brutality across the country,[73] they have defied gendered notions of respectable citizenship, affirming one another through their demands, and in doing so beginning to heal the wounds inflicted by surveillance, paranoia, and state terror.[74]

Everyday Life at Home

Maryam and I had known each other for two years when she first began to describe the trauma she experienced in the wake of the arrest. In addition to the pain caused by Hamisi's sudden disappearance, she lives in a state of paranoia inside her own home. *Any unexpected noise,* she told me one afternoon, *reminds me of the day when they raided the house.* Glancing outside at the relatively short cement wall that encloses the backyard, she observed that it would be easy for the police to force their way into the house again.

For Muslim women who have lost family members to the war on terror, and whose homes have been subject to police raids, daily life is rife with painful memories and uncertainty about what the future holds. Yet scholarship on the war on terror is only beginning to wrestle with its gendered reverberations.[75] By virtue of the fact that Muslim men are assumed to be the primary targets of police violence in the form of enforced disappearances, renditions, or extrajudicial killings, most analysis overlooks the women who—albeit in different ways—are equally caught in the crosshairs.[76] As Ramzi Kassem observes:

> Although it has been largely invisible, "War on Terror" rendition, interrogation, and detention practices that ensnare men have a concrete and indisputable impact on women, especially spouses. From the outset, prisoners' wives struggle with the deep uncertainty that detention practices impose on their lives. Sometimes these women are present as their husbands are apprehended, and they share fully in the trauma, terror, and anxiety of that

experience . . . even when they do not witness the actual abduction, women are the first to realize and report their husbands' disappearances. From that moment on, often for many years, they must cope with not knowing how their husbands are doing and whether they will ever see them again.[77]

Indeed, Hamisi's arrest was a critical event for this family.[78] Much like other families affected by the counter-terror apparatus, they found that the violence of the home raid and Hamisi's extended imprisonment in Uganda fundamentally transformed their lives. Maryam's sons Shehab and Kareem were seven and eleven, respectively, at the time of their father's arrest. They were confused by the news that he had been taken away, and only mildly comforted by Maryam's assurances that she would challenge his arrest in court. Knowing that her children would likely face scrutiny and even harassment at school, Maryam did not attempt to shield her children from the complexity of the situation. As an activist herself, she explained to them how the government used the language of terrorism to discredit and delegitimize those who challenged the state.

At times, Maryam would joke about her position as the wife of a supposed Al-Shabaab mastermind. Because she is tall and light-skinned, store clerks and restaurant staff in her neighborhood often jest that Maryam looks like the "White Widow"—the British convert to Islam who was believed to play a role in the 2013 Westgate Mall attack, and who inspired one of the characters in *Eye in the Sky*. Because of her own readiness to mobilize financial and legal support for other families affected by counter-terror policies, some people have insinuated that perhaps Maryam herself has ties to militant groups. On one occasion, for example, a representative from the Red Cross asked Maryam to communicate with "her people" inside Al-Shabaab in order to negotiate the transport of humanitarian supplies into Somalia. As she recounted to me, laughing, *They actually sat there waiting for me to pick up the phone!*

While humor offers a modicum of respite from the stress, Maryam's doctor has expressed concern about her high blood pressure. In addition to maintaining her full-time job, she must balance the challenges of unexpected single motherhood with the strenuous labor of being "on the outside":[79] this includes attending to the legal case and the exorbitant bills that come with it; to the anxieties of Hamisi's family members; and to the emotional support that Hamisi himself requires to get by while he is in prison.

These worries and responsibilities are compounded by Maryam's embodied awareness that her actions continue to be monitored by multiple powers. Through the use of digital surveillance, Kenyan authorities have worked closely with the US government to track the presence of specific individuals in her home.[80] In one instance, a female relative received a phone call from the US embassy while she was seated in Maryam's living room, and this person was instructed to go to the embassy to follow up on a visa application she had recently submitted. Upon arrival at the embassy, she was questioned about her presence in Maryam's home that day, and told that her application had been rejected.

As the legal process dragged on, the boys' twice-yearly trips to Kampala to visit their father in prison became all the more meaningful. Maryam spoke openly with them about various aspects of the legal hurdles, and about the frustrations she has had with human rights activists who come and go, offering their support one day, and then failing to follow up—likely due to paranoia or fear of guilt by association. Occasionally, one of the boys would speak up in conversations I had with her, asking a clarifying question, or offering an observation. Maryam's commitment to proving Hamisi's innocence, and more generally to addressing the injustices of Kenya's counter-terror policies, has not gone unnoticed by the boys. In various ways, they have demonstrated their own critical consciousness about the contradictions of the war on terror. When on one occasion the prison guards tried to prevent them from entering the prison to see their father, Kareem—then aged thirteen—protested, proclaiming, *It is our right*. Maryam chuckled when she relayed this story to me, and it was clear that she was proud of her son's readiness to defend himself. Much like mothers elsewhere who have struggled to counter the effects of racism, militarism, and structural violence, Maryam in her parenting works to affirm her children's rightful place in society, and to instill critical thinking about the world around them.[81]

She is painfully aware, however, of the changes in everyday life at home that have affected them. Ramadan is when they feel this the most. Before

Hamisi's arrest, Maryam explained, *Hamisi used to take the boys to pray in the mosque in Eastleigh; for Suhoor* (the predawn meal), *they would go to their favorite restaurant nearby for pancakes and liver.* Besides the obvious absence of a father figure, the boys miss having friends and family around the house. Throughout the month of fasting, they regularly hosted people for *Iftar* (the breaking of fast). *The house used to be so full, people were seated even in the entryway,* she recounted.

The family's commitment to hospitality, which led them to open their home to relatives and acquaintances from around the world, was a source of suspicion, raising queries among intelligence officials about their ties to potentially criminal actors. When the police interrogated Maryam in the aftermath of Hamisi's arrest, they questioned her about specific individuals who had at one point spent time in her home. For Maryam and Hamisi, opening their home to those in need of shelter or a meal is a basic tenet of their faith, reflecting compassion and openness toward others. The expansion and entrenchment of the counter-terror apparatus worldwide has rendered hospitality all the more significant for traveling Muslims, who rely on trusted social relationships to navigate uncertain and unexpected restrictions on their movement.[82]

Indeed, the home is a space in which geopolitical knowledge is shared and put to use: as the counter-terror apparatus gained traction during the early 2000s, news circulated within social networks about the latest disappearances, arrests, and renditions. Visitors in their home would share stories about a friend or family member who had been affected in some way. At the same time, they would have access to dozens upon dozens of books that Maryam had collected that offered critical analysis on the war on terror—in some cases following a specific request asking me or others to carry books from the United States or Europe on our next trip to Kenya. These forms of subaltern knowledge work against the disorienting effects of the war on terror.[83] While counter-terror practices have eroded trust and social bonds, actors like Maryam worked to reconstitute these bonds by collecting information that might help families affected by detention or disappearance.

In July 2015, two days before Hamisi's brother was arrested outside the courthouse in Kampala, another person in their social network disappeared.

Latif was abducted just outside of his home in Nairobi. Family and friends anxiously circulated messages on social media with hopes of raising awareness about his disappearance. I was with Maryam at home when she heard the news, and she recounted to me the ways in which Hamisi used to offer whatever help he could to Latif whenever he needed it. *He used to come home a lot,* she told me. *He needed money for things like electricity and Hamisi would assist him.* As she processed out loud what had just happened to Latif, she feared that another acquaintance in their network could be the police's next target. She quickly texted him, cautioning him against moving around the city alone.

Conclusion

In 2016, Hamisi was finally acquitted of all charges. As Maryam recounted to me when I returned to Kenya for a follow-up research visit that year, he had planned for this day: convinced that the evidence presented by the prosecuting attorneys would not hold, he had already given away many of the belongings that he had accumulated in prison over the years, anticipating that he would no longer need them. But Maryam's sense of relief was quickly weighed down by the uncertainty of what would happen next. Would Hamisi be allowed to return home to Kenya? Would he be any safer, or any closer to living a normal life outside of prison than he was inside? That Maryam wrestled with this question was a painful reminder of the reality that seemingly exceptional sites (like the prison) may not be so exceptional after all, as Maryam wondered if Hamisi's home would ultimately be just as unsafe for him as his prison cell.[84]

Ultimately, she had less than twenty-four hours to preoccupy herself with what was next. Together with the four others who had been acquitted, Hamisi was rearrested from his mother's home in Kampala by plainclothes officers. For several days, Maryam was unable to obtain any information on their whereabouts. Within the family, rumors circulated about which government was responsible for his rearrest. Maryam was convinced that it was the Kenyans, who did not want Hamisi to return home. Those present in court, including representatives from the International Commission of Jurists, had observed that the FBI officials were unhappy with the ruling when the verdict came in. Perhaps they had convinced the Ugandan authorities to ignore the judge's decision. In the midst of the confusion, Maryam settled for her only source of certainty when she learned that Hamisi had resurfaced in Luzira Prison in Kampala. At least she knew he was alive.

It would be another two years before Hamisi was released and sent home to Kenya. In that time, inquiries mounted from friends and family members about whether Maryam would consider divorcing her husband in order to remarry. The unspoken assumption contained in these inquiries was that Hamisi would never return—either he would remain in prison indefinitely, or he would be killed. Maryam relayed to me how difficult it was to retain any sense of hope when those around her had effectively given up. In the meantime, she continued to face restrictions on her ability to travel. Following her latest attempt to obtain a visa to the United Arab Emirates, she was advised to contact INTERPOL. She texted me frantically to inquire whether I knew anyone who worked at INTERPOL *I don't know where to begin!* she said despondently.

Despite our various efforts to learn more and seek legal advice, information was hard to come by. This meant that Maryam was never able to visit Hamisi in prison in Uganda. When he was finally released in late 2018, they had spent more than eight years apart. Even as she processed what it would mean on an emotional level for them to reconnect and live under the same roof again after so long, lingering memories of the police incursion at the time of his arrest in 2010 left her unsure about whether it would even be safe for him to return to their own home.

For women like Maryam who have lost loved ones to the war on terror, daily life is haunted by painful memories and uncertainty about the future. This chapter has argued that the intrusion of the war on terror into the homeplace—whether coercively through counter-insurgent policing, or socially through calls for mothers to monitor children for signs of "extremism"—expands the geographies and technologies through which life is regulated and policed. My goal has been not to dwell on violence and victimization, but to shed light on everyday forms of worldmaking in the face of uncertainty. Over the years, Maryam has worked to restore and reclaim her home as a site of dignity, critical consciousness, care, and community.

Like bell hooks, who underscores the subversive potential of the homeplace in the midst of an oppressive reality, she has raised her sons to survive in a political context where they are likely to be viewed and treated with suspicion indefinitely.[85] She has instilled a sense of curiosity in them, leading them to be inquisitive rather than passive. Shehab, already a skilled football player, wants to play professionally. Kareem, now in his early twenties, has composed poetry about his father, and as a teenager he devoted a school history project to studying the anticolonial Land and Freedom Army. Like his mother, he seeks knowledge that can empower him to process uncertainty, so that he, too, is prepared for what is to come.

5 ON FRIENDSHIP AND FREEDOM DREAMS

> In friendship, then, is our resistance to the divisive and fragmenting lies
> of structural power; the seeds of global compassion, generosity, empathy
> and love; and the foundation of a world that works on behalf of life.[1]

IN APRIL 2015, two weeks after the deadly attack on Garissa University
in northeastern Kenya by Al-Shabaab, the government's interior secretary
announced an amnesty for "radicalized" youth:

> The Government hereby calls upon all individuals who had gone to Somalia
> for training and wish to disassociate themselves with terrorism to report to
> National government offices. We are in the process of creating mechanisms
> to rehabilitate youth who have been radicalized and those who are vulner-
> able to exploitation and radicalization, and will consider granting amnesty
> and appropriate reintegration support.[2]

The following day however, a billboard containing the names and pictures
of eight young men with the caption: *Wanted! Dead or Alive* was erected in
downtown Mombasa. News outlets reported that these individuals were
suspected of involvement in the Garissa attack. The contradiction between
the two government-issued statements was not lost on young Muslim men
in Mombasa: how could the state simultaneously refer to a group of citizens
as deserving of protection *and* as a threat, punishable by death? It was not
long before a few residents attempted to dismantle the *Wanted* billboard,
with supporters defending their actions on social media on the grounds

that the young men in the photos were their brothers, and not criminals as the state had alleged.

Since the Kenyan military's invasion of Somalia in October 2011, Al-Shabaab attacks inside Kenya have raised questions and concerns about the spillover effects of the war, and about the recruitment of Kenyan Muslims onto the "wrong" side of this war. In Mombasa, Al-Shabaab leaders actively exploited longstanding political and economic grievances among the Muslim population in order to draw young people to Somalia. Others were lured by the Kenyan military, which in 2009 trained 2,500 recruits from northeastern Kenya (primarily Kenyan Somalis and Somali refugees) to fight *against* Al-Shabaab; some of these recruits are now believed to have defected and joined forces with the militant organization.[3]

A few days after the incident with the *Wanted* billboard, I was sitting with Mohideen and Fahad, two young men from the Majengo neighborhood in Mombasa. Both in their early twenties, they defended the actions of the youth who sought to dismantle the billboard. They were tired of the seemingly endless suspicion and criminalization of young Muslim men like themselves. It was rare that a week would pass without news circulating in Mombasa about the arrest, disappearance, or extrajudicial killing of young men identified by the state as terror suspects. Whenever I asked about the latest incident, they had a story.

Vijana wengi walishikwa (So many youths have been arrested), Fahad told me. *Everyone I know, and all of their close friends. Our classmate was just picked by the police in Majengo. We are the same, we have all faced arrest.* In addition to alluding to a shared political identity as young men under constant suspicion, the two were haunted by the question of what had happened to their peers who never returned home.

In February 2014, Mohideen was among more than one hundred young men who were swept up in a police raid of Masjid Musa. This particular mosque was associated with the sermons of Aboud Rogo and Abubaker Sharif, both of whom called for young people to join Al-Shabaab on the grounds that the Kenyan security apparatus and its partners had been unjustly targeting the country's Muslim minority population. In the years leading up to and following the police raid, Kenya's Anti-Terrorism Police Unit (ATPU), trained and backed by the US and UK governments, has been deployed to city streets in search of suspected militants. Those identified as suspects have been arrested, disappeared, and in some cases gunned down in broad daylight.[4] Between 2012 and 2016, more than eighty people from the coast—including Rogo and Sharif themselves—were either killed or disappeared by agents operating within specialized counter-terror police units like the ATPU.[5]

Mohideen and I spent many afternoons discussing the ways in which he and his peers experienced and made sense of police violence and the uncertainties of life under constant suspicion. Our conversations often began by catching up on the latest news, and sometimes he would raise an incident from the past that had marked him in a particular way—whether it was his month in prison or his confusion about Aisha, the young woman he once wanted to marry. Mostly, he lamented the ways in which his arrest has affected him and those closest to him. In addition to disappointing family members who provided funds for his school fees, Mohideen dwelled on how his arrest made Fahad the subject of surveillance. Besides his concern for Fahad's physical safety, Mohideen worried about the ways in which life circumstances might strain their friendship.

Mohideen navigates his daily life with a keen awareness that he is being watched, and connects his experiences of surveillance to wider forces. *The way the Kenyan guys work,* he explained to me, *it's based more on monitoring your whereabouts; who you associate with; it's the higher-up guys (the Americans and Israelis) who monitor electronic stuff; then they share the info with Kenya and tell them who to kill.* For Mohideen, an understanding of the relationship between "eyes on the street" and "eyes in the sky" is a form of everyday geopolitical knowledge that is indispensable not simply for his own survival, but also for his ability to protect his friends.[6] When he was released from prison, he actively avoided contact with Fahad for several months as a strategy to protect him from guilt by association. But this strategy backfired when Fahad was arrested a few months later, and Mohideen believes that he alone was the reason that his friend suffered the confusion and humiliation of arrest. When Fahad was released, Mohideen recounted, *he didn't want to speak to me or hang out with me; he was scared.* The extent to which Mohideen was preoccupied with the consequences of his arrest for his friends points to the intimate domains through which the war on terror is lived. Just as we saw in chapter 4, the war on terror seeps into spheres that we might otherwise think of as private, and as separate from the more "public" sphere of political violence.

This chapter explores how surveillance, suspicion, and policing shape everyday socialities and modes of self-making among young Muslim men in Mombasa. I situate the micro-interactions of daily life against the backdrop of the war on terror's portrayals of young Muslim men as one-dimensional characters whose "manipulated minds" are purportedly in need of monitoring and reform. In doing so, I demonstrate how the war against Al-Shabaab is waged on highly gendered terrain: contemporary calls to rehabilitate (primarily male) "violent extremists" present decontextualized male figures stripped bare of the social and political histories that animate their lived realities. The friendship between Mohideen and Fahad, I suggest, offers insights into shared struggles to redefine and remake the self in the face of criminalization.

* * *

Kenya has a long history of spying on its citizens: the ideologies underpinning the colonial intelligence apparatus, consolidated in the context of anticolonial resistance, ensured that the newly independent state would inherit a temperament of nervous suspicion towards its own population.[7] Intelligence-gathering powers concentrated around the presidency and the Special Branch (the intelligence unit of the police), and these entities relied heavily on networks of informants.[8] In addition to monitoring the population for subversive actors, the state has relied on surveillance to distinguish between so-called insiders and outsiders, and in doing so, to legitimate a militarized response against perceived threats to national security.

More recently, the war on terror has enabled the Kenyan state to vastly expand its surveillance capabilities, as logics of anticipatory preemption allow it to justify broad-sweeping data collection in the name of preventing future threats to the public.[9] In addition to the acquisition of unmanned drones, legislation adopted in 2012 authorized the National Intelligence Service (NIS) to intercept communication content, acquire call data, and search homes without the need for a warrant. In 2014, national and international media outlets reported that the CIA and the US National Security Agency had been secretly monitoring telecommunications systems in Kenya through a program called MYSTIC.[10] And a 2017 report by Privacy International revealed that intercepted content has been abused to spy on, profile, and track terror suspects across Kenya, often leading to their arrest, torture, and disappearance.[11] These developments illustrate how intelligence and information have been weaponized as instruments of war.

Scholars have documented the disciplinary effects of surveillance and policing in the post-9/11 era, pointing to the impact of perceived or suspected criminal ties on families, communities, and social relationships.[12] The cumulative burden of surveillance and racial profiling contributes to uncertainty, suspicion, and distrust, as everyday acts are shaped by the knowledge or perception of being watched. As Sunaina Maira observes of the US context, "strategies of living with, accommodating, or resisting surveillance are now part of the coming-of-age experience of the 9/11 generation."[13] Within Muslim populations under scrutiny, it is one's proximity to state surveillance operations—whether as a potential criminal or informant—that works to erode kinship and social bonds, as paranoia drives people apart.

Yet even as these modes of power are now prevalent in Mombasa, they are not all-encompassing. Indeed, as scholars have observed in other contexts, it is precisely the uncertainty and insecurity resulting from surveillance and policing that leads to a complementary drive "to seek safety in the familiar—in longtime friends and allies and within family."[14] As I illustrate here, young men like Fahad and Mohideen draw on reciprocal relations of care and trust in order to make sense of their experiences, and to survive in the midst of paranoia and uncertainty. Existing in the shadows of more overt forms of resistance, their friendship constitutes a practice of freedom, an imaginative place in which to process shared experiences, and to chart new possibilities for the future.

The Friendly "Terrorists"

In 1969, anthropologist Robert Paine observed that scholars have generally overlooked the role of friendship in the construction and maintenance of social relationships, focusing instead primarily on kinship.[15] This has been especially true of anthropological studies of Africa, with problematic implications that friendship is not socially significant in the African con-text.[16] In addition to offering forms of emotional support and guidance, friendships provide a space for reflection, humor, affirmation, and self-in-vention. As Sandra Bell and Simon Coleman articulate, "through the ambi-guities and ambivalences involved in establishing and keeping friendships alive, we learn about how others see us and therefore, in some sense, how to view ourselves."[17] David Scott directs our attention to solidarities that are of-ten overlooked, namely, how Black slaves in the Americas learned *together* to practice freedom on the run from the plantation. With these histories in mind, Scott proposes that we think of friendship as "a quotidian art of learning to live and think together *differently*." Friendship is never devoid of tension, but is nonetheless generative of productive creativity, "driven by a desire to think together with a view toward activating something new."[18]

Bonds of friendship have been integral to anti-imperial political struggle and solidarity, often across continents: Malcolm X, for example, invoked his friendship and brotherhood with Zanzibari revolutionary Abdulrahman Babu to point to the more intimate dimensions of anticolonial struggles:

> So, brothers and sisters, again at this time, a very good friend of mine. I'm
> honored to call him my friend. He treated me as a brother when I was in
> Dar es Salaam. I met his family, I met his children—he's a family man. Most
> people don't think of revolutionaries as family men. All you see him in is
> his image on the battle-line. But when you see him with his children and
> with his wife and that atmosphere at home, you realize that revolutionaries
> are human beings too. So here is a man who's not only a revolutionary, but
> he's a husband—he could be yours; he's a father—he could be yours; he's a
> brother— he could be yours. And I say he is ours. Sheik Babu.[19]

Kenyan poet Abdilatif Abdalla, imprisoned in the late 1960s by the Jomo Kenyatta government for his political writings, playfully recounts how a friend protected the "secret" of his small acts of resistance in school during the colonial era:

> When I was attending primary school . . . I used to secretly and whisper-
> ingly substitute the word "Queen" with "Kenyatta" because I believed that

he deserved that prayer more due to the fact that he was fighting for the rights of our country and its people. (There was only one student friend who knew about this "subversive and seditious" act of mine and, thank God, he never betrayed me to the school authorities.)[20]

In exile, friendships between Abdalla and Ngũgĩ wa Thiong'o provided a vital link in diaspora activism and organizing.[21] As former political prisoners themselves, both worked with the Trinidadian poet and intellectual John La Rose at the London-based Committee for the Release of Political Prisoners in Kenya. As Ngũgĩ wa Thiong'o recounts,

> Our friendship in a way was really formed by struggle . . . I was detained at the same prison, and from my block I could see the block where Abdilatif was imprisoned some years earlier. . . . It was only in 1982 in London through the Committee for the Release of Political Prisoners in Kenya (CPRK) that we met. After working together in the CPRK for about five years, we moved to another stage politically, but also personally. With other Kenyans in London, we then formed the United Movement for Democracy in Kenya, taking its acronym UKENYA from its Kiswahili name, Umoja wa Kupigania Demokrasia Kenya. In this organisation one had to prove oneself in order to be trusted with tasks given. So we all went through a phase of testing each other. That's when our friendship became even stronger.[22]

Other friendships were forged inside prison itself: Willy Mutunga met his lifelong friend and fellow activist Alamin Mazrui during his year-long detention in 1982–83. Arrested for the possession of "seditious" material, Mutunga was dismissed from his job at the University of Nairobi. Over tea one afternoon in Nairobi, the former chief justice recounted to me when he first met Mazrui, who was arrested two weeks after the public performance of his play, *Kilio cha Haki* (Cry for Justice): *I was thirty-five. He was thirty-four. We were both Marxist-Leninists-Maoists. Our friendship, nay comradeship, grew by leaps and bounds in detention.*

Each of these examples points to the ways that intimate relationships of reciprocal trust and solidarity are forged in contexts of political oppression,

FIGURE 9. Abdilatif Abdalla and Ngugi wa Thiong'o. Source: Abdilatif Abdalla. Reprinted with permission.

sustaining broader struggles. While this chapter retains a focus on male homosociality, it is *not* attempting to tell a story of subaltern resistance. Here, one must acknowledge, too, that the revolutionary subject is often—if not always—imagined as male. Instead, I explore more mundane strategies of survival, or what some have referred to as "a poetics of living rebellion."[23] As Robin D. G. Kelley observes, "In the poetics of struggle and lived experience, in the utterances of ordinary folk, in the cultural products of social movements, in the reflections of activists, we discover the many different cognitive maps of the future, of the world not yet born."[24] Kelley is in dialogue with Aimé Césaire, who opened a 1945 essay with the provocation that "poetic knowledge is born in the great silence of scientific knowledge. . . . what presides over the poem, is not the most lucid intelligence, the sharpest sensibility, or the subtlest feelings, but experience as a whole."[25] For Kelley, poetry is not limited to the formal "poem" but is also "a revolt: a scream in the night, an emancipation of language and old ways of thinking."[26] Alongside Kelley and Césaire, I take inspiration from Orisanmi Burton, whose study

of Black masculine care work within and beyond US prisons illustrates that
intimacy and care constitute subtle forms of collective rebellion:

> When we care for each other and create dense webs of connection, inter-
> dependence, accountability, and intimacy among ourselves, we establish a
> layer of protection against the genocidal technologies of domestic warfare.
> While there is nothing inherently radical or revolutionary about survival,
> this defensive shield creates furtive spaces and fleeting moments in which
> defiant Black life can be nurtured through stories of past, present, and fu-
> ture struggle."[27]

Burton illustrates how intimacy itself becomes a form of political praxis,
animating political education, debate, and collective theorization.[28] Building
on these insights, this chapter questions the tendency of security actors to
pathologize young Muslim men as violent extremists. During the period of
my extended research, images of frustrated, angry young Muslim men on the
coast featured regularly in the Kenyan media, contributing to perceptions of
their purportedly threatening and criminal behavior. Fahad and Mohideen
are deeply aware that the public's reading of them occurs primarily through
the lens of gender, race, and religion, and that they are seen as problems requiring governmental intervention. They know that being read as a "radical"
or "extremist" has consequences for their life chances, particularly as local
political elites clamor to position themselves on the "right" side of the war
on terror, and to obtain funding on issues related to security.

I approach friendship as a site to reimagine and remake the self in the
face of criminalization and dehumanization, wherein young men claim a
different gendered subjectivity that distances itself from the image of the
violent Muslim male.[29] Counter-insurgency tactics, as we know from Frantz
Fanon, are designed with an explicit plan of "separating the people from
each other, of fragmenting them, with the sole objective of making any co-
hesion impossible."[30] The effects of this form of warfare are felt not only in
social relationships, but equally within individuals themselves. As Sharika
Thiranagama observes, war is something that happens "to" people, and at the
same time makes them: every making is also an unmaking. In inaugurating

new forms of subjectivities, war gives life to "particular kinds of biographies, bodily regimes, manners of coping."[31]

In the time I spent with Mohideen and Fahad, they regularly referred to themselves as "friendly terrorists," self-consciously appropriating stereotypical discourses that associate young Muslim men with terrorism. By adopting this language, they reclaimed it as their own, denying its shaming qualities and endowing it with dignity, as well as humor.[32] Leisure activities on the weekends, such as bowling, going out for ice cream, or visiting the beach, provided an escape, an opportunity to reflect on their shared anxieties and to create a sense of normalcy in an otherwise uncertain political context.[33] These small actions of simply "getting by" themselves have political potential.[34] As Lori Allen observes, the processes of managing everyday survival may be too nebulous to constitute an "event" in the form of a structural shift or public outburst, but nonetheless have productive political potential.[35]

While I draw inspiration from others who have sought to tell a fuller story about Muslim youth in the context of the war on terror, I am similarly skeptical about the desire to "know" this population, as it risks reifying mainstream fixations with, and even pathologizing, seemingly exceptional others. Perhaps more significantly, it risks contributing to the surveillance of an already heavily surveilled population.[36] It is worth noting that I did not seek out young men like Mohideen as an object of study, precisely because I did not want to contribute yet another layer of surveillance. It was through our chance meeting at the youth association in 2014 that he and I gradually began to develop our own friendship. While my own positionality as a woman and an outsider inevitably shaped our interactions (both limiting and potentially expanding what could be shared), I came to appreciate how storytelling among friends pulls ethnographers into "relations of intersubjective obligation that shape their anthropological practice of listening and writing."[37] My hope is that the stories shared here might deepen our understanding of the lived realities of the war on terror.

War of Frames

In her book *Frames of War*, Judith Butler explores the epistemological frames that work to differentiate lives we can apprehend from those we cannot. States and empires construct particular frames—often relying on film and media—to legitimize the decision to go to war, and to shape popular understandings of the purported enemy. As Butler explains, these frames emerge and fade depending on broader operations of power. The frame can be exposed as a ruse—as was the case in the early stages of the Iraq war, when investigative journalists released images of widespread torture and abuse at Abu Ghraib, a notorious prison of the Saddam Hussein regime that became one of the largest detention centers run by the US military. Butler notes that US officials sought to prevent the circulation of these images in order to limit the potential outrage that would ensue, anticipating that it could turn public opinion *against* the Iraq war. Outrage in the face of injustice, she writes, has enormous political potential: "To call the frame into question is to show that the frame never quite contained the scene it was meant to limn, that something was already outside . . . something exceeds the frame that troubles our sense of reality."[38]

As I suggested at the start of this chapter, young men in Mombasa objected to the ways in which the *Most Wanted* billboard depicted them and their peers as "terrorists." Mohideen's expression of support for the youth who attempted to dismantle the billboard was motivated by a social inclination to protect his peers from the effects of surveillance and criminalization. At the time the billboard was erected, the rise in incidents of young people traveling to Somalia to join Al-Shabaab was an uncontested reality. For Mombasa residents, questions about crime, drug use, and "radicalization" were intimate everyday concerns. *What is happening to our youth?* many people I spoke to would ask in frustration. *Hawana maadili*, they would say, *they have no values.* Others pointed to the high levels of unemployment (twice the national average) and resulting susceptibility to criminal activities. Because young people are in many ways seen as living embodiments of the future, the seeming "crisis" of the youth (a common focus of discussion across the continent and beyond) is integrally tied to wider anxieties and uncertainties about jobs, the economy, and social reproduction.[39]

In the 1980s, the Mombasa port gained importance as a transit hub and point of entry for heroin from Afghanistan, contributing to domestic consumption.[40] Young men along the coast began to spend what little money they

had on heroin, and by the early 1990s, community and religious leaders identified drug abuse as a serious public health issue: the use of unclean needles
contributed to a drastic rise in HIV transmission.[41] Muslims in Mombasa
have hypothesized that the Kenyan government has deliberately facilitated
the flow of drugs along the coast in order to quell or numb widespread dissent. It is partly in this context that Islam has been invoked as a means to
restore social and moral order on the coast.[42]

Young people themselves are attempting to make sense of and address
these realities.[43] In October 2014, I was invited to discuss my research with
members of a Mombasa youth association, and it was in this context that I
first met Mohideen. As was often the case during my time in Kenya, I was
introduced as a "security expert." The organization's members (Christian
and Muslim, male and female, mostly middle-class and working toward a
college degree) likely expected someone who would offer concrete policy
recommendations for Kenya to enhance its security in the face of "terrorist" attacks, but I inevitably confused them by raising questions about what
"security" actually means. We discussed government initiatives like *nyumba
kumi*, and the members shared their concerns about the lack of clarity and
structure underpinning these community policing programs. As some of
the young people explained, the idea that anyone with knowledge of or ties
to "wanted" suspects would consider sharing information with the police
was absurd—not simply because one could suddenly be labeled a suspect
oneself, but also because it risked alienation and reprisal from one's friends,
neighbors, and community members. Though Mohideen was quiet during
the discussion, he approached me afterward and expressed his agreement
about the need to interrogate terms deployed by government and the media.
He confirmed what the others had shared about the ways in which the state's
use of religious leaders and chiefs as informants was fracturing social trust
and exacerbating already existing intergenerational tensions.

Even as Mohideen acknowledged that young people from Mombasa had
traveled to Somalia to join Al-Shabaab, the billboard displaying *Most Wanted*
suspects in Mombasa was incommensurate with his understanding of reality.
In his assessment, far more young Muslims were affected by surveillance and
policing than by the potential lure of Al-Shabaab. As he and Fahad recounted

the ways in which police arrests and disappearances had touched on nearly every friendship they had, it became clear to me that their reasoning was informed by embodied experiences of what criminalization does to oneself, one's circle of friends, and one's sense of dignity. It is their proximity to similarly affected young men that troubles the frames constructed by the state and its donor-partners in the war on terror.

Here we begin to trace the contradictory workings of surveillance, which has the potential to instill fear, yet also may provoke the opposite effect, producing challenges to infrastructures of power and intelligence gathering.[44] On November 29, 2013, for example, a group of young men interrupted Friday prayers at Mombasa's Sakina mosque. In their confrontation with the imam of the mosque, they accused him of working as an informant, and of failing to condemn the state's injustices against the Muslim population.

When we talked about what had unfolded that day, Mohideen shook his head cynically, indicating his solidarity with the youth. Most religious leaders on the coast were caught up in what he referred to as the counterterror business, which was thriving thanks to the growing international spotlight on insecurity in the region.[45] *Have you noticed,* he asked me, *that now the Sheikhs drive big cars?* While I hadn't taken note of the fancy cars, I had heard regularly from many of my interlocutors that the cultivation of religious and NGO leaders as informants was fracturing social trust and exacerbating already existing intergenerational tensions. The failure of the local political and religious leadership to address these widely held frustrations about co-optation means that few formal spaces exist in which to deliberate and make sense of the political situation.[46] If and when young people have sought to raise concerns—as they did when they attempted to take over Sakina mosque—their actions are either read through the lens of youth criminality, or viewed as evidence of the seeming intrinsic contradiction between Islam and reason.

Mohideen is equally cynical about seemingly humane programs that claim to assist "vulnerable" youth. As a condition for his release from prison, he was required to participate in a rehabilitation program jointly sponsored by a local NGO and the Mombasa county government. The program emphasized psychology and ideology, as well as financial and social support as a means to prevent recidivism. Mohideen described his experience to me as follows:

> There was a veiled threat that if you didn't attend the program, you would be targeted by the police, so we had to go. When we attended we were given 1K (equivalent to $10) plus free lunch; so they were luring us with the money. They said they would open an office for counseling, but there was no counselor. Only classes: during these classes they asked us questions like "Do you have nightmares?" They asked us as a group, we were 20–25 in total: "How do you feel since last Saturday? How do you feel about the police?" They were assessing our emotions on the government and the police. I would just laugh; it wasn't serious. What were we supposed to change to? What did they expect from us?

The concept of rehabilitation underpinned the establishment of modern prisons and remains the basis for maintaining them. As Michel Foucault observed, prisons ultimately function as a method of social control, producing the delinquent as a subject in need of monitoring and reform.[47] In the context of conventional warfare, the purpose of detention was to disable and warehouse enemy combatants rather than punish or rehabilitate them.[48] But as Laleh Khalili notes in her discussion of confinement in counter-insurgency contexts, detention camps housed "not only suspected enemy combatants but also vast numbers of non-combatants swept up in 'mop up' operations."[49] As anticolonial movements gained ground in the aftermath of World War II, counter-insurgency became an important tactic both of conventional military operations and of civilian-centered transformation in soon-to-be former colonies. The emergence of liberal programs of rehabilitation can be traced to the 1940s, when the British developed reeducation programs for Greek communists on the island of Makronisos. Drawing on their experience in Greece, they deployed a similar strategy against nationalists in Malaya beginning in 1949.[50] And in the face of growing anticolonial resistance in Kenya, British officials declared a state of emergency in 1952, intending to replicate the Malaya model. The British referred to the insurgency either as a disease or as the product of witchcraft, and reasoned that "rehabilitation" in detention facilities would serve the dual purpose of quarantine and diagnosis and treatment.[51]

Today, the doctrine of "countering violent extremism"—introduced in 2005 by the Bush administration—creates a new category of risky populations. The degree to which policymakers repeatedly make reference to the "violent extremist" as a singular, monolithic subject overlooks the process of its construction as a category. Questions about *who decides* who should fall into this category, about whether and how the violent extremist should be provided amnesty or protection, and under what terms and conditions are all political questions, raising new problematics for debate about sovereignty, citizenship, and belonging. Moreover, the preoccupation with risk and preemption constructs rehabilitation not simply as a pragmatic, but as the *moral responsibility* of institutions dedicated to peace and security. Converging under the label "human security," an array of non- and intergovernmental organizations work alongside states to develop gendered and racialized projects of rescue and reform.[52] It is here that seemingly benign entities like human rights and humanitarian organizations are increasingly drawn into the interlinked domains of compassion and repression, tasked with managing and policing the populations they claim to serve.[53]

Since 2014, the Kenyan state has worked closely with local, national, and supranational organizations to promote "rehabilitation" programs for so-called extremist youth, promising amnesty to those who participate. Yet calls for rehabilitation are occurring in an uncertain political context: because the Kenyan military is engaged in ongoing combat against Al-Shabaab in Somalia, the targets of rehabilitation programs are not limited to former combatants, but can equally include actors suspected of *potential* ties to militant groups. The aid regime's attempt—using Kenyan NGOs as intermediaries—to achieve clarity has resulted in more, rather than less, uncertainty. Indeed, the lack of clarity on who qualifies as an extremist, not to mention what rehabilitation entails in practice, is the source of profound uncertainty and unease for young Muslim men targeted by surveillance and policing. Would qualification as a "radical" require possession of a weapon? adherence to a particular ideology? membership in a specific organization? or simply a passing interest in certain ideas and organizations?

I learned that many Mombasa residents are skeptical of rehabilitation as a path toward restoring so-called normalcy. They worry that even rehabilitation programs could be used to rationalize the surveillance and indefinite detention—if not outright killing—of anyone suspected of involvement with a militant group. These concerns are not unwarranted: in January 2016, a young man who turned himself in to the police with hopes of admittance to a rehabilitation program disappeared.[54] At the same time, entities that would be expected to offer care or protection from the security apparatus deploy language that is more akin to military strategy. For example, the United Nations recognizes that individuals who voluntarily subject themselves to a rehabilitation program may be held indefinitely if they are determined to be a "security threat."[55] Even as humanitarian rationales are invoked to invite young people to abandon ideas about violent confrontation, the reality of ongoing military operations in Somalia means that "rehabilitation" effectively augments the reach of the war on terror to govern more bodies and spaces.

Indeed, Mohideen astutely observed that the rehabilitation program he participated in failed to account for the continued impact of policing and surveillance on everyday life, and of the trauma precipitated by his own arrest and imprisonment. When the program ended, he knew that he would need support to process what he had experienced in prison. *Al-Shabaab have PTSD too*, he said to me half-jokingly. While the most obvious step would be to reach out to friends, Mohideen was forced to calculate whom he could and could not afford to interact with. And while he raised the possibility of creating an informal space for discussion and mutual support, he was again confronted with the risks: any such gathering would be viewed with suspicion, particularly if it was not operating within a liberal governance framework. There are no rehabilitation programs designed for victims of counter-terror policies; but any such initiative—even if it were staffed with the appropriate psychosocial and spiritual support—comes with the risk that the personnel would be called upon to extract intelligence.[56] Mohideen shared his fears about the possibility of rearrest, of being compelled to work as a police informant, and about the implications of his own arrest for his friends.

"Even the so-called heartless jihadists fear death"

When he was sixteen, Mohideen's family moved from Kaloleni to the nearby neighborhood of Majengo. This was in 2008, roughly when Sheikh Aboud

Rogo began delivering lectures at Masjid Musa.[57] Mohideen recounted to
me his early impressions of Rogo:

> During Ramadan, people said, Let's go hear Rogo, he's more of an entertainer;
> the pro-jihadists would go, the moderates would go. He would critique the
> government in the same way Sheikh Balala did; he said, "If you are stopped by
> the police, you don't ask why he's stopping you, you just pay the bribe. Why do
> you do this? Why don't you stand up for your rights?" People were provoked.

Rogo did not limit his criticism to the Kenyan government. According
to Mohideen, he was one of the few public figures to expose the hypocrisy
of coastal religious leaders:

> He showed us how Raila Odinga made false promises about helping us appeal
> the antiterror law, and how some of the Muslim leaders were corrupt. He even
> managed to catch them on film discussing how to distribute funds to youth
> to support specific political candidates. Rogo was more of a politician than a
> scholar. I liked him for his politics.[58]

Rogo's lectures became a popular gathering space for debate related to Islam,
democracy, and citizenship. As policymakers fixate on Al-Shabaab recruitment and the purported manipulation of young minds by figures like Rogo,
left unexplored is the role of critical reflection and exchange as young Muslim
men attempt to understand, interrogate, and evaluate the world.[59] The fact that
Mohideen was drawn to this space did not mean that he failed to think for
himself. His own understandings of Islam and politics revealed a clear depar-
ture from many of the ideas and ideologies commonly associated with Rogo.[60]
By February 2014, the controversial preacher was dead. As rumors spread
that his death in August 2012 was the work of Kenya's antiterror police unit,
Mohideen joined hundreds of demonstrators on the streets of Mombasa, but
was ultimately troubled by the violence that unfolded.[61] He resolved to focus
on his studies. But when the government issued statements in February 2014
forbidding young people from attending an upcoming gathering at Masjid
Musa, he was provoked:

I wasn't planning to go to Masjid Musa that day. But when I heard the govern-
ment was restricting people, I said, This is our right, our right of expression! It
changed my mind. But you know, when the police entered the mosque, I was
crying—I heard gunshots and I was hiding in a corner and I thought, I can
never die this way. I was really scared, and I sat on the corner of the masjid
and was just thinking about my family, my mom. You see, even the so-called
heartless jihadists, they fear death.

Once he reached Shimo la Tewa prison, officers called in the suspects
one by one.

When they called my name, my heart was racing, I couldn't stand it. One of
the officers laughed at me, and the others joined in. They were laughing at
my clothes because they were covered in blood. At first, I wanted to tell them
I wasn't supposed to be there; other guys said, "I was just passing by," or "I
went for the pilau!" But I decided no, I would tell them directly: I wanted to be
there. For me it was never about hearing about jihad; my problem was, since
when does the government care about what happens in the masjid—why do
you want to interfere in our matters? They are saying Al-Shabaab will come
into the mosque—seriously? How dumb to congregate in a mosque and just
wait to be arrested. So for me it was like a form of protest, and that's what
happened.

He described the pressure he faced to become an informant:

They wanted me to work for them. They said, "We will help you, we will pro-
tect you." I could never accept that. Another officer asked, "Which madrasa
did you go to?" Back in my mind I said, Really? . . . because the madrasa I
went to has nothing to do with my "radicalization." In fact it's the reason why
I left it and resorted to the mosque teachings. I responded to the officer, but he
was not interested, maybe he expected something else.

When the first group of young people who had been arrested with him
were released, Mohideen grew more paranoid. He managed to get access

to a phone and called his brother in order to ask him to delete his social media accounts.

> *It was a huge hit on me when the first lot was released, and I was still inside.*
> *I was scared. We never knew what criteria they were using to release, so I had*
> *to take my precautions. But I didn't tell my family how scared I was. When my*
> *brother and his wife visited me, we talked about other things. When you have*
> *been strong, people barely ask how you are really taking it all up.*

Mohideen was finally released after nearly one month in prison. Security officials made clear that he did not have a choice in whether or not to participate in the rehabilitation program: failure to attend risked further scrutiny and even his rearrest. As Mohideen anticipated, the program did not help him process the trauma he had experienced in the wake of the police raid and subsequent interrogations. Despite the stated aim of "reintegrating" young men like him into mainstream society, he continues to feel out of place—both in relation to members of his immediate community, and as a Muslim young man who is read by the state and the wider world as a thug, a criminal, and a would-be "terrorist."

Road Trips, "Free" Trips, and Prison Memories

I first met Fahad on a visit to South Coast. In the weeks and months to follow, I would join Fahad and Mohideen on their weekend outings. Both young men were busy during the week either working or attending class, making weekends the primary times when they had an opportunity to relax. We made trips to the beach or the lighthouse, often preceding or following a stop for ice cream in Old Town. Movement after dark came with the risk of harassment by police at pop-up security checkpoints: these mobile, flexible police maneuvers increasingly shape daily life in Mombasa and Nairobi, and are designed to match the amorphousness of the so-called enemy. While Fahad reassured us that an offering of *kitu kidogo* (something small) would guard against trouble, the mere sight of a police truck triggered sardonic references to *gari bure*, understood as a "free ride" to the police station.

When Mohideen texted to invite me to join them for the first time, he explained that he was not sure whether Fahad would talk about his own arrest. In the car the next day, however, hardly ten minutes had passed before the two began to compare notes about their prison experiences. *Fahad has so many stories,* Mohideen said, turning the volume down on the radio. *He has been through a lot.* Fahad intervened in an attempt to recognize the harsher conditions that Mohideen had endured while inside. *I was not in "max" like him,* Fahad explained.[62] *We would sit around playing cards!* I quickly learned that it was not in Fahad's character to dwell on serious matters. *Twende Tanga!* he suddenly proposed. *Let's go to Tanga. Road trip!*

Eventually, Fahad recounted some of the details of his arrest. He had been traveling north along the Mombasa–Malindi highway by car with his brother and was arrested in a small town north of Malindi. When the police began interrogating him, they showed him pictures that they had been collecting for several months. *I realized they had been tracking me for a long time—they even knew about my girlfriend, I couldn't believe it.*

In addition to processing their embodied experiences of surveillance (on the phone, on the street, in school, and in the mosque), they shared their anxieties about marriage and job security. Fahad spoke of his search for the right girl to marry; Mohideen poked fun at him for his boyish ideas about love and romance. *The only thing that motivated me in high school,* Fahad shared proudly, *was wanting to impress girls.* Mohideen was more pragmatic about romance, reasoning that he needed job security before making such a decision. While the shared experience of prison time in some ways marks a rite of passage among young Muslim men in Mombasa, it is not recognized as such by society.[63] Whether or not they were ever charged with a crime, social awareness of an arrest or time served inhibits their ability to fulfill traditional heteropatriarchal roles of starting and providing for a family.[64]

They each recounted and tried to make light of their biggest fear—rape—as well as the ways in which they made prison survivable, using whatever money they had to negotiate access to phones and phone credit. Fahad even managed to call his girlfriend Noura in Canada. He would later describe to me how his arrest ultimately led to their break-up, as her parents, who are from Mombasa, no longer trusted Fahad. *They don't understand,* Mohideen interjected, *they think that he is bad somehow just because of this arrest.* Inevitably, the discussion would change tone as one or the other sought to make light of the situation. Mohideen half-joked that he had enjoyed his time inside: *I learned a lot, I met many people!* Because he was compelled to wear a tag that identified him as "Al-Shabaab," Mohideen claimed to have garnered respect from the Somali inmates, *especially the pirates,* he said, laughing.

Whenever the conversation shifted to politics, Fahad lost interest, and this pattern was a source of debate between the two young men. *You can't just be silent!* Mohideen would say to him. *Things are happening, we can't ignore it!* Fahad would retort with a simple *Sipendi siasa* (I don't like politics). Whereas Fahad revealed a sense of resignation about the state of affairs (including selfish or misinformed religious leaders), Mohideen encouraged him to be more engaged. In my remaining months in Kenya, Fahad began to attend events hosted by the local youth association where I first met Mohideen. But he would regularly report back about how "boring" these gatherings were, which inevitably led Mohideen to laugh and try yet again to convince him of the importance of participating in discussions that affect them.

Conclusion

Discourses about youth criminality and extremism on the Kenyan coast are both racialized and gendered, focusing primarily on young Muslim men. Pathologies of male youth criminality render them hypervisible in the political imagination, reproducing stereotypes of the figure of the Muslim male "terrorist." Calls to rehabilitate young men identified as violent extremists present decontextualized actors stripped bare of the social and political histories—and forms of power—that animate their lived realities. As such, young men like Fahad and Mohideen become homogenized figures: policymakers and security experts alike assume that their lives are governed predominantly by economic or political interests that take shape in the public sphere.[65]

The more that discourses of violent extremism permeate national media and civil society spaces, the more that essentialist ideas about young Muslim men circulate not only among the political elite, but in everyday interactions between Muslims themselves. One afternoon, I observed an exchange between Mohideen and Rahma, a young woman blogger in her early twenties. The two had met at an NGO gathering for youth, where Rahma expressed an interest in learning from Mohideen what had motivated him to attend the sermon at Masjid Musa on the fateful day that led to his arrest. As we sat together, Rahma grew increasingly confused by the stories Mohideen shared with her about his life. In short, his interests and political inclinations did not fit the mold so often outlined in the media, or at NGO workshops on peace and security. For one, Mohideen explained that he had no desire to join Al-Shabaab, but was keen to find a space that allowed for critical reflection on the war on terror and its effects on Muslims around the world. But Rahma was most taken aback when Mohideen spoke at length about his love for a young woman named Amina.

Wait, so you are portraying yourself as a Mujahid and then you have love issues?! Rahma asked, shocked by the notion that someone like Mohideen would be preoccupied by love.

You mean Mujahids don't have love issues?! Mohideen retorted, laughing. *So we are just heartless?* he said, provoking her. This exchange (just a snapshot from a two-hour conversation) revealed that Mohideen's ideas about religion and politics were far more complex than Rahma had assumed. Rahma was unable to fit him into any of the neat categories that she had been socialized to look for, and was confounded by the notion that Mohideen was preoccupied by matters that, in her estimation, were irrelevant to the topic at hand.

Against the backdrop of the war on terror and its one-dimensional portrayals of young Muslim men in East Africa, this chapter has explored the intimate sphere of friendship as a source of reciprocal trust and solidarity for two young men in Mombasa. The time I spent with Fahad and Mohideen revealed how integral their friendship is to their ability to make sense of the world they inhabit, and to find humor and solace in the face of surveillance and policing. Leisure activities like road trips and other outings constitute one of the strategies they employ to reflect on their shared experiences of criminalization, and to create a sense of normalcy in the context of uncertainty. Exploring these everyday, mundane practices of "getting by" helps shed light on masculinities-in-the-making: namely, on contingent, constantly shifting modes of self-making that complicate hegemonic representations, as well as the multivalent ways in which young Muslim men in Mombasa experience and navigate the war on terror.[66] The ways in which Fahad and Mohideen collectively make sense of their situation and carve out strategies of survival are productive of new modes of worldmaking that resist dehumanization. In this sense, their friendship emerges as itself a practice of freedom, an imaginative place to remake the world, and to chart new possibilities for the future.

In the meantime, however, they continue to wrestle with paranoia and the rupturing of their social worlds precipitated by surveillance. A few months after I left Kenya in August 2015, Mohideen and I caught up over the phone. He shared that his friend Abdul had recently been approached to work as an informant. The intimate nature of the recruitment process was what troubled Mohideen the most. Abdul had met a young woman on their college campus who expressed interest in getting to know him; Abdul understood her interest to be romantic in nature, only to later glean that she worked for Kenyan intelligence. Because Mohideen still grapples with the possibility that he himself remains closely monitored by the government, his anxieties resurfaced when he heard all this from Abdul. Minutes after we ended our phone conversation, he sent me a text: *I should tell you something. I just freaked out n deleted my What'sApp hahaaha. I don't know wats next. I'm really scared nowadays. I need my mojo back.*

CONCLUSION

IN JULY 2022, one year before Kenya formally announced that it would lead a multinational intervention in Haiti, Kenya's ambassador to the United Nations delivered a striking speech to the UN Security Council, where Kenya served as a nonpermanent member at the time. Invoking the world-historical significance of Haiti's "magnificent" revolution in 1791 that "struck the first critical blow to the mass enslavement of African peoples, and the colonial tyranny and racism it was founded upon," Ambassador Martin Kimani proclaimed that Africans are indebted to the Haitian people. It was on the basis of a shared history of struggle against colonialism and racism that the Kenyan official declared, "Africa owes you every support."[1]

Contending that the solution to Haiti's deteriorating security situation could be found in a stable government based on strong institutions, Ambassador Kimani expressed sympathy with the challenges that come with this process. Kenya, he observed, had experience pulling itself "back from the brink of collapse" (referring to the 2007–8 postelection violence) and could share the lessons it learned. Rather than a charitable offer of support, Kimani's framing was one of obligation, a debt owed to the Haitian people in the name of Pan-African solidarity.

It is increasingly clear that contemporary invocations of Pan-Africanism—particularly when wielded by state officials—mystify and obscure what are often conflicting interests and ideological positions. Even as they are suggestive of racial unity and anti-imperialism, these vocabularies are often imbricated in militarized interventionism, demonstrating again the intricate entanglement of war-making and race-making in today's world. What is significant here is not simply that difference functions as a justification for war and militarized intervention, but that war becomes an avenue to remake race. As the image of the white Euro-American savior is replaced with that of the Black African comrade, we become attuned to shifting significations with regard to race and Blackness, wherein the affirmation of some (e.g., Kenya as an emerging Global South leader on the global stage) is inextricably entwined in the subjugation of others.

The fact that Ambassador Kimani articulated these words *one year before* the US government dispatched a delegation of officials to Nairobi—ostensibly to convince the Kenyan government to lead the mission—is equally significant. One need only peruse the archives of the Kenyan Ministry of Foreign Affairs to discover that Kenya has been positioning itself to assume a more active role in the Caribbean since at least 2021, when it hosted an *Arria Formula* meeting on the situation in Haiti following the first Africa–Caribbean Community (CARICOM) Summit—held under the chairmanship of (then) President Kenyatta—in September 2021.[2] Here we become privy to South-South relationalities that are often overlooked by analysis that continues to privilege an imperial "center." As I have demonstrated, a view from the Global South allows for new ways of seeing and apprehending global affairs, decentering lingering ideas about unidirectional modes of power in favor of pluriversal trajectories and epistemologies. Using Kenya as a window into the politics of war-making as a form of worldmaking, we begin to see how African political leaders, rather than simply following externally imposed directives, have actively shaped the politics of interventionism in numerous ways. This necessitates a theoretical and analytical consideration of coauthorship, and of relationality and interdependence.

It is by wrestling with imperial *entanglements* that we can more clearly discern relationships and associations that are either denied or deliberately obscured. As Ann Stoler reminds us, "beyond the actual connection of things," sometimes "the political task is to identify how things get cut off from one another in our conceptualizations. What prevents people, rela-tions, things, from being seen as proximate, implicated, and dependent?" Indeed, the US imperial script, observes Zainab Saleh, is based on a "politics of concealment," one that disaggregates people and places from one another.

What is perhaps most striking about mainstream media reporting on the proposed Kenyan-led intervention in Haiti is that Kenya is presented as a sovereign, bounded, geographic entity disconnected from histories of empire, including its decades-long post-9/11 security partnership with the United States. This obfuscation (which suits Kenyan and US officials alike) ensures that analysts speak only in general terms about "the Kenyan police," occlud-ing the fact that the Kenyan state has collaborated closely with the United States to train and equip elite *paramilitary* units that possess—according to the US Institute of Peace— "extensive experience in these kind of gray-area operations."[3] Within these paramilitary units are special operations forces trained and financed by the CIA, which is not subject to human rights vet-ting restrictions required by the Leahy Law. Analysts who have questioned whether the Kenyan "police" are capable of defeating Haiti's "fearsome gangs" fail to account for the human impact of militarized interventionism and must also ask what constitutes success, given the large number of Kenyan families who have lost relatives to the deadly practices of these combat-trained units.

The plan to intervene in Haiti should prompt new questions about the horizontal circuits through which counter-insurgency strategies have his-torically been transmitted from one location to another. In these instances, as Laleh Khalili explains, "bureaucrats and military elites actively study and borrow each other's techniques and advise one another on effective ruling practices."[4] Whereas Global South states have historically served as laborato-ries for Euro-American imperial powers to test new techniques of control, it is increasingly clear that our analytical lens should not be limited to North–South relations, but instead account for entanglements "within, between, and across different (post)colonial contexts."[5] For example, it is likely that Kenya—much like Brazil before it— intends to use Haiti as a laboratory for its own future pacification efforts, whether at home or abroad. But if we continue to analytically relegate countries like Kenya to the periphery of the global order, we fail to grasp the fuller, more complex picture of dynamics at play.

Meanwhile, given the widely critiqued history of US interventionism in Haiti, the Biden administration has sought to disassociate itself from this history and avoid being seen to play a direct role in the most recent calls to "restore stability" to the country.[6] Much as it did in the case of Somalia, the United States has turned to its security "partners" to assume a leadership role.[7] Here, the objective is to convince the American public that the United States is not embroiling itself in yet another foreign conflict, and to persuade the citizens of the country in question (Somalia, Haiti), that the interveners are comrades rather than colonizers. Strategically downplayed is the fact that (along with at least $100 million in financial backing) the United States will be providing "logistical support" to the mission in Haiti, including intelligence sharing, communications, and air power—meaning that this is as much a US-led mission as a Kenyan-led one.

The shift away from overt displays of US power has been accompanied by carefully choreographed performances of racial equality among nation-states on the global stage. While US foreign policy makers have long sought to craft an image of racial progress at home, the championing of "African solutions" points to an emergent mythology of equality that purportedly undergirds US commitments to multilateralism. It also suggests a growing recognition among US political leaders that America's power is closely linked to, if not dependent on, its African "partners"—particularly amid growing competition with China, Russia, and other powers. It is not insignificant that Secretary of Defense Lloyd Austin (the first Black man to hold this office) traveled to Kenya, Djibouti, and Angola in September 2023 with the stated objective of working "as equals towards shared goals." And it is not insignificant that Secretary Austin invoked the legacy of the slave trade during his time in Angola: "We all know that the United States and Angola were first connected by the slave trade," he declared. "And four centuries ago, slavers from far away put the men, and women, and children of this country into shackles—people who looked just like you and me. The horrors of slavery will always be a part of the shared history of our two countries. And we must never forget them."[8] Defense Secretary Austin's emotive reference to shared histories in relation to the slave trade serves as yet another reminder that war-making and race-making are deeply intertwined, with race operating as a basis on which to articulate bonds of solidarity and connection as much as it functions to divide. Officially, the United States presents itself—embodied in figures like Secretary Austin—as having overcome its racist past. And by employing the rhetoric of "equals," "partners," and "shared goals," US officials creatively paper over and obscure lingering structural inequalities. Race and power don't disappear but instead are reconfigured.

Indeed, Kenya's rise as a Global South leader is predicated on its seeming exceptionalism. Even as Kenyan officials invoke the language of Pan-African-ism in relation to Haiti, they position Kenya in direct *contrast* to Haiti. Just as they did in relation to Somalia, Kenyan leaders have invested considerable time and effort to distinguish themselves from uncivilized "terrorists" and "gangsters," and thereby to cultivate a paternalistic sense of responsibility and superiority in relation to a people who were once seen as equals in shared struggles for liberation. The construction of an "us" (Kenya) versus "them" (Haiti) is contingent on severing transregional bonds of solidarity, long viewed by empire as threatening.[9]

Lest we forget: writer and former political prisoner Ngũgĩ wa Thiong'o once taught a class on C. L. R. James's *The Black Jacobins*—an impassioned historical account the Haitian revolution—at the University of Nairobi. As Ngũgĩ explained to his students at the time (in the 1970s), James recognized the centrality of Haiti to the very idea of Africa, and he wrote *The Black Ja-cobins* with Africa in mind, suggesting (in Ngũgĩ's analysis) that "what the Haitians had done to counter plantation slavery could be replicated in Africa and the entire Caribbean region in the twentieth century."[10] For encouraging his students to draw connections between seemingly distinct struggles, and for daring Kenyans more broadly to dream of a more just world, Ngũgĩ was detained and charged for "dangerous" utterances and activities, and forced into exile.

Beyond official narratives are ordinary people who engage in everyday memory-work that are productive of radically different accountings of the past, and that are generative of new lifeworlds.[11] Today, Kenya's proposed in-tervention in Haiti has prompted new conversations and exchanges between Kenyan and Haitian activists who are keen to learn from one another. The result has been a growing recognition not only of the two countries' shared histories of revolt against imperial subjugation and exploitation, but of a more recent shared history as sites for experimenting and refining the art of counter-insurgency.[12] Indeed, although neither Kenya nor Haiti is widely understood to be a site directly targeted by the war on terror, both serve as an important reminder that we cannot limit our understanding of the human impact of the post-9/11 application of counter-insurgency military strategy to the geographies of Iraq, Afghanistan, and Somalia.[13] Rather than be set against one another—as Kenya's proposed intervention in Haiti is anticipated to do—we may soon hear Kenyans and Haitians declaring in unison, "This is not our war, this is not the war of Black and Third World peoples. This is not a war for us, this is a war against us wherever we are—whether in Europe, the United States, or any part of the Third World."[14] Indeed, empire's latest iteration of war-making in Haiti may give way to unexpected outcomes—spawning rather than severing transnational solidarities, forging rather than disrupting the exchange of knowledge, opening rather than foreclosing political possibility.[15] Other worlds are on the horizon.

ACKNOWLEDGMENTS

I have been extremely fortunate to receive the support, guidance, and friendship of so many people over the years. A few people deserve special mention at the outset for the vital role they played in facilitating initial contacts for my research in Kenya: Hussein Abdullahi, Ann Biersteker, Abdullahi Boru Halakhe, Al-Amin Kimathi, Firoze Manji, Athman Lali Omar, Ali Skandr, Mohamed Yunus Rafiq, and John Kiarie Wa'Njogu.

During the longer phase of research and beyond, I am grateful for the generosity and spirited engagement of a wide array of people, including Abdilatif Abdalla, Nuru Abdalla, Hassan Abdille, Simon Addison, Steve Akoth, Ahmed Alaidarus, Asma Alamin, Francis Auma, Evonne Baya, Abdalla Bujra, Ngala Chome, Mohamed Daghar, Ali Fujo, Gacheke Gachihi, Patrick Gathara, Paul Goldsmith, Mboto Hassan, Yusuf Hassan, Salma Hemed, Jonathan Horowitz, Irungu Houghton, Adam Hussein, Mohamed Jaafar, Parselelo Kantai, Masumbayi Katumanga, Hussein Khalid, Khelef Khalifa, Wangui Kimari, Lubna, Yusuf Lule, Alamin Mazrui, Ahmed Mohiddin, Willy Mutunga, Hassan Ole Naado, Anne Ngare, Mahmoud Noor, Abdul Noormohamed, Onyango Oloo, Rabia Omar, Suhayl Omar, Abdikadir Ore Ahmed, Mohamed Osman, Mutuma Ruteere, Hassan Sarai, Clara Usiskin, Muthoni Wanyeki, and Rasna Warah. It was by chance that I stumbled upon Khaled Twahir, whom I quickly hired as my research assistant. I learned a tremendous amount from him and am grateful for our friendship. Zahra Moloo was a near constant companion in Mombasa, and my wider Mombasa Raha crew kept me sane when the research proved stressful. There are many others whom I am unable to name, whom I thank for their willingness to share their stories and insights.

At Yale, I was fortunate to work with Kamari Clarke, Doug Rogers, Inderpal Grewal, and Narges Erami. They were thoughtful and engaged readers of my work and have been a consistent source of support. In addition to their exceptional scholarly interventions, Kamari and Inderpal have inspired me beyond words as generous mentors and as models of politically engaged scholarship. Many others were supportive throughout my time at Yale. I would like to thank Jafari Allen, Sean Brotherton, Michael Denning, Zareena Grewal, Louisa Lombard, Dan Magaziner, Mike McGovern, Sara Shneiderman, Kalyanakrishnan Sivaramakrishnan, David Watts, and Jonathan Wyrtzen, with a special shout-out to Connie Busky, Marleen Cullen and Francesco D'Aria for the laughter and friendship. I have fond memories of our cohort potlucks. Thank you to Sahana Ghosh, Nilay Erten, Ryan Jobson, Gabriela Morales, Caroline Merrifield, and Sayd Randle for the food, fun, and conversation over the years!

The fieldwork on which this book is based was funded by grants from the Social Science Research Council, the Henry Luce Foundation, and the MacMillan Center at Yale University. The University of California President's Postdoctoral Fellowship afforded me invaluable time to write, as did the Career Enhancement Fellowship funded by the Institute for Citizens and Scholars. I am grateful to Haki Africa and the University of Nairobi for providing institutional support while I was in Kenya, to the University of California Humanities Research Institute (UCHRI) for a grant that enabled me to convene a book manuscript workshop, and to the University of California Hellman Fellows Fund, which allowed me to conduct follow-up research in 2021–22. I am fortunate to have wonderful colleagues in the Department of Anthropology at UCI who have been a consistent source of support. Deep appreciation to Kristin Peterson in particular for being a generous mentor while I was a UC President's Postdoctoral Fellow.

I had a fabulous group of readers for my book manuscript workshop in May 2022. My deep gratitude to Hannah Appel, Jatin Dua, Wangui Kimari, Kristin Peterson, and Jeremy Prestholdt for their generosity and engagement, and to Orlando Lara for helping me take notes! Both before and after the workshop, several people generously read draft chapters and in some cases the full manuscript. Much appreciation to Bina Ahmed, Yousuf Al-Bulushi, Tawfiq Alhamedi, Lisa Bhungalia, Gabriel Dattatreyan, Sahana Ghosh, David Theo Goldberg, Sean Jacobs, Darryl Li, Sabine Mohamed, Zahra Moloo, Willy Mutunga, Ahmed Sharif Ibrahim, and Madiha Tahir.

I am grateful to the staff at Stanford University Press, especially my editor Daniel LoPreto for his unwavering support and excitement about the project. Sincere gratitude to the two reviewers who provided exceptionally constructive feedback. I thank Princeton University Press for allowing me to reprint a section of chapter 2, which was published as "Securing Paradise" in *The Anthropology of White Supremacy*. A version of chapter 3 was previously published as "Citizen-Suspect: Navigating Surveillance and Policing in Urban Kenya," in *American Anthropologist*.

I have participated in a number of reading groups, workshops, and conferences where I benefited from exchanges that enriched my thinking, including the 2013 SSRC DPDF cohort on Critical Approaches to Human Rights. Thanks to Kristin Peterson for including me in the Africa Political Economy conversations, which led to several productive collaborations, and to Munira Khayyat and Smriti Upadhyay and the participants in the May 2023 Theory from the South workshop at the American University of Cairo, where I shared and received helpful feedback on the draft introduction to the book.

So many people have been generous interlocutors, mentors, and sources of friendship, inspiration, and support. Sahana Ghosh and Madiha Tahir are dear friends and co-conspirators, whose fierce principles, brilliant minds, humility, and groundedness I deeply admire. Both have read countless drafts of my work and have been steady writing companions. In the years leading up to my decision to pursue a PhD, Yousuf Al-Bulushi, Anjali Kamat, and Darryl Li each helped me process whether it was the right move, gently encouraged me to take the plunge, and have continued to support me along the way. Since arriving at UCI, I've been especially grateful for the comradeship of Sandra Harvey, Anneeth Kaur Hundle, Lilith Mahmud, Kristin Peterson, and Chelsea Schields. In Long Beach, Bahar Mirhosseini and Bina Ahmed have been my steady champions in the final stretch of the writing process. Thank you!

I also wish to express my sincere gratitude to Ali Abdi, Lila Abu Lughod, Adekeye Adebajo, Omolade Adunbi, Attiya Ahmad, Zohra Ahmed, Hisham Aidi, Hayal Akarsu, Amna Akbar, Imad Akbar, Anthony Alessandrini, Amanda Alexander, Paul Amar, Hannah Appel, Elizabeth Ault, Wossen Ayele, Hamzah Baig, Sophia Balakian, Victoria Bernal, Catherine Besteman, Tom Boellstorff, Amahl Bishara, Amiel Bize, Robert Blunt, Adam Branch,

Orisanmi Burton, Ray Bush, Darren Byler, Horace Campbell, Roosbelinda Cárdenas, Jessica Cattelino, JM Chris Chang, Kizzy Charles-Guzman, Charmaine Chua, Kamari Clarke, Ayça Çubukçu, Gavriel Cutipa-Zorn, Omar Dahi, Gabriel Dattatreyan, Sohail Daulatzai, Jatin Dua, Mariam Durrani, Sally Eberhardt, Abdi Latif Ega, Nisrin Elamin, Zachary Obinna Enumah, Shirley Feldman, Joan Flores-Villalobos, Benjamin Fogarty-Valenzuela, Kim Fortun, Aisha Ghani, Zoe Goodman, Fadila Habchi, Sherine Hamdy, Ian Head, Muneira Hoballah, Saida Hodžić, Danny Hoffman, Peter James Hudson, Angela Jenks, Mohamad Junaid, Leili Kashani, Ramzi Kassem, Laleh Khalili, Munira Khayyat, Eleana Kim, Wangui Kimari, Paul Kramer, Kai Kresse, Virginie Ladisch, Annie Lai, Vivian Lu, Lora Lumpe, Sunaina Maira, Zachariah Mampilly, Constantine Manda, Eddie Mandhry, Mark Fathi Massoud, Biju Matthew, Najwa Mayer, Brittany Meché, Julia Mellinghoff, Elizabeth Miles, Ali Mir, Zachary Mondesire, Corinna Mullin, Keith Murphy, Curtis Murungi, Kambale Musavuli, Brian Mwiti, Tejasvi Nagaraja, Nadim Naser, Vasuki Nesiah, Sobukwe Odinga, Valerie Olsen, Sam Opondo Okoth, Diana Pardo Pedraza, Prachi Patankar, Jemima Pierre, Michael Ralph, Junaid Rana, Sayd Randle, Muhammad Abdur Raqib, Negar Razavi, Justin Richland, Mubbashir Rizvi, Sahar Romani, Amy Ross, Brahim Rouabah, Mutuma Ruteere, Jeremy Scahill, Manuel Schwab, Sherene Seikaly, Namir Shabibi, Anooradha Siddiqui, Devin Smart, SA Smythe, Damien Sojoyner, Chandra Sriram, Mayssoun Sukarieh, Ngũgĩ wa Thiong'o, Sharika Thiranagama, António Tomás, Clara Usiskin, Penny Von Eschen, Syed Mir Waleed, Emira Woods, Alden Young, Salvador Zárate, and Elleni Centime Zeleke.

Finally, to my family. I simply would not have made it this far without the love, nourishment, and unwavering support of my parents Kathy and Mussa, and of my brother Yousuf. I have learned so much from each one of them and continue to be inspired by their commitment to and belief in the possibility of a more just and peaceful world.

NOTES

Preface

1. Kagwanja and Southall, "Kenya's Uncertain Democracy"; Branch, *Kenya: Between Hope & Despair;* Clarke, *Affective Justice.*

2. See the Truth, Justice, and Reconciliation Commission, Commission of Inquiry into the Post-Election Violence (Waki Report).

3. See especially Prestholdt, "Kenya, the United States, and Counterterrorism."

4. Seeseman, "Kenyan Muslims, the Aftermath of 9/11, and the 'War on Terror.'"

5. See, for example, Niang, *The Postcolonial African State in Transition.*

6. Feldman, *The Migration Apparatus.*

7. Gill, *School of the Americas.* See also Saleh, *Return to Ruin.*

8. See especially Mutunga, *Constitution-Making from the Middle;* Murungi, "The Letter & the Spirit."

9. Stoler, *Imperial Debris,* 4.

10. Stoler, *Imperial Debris,* 7–8.

11. For more on the rise of Oman's transoceanic empire in the eighteenth and nineteenth centuries, see Bishara, *A Sea of Debt;* on precolonial racial thought, see Glassman, *War of Words, War of Stones.*

12. See Bezabeh, *Subjects of Empires, Citizens of States;* Bishara, *A Sea of Debt;* Glassman, *War of Words, War of Stones;* Hopper, *Slaves of One Master;* McIntosh, *The Edge of Islam.*

13. See especially Coronil, "Beyond Occidentalism"; Trouillot, *Silencing the Past;* Trouillot, *Global Transformations;* Lowe, *The Intimacies of Four Continents.* Writing against longstanding anthropological notions of the "local," Trouillot insists on situated, intersectional *location:* "One needs a map to get there, and that map necessarily points to other places without which localization is impossible." Trouillot, *Global Transformations,* 122.

14. For more on these elisions, and on the significance of connections, entanglements, and interdependencies see Du Bois, *The World and Africa;* Cooper, *Africa in the World;* Prestholdt, *Domesticating the World;* Lowe, *The Intimacies of Four Continents;* Trouillot, *Global Transformations;* Ferguson, *Global Shadows;* Appel, *The Licit Life of Capitalism.*

15. Ho, "Empire through Diasporic Eyes"; Von Eschen, *Race against Empire;* Horne, *Mau Mau in Harlem;* Tolan-Szilnik, *Maghreb Noir.*

16. Ho, "Empire through Diasporic Eyes," 240.

17. On the need for greater consideration of the power relations, including those of nationality, gender, race, and citizenship, that shape a researcher's ability to pursue the study of security regimes, see Al-Bulushi, Ghosh, and Grewal, "Security Regimes."

18. In August 2010, Ugandan authorities arrested a Kenyan activist who traveled to Kampala to arrange legal representation for the Kenyan citizens held in connection with the bombings. In April 2011, four Kenyans who traveled to Kampala to meet the Ugandan attorney general about the Kenyan suspects were denied entry and deported back to Kenya. One year later, a British lawyer was detained, deported, and banned from reentering Kenya for working on the same cases of the Kenyan men who were held in Uganda for their alleged involvement in the 2010 bombings. For more, see Usiskin, *America's Covert War in East Africa.*

19. Abboud et al., "Towards a Beirut School of Critical Security Studies," 280.

Introduction

1. With the exception of names of public figures, I use pseudonyms for most individuals throughout the book.

2. See Justice Forum, "East African Renditions."

3. "Rendition" refers to the government-sponsored abduction and extrajudicial transfer of a person from one country to another with the purpose of circumventing the former country's laws on interrogation, detention, and torture.

4. One of the detainees reported that they were interrogated by officials from the United States, United Kingdom, France, Italy, Switzerland, Israel, Pakistan, and Libya. See Muslim Human Rights Forum, *Horn of Terror,* 11.

5. Muslim Human Rights Forum, *Horn of Terror,* 11.

6. In contrast to Afghanistan and Iraq, where Muslim women were constructed as victims in need of saving, women in East Africa have been subjected to rendition and inhumane prison conditions. In the context of the transnational border operation of 2007, for example, at least nineteen women were apprehended and held for weeks—if not months—without being charged. Several of these women were pregnant, and some were accompanied by children. As Malinda Smith explains, some of them were held because their husbands or brothers were persons of interest, while others "were reportedly tortured in the belief that because of family ties, they had information on the Islamic Courts Union." See Smith, "Africa, 9/11 and the Temporality and Spatiality of Race and Terror"; Muslim Human Rights Forum, *Horn of Terror.* On the politics of "saving" Muslim women, see Abu Lughod, *Do Muslim Women Need Saving?*

7. Agina, "Osama Agents Back in Kenya," *The Standard,* 2008.

8. For exceptions, see Muslim Human Rights Forum, *Horn of Terror;* Human Rights Watch, *"Why Am I Still Here?";* Qureshi, "War on Terror"; and Usiskin, *America's Covert War in East Africa.* Alex Lubin characterizes the US-led war on terror as "both a material war with serious geopolitical outcomes, especially for its targets, as well as a discursive battle about the meaning of US empire." See Lubin, *Never-Ending War on Ter-*

ror, 8. I would add that the question of violence—how it is represented, legitimated, and deployed—is central to the war on terror.

9. See Muller, "Entangled Pacifications."

10. Kenyan counter-terror forces have also been trained by Israel and the United Kingdom. See Gidron, *Israel in Africa;* Shabibi, "Revealed: The CIA and MI6's Secret War in Kenya." Shabibi explains that many operations believed to have been conducted by the Anti-Terror Police Unit (ATPU) were later revealed to have been led by the CIA-backed Rapid Response Team, a clandestine "special team" of the Kenyan paramilitary General Service Unit's Recce Company.

11. See Bhungalia, *Elastic Empire;* Hoffman, *The War Machines;* Singh, *Race and America's Long War;* Turse, *The Changing Face of Empire;* Parks and Kaplan, *Life in the Age of Drone Warfare;* Kaplan, *Aerial Aftermaths;* Moyn, *Humane.*

12. See Hoffman, "Geometry after the Circle"; Segell, "Including Africa Threat Analysis in *Force Design 2023.*"

13. Bachmann, "Policing Africa," 120. See also Gould and Demmers, "An Assemblage Approach to Liquid Warfare"; Hoffman, "Geometry after the Circle." As Bachmann explains, the US military has "taken counterinsurgency thinking and practice to non-war spaces," making Africa an experimental site where new ideas about stabilization can be tested. Bachmann notes that the key pillars of the US military's stability operations doctrine intersect with concerns of police science. Specifically, "the simultaneous deployment of civil affairs teams and special operations forces gradually leads to a normalization of preventative military activity aimed at fostering a notion of 'good order' in so-called fragile contexts. It is in this sense that we understand the activities subsumed under the label 'stabilization' as a form of policing." Bachmann, "Policing Africa," 120.

14. As scholars remind us, a singular fixation with military omnipotence has the effect of upholding the liberal myth of the war/police distinction. See especially Neocleous, *A Critical Theory of Police Power;* Bachmann, Bell, and Holmqvist, *War, Police, and Assemblages of Intervention;* Tahir, "Violence Work and the Police Order." On the significance of policing in counterinsurgency, see Khalili, *Time in the Shadows;* Bachman, "Policing Africa"; Yonucu, *Police, Provocation, Politics;* Singh, *Race and America's Long War;* Schrader, *Badges without Borders.*

15. I am in dialogue with scholars who attend to the routinized structural violence that constitutes the social condition of war. In the words of Robin Kelley, the consequences for those targeted "ought not to be measured merely by the destructive force of American-made F-15s, cluster bombs, and white phosphorus, but also by the everyday routine" of policing and organized abandonment. See Kelley, "Thug Nation"; see also Khayyat, *A Landscape of War;* Lubkemann, *Culture in Chaos;* Hermez, *War Is Coming;* Burton, *Tip of the Spear.*

16. A 2016 report by the Congressional Research Service stated that the United States provided more than $8 million in antiterrorism law enforcement support to Kenya annually, the largest such allocation to any sub-Saharan African country. Financial support to the Kenya Defence Forces for counter-terrorism-related training and equipment

increased more than threefold since 2013, and was projected to reach over $120 million in 2016. See Blanchard, "Kenya: In Focus."

17. Blanchard, "Kenya: In Focus."

18. Abrahamsen, "Return of the Generals."

19. As Laleh Khalili observes, "the very 'humanization' of asymmetric warfare and the application of liberal precepts to its conduct have legitimated war making as political intervention." Khalili, *Time in the Shadows*, 3. Writing about the obfuscating language of prisons (e.g., "correctional institutions"), Orisanmi Burton argues that "these nomenclatural reforms and euphemistic baptisms were part of a broader strategy of psychological warfare through which counterinsurgency intellectuals aimed to present a benign public image without in any way altering their repressive and dehumanizing function within the social order." Burton, *Tip of the Spear*, 17–18. See also Dillon and Reid, *The Liberal Way of War*; Basham, *War, Identity, and the Liberal State*; Bachmann, Bell and Holmqvist, *War, Police, and Assemblages of Intervention*; Tudor, *Blue Helmet Bureaucrats*; Amar, *The Security Archipelago*; Greenburg, *At War with Women*; Moyn, *Humane*; Abrahamsen, "Return of the Generals"; Gelot and Sandor, "African Security and Global Militarism"; Orford, "Muscular Humanitarianism."

20. On the idea of military normal, see Lutz, "The Military Normal." On how African states have capitalized on the military normal, see Branch, *Displacing Human Rights*; Schmidt, *Foreign Intervention in Africa after the Cold War*; Epstein, *Another Fine Mess*; Bachmann, "Governmentality and Counterterrorism."

21. See "National Police Service Annual Report, 2021."

22. See especially Namir Shabibi, "Revealed: The CIA and MI6's Secret War in Kenya."

23. For more, see especially Niang, "Coups, Insurgency, and Imperialism in Africa"; Ake, *Democracy and Development in Africa*; Mkandawire, "Disempowering New Democracies and the Persistence of Poverty."

24. For more on the intersection of war-making and race-making, see Singh, *Race and America's Long War*; Man, *Soldiering through Empire*; Daulatzai, *Black Star, Crescent Moon*; Goldberg, "Militarizing Race"; Kapadia, *Insurgent Aesthetics*; Edwards, *The Other Side of Terror*; Rana, *Terrifying Muslims*; Li, *The Universal Enemy*; Mbembe, *Critique of Black Reason*.

25. See especially Mamdani, *Good Muslim, Bad Muslim*. Mamdani interrogates the assumption among Western analysts that the political subjectivities of Muslims are shaped primarily by their religion or culture. He traces the modern roots of what he calls "culture talk" to the days of European colonialism, where theories of cultural difference between the colonizers and the colonized functioned to legitimize colonial rule. Culture talk ascribed modernity, rationality, and humanism to the Occident while ascribing a cultural "lack" in these traits among inhabitants of the Orient, and the Muslim world in particular. Mamdani insists that we turn this cultural theory of politics on its head, arguing that culture talk dehistoricizes the construction of political identities. See also Daulatzai, *Black Star, Crescent Moon*; Grewal, *Islam Is a Foreign Country*; Li, *The Universal Enemy*.

26. See Hirsch, *In the Moment of Greatest Calamity*.

27. See Omeje, "The War on Terror and the Crisis of Postcoloniality in Africa"; Prestholdt, "Kenya, the United States, and Counterterrorism."

28. As Wanjiru Kamau observes, the US and UK governments both imposed restrictions on their citizens' ability to travel to Kenya in response to delays in the implementation of Kenya's "Suppression of Terrorism Bill," which closely resembled the US Patriot Act. Kenyan political leaders characterized this strategy as tantamount to economic sanctions, given that the country relied so heavily on tourism as a source of hard currency. Kamau, "Kenya and the War on Terrorism."

29. I draw on the work of many others who similarly argue about the centrality of seemingly marginal places and populations to global and imperial processes. See Trouillot, *Global Transformations*; Ong, *Flexible Citizenship;* Coronil, "Beyond Occidentalism"; Stoler, *Imperial Debris*; Ferguson, *Global Shadows;* Kramer, *Blood of Government;* Mbembe, "At the Edge of the World"; Metcalf, *Imperial Connections*; Moyd, *Violent Intermediaries*; Shields, *Offshore Attachments*; Hanieh, *Money, Markets, and Monarchies;* Amar, *The Security Archipelago;* Hönke and Müller, eds., *The Global Making of Policing;* Hart, "Denaturalizing Dispossession"; Razavi, "Navigating the 'Middle East' in Washington"; Tahir, "The Distributed Empire of the War on Terror"; Rhys Machold, "India's Counterinsurgent Knowledge."

30. Nesiah, "An Un-American Story of the American Empire." As Nesiah writes there, "Not just unidirectional from center to periphery, American empire is also constituted and destabilized through the complex, ambiguous, and ever shifting dialectic of historical circumstances and political projects through which the subjects of empire engage the world, and in that process, shape it" (1453). See also Lutz, "Empire Is in the Details"; Li, "From Exception to Empire." We must also be attentive to the shifting geopolitical landscape and the potential waning of US hegemony. While the United States continues to wield outsized military power on the continent, it is facing stiff competition in East Africa and the Horn, where China, Turkey, India, and the Gulf States have a growing presence.

31. See especially Trouillot, *Silencing the Past*; Grovogui, *Beyond Eurocentrism & Anarchy*; Khayyat, *A Landscape of War*; Prestholdt, *Domesticating the World;* Gopal, *Insurgent Empire*; Getachew, *Worldmaking after Empire;* Sabaratnam, "IR in Dialogue"; Sharp, "Subaltern Geopolitics"; Amar, *The Security Archipelago;* Vitalis, *White World Order, Black Power Politics*; Shilliam, *Decolonizing Politics*; Thornton, *Revolution in Development;* Heredia and Wai, *Recentering Africa in International Relations*.

32. Nyerere, *Stability and Change in Africa*, 2.

33. Ngũgĩ wa Thiong'o, *Moving the Centre*, 4.

34. Ngũgĩ wa Thiong'o, *Moving the Centre*, 4.

35. Getachew, *Worldmaking after Empire*; see also Lee, *Making a World After Empire;* Prashad, *The Darker Nations*.

36. Shohat, "Notes on the 'Post-Colonial,'" 100. See also Vitalis, "The Midnight Ride of Kwame Nkrumah and Other Fables of Bandung (Ban-doong)"; Bardawil, *Revolution and Disenchantment;* Hundle, *Insecurities of Expulsion*.

37. Long before US officials worried about the figure of the Muslim "terrorist" in East Africa, they were preoccupied with the possibility that the spirit of the anticolonial struggle in Kenya would spread to Black America. As Gerald Horne explains, "So concerned were the U.S. authorities . . . that when in 1968 the Federal Bureau of Investigation (FBI) expanded their notorious COINTELPRO—or counter-intelligence program—one of their chief goals was to 'prevent the coalition of militant black nationalist groups' that 'might be the first step toward a real 'Mau Mau' in America, the beginning of a true black revolution." Horne, *Mau Mau in Harlem*, 13. See also Osborne, "Mau Mau Are Angels"; Alvarado, "Mau Mau as Method."

38. Ruth Wilson Gilmore defines racism as "group-differentiated vulnerability to premature death." Gilmore, *Golden Gulag*.

39. Getachew also accounts for the destructive potential of worldmaking, characterizing European imperialism "as itself a world-constituting force that violently inaugurated an unprecedented era of globality." Getachew, *Worldmaking after Empire*, 3. Fadi Bardawil astutely notes that while the intellectual and theoretical project of decentering the West "is staged as a liberatory act of decolonization, its decentering in practice does not necessarily usher in an era of progressive politics." Bardawil, *Revolution and Disenchantment*, xv–xvi.

40. See especially Ong, "Worlding Cities, or the Art of Being Global"; Escobar, *Pluriversal Politics*; Rofel and Rojas, *New World Orderings*. Rofel and Rojas emphasize the significance of history, culture, and imaginative processes.

41. For more on the vast assemblage of US military bases, see Lutz and Enloe, *The Bases of Empire*; Vine, *Base Nation*.

42. See Turse, "The U.S. Military Says It Has a 'Light Footprint' in Africa." As defined by the US military, a cooperative security location (CSL) is "a host-nation facility with little or no permanent U.S. personnel presence, which may contain prepositioned equipment and/or logistical arrangements and serve both for security cooperation activities and contingency access."

43. See especially Scahill, *Dirty Wars*; Turse *Tomorrow's Battlefield*.

44. On AFRICOM as geopolitical assemblage, see Moore and Walker, "Tracing the US Military's Presence in Africa."

45. As feminist geographers have long reminded us, cartography was an integral component of the masculine imperial imagination during the colonial era, largely because of its distancing and objectifying effects. Caren Kaplan observes that "the challenge for those of us who study the history of visuality in relation to military technologies is to avoid remythologizing and promoting the narratives generated by colonial occupations and asymmetric warfare." Kaplan, *Aerial Aftermaths,* 210. And as Ronak Kapadia implores, we need "alternative systems of knowing, feeling, and living with and beyond forever warfare." Kapadia, *Insurgent Aesthetics,* 12. For further discussion, see Dowler and Sharp, "A Feminist Geopolitics?"; Rofel, "Modernity's Masculine Fantasies"; Grewal, *Transnational America*; Hyndman, "Mind the Gap"; Coronil, "Beyond Occidentalism"; Sparke, *In the Space of Theory*.

46. See Mamdani, *Good Muslim, Bad Muslim*; McFadden, "Interrogating Americana"; Mama, "Beyond Survival"; Minter, *Apartheid's Contras*.

47. Hecht, "Introduction," in *Entangled Geographies*, 2. On the fascination with drones specifically, see Parks and Kaplan, *Life in the Age of Drone Warfare*; Kaplan, *Aerial Aftermaths*.

48. Paul Kramer characterizes this singular focus on US actors and institutions as a form of nationalist transnationalism that is limited by a tendency to pose US-oriented questions. Kramer, "How Not to Write the History of U.S. Empire." As Zoe Samudzi observes, "adoration and disgust are two sides of the same Americentric coin." Samudzi, "Journey from the Center of the World."

49. See especially Coburn, *Under Contract;* Li, "Offshoring the Army"; Hoffman, "Geometry after the Circle"; Moore, *Empire's Labor;* Tahir, "The Distributed Empire of the War on Terror."

50. Li, "From Exception to Empire"; Tahir, "The Distributed Empire of the War on Terror"; Bhungalia, *Elastic Empire;* Gregory, "Dirty Dancing."

51. Tahir, "The Distributed Empire of the War on Terror."

52. See especially Ṣóyẹmí, "Making Crisis Inevitable."

53. Adebajo, "Africa, African-Americans, and Avuncular Sam."

54. Ahmed, "Towards a Law and Political Economy Approach to the War on Terror."

55. The International Monetary Fund (IMF) approved a $2.34 billion loan to Kenya in 2021, triggering protests about what this would mean for the country's economic sovereignty. See Warah, "Why Kenyans Fear Another IMF Loan," May 2021. See also "Kenya Vote Backdrop Is Anger over Living Costs, Debt," *Washington Post*, 8 August 2022.

56. The Kenyan Ministry of Defense states on its website that "UN peace operations offer Kenyan soldiers and police a rare opportunity to obtain UN allowances that are ordinarily not offered by the KDF (Kenya Defence Forces) . . . Due to the huge sums involved, remittances—including from peacekeepers—are now being recognized as an important contributor to the country's growth and development." See "Kenya's Peacekeeping Missions."

57. SIPRI, "Trends in World Military Expenditure, 2021," April 2022.

58. For more on the significance of ideology, culture, and the imagination, see Gregory, *The Colonial Present;* Lubin, *Never-Ending War on Terror;* Kapadia, *Insurgent Aesthetics.*

59. Li, *The Universal Enemy,* 5

60. See also Neocleous, "The Police of Civilization."

61. As Ferguson observes, "Yearnings for cultural convergence with an imagined global standard . . . can mark not simply mental colonization or capitulation to cultural imperialism, but an aspiration to overcome categorical subordination." Ferguson, *Global Shadows*, 20.

62. Haugerud, *The Culture of Politics in Modern Kenya.*

63. Quoted in Branch, *Kenya: Between Hope and Despair*, 19.

64. See especially Njoya, "Invisible Citizens"; see also Kessler and Kabukuru, "Shadow Diplomacy: African Nations Bypass Embassies, Tap Lobbyists."

65. Fisher, "Some More Reliable Than Others."

66. Epstein, *Another Fine Mess*. While Kenya, Uganda, and Ethiopia are all troop-contributing countries to AMISOM, all three militaries have simultaneously engaged in unilateral military operations in Somalia.

67. See Donelli, "Rwanda's Military Diplomacy."

68. Noting the interventions of non-Western powers like Iran and Turkey in Syria, Fadi Bardawil observes that such interventions "can be condemned morally and politically, but critical theories don't have the resources to apprehend them conceptually." Bardawil, *Revolution and Disenchantment*, xvii.

69. See, for example, Visweswaran, "Occupier/Occupied"; Heredia and Wai, *Recentering Africa in International Relations*. And as Siba Grovogui observes, "Our inability to understand that Africa actually sees itself as a part of the world, as a manager of the world, has so escaped us today that in the case of Libya for instance, when people were debating, you saw in every single newspaper in the world, including my beloved *Guardian*, that the African Union decided this, but the International Community decided that, as if Africans had surrendered their position in the international society to somebody: to the International Community. People actually said that! The AU, for all its 'wretchedness', after all represents about a quarter of the member states of the UN. And yet it was said the AU decided this and the International Community decided that. The implication is that the International Community is still the West plus Japan and maybe somebody else, and in this case it was Qatar and Saudi Arabia: 'good citizens of the world,' very 'good democracies' etc. That's how deeply-set that is, that people don't even check themselves. Every time they talk they chuck Africa out of the World. Nobody says, America did this and the International Community decided that. All I am saying is that our mindscapes are so deeply structured that nothing about Africa can be studied on its own, can be studied as something that has universal consequence." Creutzfeldt, "Siba Grovogui on IR Theory as Theology."

70. Most scholars contend that Kenya's decision to invade was made independently of US influence or pressure. Some have pointed to the fact that Kenyan officials sought US support well in advance of the incursion but were "curtly rebuffed." See Anderson and McKnight, "Kenya at War." Beyond the official rhetoric of protecting its territorial integrity and national security, Kenya was keen to secure the area near the border with Somalia to ensure that it remained safe for investment and economic development, including oil exploration. The invasion also came at a time when the International Criminal Court (ICC) investigations into crimes related to the 2007 postelection violence risked jeopardizing Kenya's image abroad, and came with the dangerous potential for renewed ethnic tensions within the country. War against a foreign enemy became a convenient distraction from both issues. For more, see Wanyeki, "Foreign Policy and Regional Relations"; Anderson and McKnight, "Kenya at War"; Rosen, "Strategic Posture Review"; Olsen, "The October 2011 Kenyan Invasion of Somalia"; Gathara, "The Guns of October."

71. For more on this topic see Enloe, "Masculinity as Foreign Policy Issue"; Lewis, *Empire State-building*; McFadden, "Plunder as Statecraft"; Decker, *In Idi Amin's Shadow*.

72. Otuki, "Nairobi leads EA Arms Race with Sh96 Billion Military Budget," *Business Daily Africa.*

73. Kenyan military spending has since surpassed the $1 billion per year mark, hovering around $1.1 billion since 2017. It is worth noting that the size of the Kenyan military is considerably smaller than those of neighboring Ethiopia and Uganda.

74. In contrast to mainstream conceptualizations of geopolitics that continue to privilege Eurocentric ideas about disembodied actors operating only in official "public" and "global" realms, I am in dialogue with feminist scholars who foreground the significance of affect and emotion, and who insist that we scrutinize what kinds of sites are relevant for our understandings of war, empire, and geopolitics. A feminist analytic of scale interrogates the very constitution of the macro-picture while attending to the intimate, the embodied, and the everyday. See especially Massaro and Williams, "Feminist Geopolitics"; Smith, *Intimate Geopolitics*; Clarke, *Affective Justice*; Schields, *Offshore Attachments*; Flores-Villalobos, *The Silver Women*; Zeleke, *Ethiopia in Theory*; Baik, *Re-encounters*; Ghosh, "Parade-Charade."

75. See especially Aretxaga, "Maddening States"; Green, "Fear as a Way of Life"; Masco, *The Theater of Operations*; Ali, *Delusional States*; Rashid, *Dying to Serve*; Zia, *Resisting Disappearance*; Ghosh, *A Thousand Tiny Cuts.*

76. I concur with other scholars that we must address and think critically about the question of political violence, particularly with a view toward interrogating the paradigm of national security that authorizes more violence in response to perceived threats. See especially Asad, "Thinking about Terrorism and Just War"; Mamdani, *Good Muslim, Bad Muslim*; Li, *The Universal Enemy*. In dialogue with abolition feminists, I concur that the time has come to re-imagine new modes of relationality and collective safety. See Kaba, *We Do this 'Til We Free Us*; Davis et al, *Abolition. Feminism. Now.*

77. See especially Mudimbe, *The Invention of Africa*; Grovogui, "Come to Africa"; Mbembe, *On the Postcolony*; Pierre, *The Predicament of Blackness.*

78. Jones, "'Good Governance' and 'State Failure,'" 62–63.

79. See especially Grovogui, "Come to Africa"; Shilliam, "What the Haitian Revolution Might Tell Us about Development, Security, and the Politics of Race"; Jones, "'Good Governance' and 'State Failure'"; Wai, "Neopatrimonialism and the Discourse of State Failure in Africa"; Pierre, *The Predicament of Blackness.*

80. Grovogui, "Come to Africa."

81. On the notion of "cultural coding," see Springer, "Violence Sits in Places?"

82. Kramer argues for "the necessity of examining metropole and colony in a single, densely interactive field" in order to grasp the inseparability of "the racial remaking of empire and the imperial remaking of race." Kramer, *The Blood of Government*, 2–3. See also Clarke and Thomas, eds., *Globalization and Race.*

83. Mungai, "The Whiteness Conference." Avery Gordon uses the language of haunting as "one way in which abusive systems of power make themselves known, and their impacts felt in everyday life, especially when they are supposedly over and done with." Gordon, *Ghostly Matters*, xvi. See also Stoler, *Haunted by Empire.*

84. Pierre, *The Predicament of Blackness*, 5.

85. Pierre, *The Predicament of Blackness,* 5. As she elaborates, "The overall scholarly interest in 'ethnic conflict' or indigenous cultural traditions belies the continent's relation to global racialized hierarchies against and through which these local events develop."

86. For more on racial liberalism and its relationship to US empire see Von Eschen, *Race against Empire*; Singh, *Race and America's Long War.*

87. For more on the intersectionality of race and religion, see Guner, "Transnational Muslim Crossings and Race in Africa"; Young and Weitzberg, "Globalizing Racism and De-Provincializing Muslim Africa"; Tounsel, *Chosen Peoples.*

88. Mazrui "Afrabia: Africa and the Arabs in the New World Order"; Gubara, "Revisiting Race and Slavery"; Aidi et al., "And the Twain Shall Meet"; Li, "Captive Passages"; Fadlalla, *Branding Humanity*; Ware, *The Walking Qur'an.*

89. More than one-sixth of the world's Muslims live south of the Sahara (compared to one-tenth in North Africa). See Ware, *The Walking Qur'an,* 17.

90. For more, see Ware *The Walking Qur'an*; Marsh, "Compositions of Sainthood."

91. Gross-Wyrtzen, "There Is No Race Here"; see also Malkki, "National Geographic"; Prestholdt, "Politics of the Soil"; Chome, "Uses of Race."

92. See especially Hofmeyr, "The Complicating Sea"; Srinivas et al., *Reimagining Indian Ocean Worlds*; Bertz, *Diaspora and Nation in the Indian Ocean*; Besteman, *Unraveling Somalia: Race, Class and the Legacy of Slavery*; Hundle, *Insecurities of Expulsion*; Mahajan, "Notes on an Archipelagic Ethnography"; Young and Weitzberg, "Globalizing Racism and De-Provincializing Muslim Africa"; Aidi et al., "And the Twain Shall Meet"; Goldberg, "Racial Comparisons, Relational Racisms." In his study of racial thought in nineteenth- and twentieth-century Zanzibar, Jonathan Glassman (*War of Words*) challenges the notion that European colonialism was the only source of ideas about difference, pointing to the significance of Zanzibari discourses about race, ethnicity, and notions of Arab supremacy. Precolonial Swahili words like *Ustaarabu* (civilization) and *Mstaarabu* (civilized person) for example, contained within them the figure of the Arab as civilized, and as source of civilization. Glassman, *War of Words.*

93. Mamdani, "Beyond Settler and Native." As Weitzberg explains, Isaaq and Harti Somalis were initially classified as nonnative under the Somalia Exemption Ordinance (1919) but later lost many nonnative privileges. Weitzberg, *We Do Not Have Borders.* See also Turton, "Somali Resistance to Colonial Rule."

94. Africans were ethnicized as "natives" and subject to customary law, whereas Europeans, Asians, and Arabs were racialized as "nonnatives" and governed by civil law. These processes of differentiation legitimated the introduction of separate laws that governed the lives of "natives" and "nonnatives." Mamdani, *Citizen and Subject.*

95. Ng'weno and Aloo, "Irony of Citizenship," 145.

96. I join other scholars in foregrounding the politics of location for theorizations of race, even as we attend to continuities in processes of race and racialization across time and place. Paul Zeleza, for example, insists that scholars confront the epistemic hegemony of the Euro-American world system in shaping monolithic notions of Blackness, even among scholars and activists committed to Pan-Africanism. Zeleza, "Rewriting the

African Diaspora." Annie Olaloku-Teriba similarly notes what she refers to as "the subsumption of 'Africanness' by an Americanised conception of blackness," observing that US theorizations of Blackness have become "unmoored from time and space." Olaloku-Teriba, "Afro-Pessimism." Emmanuel Akyeampong scrutinizes African American invocations of Africa as the homeland of Black people, noting that the continent continues to be imagined as "the place of Blacks where race, geography, and polity overlap(ped) naturally." Akyeampong, "Race, Identity, and Citizenship in Black Africa," 299. And as Keguro Macharia observes, "The history of blackness as a shared category is marked by disagreement, disavowal, and ambivalence, from those who distinguish themselves as 'African, not black,' to those who police blackness as a product of Atlantic slavery and thus unavailable to other populations." Macharia, *Frottage*, 6. See also Li, "Captive Passages"; Tageldin, "The Place of Africa, in Theory."

97. Clarke, "Mapping Transnationality."

98. See especially Kindy, *Life and Politics in Mombasa*; Willis, *Mombasa, the Swahili, and the Making of the Mijikenda*; Kresse, *Philosophising in Mombasa*; McIntosh, *The Edge of Islam*.

99. Muslims constitute 20–30 percent of Kenya's predominantly Christian population, although conflicting reports exist on the exact figure. See Ndzovu, *Muslims in Kenyan Politics*.

100. On the post-9/11 racialization of Islam and Muslims, see Rana, *Terrifying Muslims*; Maira, *The 9/11 Generation*; Fernando, *The Republic Unsettled*; Kundnani, "Islamophobia as Ideology of U.S. Empire"; Li, "Captive Passages."

101. See Kapadia, *Insurgent Aesthetics*.

102. Muriithi, "Stop Targeting Somalis, Says Raila," *Daily Nation*, 12 April 2014.

103. See Nanjala Nyabola, "The Politics of Identity and Belonging in Kenya," *Al-Jazeera*, 23 June 2014.

104. For more on the Shifta War, see especially Whittaker, *Insurgency and Counterinsurgency in Kenya*; Weitzberg, *We Do Not Have Borders*. Weitzberg astutely observes that the terminology of secession naturalizes the nation-state framework as the paradigmatic basis for political community. What she describes as a fabled dilemma between separatism and integration obscures the manifold ways that ethnic Somalis "felt loyalty to a variety of overlapping, and at times, competing nationalist visions," yet decolonization "provided little space for flexible notions of citizenship" (109–10). See also Aidid, *Pan-Somali Dreams*.

105. Whittaker, *Insurgency and Counterinsurgency in Kenya*; Branch, *Kenya: Between Hope and Despair*.

106. For more, see Whittaker, *Insurgency and Counterinsurgency in Kenya*.

107. Weitzberg, *We Do Not Have Borders*, 145.

108. Thomas, "Can Black Lives Matter in a Black Country?"

109. I borrow the notion of a "long war on terror" from Edwards, *The Other Side of Terror*. On the violent legacies of colonial rule and colonial-era counter-insurgency practices in Kenya, see especially Sahle, "Fanon and Geographies of Political Violence in the Context of Democracy in Kenya"; Kimari, "The Story of a Pump"; Kimari and

Pfingst, "Carcerality and Legacies of Settler Colonial Punishment in Nairobi"; Ossome, *Gender, Ethnicity, and Violence in Kenya's Transitions to Democracy*; Branch, *Kenya: Between Hope and Despair.*

110. I borrow this language of liberal piety from Vora, *Teach for Arabia.*

111. On the tensions at the heart of secular democracy see Asad, *Formations of the Secular*; Agrama, *Questioning Secularism*; Fernando, *The Republic Unsettled*; Mahmood, *Religious Difference in a Secular Age.*

112. See Gifford, *Christianity, Politics, and Public Life*; Haugerud, *The Culture of Politics in Modern Kenya.*

113. See Mwakimako, "Christian-Muslim Relations in Kenya"; Bakari, "A Place at the Table"; Ndzovu, *Muslims in Kenyan Politics.*

114. See Gifford, *Christianity, Politics, and Public Life*; Deacon and Lynch, "Allowing Satan In?"

115. Mahmood, *Religious Difference in a Secular Age.*

116. For more on the body and the sensorial in contexts of surveillance, war, occupation, and insecurity, see Aretxaga, "Maddening States"; Thomas, *Exceptional Violence*; Hermez, *War Is Coming*; Kapadia, *Insurgent Aesthetics*; Ghosh, "Everything Must Match"; Zia, *Resisting Disappearance*; Junaid, "Counter-Maps of the Ordinary."

117. Ann Stoler suggests that our conceptual vocabularies have been "more brittle, more constrained than imperial forms themselves" (*Duress*, 180). She proposes the concept of "imperial formation" in order to shift the emphasis from notions of "clearly bordered and bounded polities" to "scaled genres of rule that in their very making thrive on opaque taxonomies" (*Duress*, 177). Unlike empires, she writes, imperial formations are "processes of becoming, not fixed things" (*Imperial Debris*, 8). Stoler disrupts categorical distinctions like colonizer/colonized and insists that we contend with entanglement. As she writes, "The 'interior' and 'exterior' spaces of imperial formations may not correspond to the common geographical designations that imperial architects scripted themselves. Terms like metropole and colony, core and periphery presume to make clear what is not" (*Imperial Debris*, 19).

118. While the United States continues to wield outsized military power on the continent, it is facing stiff competition in East Africa and the Horn, where China, Turkey, India, and the Gulf States have a growing presence.

119. I follow the work of many others who have made a similar observation. See Enloe, *Bananas, Beaches, and Bases*; Lutz, *Homefront*; Mama and Okazawa-Rey, "Militarism, Conflict, and Women's Activism"; Terry, *Attachments to War*; Kaplan, Kirk, and Lea, "Everyday Militarisms"; Baik, *Reencounters*, Ghosh, *A Thousand Tiny Cuts*; Bhungalia, *Elastic Empire*; Pedraza et al., "Domestication of War."

120. See Stoler, *Imperial Debris.*

Chapter 1

1. For more, see Okwembah, "#weareone"; Gluck, "Security Urbanism"; Okech, "Boundary Anxieties"; Harrington, "#weareone: Blood Donation, Terrorism and Dreams of Inclusion in Kenya."

2. KTN News, "Kenya Has Triumphed over Terrorists: Uhuru Kenyatta," 24 September 2013.

3. Munene, "Kenya Must Emerge Stronger from Attack on Westgate Mall," *The Standard*, 28 September 2013.

4. See Migue and Oloch, *Operation Linda Nchi*.

5. See Molony, "Social Media Warfare and Kenya's Conflict with Al Shabaab in Somalia."

6. For more on the significance of the home front see Lutz, *Homefront*;

7. Lutz, "The Military Normal"; Bernal, *Nation as Network*.

8. Cited in News 24, "Forgetting Westgate." For more, see especially Gathara, "Five Years after the Westgate Mall Attack, a Culture of Silence Still Haunts Kenya"; Purdekova, "Memory as Vulnerability." As Purdekova observes in dialogue with Gathara, to memorialize would be to acknowledge Westgate as a site of visceral security failure; to forget by leading "normal lives" is to engage in an act of defiance.

9. Gathara, "Five Years after the Westgate Mall Attack."

10. Gathara, "Five Years after the Westgate Mall Attack."

11. Kumar, "See Something, Say Something."

12. "The Untold Story of KDF War against Al-Shabaab Fighters" *Daily Nation*.

13. See also Migue and Oloch, *Operation Linda Nchi*.

14. Branch, *Displacing Human Rights*; Epstein, *Another Fine Mess*; Wilson, *The Threat of Liberation*; Rizvi, *The Ethics of Staying*; Ali, *Delusional States*; Byler, *Terror Capitalism*.

15. Although the Constitution permits the deployment of military forces to "restore peace in any part of Kenya affected by unrest or instability," it stipulates that the decision to deploy may "only be made *with the approval* of the National Assembly. However, the Kenya Defence Force Act (Amendment 2016) allows for interference by the KDF domestically for a period of seven days *without* informing or receiving approval from the Parliament. See Wabuke, "Mapping the Legal Contours for Internal Deployment of Military Forces in Kenya."

16. Gitau, "Civil Military Relations in an Era of Violent Extremism."

17. Lutz, *Homefront*.

18. Lutz, "A Military History of the American Suburbs," 903.

19. Lutz, "A Military History of the American Suburbs," 903.

20. Asad, "Thinking about Terrorism ands Just War," 1; see also Mamdani, *Good Muslim, Bad Muslim*.

21. See Ali, *Delusional States*; Rashid, *Dying to Serve*; Ghosh, *A Thousand Tiny Cuts*.

22. Lutz, "The Military Normal."

23. Mama, "Beyond Survival"; Gusterson, "Anthropology and Militarism"; Rashid, *Dying to Serve*.

24. Mama and Okazawa-Rey, "Militarism, Conflict and Women's Activism in the Global Era," 100.

25. Mazrui, "On Heroes and Uhuru-Worship"; Carrier and Nyamweru, "Reinventing Africa's National Heroes."

26. See Lonsdale and Odhiambo, *Mau Mau and Nationhood*; McIntosh, *Unsettled*. As Robert Blunt observes, the hesitancy around the figure of the Mau Mau continues to haunt the present day, informed by "the trauma of deep betrayals and endless cycles of violence and counterviolence between social intimates." Blunt, *For Money and Elders*, 68–69. In part, these divisions were exacerbated by the fact that the Mau Mau represented not only an anticolonial politics, but also class struggle: they called for bread and land alongside freedom. Threatened by these calls for economic redistribution, the ruling class has worked to shape national debate around recognition rather than redistribution. "Elites," writes Daniel Branch, "have encouraged Kenyans to think and act politically in a manner informed first and foremost by ethnicity, in order to crush demands for the redistribution of scarce resources." Branch, *Kenya: Between Hope and Despair*, 16. As McIntosh notes, it was not until the mid-2000s that the reframing of Mau Mau as liberation heroes gained some traction with the publication of scholarly works by David Anderson and Caroline Elkins. Even then, Daniel Branch observes that these books have been used as "intellectual props" by the government in its attempt to privilege Kikuyu history, sidelining the many ethnic groups that either opposed the insurgency or feared Kikuyu hegemony.

27. D. Branch, *Defeating Mau Mau, Creating Kenya*. Moreover, as Timothy Parsons explains, popular nationalist narratives have long celebrated the idea that many Mau Mau had fought in World War II, and that they drew upon their combat experience in the war to confront the British. "By assuming that all Kenyan soldiers were infantrymen, popular and professional historians alike have failed to realize that most Kikuyu veterans actually served in labor and specialist units. This means that their main contributions to the KLFA (Kenya Land and Freedom Army) was clerical and logistical rather than tactical." Parsons, "Mau Mau's Army of Clerks," 287.

28. See, for example, Migue and Oloch, *Operation Linda Nchi*.

29. Jacobs and Isbell, "Seven Years In."

30. On the notion of critical events, see Veena Das, *Critical Events: An Anthropological Perspective on Contemporary India*.

31. See especially Pierre, *The Predicament of Blackness*.

32. See Enloe, *The Morning After*; Enloe, *Bananas, Beaches, and Bases*; Mama, "Khaki in the Family"; "Beyond Survival"; Higate, ed., *Military Masculinities: Identity and the State*; Eichler, *Militarizing Men*; Decker, *In Idi Amin's Shadow*; Moyd, *Violent Intermediaries*; McFadden, "Plunder As Statecraft"; Henry, "Problematizing Military Masculinity."

33. See McEvoy, "Shifting Priorities"; Wanyeki, "Foreign Policy and Regional Relations."

34. Mama, "Beyond Survival," 32–33.

35. McFadden, "Plunder As Statecraft," 152.

36. Mama "Beyond Survival"; see also Musila, "Violent Masculinities"; McFadden, "Plunder As Statecraft"; Lindsay and Miescher, eds., *Men and Masculinities in Modern Africa*.

37. McFadden, "Plunder As Statecraft," 138.

38. See Rodney, *How Europe Underdeveloped Africa*.

39. Katumanga, "Post-colonial State-Military Relations," 414. See also Parsons, "The Lanet Incident."

40. Parsons, "The Lanet Incident."

41. Ngũgĩ wa Thiong'o, *Homecoming*; Odhiambo, "Democracy and the Ideology of Order in Kenya"; Lewis, *Empire State-Building*; Morton, "Agamben and Colonialism"; D. Branch, *Kenya: Between Hope and Despair.*

42. Keren Weitzberg rightly observes that the language of secession implies a certain acceptance of a national lens. As she writes, "Thinking about the northern campaign as a separatist movement naturalizes its place within Kenya, obscures the extent of the north's isolation, and projects an idea of indivisible territorial sovereignty." Weitzberg, *We Do Not Have Borders,* 97.

43. Weitzberg, *We Do Not Have Borders,* 121.

44. Weitzberg, *We Do Not Have Borders,* 121.

45. Branch, *Kenya: Between Hope and Despair*, 29.

46. Beyond claims of territorial integrity, historians have noted that Kenyan leaders and their Western allies had economic considerations in mind—namely, prospects for oil reserves in northern Kenya. See D. Branch, *Kenya: Between Hope and Despair*; Weitzberg, *We Do Not Have Borders.*

47. Derived from the Amharic expression for banditry, *sheftenat*, which stems from the verb *shaffata* (to rebel), was traditionally associated with violence that combined partisan warfare with organized livestock stealing. Beginning in the 1940s, however, the term acquired nationalist overtones, and was used to describe individuals engaged in subversive antistate activity. See Crummey, "Banditry and Resistance."

48. Hannah Whittaker observes that the British employed tactics of collective punishment not only in East Africa but also in British Palestine where the 1924–25 Collective Responsibility and Punishment Ordinance became a key feature of colonial repression. Whittaker, *Insurgency and Counterinsurgency in Kenya.*

49. See Branch, *Kenya: Between Hope and Despair*, 27.

50. See Anderson, "Remembering Wagalla"; also Turton, "Somali Resistance to Colonial Rule."

51. Whittaker, *Insurgency and Counterinsurgency in Kenya*, 643.

52. For more on the Wagalla massacre, see Sheik, "Blood on the Runway"; Anderson, "Remembering Wagalla"; Whittaker, *Insurgency and Counterinsurgency in Kenya*; Weitzberg, *We Do Not Have Borders*; Kantai, "The Rise of Somali Capital."

53. See "Somalia Hosts Regional Summit to Discuss Fighting al-Shabab," *Al-Jazeera,* February 2023. https://www.aljazeera.com/news/2023/2/1/somalia-hosts-regional-summit-to-discuss-fight-against-al-shabaab

54. For more see Nkrumah, *Neo-Colonialism*; Ijomah, *The African Military Interventions*; Getachew, *Worldmaking after Empire.*

55. Nkrumah, *Neo-Colonialism*; see also Forte, *Slouching Towards Sirte*; Esmenjaud, "Africa's Conception of Security in Transition"; Imojah, "The African Military Interventions."

56. Nkrumah, *Neo-Colonialism.*

57. See Charles Quist-Adade, "How Did a Fateful CIA Coup . . .," *Monthly Review* (2021). https://mronline.org/2021/02/25/how-did-a-fateful-cia-coup-executed-55-years-ago-this-february-24-doom-much-of-sub-saharan-africa/.

58. Baimu and Sturman, "Amendment to the African Union's Right to Intervene"; Forte, *Slouching Towards Sirte*; Adi, *Pan-Africanism*.

59. Chapter VII of the UN Charter still requires that the African Union obtain UN Security Council authorization to launch an intervention. See Ferim, "African Solutions to African Problems"; Coning, Gelot, and Karlsrud, *The Future of African Peace Operations*.

60. Mamdani, "Responsibility to Protect or Right to Punish?"; Mepham and Ramsbotham, "Safeguarding Civilians"; Kioko, "The Right of Intervention." Libya argued that the AU should have the right to intervene in cases of external (i.e., Western) aggression against African states. See Kioko, "The Right of Intervention."

61. Abrahamsen, "Return of the Generals," 26.

62. See Odinga, "We Recommend Compliance."

63. International Crisis Group, "Somalia's Islamists," 2005. Available at https://www.crisisgroup.org/africa/horn-africa/somalia/somalias-islamists.

64. See Prestholdt, "Fighting Phantoms"; Malito, "Building Terror While Fighting Enemies." As Prestholdt observes, intelligence officials ultimately found little evidence of an Al-Qaeda connection at that time.

65. Rawlence, *City of Thorns*.

66. See Elmi, "Revisiting United States Policy toward Somalia"; Harper, *Getting Somalia Wrong?*; Scahill, *Dirty Wars*; Besteman, *Global Militarized Apartheid*.

67. As Abdi Samatar elucidates, the African Union, Arab League, and the Intergovernmental Authority on Development (IGAD) all demanded that Ethiopia withdraw. See Samatar, "Ethiopian Occupation, American Terror."

68. Wondemagegnehu and Kebede, "AMISOM: Charting a New Course for African Union Missions," 203.

69. The Kenyan government's invocation of self-defense (drawing on Article 51 of the UN Charter) enabled it to legitimize its actions *through* international law rather than in breach of it. Here it is worth recalling Laleh Khalili's observation that "what distinguishes warfare by powers that claim adherence to liberal principles is the invocation of law and legality as structuring the conduct of war." Khalili, *Time in the Shadows*, 4.

70. As Danny Hoffman observes of contemporary counterinsurgency strategy: "It is too late to simply police borders and build walls." Flexibility and adaptability are key to security forces' ability to "arrest African threats the moment they emerge, wherever they emerge—and whatever form they might take." Hoffman, "Geometry after the Circle," 106.

71. David Throup, "Kenya's Intervention in Somalia," CSIS.

72. Williams, "Joining AMISOM."

73. United Nations, "Report of the Monitoring Group on Somalia and Eritrea pursuant to Security Council Resolution 2182 (2014)," 19 October 2015.

74. For more on AMISOM's rules of engagement, see Wondemagegnehu and Kebede, "AMISOM: Charting a New Course for African Union Missions."

75. See Coning, Gelot, and Karlsrud, *The Future of African Peace Operations.*

76. United Nations, *Report of the Monitoring Group on Somalia and Eritrea pursuant to Security Council Resolution 1916* (2011), 44. See also Epstein, *Another Fine Mess.*

77. United Nations, "Report of the Monitoring Group on Somalia and Eritrea pursuant to Security Council Resolution 2182 (2014)," 19 October 2015.

78. It is estimated that AMISOM fatalities ranged from 1,483 to 1,884 for the period between March 2007 and December 2018. See Williams, "An Update," https://theglobalobservatory.org/2019/09/update-how-many-fatalities-amisom-has-suffered. See also Besteman, *The Costs of War in Somalia.*

79. See Besteman, *The Costs of War in Somalia.* On EU spending, see Barigaba, "ATMIS troops Demand Pay Arrears as Mission Ends," *East African.*

80. See Blanchard, "Al-Shabaab," *Congressional Research Service*, 2020. See also "Why the U.S. Military Is in Somalia," US Africa Command Public Affairs, 29 November 2017.

81. See De Waal, *The Real Politics of the Horn of Africa;* Campbell, "War on Terror as Business."

82. Bearak, "In Kenya, Soldiers Traumatized by the US-backed War in Somalia Often Face Discipline instead of Treatment," *Washington Post,* April 2019.

83. See "Wikileaks: Museveni Discredits Kenya Army." https://www.monitor.co.ug/News/National/688334-1233186-a5fobfz/index.html.

84. Gaitho, "Kenya's Foray against Al-Shabaab Will Not Be Easy But It Is Necessary."

85. Mathiu, "Kenya Has No Choice on the Matter of Al-Shabaab." https://www.nation.co.ke/kenya/blogs-opinion/blogs/mutuma-mathiu/kenya-has-no-choice-on-this-matter-of-al-shabaab-the-war-must-go-on--787454.

86. Macharia, "War as Viagla." Drawing on bell hooks, Musila astutely cautions against fixating only on emasculation, as it risks excluding women's experiences.

87. See https://www.theeastafrican.co.ke/tea/news/east-africa/how-war-boosts-kenya-s-regional-global-clout--1305866.

88. N'Diaye, "How Not to Institutionalize Civilian Control"; Branch and Cheeseman, "Democratization, Sequencing"; Gathara, "The Guns of October."

89. Cynthia Enloe observes that militarized forms of manliness are prevalent within the militaries of modern states. Her conceptualization of militarized masculinity highlights the ways in which military institutions are important sites for the production of both gender and culture. Particular forms of martiality (those associated with men exclusively) are valorized, thereby shaping the glorification of men's participation in war. See Enloe, *The Morning After;* Enloe, *Bananas, Beaches, and Bases.* Since Enloe's pioneering work, scholars have expanded upon and complicated her theorization of militarized masculinity, pointing to the plurality and diversity of militarized masculinities, and looking beyond the institution of the military itself to reflect on the co-constituting processes of gender and military socialization. See especially Higate, *Military Masculinities: Identity and State;* Duncanson, "Forces for Good?"; Henry and Netantel,

"Militarisation as Diffusion"; Amar, "Middle East Masculinity Studies"; Musila, "Violent Masculinities."

90. See "The President and His Uniform," *Daily Nation,* December 2014.

91. Musila, "Phallocracies"; Musila, "Violent Masculinities." Musila's analysis allows for an understanding of masculinities as multiple and dynamic, evolving according to different historical contexts.

92. Musila, "Phallocracies," 43.

93. Musila, "Violent Masculinities," 154. See also McClintock, *Imperial Leather.*

94. See Maruska, "When Are States Hypermasculine?"

95. See especially Goldberg, "Militarizing Race"; Singh, *Race and America's Long War;* Edwards, *The Other Side of Terror.*

96. Adesanmi interrogates the very framing of "African solutions to African problems," suggesting that the construction of the "problem" requires scrutiny, as does the construction of the problem as "African." See Adesanmi, *Who Owns the Problem?*

97. See also Man, *Soldiering for Empire.* Of significance for Singh is that "if blackness has been the principal figure and ground for defining and enacting a racialized *inhumanity,* particularly in U.S. history, it has also proved to be analogically flexible and part of a heterogeneous repertoire of racializing motifs that have informed the creation of a military-police apparatus at home and abroad." Singh, *Race and America's Long War,* 147.

98. Edwards, *The Other Side of Terror,* 9–10.

99. "Kenya Lobbying for UN Security Council Slot," https://www.the-star.co.ke/news/2019-04-13-kenya-lobbying-for-un-security-council-slot/.

100. https://www.youtube.com/watch?v=bAawso1uKhY.

101. Makau Mutua, @makaumutua, Twitter, 28 December 2019. https://twitter.com/makaumutua/status/1211074669757026304?s=19.

102. Razack, *Dark Threats, White Knights,* 10.

103. Lubin makes this observation in his analysis of the American film *Zero Dark Thirty.* See Lubin, *Never-Ending War on Terror,* 85.

104. On enforcement masculinities, see Highgate, "Martial Races and Enforcement Masculinities."

105. Enloe, *The Morning After,* 73. See also Rashid, *Dying to Serve.*

106. "Message from His Excellency the President," in *Gender Policy,* Ministry of Defense, May 2017. http://www.mod.go.ke/wp-content/uploads/2017/05/gender-policy.pdf.

107. See especially Greenburg, *At War with Women.* Greenburg (8) argues that "women's integration into previously male and masculinist military domains, along with military praise for their unique contributions, calls for a concept of military femininity akin to more robust theorizations of military masculinity." See also Grewal, *Saving the Security State;* Abu-Lughod et al., *The Cunning of Gender Violence;* Hunt, "Embedded Feminism"; Nesiah, "Feminism as Counter-Terrorism."

108. See Mesok, "Affective Technologies of War"; Greenburg, *At War with Women.*

109. For similar discussions in other contexts see Rashid, *Dying to Serve;* Greenburg, *At War with Women.*

110. Ironically, as Darryl Li observes, the traits that make for a good mujahid are qualities "not conventionally associated with soldiering or even masculinity, such as calmness, humility, and leniency." See Li, *The Universal Enemy*, 109–10. For more on what Duncanson refers to as peacekeeper masculinities, see Duncanson, "Forces for Good?" On cosmopolitan militarism see Kuus, "Cosmopolitan Militarism?"

111. Suttner, "Masculinities in the ANC-led Liberation Movement"; Gqola, "The Difficult Task of Normalizing Freedom."

112. See especially Wedeen, *Ambiguities of Domination*.

113. I borrow the phrase "disposition of disregard" from Stoler, *Along the Archival Grain*.

114. "Kenyan Soldiers Killed in Somalia: The Shroud of Secrecy," BBC News, 21 March 2022. https://www.bbc.com/news/world-africa-60826313.

Chapter 2

1. See especially Mazrui and Shariff, *The Swahili*; Willis and Chome, "Marginalization and Political Participation on the Kenya Coast"; Mwakimako and Willis, "Islam, Politics and Violence on the Kenya Coast."

2. Yousuf Al-Bulushi reminds us of the importance of defetishizing the state as the principal unit of analysis in order to account for continuities in processes of race and racialization across time and place. He documents the extent to which Cedric Robinson's theory of racial capitalism was shaped by his engagement with world-system analysis. See Y. Al-Bulushi, "Thinking Racial Capitalism and Black Radicalism from Africa"; see also Beliso de Jesus and Pierre, "Anthropology of White Supremacy."

3. Attending to the spatial dimensions of racialization under colonial rule, Frantz Fanon describes the colonial world as one that is divided into compartments, and insists that we attend to its geographical layout: "The zone where the natives live is not complementary to the zone inhabited by the settlers." He continues: "The town belonging to the colonized people . . . is a place of ill fame, peopled by men of evil repute. They are born there, it matters little where or how; they die there, it matters little where or how." Fanon, *Wretched of the Earth*, 39.

4. Said, *Orientalism*.

5. Nation Media Group, "Jewel in the Crown of Tourism in Kenya," quoted in Eisenberg, "Hip-Hop and Cultural Citizenship on Kenya's 'Swahili Coast.'"

6. Following the 2011 kidnappings of European tourists from Lamu by Al-Shabaab, the *Guardian* referred nostalgically to Lamu as what had been "one of the most peaceful places in Kenya, and perhaps the most beautiful too—a Swahili island paradise of warm, deep-blue water, golden sands and ancient, narrow streets where cars are banned and donkeys rule." See "Kenya Kidnap Attacks by Somalis Drive Terrified Tourists Out of Paradise Islands," *Guardian*, 4 October 2011.

7. For the fiscal year 2015–16, the State Department sought to provide $40 million in assistance related to countering violent extremism (CVE) in East Africa. See White House, "U.S. Support for Peace, Security, and Countering Violent Extremism in Africa," Office of the Press Secretary, 27 July 2015.

8. See also Seeseman, "Kenyan Muslims."

9. Scholars of Kenya have documented political invocations of Islam and the rise of "Islamist ideology," noting the range and diversity of perspectives over time. In these studies, articulations of victimization in relation to Islam and Muslims are often minimized as narratives that are politicized or capitalized upon. See, for example, Mwakimako and Willis, "Islam, Politics and Violence on the Kenya Coast"; Chome, "From Islamic Reform to Muslim Activism."

10. See especially Mamdani, *Good Muslim, Bad Muslim*.

11. See Trouillot, *Peasants and Capital*; see also Bonilla, *Non-Sovereign Futures*; Bonilla et al., eds., *Trouillot Remixed*.

12. I am especially inspired by Sarah Ihmoud's theorization of "the politics of staying in place," which she defines as an ethically based collective response to what she views as Israel's ongoing policies of colonization in Jerusalem. See Ihmoud, "Murabata."

13. On knowledge-making as worldmaking, see Zhan, *Other-worldly*; Kamola, *Making the World Global*; Kapadia, *Insurgent Aesthetics*.

14. Omi and Winant, *Racial Formation in the United States*, 68.

15. See Prestholdt, "Politics of the Soil"; Hofmeyr, "The Complicating Sea"; Srinivas et al., *Reimagining Indian Ocean Worlds*; Mahajan, "Notes on an Archipelagic Ethnography"; Lori, *Offshore Citizens*; Hundle, *Insecurities of Expulsion*.

16. Mamdani, *Citizen and Subject*; Weitzberg, *We Do Not Have Borders*.

17. Lee, "The Native Undefined."

18. Powell, *A Different Shade of Colonialism*; Glassman, *War of Words, War of Stones*; Brennan, *Taifa*; Bertz, *Diaspora and Nation*; Hundle, *Insecurities of Expulsion*; Young and Weitzberg, "Globalizing Racism and De-Provincializing Muslim Africa"; Mamdani, "Trans-African Slaveries Thinking Historically"; Gubara, "Revisiting Race and Slavery"; Li, "Captive Passages."

19. Glassman, *War of Words*.

20. Glassman, *War of Words*, 30.

21. Glassman, *War of Words*, 31.

22. As just one example, these Zanzibari intellectuals replaced a Bantu-derived term for civilization (*uungwana*) with *ustaarabu*, derived from Arabic, which translates as the act of becoming an Arab. See Glassman, *War of Words*.

23. Ndzovu, *Muslims in Kenyan Politics*, 22–24.

24. Glassman, *War of Words*; Ndzovu, *Muslims in Kenyan Politics*.

25. See especially Prestholdt, "Politics of the Soil"; also Brennan, *Taifa*; Glassman, *War of Words*; Salim, "The Movement for 'Mwambao' "; Chome, "Uses of Race."

26. The Arab-dominated Coastal League campaigned for reintegration with Zanzibar. The Coast African Political Union (CAPU), dominated primarily by Mijikendas, called for secession of the Coast Province.

27. For a recounting of the heated exchange between Tom Mboya and Sheikh Abdullahi Nassir about race and autochthony in relation to the coast, see Prestholdt, "Politics of the Soil." When Mboya instructed Nassir, based on his partial Arab ancestry, to "go back to Arabia," Nassir responded in kind. Alluding to Luo claims to have mi-

grated south from the Sudan, Nassir countered that by Mboya's logic he could "go back to the Sudan."

28. Chome, "Uses of Race."

29. Rural-to-urban migration to Mombasa in the 1990s contributed to significant demographic changes. What was once a predominantly Muslim urban center was soon dominated by Christians. See Chome, "From Islamic Reform to Muslim Activism"; Gona, "Changing Political Faces in Kenya's Coast."

30. Exact figures are disputed. As Ndzovu explains, "non-Muslim sources typically estimate the Muslim population to be between 5 and 8 percent, whereas Muslim sources propose higher figures of between 25 and 35 percent." The government census has generally been rejected by Muslim leaders as a gross underestimate. See Ndzovu, *Muslims in Kenyan Politics,* 8–9.

31. Kresse, "Muslim Politics in Postcolonial Kenya"; Mwakimako and Willis, "Islam, Politics and Violence on the Kenya Coast"; Willis and Gona, "Pwani C Kenya?"; Chome, "Uses of Race"; Seesemann, "Kenyan Muslims."

32. Westerlund and Rosander present a historically indigenous "African" Islam in contrast to a "foreign" Islam that disturbs the previously stable religious and political fabric of the continent. See Westerlund and Rosander, *African Islam and Islam in Africa.*

33. Li, "Taking the Place of Martyrs," 18.

34. Li, "The Universal Enemy," 356–57.

35. Li, *The Universal Enemy.*

36. Mamdani, *Good Muslim, Bad Muslim,* 15, 17.

37. Springer, "Culture of Violence or Violent Orientalism?"

38. Brown, Shapiro, and Watts. "Al-Qaida's (Mis)Adventures in the Horn of Africa," 51.

39. For similar discussions about tourism and the production of the coast as exotic space, see Kasfir, "Tourist Aesthetics in the Global Flow"; Walley, "Our Ancestors Used to Bury their 'Development' in the Ground"; Hillwaert, *Morality at the Margins.*

40. See, for example, Richards, "More Trouble in Paradise."

41. The British colonial system in East Africa classified Arabs and Somalis as nonnative citizens. These "subject races," as Mamdani observed, enjoyed legal protections not afforded to their "native" counterparts, yet they also point to the presence of an internal African "other." See Mamdani, "Beyond Settler and Native as Political Identities."

42. Pierre, *The Predicament of Blackness,* 12.

43. As Dane Kennedy has documented, the dominant element within the white population consisted of aristocrats, even if they were a numerical minority. Poor whites posed a threat to ideologies of white supremacy. Kennedy, *Islands of White.* See also Jackson, "White Man's Country."

44. See especially Gonzalez, *Securing Paradise*; and Jackson, "White Man's Country."

45. Padmore, "Behind the Mau Mau," 357.

46. See Berman, *Germans on the Kenyan Coast.*

47. Berman, *Germans on the Kenyan Coast.*

48. See Musila, *A Death Retold in Truth and Rumor*; McIntosh, *Unsettled.*

49. Musila, *A Death Retold in Truth and Rumor*, 151

50. Musila, *A Death Retold in Truth and Rumor*, 159–60.

51. For more on the significance of property law for the historical development of racial capitalism, see Bhandar, *Colonial Lives of Property*.

52. Shadle, *The Souls of White Folk*, 17.

53. Lipsitz, *The Possessive Investment in Whiteness*, vii.

54. Ngũgĩ wa Thiong'o, *Wrestling with the Devil*, 46.

55. Smith, *Bewitching Development*; Luongo, "If You Can't Beat Them, Join Them"; Sahle, "Fanon and Geographies of Political Violence."

56. See Dyer, *White: Essays on Race and Culture*.

57. Elkins, *Imperial Reckoning*, 48–49.

58. Ngũgĩ wa Thiong'o, *Wrestling with the Devil*, 20.

59. Fanon, *Wretched of the Earth*; Stoler, *Duress*.

60. Ngũgĩ wa Thiong'o, *Decolonizing the Mind*, 3.

61. Ngũgĩ wa Thiong'o, *Decolonizing the Mind*, 3.

62. On whiteness as ideology, see Hesse, "Racialized Modernity"; Pierre, *The Predicament of Blackness*. See also Mungai, "The Whiteness Conference."

63. See Mazrui and Noor Shariff, *The Swahili*; Berman, *Germans on the Kenyan Coast*; McIntosh, *Unsettled*.

64. Mazrui and Noor Shariff, *The Swahili*, 141.

65. Smart, "Safariland," 147.

66. Smart, "Safariland," 139.

67. Smart, "Safariland."

68. See especially Bruner and Kirshenblatt-Gimblett, "Maasai on the Lawn"; Bruner, "The Maasai and the Lion King"; Jackson, "White Man's Country"; Musila, *A Death Retold in Truth and Rumour*.

69. Bruner, "The Maasai and the Lion King," 882.

70. Bruner and Kirshenblatt-Gimblett, "Maasai on the Lawn," 457.

71. Jackson, *White Man's Country*, 345.

72. Jackson, *White Man's Country*, 355.

73. Bruner, "The Maasai and the Lion King."

74. In 2008, the government of Kenya hired Chlopak, Leonard, Schechter & Associates to lobby policymakers and burnish the country's reputation in Washington, New York, and other cities. See Aaron Kessler and Wanjohi Kabukuru, "Shadow Diplomacy: African Nations Bypass Embassies, Tap Lobbyists," *Huffington Post*, July 2013.

75. Njoya, "Invisible Citizens."

76. Njoya, "Invisible Citizens."

77. Smart, "Safariland," 151.

78. Ogada on Twitter, August 2021. https://twitter.com/m_ogada/status/1428999758702600193.

79. Njoya on Twitter, June 2020. https://twitter.com/wmnjoya/status/1272468056653127681?s=20&t=NdUvom-58JQAmj1fQZ2XQA.

80. Mungai, "The Whiteness Conference."

81. See especially Pierre, *The Predicament of Blackness,* for a similar discussion in relation to Ghana.

82. Smart, "Safariland."

83. See especially Open Society Foundations and MUHURI, "We are Tired of Taking You to the Court"; Al-Jazeera, *Inside Kenya's Death Squads.*

84. With the new Constitution in place, ethnic minorities (especially Arabs, Asians, Somalis, and Nubians) who had long confronted discriminatory vetting processes in their effort to obtain passports and other identification documents, technically no longer needed to prove their citizenship by providing extra paperwork documenting that their parents or grandparents had been born in Kenya. See Ng'weno and Aloo, "Irony of Citizenship."

85. Mamdani, *Define and Rule.*

86. For more on these tensions see Asad, *Formations of the Secular*; Agrama, *Questioning Secularism*; Fernando, *The Republic Unsettled*; Mahmood, *Religious Difference in a Secular Age.*

87. See especially Khalil, *Time in the Shadows.*

88. For more on this theme see Cattelino, "The Difference that Citizenship Makes"; Feldman, *Police Encounters.*

89. See also Kundnani, *The Muslims Are Coming.*

90. A. Mazrui, "Magimbo: Political, Economic, and Military" (unpublished paper, cited in Mazrui and Sharif, *The Swahili*). See also Mazrui, "Religious and Ethnic Revival in Africa: Has Lord Lugard Been Vindicated?" Lord Lugard Lecture at SOAS, University of London. It is possible that Mazrui was in dialogue with the work of Robert Allen (*Black Awakening in Capitalist America;* "Reassessing the Internal (Neo) Colonialism Theory"). It is worth noting that the secessionist Mombasa Republican Council Manifesto of 2010 demands independence from "the bad colonial leadership from Kenya" (*uongozi mbaya wa kikoloni kutoka Kenya*). See Kresse, *Swahili Muslim Publics and Postcolonial Experience.*

91. For more on the Mombasa Republican Council, see Mwakimako and Wills, "Islam, Politics and Violence on the Kenya Coast"; Willis and Gona, "Pwani C Kenya?"; Willis and Chome, "Marginalization and Political Participation on the Kenya Coast"; Prestholdt, "Politics of the Soil"; Kresse, *Swahili Muslim Publics and Postcolonial Experience.*

92. Prestholdt, *Icons of Dissent,* 143.

93. Prestholdt, *Icons of Dissent,* 144.

94. Prestholdt, *Icons of Dissent.*

95. See Trouillot, "Peasants and Capital"; Bonilla, *Non-Sovereign Futures*; Bonilla et al., *Trouillot Remixed.*

96. Kimari, "War-talk."

97. Kimari, "War-talk," 708.

98. Moloo, "Mombasa Bloodshed and Alleged Police Impunity," *Al-Jazeera.*

99. See Haki Africa, "What Do We Tell the Families?"

100. See Bhungalia, *Elastic Empire,* 25.

Chapter 3

1. The bombings took place in two locations where patrons were watching the 2010 FIFA World Cup.

2. Mutuma Ruteere, "Mission to Repress: Torture, Illegal Detentions, and Extrajudicial killings by the Kenyan Police," Kenya Human Rights Commission, 1998.

3. Kenya National Commission on Human Rights, "The Cry of Blood: Report on Extra-Judicial Killings and Disappearances," Nairobi, 2008.

4. See *Report of the Truth, Justice, and Reconciliation Commission*. Nairobi: Truth Justice, and Reconciliation Commission (TJRC), 2013.

5. I depart from much of the analysis on police reform in Kenya, which remains wedded to methodological nationalism.

6. See Beckett "Phantom Power." For more on the opacity of US power and its social effects, see Sean T. Mitchell, "Paranoid Styles of Nationalism after the Cold War," in *Anthropology and Global Counterinsurgency*, ed. Beckett.

7. Peterson, *Speculative Markets*, 7.

8. Bishara, "Driving While Palestinian."

9. I conceive of an assemblage as an emergent, ad hoc grouping of heterogeneous actors that are nevertheless characterized by collective synergy. For more, see Deleuze and Guattari, *A Thousand Plateaus*; Bachmann, Bell, and Holmqvist, *War, Police, and Assemblages of Intervention*; Hoffman, *The War Machines*; Hoffman, "Geometry after the Circle"; Gould and Demmers, "An Assemblage Approach to Liquid Warfare"; Stalcup, "Interpol and the Emergence of Global Policing." The notion of the assemblage allows for an understanding of empire as "composed of plural forms, strategies, justifications, and disguises." McGranahan and Collins, "Ethnography and U.S. Empire," 10.

10. Ong, "Worlding Cities, or the Art of Being Global," 12.

11. International Crisis Group, *Overkill*.

12. For a critical reconsideration of the "laboratory" thesis, see Rhys Machold, "Reconsidering the Laboratory Thesis." Machold questions the assumption that security strategies circulate seamlessly from one geography to another and rightly argues that we need more precision on *what* travels and *how* it travels, as well as the practical consequences of these circulations.

13. Hoffman, "Geometry after the Circle," 100.

14. Hoffman, "Geometry after the Circle."

15. Bhungalia, *Elastic Empire*.

16. In these instances, the US military often relies on "127e" programs, made possible by an obscure US budgetary authority that allows the Pentagon to bypass congressional oversight. See "What Can Secretive Funding Authority Tell Us about Pentagon's Use of Force Interpretations." https://www.lawfareblog.com/what-can-secretive-funding-authority-tell-us-about-pentagons-use-of-force-interpretations.

17. Bhungalia, *Elastic Empire*, 5.

18. Tahir, "The Distributed Empire of the War on Terror."

19. Stuart Hall made this observation of the United Kingdom in *Policing the Crisis*.

20. Kimari, "The Story of a Pump."

21. For more on the uses and effects of these tactics in Kenya, see Balakian, "Money Is Your Government"; Gluck, "Security Urbanism and the Counterterror State in Kenya." For an analysis of flexible, pop-up warfare, see Gould and Demmers, "An Assemblage Approach to Liquid Warfare."

22. Namir Shabibi, "Revealed: The CIA and MI6's Secret War in Kenya," *Daily Maverick,* 28 August 2020. See also Namir Shabibi, "The Militarisation of US/Africa Policy: How the CIA Came to Lead Deadly Counter-Terrorism Operations in Kenya," *Daily Maverick,* 28 August 2020,

23. According to the US State Department, the Leahy Law refers to two statutory provisions prohibiting the US government from using funds for assistance to units of foreign security forces where there is credible information implicating that unit in the commission of gross violations of human rights. For a discussion of the contradictory effects of the Leahy Law, see Tate, *Drugs, Thugs, and Diplomats.*

24. According to the investigative report by the *Daily Maverick,* the US and UK governments play a key role in identifying, tracking, and fixing the location of targets, as well in decisions determining their fate: kill or capture.

25. See Omeje and Mwangi Githigaro, "The Challenges of State Policing in Kenya." As N'diaye extrapolates, the Kenyan security apparatus has long been shaped by its cooperation with foreign powers like the United States, United Kingdom, and Israel. N'diaye, "How Not to Institutionalize Civilian Control."

26. "Israeli Firm Lands Kenyan ID Project, Aimed at Stemming Terror," *Haaretz,* November 2014.

27. Pakistan has also been contracted to provide biometric e-passport software for Kenya. See "Kenya Seeks NADRA Collaboration, Expertise on Digital ID Project"; "NADRA to Undertake Kenya's National Identity Management Project."

28. See PrivacyInternational, *Track, Capture, Kill.*

29. Muslim Human Rights Forum, *Horn of Terror: Report of US-Led Mass Extraordinary Renditions from Kenya to Somalia, Ethiopia and Guantanamo Bay*; Open Society Foundation and Muhuri, "We Are Tired of Taking You to the Court"; Haki Africa, "What Do We Tell the Families?"; KNCHR, "The Error of Fighting Terror with Terror."

30. Tate, *Counting the Dead,* 118.

31. Tate, *Counting the Dead,* 108.

32. Bishara, "Driving While Palestinian," 37.

33. Rancière, *Disagreement,* 30.

34. Ngũgĩ wa Thiong'o, *Moving the Centre,* 94

35. Tate, *Counting the Dead,* 292.

36. Taussig, *Defacement,* 6.

37. Masco, *The Theater of Operations,* 123.

38. For more on the management of "dangerous knowledge," see especially Robinson, *Body of Victim, Body of Warrior*; and Thiranagama and Kelly, *Traitors.*

39. Beckett, "Phantom Power," 49.

40. Aretxaga, "Maddening States," 396.

41. For Benjamin, police power is *both* tangible and intangible; it is the formless and intangibility of power that contributes to its spectral effects. "Benjamin, Critique of Violence."

42. See also Maira, *The 9/11 Generation*; Maqsood, "The Social Life of Rumors."

43. Asad, "Thinking about Terrorism and Just War."

44. See Feldman, *Police Encounters*, 54.

45. In July 2012, one month before his death, the UN Security Council imposed a travel ban and asset freeze on Rogo, stating he had provided "financial, material, logistical or technical support to al-Shabab."

46. "Riots Break Out in Mombasa after Killing of Muslim Cleric," *Associated Press*, 27 August 2012.

47. Mwakimako, "Christian-Muslim Relations in Kenya."

48. See Ndzovu, "The Politicization of Muslim Organizations."

49. That all of the suspects held in connection with the bombings were detained at Luzira serves as an important reminder of the more conventional sites that constitute the global network of detention centers tied to the war on terror. As Darryl Li observes, "For each extraterritorial and extraordinary prison like Guantanamo, there are many more 'ordinary' prisons and detention sites run by other governments in their own territory." Li, "From Exception to Empire," 457.

50. See especially Kimathi and Butt, *Horn of Terror*. For a discussion of counter-mapping as counter-hegemonic practice in Kashmir, see Junaid, "Counter-Maps of the Ordinary."

51. See especially Stoler, *Duress*; Kimari and Ernstson, "Imperial Remains and Imperial Invitations."

52. Stoler, *Duress*, 33.

53. Throup, "Crime, Politics, and the Police in Colonial Kenya," 129; Ruteere and Pomerolle, "Democratizing Security or Decentralizing Repression?"

54. Rather than approach surveillance "as something inaugurated by new technologies," Simone Browne reminds us, we must contend with the ways that colonial measures like the kipande "worked to structure social relations and institutions in ways that privilege whiteness." Browne, *Dark Matters*, 17.

55. The kipande is an apt illustration of how racial capitalism "was enacted and routinized through mundane, daily techniques of registration and identification." Weitzberg, "Biometrics, Race Making, and White Exceptionalism," 41.

56. Ruteere and Pommerolle, "Democratizing Security or Decentralizing Repression?"

57. Ruteere and Pommerolle, "Democratizing Security or Decentralizing Repression?"; Throup, "Crime, Politics, and the Police in Colonial Kenya."

58. Throup, "Crime, Politics and the Police in Colonial Kenya" (quote); Oloka-Onyango, "Police Powers, Human Rights and the State in Kenya and Uganda."

59. I borrow the term "criminal type" from Siegel, *A New Criminal Type in Jakarta*.

60. See especially Kresse, "Kenya Twendapi?"

61. Amutabi, "Intellectuals and the Democratisation Process in Kenya"; Gimode, "The Role of the Police in Kenya's Democratisation Process."

62. Ndzovu, *Muslims in Kenyan Politics*; Gifford, *Christianity, Politics, and Public Life in Kenya.*

63. See Ndzovu, *Muslims in Kenyan Politics*; Bakari, "A Place at the Table"; Chome, "Uses of Race." Bakari links SUPKEM's formation with broader attempts by the state "to control various segments of Kenyan society, from trade unions to religious organizations, in the name of centralized decision-making."

64. Bakari, "A Place at the Table," 29. Bakari reminds us that among the notable sympathizers of the IPK was Reverend Dr. Timothy Njoya, "the iconoclastic Yale-educated theologian who was the most determined critic of the regime."

65. See Bakari, "A Place at the Table." Prestholdt notes that unlike most Islamist parties elsewhere in the world, the IPK was not ideologically driven but rather used Muslim identity to mobilize support. See Prestholdt, *Icons of Dissent.*

66. Ndzovu, *Muslims in Kenyan Politics.*

67. McIntosh, *The Edge of Islam*; Kresse, "Muslim Politics in Postcolonial Kenya."

68. Mazrui and Noor Shariff, *The Swahili*; author interview with former IPK member, 2015.

69. Prestholdt, *Icons of Dissent*, 150.

70. Mazrui, "The Black Intifadah?"

71. Ndzovu, *Muslims in Kenyan Politics*; Prestholdt, "Kenya, the United States, and Counterterrorism." The state has long worked to manipulate historical categorizations of racial difference. However, the IPK was ultimately unable to mobilize the majority of Muslims based on their religious identity. The Digos, Bajunis, and Somalis all identified themselves in their ethnic categories first and as Muslims second. See Ndzovu, *Muslims in Kenyan Politics.*

72. Oded, "Islamic Extremism in Kenya"; Prestholdt, "Kenya, the United States, and Counterterrorism."

73. Prestholdt, "Kenya, the United States, and Counterterrorism." Ironically, Moi himself was receiving funds from leaders in the Middle East. As Bakari observes, although Moi was more anti-Muslim in his public pronouncements, his business interests remained untainted by this rhetoric. See Bakari, "A Place at the Table."

74. Although the state characterized Balala as the spiritual leader of the IPK—and, by implication, of Kenya Muslims—he was neither. See Bakari, "A Place at the Table."

75. Ndzovu points to the role of other scholars like Oded in contributing to these misrepresentations. See Ndzovu, *Muslims in Kenyan Politics*; Oded, "Islamic Extremism in Kenya."

76. Chome, "Uses of Race."

77. Kamau, "Kenya and the War on Terrorism"; Seeseman, "Kenyan Muslims, the Aftermath of 9/11, and the 'War on Terror' "; Mogire and Mkutu Agade, "Counter-Terrorism in Kenya."

78. See, for example, "Kenya Denies the Existence of Police Death Squads," *Business Standard,* 10 December 2014.

79. "Kenyan MPs Back Security Law after Heated Debate," *BBC News,* December 2014.

80. On fear as integral to the affective infrastructure of the security state, see Masco, *The Theater of Operations.*

81. For more see Grewal, *Saving the Security State*; Presley, "The Mau Mau Rebellion"; Tibbetts, "Mamas Fighting for Freedom in Kenya"; White, *The Comforts of Home*.

82. Scahill, "The CIA's Secret Sites in Somalia."

83. Junaid, "Counter-Maps of the Ordinary," 13.

84. See also Jeganathan, "Checkpoint."

85. See Bhungalia, *Elastic Empire*, 26.

86. Mitchell, "Empire as Accusation, Denial, and Structure," 369, 377.

87. See Prestholdt, "Fighting Phantoms."

Chapter 4

1. *Buibui* is the Kiswahili phrase for hijab.

2. Human Rights Watch, "Kenya: End Abusive Roundups."

3. See, for example, Mawiyoo, "'You Are All Terrorists': The Sanitization of a Nairobi Suburb."

4. "Police Gun Down Alleged Terrorist in Morning Raid," *Daily Nation,* 14 September 2014.

5. See *US Army Counterinsurgency Field Manual.*

6. Bhungalia, *Elastic Empire*, 8. See also Bell, "Civilianising Warfare."

7. Khalili, "Gendered Practices of Counterinsurgency," 4.

8. See especially Greenburg, *At War with Women;* Smith, *Intimate Geopolitics.*

9. See especially Enloe, *Bananas, Beaches, and Bases;* Hyndman, "Mind the Gap"; Dowler and Sharp, "A Feminist Geopolitics?"; Brickell, "Geopolitics of Home"; Puar, *Terrorist Assemblages;* Grewal, *Saving the Security State;* Pratt, *Embodying Geopolitics;* Greenburg, *At War with Women;* Smith, *Intimate Geopolitics;* Shalhoub-Kevorkian, *Security Theology;* Schields, *Offshore Attachments;* Flores-Villalobos, *The Silver Women;* Arondekar and Patel, "Geopolitics Alert."

10. Brickell, "Geopolitics of Home," 57.

11. For an example of literature that reproduces the notion that insurgents "hide" within civilian spaces, see Bailliet, "War in the Home."

12. "Kenyan Leader Vows to Crush al-Shabab after Massacre," *Al-Jazeera,* 5 April 2015.

13. Khalili, *Time in the Shadows.*

14. See especially Khalili, *Time in the Shadows;* Weizman, "Walking through Walls"; Bailliet, "War in the Home."

15. See "How Osama bin Laden Was Located and Killed," *New York Times,* 8 May 2011.

16. Weizman, "Walking through Walls," 15.

17. See Gusterson, *Drone.* In February 2016, Kenya purchased a Boeing-manufactured ScanEagle drone from the United States in order to conduct aerial surveillance inside Kenyan borders. In 2020, the US military sought White House approval to expand the counter-terrorism drone war to Kenya. See "U.S. Military Seeks Authority to Expand Counterterrorism Drone War to Kenya," *New York Times,* 15 September 2020.

18. hooks, *Yearning,* 41.

19. hooks, *Yearning,* 41.

20. Shalhoub Kevorkian, *Security Theology,* 177.

21. Fanon, *A Dying Colonialism,* 118–19.

22. Gordon, *Ghostly Matters,* xvi.

23. See Stoler, *Imperial Debris.*

24. Ihmoud, "Murabata," 514.

25. Zia, *Resisting Disappearance.*

26. Khayatt, *A Landscape of War.* See also Thiranagama, *In My Mother's House;* Lubkemann, *Culture in Chaos;* Smith, "Facing the Dragon."

27. Salem, "Haunted Histories."

28. I borrow the term "will to life" from Khayyat, *A Landscape of War.*

29. I am indebted to conversations with Narges Erami for the "politics of warning" formulation.

30. Greenburg, *At War with Women,* 6–7.

31. Kilcullen, "Twenty-Eight Articles."

32. As Darryl Li writes, "One of the distinguishing and largely overlooked features of the Global War on Terror is a suspicion of mobility, exchange, and cosmopolitanism on terms not defined or controlled by the west." Li, "The Universal Enemy." See also Ho, "Empire through Diasporic Eyes."

33. See Rana, *Terrifying Muslims;* Li, *The Universal Enemy.*

34. See especially Aretxaga, "A Fictional Reality"; Prestholdt, "Phantom of the Forever War"; Zulaika and Douglas, *Terror and Taboo.*

35. See especially Stoler, *Haunted by Empire;* Grewal, *Saving the Security State;* Shalhoub-Kevorkian, *Security Theology;* Weizman, "Walking through Walls."

36. See especially Cooke, *Women and the War Story;* Rygiel and Hunt, *(En)Gendering the War on Terror.*

37. Grovogui, "Come to Africa," 428. On imaginative geographies see Said, *Orientalism;* and Gregory, *The Colonial Present.*

38. Visuality has been an integral instrument of power, from the slave plantation to the war on terror. See Browne, *Dark Matters;* Mirzoeff, *The Right to Look.*

39. The female character was clearly inspired by stories about the so-called "White Widow," whom the Kenyan state charged with masterminding the 2013 Westgate Mall attack in Nairobi.

40. In one film review published by the *Telegraph,* the reviewer refers to the home as a "hut," and to the neighborhood of Eastleigh as a "shantytown."

41. See Asad, "Thinking about Terrorism and Just War."

42. Feldman, "Empire's Verticality."

43. Fanon, *Black Skin, White Masks;* Feldman, "Empire's Verticality"; McClintock, "Paranoid Empire"; Rana, *Terrifying Muslims.*

44. I unpack this further in Al-Bulushi, "From the Sky to the Streets, and Back," arguing that the film reproduces the notion that Kenyan leaders merely follow the political directives and strategic aspirations of their more powerful counterparts in the United States and United Kingdom.

45. Butler, *Frames of War;* Mackie, "The Afghan Girls."

46. Khalili, *Time in the Shadows.*

47. For a discussion of intent in relation to the legitimation of "just" wars, see Asad, "Thinking about Terrorism and Just War."

48. For a discussion of the politics of humanity in the context of the war on terror, see Asad, *On Suicide Bombing;* Devji, *Terrorist in Search of Humanity.*

49. Laura Wexler, *Tender Violence.*

50. For more see especially Aroussi, "Strange Bedfellows"; Mesok, "Beyond Instrumentalisation"; Gitau, "Civil-Military Relations"; Rabasa, "Radical Islam in East Africa."

51. See Africa Center for Strategic Studies, "Preventing Youth Radicalization in East Africa"; El-Amraoui and Ducol, "Family-Oriented P/CVE Programs."

52. Bachmann, "Governmentality and Counterterrorism"; Rabasa, "Radical Islam in East Africa."

53. For more on this topic see especially Nesiah, "Feminism as Counter-Terrorism"; Mesok, "Affective Technologies of War"; Mesok, "Beyond Instrumentalization"; Greenburg, *At War with Women.*

54. Greenburg, *At War with Women.*

55. Khalili, "Gendered Practices of Counterinsurgency," 9.

56. Grewal, "Security Moms," 29. Ironically, as Katherine E. Brown has observed, the counter-terror apparatus reduces women to their roles in the family unit, all the while critiquing the Islamic State for doing the same. See Brown, *Gender, Religion, Extremism.*

57. Grewal, *Saving the Security State,* 123.

58. For more on the instrumentalization of gendered labor by the US military, see Greenburg, *At War with Women;* Mesok, "Affective Technologies of War."

59. Schlaffer and Kropiunigg, "A New Security Architecture: Mothers Included!"

60. For more, see McClintock, *Imperial Leather;* Grewal, *Home and Harem;* Stoler, *Haunted by Empire;* Hunt, "Domesticity and Colonialism in Belgian Africa"; Hunt, *A Nervous State;* Santoru, "The Colonial Idea of Women and Direct Intervention"; Feichtinger, Malinowski, and Richards, "Transformative Invasions."

61. White, *The Comforts of Home,* 4.

62. White, *The Comforts of Home,* 4.

63. White, *The Comforts of Home,* 15.

64. More than eight thousand women were detained at Kamiti Prison Camp over the course of the Emergency period. See Presley, "The Mau Mau Rebellion, Kikuyu Women, and Social Change."

65. See Bruce-Lockhart, "'Unsound' Minds and Broken Bodies"; Santoru, "The Colonial Idea of Women and Direct Intervention."

66. McClintock, *Imperial Leather;* Grewal, *Saving the Security State.*

67. Greenburg, *At War with Women,* 20.

68. See Aroussi, "Strange Bedfellows."

69. See Aroussi, "Strange Bedfellows."

70. For more see Gitau, "Civil-Military Relations"; Mesok, "Beyond Instrumentalization."

71. Mesok, "Beyond Instrumentalization," 9.

72. Mesok, "Beyond Instrumentalization," 9.

73. See Kimari, "Kenyan Mothers Take on Police Violence."

74. For more on the history of women's resistance in Kenya, see Presley, "The Mau Mau Rebellion, Kikuyu Women, and Social Change"; Tibbetts, "Mamas Fighting for Freedom in Kenya"; Brownhill, *Land, Food, Freedom*.

75. See, for example, Hunt and Rygiel, eds., *(En)Gendering the War on Terror*; Huckerby and Satterthwaite, eds., *Gender, National Security, and Counter-terrorism*; Puar, *Terrorist Assemblages*; Perera and Razack, *At the Limits of Justice*; Grewal, *Saving the Security State*; Greenburg, *At War with Women*; Mesok, "Beyond Instrumentalization."

76. Huckerby and Satterthwaite, "A Gender and Human Rights Approach to Counterterrorism."

77. Kassem, "Gendered Erasure in the Global 'War on Terror'"; see also Brittain, *Shadow Lives*.

78. See Das, *Critical Events*.

79. Gilmore, *Golden Gulag*.

80. According to a 2016 report published by Privacy International, "The police services and NIS (National Intelligence Service) can access Kenyans' communications data formally, with the consent and cooperation of telecommunications operators. But the NIS also has direct access to Kenya's telecommunications networks, which allows for the interception of both communications data and content. Privacy International, "Track, Capture, Kill," 19. See also Kelley, "CIA Monitoring Calls in Kenya"; "How Kenya's Security Spending, Spying Changed after Westgate Attack." Spending on the National Intelligence Service more than tripled between 2013 and 2023, rising to $301.4 million.

81. See hooks, *Yearning*.

82. Amahl Bishara similarly observes that movement in Israel and the West Bank requires assistance from people along the way, as Israeli policies and restrictions often change unexpectedly. See Bishara, "Driving While Palestinian."

83. I am indebted to Amahl Bishara's notion of the "politics of disorientation" that characterizes Israel's system of closure, whereby Palestinians are regularly compelled to change their driving routes in response to unexpected road closures. See Bishara, "Driving While Palestinian." In my context, it is the lack of predictability or certainty around which governing body is authorizing counter-terror policies that is disorienting.

84. For other work that problematizes the notion of seemingly exceptional detention sites, see Coutin, "Confined Within"; Martin and Mitchelson, "Geographies of Detention and Imprisonment"; Li, "From Exception to Empire."

85. hooks, *Yearning*.

Chapter 5

1. Chowdhury and Philipose, *Dissident Friendship*.

2. See "Kenya Announces Amnesty and Reintegration to Youth Who Denounce Al-Shabaab." http://www.standardmedia.co.ke/article/2000158358/kenya-announces-amnesty-and-reintegration-to-youth-who-denounce-al-shabaab.

3. See Lind, Mutahi, and Oosterom, "Tangled Ties."

4. See KNCHR, "The Error of Fighting Terror with Terror."

5. Haki Africa, "What Do We Tell the Families?"

6. A growing number of scholars have demonstrated that techno-fetishism—particularly in relation to drones—risks overlooking low-tech modes of monitoring and control (e.g., eyes on the street), upon which the more technologically advanced modes of surveillance remain reliant. See Donovan et al., "Introduction: ASR Forum on Surveillance in Africa"; Kaplan and Parks, *Life in the Age of Drone Warfare*; Ghosh, "Everything Must Match."

7. See Boinett, "The Origins of the Intelligence System in Kenya."

8. In what some believe to be a direct reference to one of President Moi's trusted spies in the 1980s, a character in Ngũgĩ wa Thiong'o's *Wizard of the Crow* was named Sikiokuu, or "Big ear." In the novel, Sikiokuu undergoes plastic surgery to equip him with an ear that is big enough to pick up anti-Moi political gossip and relay it to the president. See Ngũgĩ wa Thiong'o, *Wizard of the Crow*; Bakari, "A Place at the Table."

9. See Masco, *Theater of Operations*.

10. See Kelley, "CIA Monitoring Calls in Kenya, Says Report," *Daily Nation*, 23 May 2014.

11. Privacy International, "Track, Capture, Kill."

12. Puar, *Terrorist Assemblages*; Grewal, "Security Moms"; Maira, *The 9/11 Generation*; Shalhoub-Kevorkian, *Security Theology*; Besteman, *Making Refuge*; Byler, *Terror Capitalism*.

13. Maira, *The 9/11 Generation*, 196.

14. See Yonucu, *Police, Provocation, Politics*, 160.

15. Paine, "In Search of Friendship."

16. Aguilar reminds us that E. E. Evans-Pritchard, for example, was more preoccupied with conceptions of kinship and marriage in his studies of Nuer social systems. Aguilar, "Localized Kin and Globalized Friends."

17. Bell and Coleman, *The Anthropology of Friendship*.

18. Scott, "Preface: Friendship as an Art of Living."

19. Breitman, *Malcolm X Speaks*, 102. Quoted in Markle, "Brother Malcolm, Comrade Babu."

20. wa Wanjiru, "Abdilatif Abdalla: My Poems Gave Me Company."

21. Bakari, "A Place at the Table."

22. Weyani Media, "We Harvest the Present from the Future We Planted Yesterday."

23. See Cordis and Ihmoud, "A Poetics of Living Rebellion."

24. Kelley, *Freedom Dreams*, 9–10.

25. Césaire, "Poetry and Knowledge."

26. Kelley, *Freedom Dreams*, 9.

27. Burton "Captivity, Kinship, and Black Masculine Care Work under Domestic Warfare," 629.

28. Burton, "Captivity, Kinship, and Black Masculine Care Work under Domestic Warfare."

29. For more on forms of self-making among young men in contexts of political uncertainty and oppression, see especially Dattatreyan, *The Globally Familiar*; Ghosh, *A Thousand Tiny Cuts*; Byler, *Terror Capitalism*; Burton, *Tip of the Spear*. Dattatreyan explores contemporary Delhi as a site of masculine becoming in a political context marked by uncertainty, threat, and possibility. Ghosh centers the social idioms of aspiration and dignity of young men who are criminalized as smugglers and criminals in the Bangladesh–India borderlands. Byler explores friendships among young Uyghur men enacted through storytelling about colonial violence in northwest China. Burton focuses on men who conceive of their incarceration in US prisons as an assault on their manhood, and who engage in rebellion as a humanizing and masculinizing process.

30. Fanon, *A Dying Colonialism*, 118.

31. Thiranagama, *In My Mother's House*, 10–12.

32. Orisanmi Burton similarly explores how the content of manhood proclaimed by Black men in US prisons is "radically different from that enacted by their captors." See Burton, *Tip of the Spear*.

33. Historians have captured how the realm of leisure (an expected site for nurturing friendships) was a terrain of struggle between colonizer and colonized in East Africa. In the 1920s and 1930s, colonial leaders viewed football, for example, as a principal arena for "covert nationalist activities." See Fair, "Kickin' It"; Kindy, *Life and Politics in Mombasa*. Colonial officials in French Equatorial Africa intervened in otherwise autonomous sports clubs, creating the "Native Sports Federation" in order to extend colonial surveillance capacities into the domain of leisure and to "prevent undesirable elements which, under the cover of sport, group together for the purposes of political agitation and provoking disorder." See Martin, "Colonialism, Youth, and Football in French Equatorial Africa," 63.

34. Allen, "Getting By the Occupation."

35. Allen, "Getting By the Occupation."

36. For more on this see especially Feldman, *Formations of Violence*; Fernando, "Ethnography and the Politics of Silence"; Maira, *Missing*; Osella, "Malabar Secrets."

37. Byler, "Anti-colonial Friendship," 153.

38. Butler, *Frames of War*.

39. See Weiss, *Producing African Futures*; Ferguson, *Global Shadows*; Hillwaert, *Morality at the Margins*.

40. Beckerleg, "Brown Sugar"; Schuberth, "The Impact of Drug Trafficking."

41. Beckerleg and Hundt, "The Characteristics and Recent Growth of Heroin Injecting."

42. Susan Beckerleg writes about what she characterizes as an Islamic revival in the coastal town of Watamu, which was at the heart of the Kenyan tourist boom and thereby directly entangled in the drug trade; local religious leaders have sought to draw young people away from heroin use through the appeal to religion and traditional values. See Beckerleg, "'Brown Sugar' or Friday Prayers."

43. For ethnographic insights on these discussions among youth in the coastal town of Lamu, see Hillewaert, *Morality at the Margins*.

44. See especially Maira, *The 9/11 Generation.*

45. For the fiscal year 2015–16, the US State Department sought to provide $40 million in assistance related to "countering violent extremism" (CVE) in East Africa. See The White House, "U.S. Support for Peace, Security, and Countering Violent Extremism in Africa" Office of the Press Secretary, 27 July 2015.

46. Tensions among Kenyan Muslims are rooted in longstanding state practices of divide and rule. See Ndzovu, *Muslims in Kenyan Politics.*

47. Foucault, *Discipline and Punish.*

48. See Berman, "Privileging Combat."

49. Khalili, *Time in the Shadows,* 142.

50. Khalili, *Time in the Shadows.*

51. See Elkins, *Imperial Reckoning*; Luongo, "If You Can't Beat Them." As Caroline Elkins explains, ethno-psychiatrists hired by the British employed the vocabulary of "normal" and "pathological" to classify populations, corresponding "rather neatly with racial categories whereby whites were always the definition of normal against which pathological blacks were defined." Elkins, *Imperial Reckoning,* 106.

52. See especially Amar, *The Security Archipelago.*

53. See especially James, *Democratic Insecurities*; Ticktin and Feldman, *In the Name of Humanity.*

54. See Yusuf, "How Kenya's Al-Shabaab Amnesty Is a Loaded Gun," *New Humanitarian,* 31 August 2016.

55. See Cockayne and O'Neil, *UN DDR in an Era of Violent Extremism.*

56. Scholars have documented the complicity of medical health professionals in torture and interrogation techniques in the context of the war on terror. See Miles, *Oath Betrayed*; Brennan, "Torture of Guantanamo Detainees."

57. Rogo was one of the early members of the Islamic Party of Kenya (IPK), founded in the early 1990s. Although he once aspired to participate in electoral politics, he was arrested and imprisoned for three years following the 2002 Kikambala hotel bombings in Mombasa, but eventually acquitted of all charges. See Seesemann, "Kenyan Muslims.'"

58. Odinga became prime minister of Kenya in 2008.

59. Hirschkind, *The Ethical Soundscape*; Watts, "Islamic Modernities?"; Marsden, "Talking the Talk."

60. See, for example, Ndzovu, *Muslims in Kenyan Politics.*

61. See Open Society Justice Initiative and MUHURI, "We Are Tired of Taking You to the Court."

62. Mohideen was held in Shimo la Tewa in Mombasa, a maximum-security prison.

63. See Peteet, "Male Gender and Rituals of Resistance," for a similar discussion in Palestine.

64. See also Jaji, "Masculinity on Unstable Ground"; Ricardo and Barker, "Young Men and the Construction of Masculinity in sub-Saharan Africa"; Ghosh, *A Thousand Tiny Cuts.*

65. See Jaji, "Masculinity on Unstable Ground"; Laurendeau, "Gendered Risk Regimes"; Waller, "Rebellious Youth in Colonial Africa"; Zilberg, *Space of Detention*.

66. I borrow the notion of masculinities-in-the-making from Dattatreyan, *The Globally Familiar*.

Conclusion

1. United Nations, "Security Council Extends Mandate of United Nations Integrated Office in Haiti for One Year, Unanimously Adopting Resolution 2645," UN Security Council 9095th meeting, 15 July 2022.

2. "Kenya's Presidency of the Security Council Advances Pan-Africanist Ideals with Meeting on Haiti." https://mfa.go.ke/kenyas-presidency-of-the-un-security-council -advances-pan-africanist-ideals-with-meeting-on-haiti/.

3. See Mines, "Haiti Needs a Political Dialogue." Kenyan news outlets indicate that officers will be picked from the Rapid Deployment Unit (RDU), Anti Stock Theft Unit (ASTU), General Service Unit (GSU), and Border Patrol Unit (BPU), all of which are "combat-trained." See Ombati, "Kenya Prepares Elite Paramilitary Units for Haiti Mission," *The Star*, 3 October 2023; Ombati, "Ruto: Reconnaissance Team to Land in Haiti Soonest," *The Star*, 15 March 2024.

4. See Khalili, "The Location of Palestine in Global Counterinsurgencies," 414.

5. See Honke and Muller, *The Global Making of Policing*.

6. For more on the history of US interventionism in Haiti, see Renda, *Taking Haiti*; James, *Democratic Insecurities*; Pierre, "Haiti: An Archive of Occupation." In March 2024, as this book went to press, US military officials declared that the United States was prepared to deploy troops as part of the multinational intervention if the crisis in Haiti worsened. At the time, Haitian prime minister Ariel Henry had announced his intention to resign following weeks of domestic pressure.

7. In July 2023, the US government sent a delegation to Nairobi to meet with Kenyan officials about Haiti. Soon thereafter, the US ambassador to the United Nations, Linda Thomas-Greenfield, announced that the United States would put forward a UN Security Council resolution authorizing Kenya to lead a multinational police force in the country. See especially "Kenya's Offer to Help Haiti Came after U.S. Delegation Visit," *Miami Herald*, 3 August 2023. While the details of the September 2023 five-year defense cooperation agreement between Kenya and the United States remain scant, political analysts understand this agreement to be a direct response to Kenya's willingness to assume a leadership role in the Haiti intervention.

8. Austin, "A Partnership of Principle and Progress: Remarks by Secretary of Defense Lloyd Austin III During a Trip to Africa." US Department of Defense, 27 September 2023.

9. See especially Coronil, "Beyond Occidentalism"; and Stoler in McGranahan and Collins, *Ethnographies of U.S. Empire*, 478.

10. See Ngũgĩ wa Thiong'o, *Something Torn and New*, 73.

11. See especially Baik, *Reencounters*; Zeleke, *Ethiopia in Theory*; Zia, *Resisting Disappearance*; Miyonga, "Archives of Emotional History."

12. In 2007, the United States launched the "Haiti Stabilization Initiative," described by the US State Department as "an innovative program that integrates security and development and strengthens government presence and local institutions in Cite Soleil, Haiti's most dangerous neighborhood and a persistent source of instability." For critical analysis of this Department of Defense–funded initiative, see Greenburg, *At War with Women*.

13. Greenburg, *At War with Women*.

14. Sivanandan, "A Black Perspective on the War."

15. I take inspiration from Orisanmi Burton, whose work sheds light on the dehumanizing and divisive effects of counter-insurgent warfare, and on collective efforts to resist domestication and brokenness: "to preserve life, dignity, sociality, and political possibility." Burton, "Captivity, Kinship, and Black Masculine Care Work under Domestic Warfare."

BIBLIOGRAPHY

Abboud, Samer, Omar S. Dahi, Waleed Hazbun, Nicole Sunday Grove, Coralie Pison Hindawi, Jamil Mouawad, and Sami Hermez. 2018. "Towards a Beirut School of Critical Security Studies." *Critical Studies on Security* 6 (3): 273–95.

Abrahamsen, Rita. 2018. "Return of the Generals? Global Militarism in Africa from the Cold War to the Present." *Security Dialogue* 49 (1–2): 19–31.

Abu-lughod, Lila. 2013. *Do Muslim Women Need Saving?* Cambridge, MA: Harvard University Press.

Abu-Lughod, Lila, Rema Hammami, and Nadera Shalhoub-Kevorkian. 2023. *The Cunning of Gender Violence: Geopolitics and Feminism*. Durham, NC: Duke University Press.

Adesanmi, Pius. 2020. *Who Owns the Problem? Africa and the Struggle for Agency*. East Lansing: Michigan State University Press.

Adi, Hakim. 2018. *Pan-Africanism: A History*. London: Bloomsbury Publishing.

Africa Center for Strategic Studies. 2012. "Preventing Youth Radicalization in East Africa."

Agrama, Hussein Ali. 2012. *Questioning Secularism: Islam, Sovereignty, and the Rule of Law in Modern Egypt*. Chicago: University of Chicago Press.

Aguilar, Mario. 1999. "Localized Kin and Globalized Friends: Religious Modernity and the 'Educated Self' in East Africa." In *The Anthropology of Friendship*, ed. Simon Coleman and Sandra Bell. New York: Berg, 169–84.

Ahmed, Zohra. 2021. "Towards a Law and Political Economy Approach to the War on Terror." *LPE Project*. 24 November 2021.

Aïdi, Hisham, Marc Lynch, and Zachariah Mampilly. 2020. "And the Twain Shall Meet: Connecting Africa and the Middle East." POMEPS Studies 40: Africa and the Middle East: Beyond the Divides.

Aidid, Safia. 2020. "Pan-Somali Dreams: Ethiopia, Greater Somalia, and the Somali Nationalist Imagination." PhD diss., Harvard University.

Ake, Claude. 1996. *Democracy and Development in Africa*. Washington, DC: Brookings Institution.

Akyeampong, Emmanuel K. 2006. "Race, Identity and Citizenship in Black Africa : The Case of the Lebanese in Ghana." *Journal of the International African Institute* 76 (3): 297–323.

Al-Bulushi, Samar. 2019. "#SomeoneTellCNN: Cosmopolitan Militarism in the East African Warscape." *Cultural Dynamics* 31 (4): 323–49.

——. 2021. "Citizen-Suspect: Navigating Surveillance and Policing in Urban Kenya." *American Anthropologist* 123 (4): 819–32.

——. 2022. "From the Sky to the Streets, and Back: Geographies of Imperial Warfare in East Africa." *Social Text* 40 (3): 37–59.

Al-Bulushi, Samar, Sahana Ghosh, and Inderpal Grewal. 2022. "Security from the South: Postcolonial and Imperial Entanglements." *Social Text* 40 (3) (152): 1–15.

Al-Bulushi, Yousuf. 2022. "Thinking Racial Capitalism and Black Radicalism from Africa: An Intellectual Geography of Cedric Robinson's World-System." *Geoforum* 132: 252–62.

Ali, Nosheen. 2019. *Delusional States: Feeling Rule and Development in Pakistan's Northern Frontier*. Cambridge, UK: Cambridge University Press.

Al-Jazeera. 2014. "Inside Kenya's Death Squads." aljazeera.com/investigations/2014/12/8/inside-kenyas-death-squads.

Allen, Lori. 2008. "Getting by the Occupation: How Violence Became Normal during the Second Palestinian Intifada." *Cultural Anthropology* 23 (3): 453–87.

Allen, Robert L. 1969. *Black Awakening in Capitalist America: An Analytic History*. New York: Anchor Books.

——. 2005. "Reassessing the Internal (Neo) Colonialism Theory." *Black Scholar* 35 (1): 2–11.

Alvarado, Christian. 2022. "Mau Mau as Method." *History in Africa* 49: 9–37.

Amadiume, Ifi. 1987. *Male Daughters, Female Husbands: Gender and Sex in an African Society*. London: Zed Books.

Amar, Paul. 2013. *The Security Archipelago: Human Security States, Sexuality Politics, and the End of Neoliberalism*. Durham, NC: Duke University Press.

——. 2012. "Global South to the Rescue: Emerging Humanitarian Superpowers and Globalizing Rescue Industries." *Globalizations* 9 (1): 1–13.

Amutabi, Maurice N. 2007. "Intellectuals and the Democratisation Process in Kenya." In *Kenya: The Struggle for Democracy*, ed. Godwin Rapando Murunga and Shadrack Wanjala Nasong'o. Dakar: CODESRIA, 197–226.

Anderson, D. M. 2014. "Remembering Wagalla: State Violence in Northern." *Journal of Eastern African Studies* 8 (4): 658–76.

Anderson, D. M., and J. McKnight. 2014. "Kenya at War: Al-Shabaab and Its Enemies in Eastern Africa." *African Affairs* 114 (454): 1–27.

Appel, Hannah. 2019. *The Licit Life of Capitalism: US Oil in Equatorial Guinea*. Durham, NC: Duke University Press.

Aretxaga, Begona. 2000. "A Fictional Reality: Paramilitary Death Squads and the Construction of State Terror in Spain." In *Death Squad: The Anthropology of State Terror*, ed. Jeffrey A. Sluka. Philadelphia: University of Pennsylvania Press.

——. 2003. "Maddening States." *Annual Review of Anthropology*: 393–410.

Aroussi, Sahla. 2021. "Strange Bedfellows: Interrogating the Unintended Consequences of Integrating Countering Violent Extremism with the UN's Women, Peace, and Security Agenda in Kenya." *Politics & Gender* 17 (4): 665–95.

Asad, Talal. 2003. *Formations of the Secular: Christianity, Islam, Modernity*. Palo Alto, CA: Stanford University Press.

———. 2007. *On Suicide Bombing*. New York: Columbia University Press.

———. 2009. "Thinking about Terrorism and Just War." *Cambridge Review of International Affairs* 23 (1): 3–24.

Atieno Odhiambo, E. S. 1987. "Democracy and the Ideology of Order in Kenya." In *The Political Economy of Kenya*, ed. M. Shatzberg. New York: Praeger.

Austin, Lloyd. 2023. "A Partnership of Principle and Progress: Remarks by Secretary of Defense Lloyd Austin III during a Trip to Africa." US Department of Defense, 27 September 2023.

Bachmann, Jan. 2012. "Governmentality and Counterterrorism: Appropriating International Security Projects in Kenya." *Journal of Intervention and Statebuilding* 6 (1): 41–56.

———. 2012. "Kenya and International Security: Enabling Globalisation, Stabilising 'Stateness,' and Deploying Enforcement." *Globalizations* 9 (1): 125–43.

———. 2014. "Policing Africa: The US Military and Visions of Crafting 'Good Order.'" *Security Dialogue* 45 (2): 119–36.

Bachmann, Jan, Colleen Bell, and Caroline Holmqvist. 2014. *War, Police, and Assemblages of Intervention*. Abingdon, UK: Routledge.

Baik, Crystal Mun-hye. 2019. *Reencounters on the Korean War and Diasporic Memory Critique*. Philadelphia: Temple University Press.

Bailliet, Cecilia M. 2007. "'War in the Home': An Exposition of Protection Issues Pertaining to the Use of House Raids in Counterinsurgency Operations." *Journal of Military Ethics* 6 (3): 173–97.

Baimu, Evarist, and Kathryn Sturman. 2003. "Amendment to the African Union's Right to Intervene: A Shift from Human Security to Regime Security?" *African Security Review* 12 (2): 37–45.

Bakari, Mohamed. 2013. "A Place at the Table: The Political Integration of Muslims in Kenya, 1963–2007." *Islamic Africa* 4 (1): 15–48.

Balakian, Sophia. 2016. "'Money Is Your Government': Refugees, Mobility, and Unstable Documents in Kenya's Operation Usalama Watch." *African Studies Review* 59 (02): 87–111.

Bardawil, Fadi A. 2020. *Revolution and Disenchantment: Arab Marxism and the Binds of Emancipation*. Durham, NC: Duke University Press.

Basham, Victoria. 2013. *War, Identity and the Liberal State: Everyday Experiences of the Geopolitical in the Armed Forces*. Abingdon, UK: Routledge.

Beckerleg, H. S. 1995. "'Brown Sugar' or Friday Prayers: Youth Choices and Community Building in Coastal Kenya." *African Affairs* 94 (374): 23.

Beckerleg, S. E., and G. Lewando Hundt. 2009. "The Characteristics and Recent Growth of Heroin Injecting in a Kenyan Coastal Town." *Addiction Research & Theory* 12 (1): 41–53.

Beckett, Greg. 2010. "Phantom Power: Notes on Provisionality in Haiti." In *Anthropology and Global Counterinsurgency*, ed. John D. Kelly, Beatrice Jauregui, Sean T. Mitchell, and Jeremy Walton. Chicago: University of Chicago Press, 39–51.

Bell, Sandra, and Simon Coleman. 1999. *The Anthropology of Friendship*. New York: Berg.

Benjamin, Walter. 1978. "Critique of Violence." In *Reflections: Essays, Aphorisms, Autobiographical Writings*. New York: Schocken Books.

Berman, Nathaniel. 2004. "Privileging Combat: Contemporary Conflict and the Legal Construction of War." *Columbia Journal of Transnational Law* 43 (1).

Berman, Nina. 2017. *Germans on the Kenyan Coast: Land, Charity, and Romance*. Bloomington: Indiana University Press.

Bernal, Victoria. 2014. *Nation as Network: Diaspora, Cyberspace, and Citizenship*. Chicago: University of Chicago Press.

Bertz, Ned. 2015. *Diaspora and Nation in the Indian Ocean: Transnational Histories of Race and Urban Space in Tanzania*. Honolulu: University of Hawaii Press.

Besteman, Catherine. 1999. *Unraveling Somalia: Race, Class, and the Legacy of Slavery*. Philadelphia: University of Pennsylvania Press.

——. 2016. *Making Refuge: Somali Bantu Refugees and Lewiston, Maine*. Durham, NC: Duke University Press.

——. 2019. *The Costs of War in Somalia*. Providence, RI: Brown University Costs of War Project.

——. 2020. *Militarized Global Apartheid*. Durham, NC: Duke University Press.

Bezabeh, Samson. 2016. *Subjects of Empires, Citizens of States: Yemenis in Djibouti and Ethiopia*. Cairo: American University in Cairo.

Bhandar, Brenna. 2018. *Colonial Lives of Property: Law, Land, and Racial Regimes of Ownership*. Durham, NC: Duke University Press.

Bhungalia, Lisa. 2023. *Elastic Empire: Refashioning War through Aid in Palestine*. Stanford: Stanford University Press.

Bishara, Amahl. 2015. "Driving While Palestinian in Israel and the West Bank: The Politics of Disorientation and the Routes of a Subaltern Knowledge." *American Ethnologist* 42 (1): 33–54.

Bishara, Fahad Ahmad. 2017. *A Sea of Debt: Law and Economic Life in the Western Indian Ocean, 1780–1950*. Cambridge, UK: Cambridge University Press.

Blanchard, Lauren Ploch. 2018."Al-Shabaab." Washington, DC: Congressional Research Service.

——. 2020. "Kenya: In Focus." Washington, DC: Congressional Research Service.

Blunt, Robert. 2019. *For Money and Elders: Ritual, Sovereignty, and the Sacred in Kenya*. Chicago: University of Chicago Press.

Boinett, Brigadier (Rtd.) Wilson. 2009. "The Origins of the Intelligence System in Kenya." In *Changing Intelligence Dynamics in Africa*, ed. Johnny Kwadjo and Sandy Africa. Global Facilitation Network for Security Sector Reform.

Bonilla, Yarimar. 2015. *Non-Sovereign Futures: French Caribbean Politics in the Wake of Disenchantment*. Chicago: University of Chicago Press.

Bonilla, Yarimar, Greg Beckett, and Mayanthi Fernando, eds. 2021. *Trouillot Remixed: The Michel-Rolph Trouillot Reader*. Durham, NC: Duke University Press.

Branch, Adam. 2011. *Displacing Human Rights: War and Intervention in Northern Uganda*. New York: Oxford University Press.

Branch, Daniel. 2009. *Defeating Mau Mau, Creating Kenya: Counterinsurgency, Civil War and Decolonization*. New York: Cambridge University Press.

———. 2011. *Kenya: Between Hope and Despair, 1963–2011*. New Haven, CT: Yale University Press.

Branch, Daniel, and N. Cheeseman. 2009. "Democratization, Sequencing, and State Failure in Africa: Lessons from Kenya." *African Affairs* 108 (430): 1–26.

Breitman G, ed. 1965. *Malcolm X Speaks: Selected Speeches and Statements*. New York: Grove Press.

Brennan, David. 2010. "Torture of Guantanamo Detainees with the Complicity of Medical Health Personnel: The Case for Accountability and Providing a Forum for Redress for These International Wrongs." *University of San Francisco Law Review* 45.

Brennan, James R. 2012. *Taifa: Making Nation and Race in Urban Tanzania*. Ohio University Press.

Brickell, Katherine. 2012. "Geopolitics of Home." *Geography Compass* 6 (10): 575–88.

Brittain, Victoria. 2013. *Shadow Lives: The Forgotten Women of the War on Terror*. London: Pluto Press.

Brown, Katherine E. 2020. *Gender, Religion, Extremism: Finding Women in Anti-Radicalization*. New York: Oxford University Press.

Browne, Simone. 2015. *Dark Matters: On the Surveillance of Blackness*. Durham, NC: Duke University Press.

Bruce-Lockhart, Katherine. 2014. "'Unsound' Minds and Broken Bodies: The Detention of 'Hardcore' Mau Mau Women at Kamiti and Gitamayu Detention Camps in Kenya, 1954–1960." *Journal of Eastern African Studies* 1055 (August): 1–20.

Bruner, Edward M. 2001. "The Maasai and the Lion King: Authenticity, Nationalism, and Globalization in African Tourism." *American Ethnologist* 4.

Bruner, Edward M., and Barbara Kirshenblatt-Gimblett. 1994. "Maasai on the Lawn: Tourist Realism in East Africa." *Cultural Anthropology* 9 (4): 435–70.

Burton, Orisanmi. 2021. "Captivity, Kinship, and Black Masculine Care Work under Domestic Warfare." *American Anthropologist* 123 (3): 621–32.

———. 2023. *Tip of the Spear: Black Radicalism, Prison Repression, and the Long Attica Revolt*. Berkeley: University of California Press.

Butler, Judith. 2009. *Frames of War: When Is Life Grievable?* New York: Verso.

Byler, Darren. 2021. "Anti-colonial Friendship: Contemporary Police Violence, Storytelling, and Uyghur Masculinity." *American Ethnologist* 48 (2): 153–66.

———. 2022. *Terror Capitalism: Uyghur Dispossession and Masculinity in a Chinese City*. Durham, NC: Duke University Press.

Campbell, Horace. 1999. "Low-Intensity Warfare and the Study of Africans at Home and Abroad." In *Out of One, Many Africas: Reconstructing the Study and Meaning of Africa*, ed. Michael O. West and William G. Martin. Champaign: University of Illinois Press.

———. "The War on Terror as a Business: Lessons from Kenya and the Somalia Interventions." *African Review* 47: 1–40.

Carrier, Neil. 2016. *Little Mogadishu: Eastleigh, Nairobi's Global Somali Hub*. New York: Oxford University Press.

Carrier, Neil, and Celia Nyamweru. 2016. "Reinventing Africa's National Heroes: The Case of Mekatilili, a Kenyan Popular Heroine." *African Affairs* 115 (461): 599–620.

Caton, Steven C. 2020. "The New Old Imperialism in the Arabian Peninsula." *History of the Present* 10 (1): 101–15.

Cattelino, Jessica R. 2004. "The Difference That Citizenship Makes: Civilian Crime Prevention on the Lower East Side." *PoLAR: Political and Legal Anthropology Review* 27 (1): 114–37.

Césaire, Aimé. 1982. "Poetry and Knowledge." *Sulfur* 5: 17.

Chau, Donovan C. 2018. "Linda Nchi from the Sky? Kenyan Air Counterinsurgency Operations in Somalia." *Comparative Strategy* 37 (3): 220–34.

Chome, Ngala. 2019. "From Islamic Reform to Muslim Activism: The Evolution of an Islamist Ideology in Kenya." *African Affairs* 118 (472): 531–52.

———. 2021. "Uses of Race: Moral Debate and Political Action in Mombasa, 1895–1990." PhD diss., Durham University, Durham, UK. http://etheses.dur.ac.uk/14251/.

Chowdhury, Elora Halim, and Philipose, Liz. 2016. "Introduction." In *Dissident Friendships: Feminism, Imperialism, and Transnational Solidarity*. Champaign: University of Illinois Press.

Clarke, Kamari. 2004. *Mapping Yorùbá Networks: Power and Agency in the Making of Transnational Communities*. Durham, NC: Duke University Press.

———. 2006. "Mapping Transnationality: Roots Tourism and the Institutionalization of Ethnic Heritage." In *Globalization and Race: Transformations in the Cultural Production of Blackness*, ed. Kamari Clarke and Deborah A. Thomas. Durham, NC: Duke University Press, 133–53.

———. 2019. *Affective Justice: The International Criminal Court and the Pan-African Pushback*. Durham, NC: Duke University Press.

Clarke, Kamari, and Deborah A. Thomas. 2006. "'Globalization and the Transformation of Race.'" In *Globalization and Race: Transformations in the Cultural Production of Blackness*, ed. Kamari Maxine Clarke and Deborah A. Thomas. Durham, NC: Duke University Press.

Coburn, Noah. 2018. *Under Contract: The Invisible Workers of America's Global War*. Stanford: Stanford University Press.

Cockayne, James, and Siobhan O'Neil, eds. 2015. *UN DDR in an Era of Violent Extremism: Is It Fit for Purpose?* United Nations University.

Cohn, Bernard. 1996. *Colonialism and Its Forms of Knowledge*. Princeton, NJ: Princeton University Press.

Cooke, Miriam. 1996. *Women and the War Story*. Berkeley: University of California Press.

Cooper, Fred. 2015. *Africa in the World: Capitalism, Empire, Nation-State*. Cambridge, MA: Harvard University Press.

Cooper, Fred, and Ann Laura Stoler. 1997. *Tensions of Empire: Colonial Cultures in a Bourgeois World*. Berkeley: University of California Press.

Coronil, Fernando. 1996. "Beyond Occidentalism: Toward Nonimperial Geohistorical Categories." *Cultural Anthropology* 11 (1): 51–87.

Coutin, Susan Bibler. 2010. "Confined Within: National Territories as Zones of Confinement." *Political Geography* 29 (4): 200–208.

Creutzfeldt, Benjamin. 2013. "Theory Talk #57: Siba Grovogui on IR as Theology, Reading Kant Badly, and the Incapacity of Western Political Theory to Travel Very Far in Non-Western Contexts." *Theory Talks* 29.

Crummey, Donald. 1986. "Banditry and Resistance: Noble and Peasant in Nineteenth Century Ethiopia." In *Banditry, Rebellion and Social Protest in Africa*, ed Donald Crummey. Heinemann.

Das, Veena. 1995. *Critical Events: An Anthropological Perspective on Contemporary India*. Delhi: Oxford University Press.

Dattatreyan, Ethiraj G. 2020. *The Globally Familiar: Digital Hip Hop, Masculinity and Urban Space in Delhi*. Durham, NC: Duke University Press.

Daulatzai, Sohail. 2013. *Black Star Crescent Moon: The Muslim International and Black Freedom beyond America*. Minneapolis: University of Minnesota Press.

Davis, Angela Y., Gina Dent, Erica R. Meiners, and Beth E. Richie. 2022. *Abolition. Feminism. Now*. Chicago: Haymarket Books.

Deacon, Gregory, and Gabrielle Lynch. 2013. "Allowing Satan In? Moving toward a Political Economy of Neo-Pentecostalism in Kenya." *Journal of Religion in Africa* 43 (2): 108–30.

Decker, Alicia C. 2014. *In Idi Amin's Shadow: Women, Gender, and Militarism in Uganda*. Athens, OH: Ohio University Press.

De Coning, Cedric, Linnéa Gelot, and John Karlsrud. 2016. *The Future of African Peace Operations: From the Janjaweed to Boko Haram*. London: Bloomsbury Publishing.

Deleuze, Gilles, and Félix Guattari. 1987. *A Thousand Plateus: Capitalism and Schizophrenia*. Minneapolis: University of Minnesota Press.

Devji, Faisal. 2005. *Landscapes of the Jihad: Militancy, Morality, Modernity*. Ithaca, NY: Cornell University Press.

———. 2008. *The Terrorist in Search of Humanity: Militant Islam and Global Politics*. New York: Columbia University Press.

Dillon, Michael, and Julian Reid. 2019. *The Liberal Way of War: Killing to Make Life Live*. Abingdon, UK: Routledge.

Donelli, Federico. 2022. "Rwanda's Military Diplomacy: Kigali's Political Use of the Military Means to Increase Prestige and Influence in Africa and Beyond." Paris: Institut français des relations internationales.

Donovan, Kevin P., Philippe M. Frowd, and Aaron K. Martin. 2016. "Introduction: ASR Forum on Surveillance in Africa: Politics, Histories, Techniques." *African Studies Review* 59 (02): 31–37.

Dougé-Prosper, Mamyrah, and Mark Schuller. 2021. "End of Empire? A View from Haiti." *NACLA Report on the Americas* 53 (1): 1–6.

Dowler, Lorraine, and Joanne Sharp. 2001. "A Feminist Geopolitics ?" *Space and Polity* 5 (3): 165–73.

Dua, Jatin. 2019. *Captured at Sea: Piracy and Protection in the Indian Ocean*. Berkeley: University of California Press.

Duncanson, Claire. 2009. "Forces for Good? Narratives of Military Masculinity in Peacekeeping Operations." *International Feminist Journal of Politics* 11 (1): 63–80.

Edwards, Erica. 2021. *The Other Side of Terror: Black Women and the Culture of US Empire*. New York: NYU Press.

Eichler, Maya. 2011. *Militarizing Men: Gender, Conscription, and War in Post-Soviet Russia*. Stanford: Stanford University Press.

Eisenberg, Andrew J. 2012. "Hip-Hop and Cultural Citizenship on Kenya's 'Swahili Coast.'" *Africa* 82 (4): 556–78.

El-Amraoui, Anaïs F., and Benjamin Ducol. 2019. "Family-Oriented P/CVE Programs: Overview, Challenges and Future Directions." *Journal for Deradicalization* 20: 190–231.

Elkins, Caroline. 2005. *Imperial Reckoning: The Untold Story of Britain's Gulag in Kenya*. New York: Henry Holt & Co.

Elmi, Afyare Abdi. 2010. "Revisiting United States Policy toward Somalia." In *Securing Africa*, ed. Malinda S. Smith. Abingdon, UK: Routledge, 173–92.

Enloe, Cynthia. 1989. *Bananas, Beaches and Bases: Making Feminist Sense of International Relations*. Berkeley: University of California Press.

———. 1993. *The Morning After: Sexual Politics at the End of the Cold War*. Berkeley: University of California Press.

———. 2000. *Manoeuvers: The International Politics of Militarizing Women's Lives*. Berkeley: University of California Press.

Epstein, Helen C. 2017. *Another Fine Mess: America, Uganda, and the War on Terror*. New York: Columbia Global Reports.

Esmenjaud, Romain. 2014. "Africa's Conception of Security in Transition." In *Handbook of Africa's International Relations*, ed. Tim Murithi. New York: Routledge, 115–24.

Fadlalla, Amal Hassan. 2018. *Branding Humanity: Competing Narratives of Rights, Violence, and Global Citizenship*. Stanford: Stanford University Press.

Fair, Laura. 1997. "Kickin' It: Leisure, Politics and Football in Colonial Zanzibar, 1900s–1950s." *Africa: Journal of the International African Institute* 67 (2): 224–51.

Fanon, Frantz. 1952. *Black Skin, White Masks*. New York: Grove Press.

———. 1963. *Wretched of the Earth*. New York: Grove Press.

———. 1965. *A Dying Colonialism*. New York: Grove Press.

Feichtinger, Moritz, Stephan Malinowski, and Chase Richards. 2012. "Transformative Invasions: Western Post-9/11 Counterinsurgency and the Lessons of Colonialism." *Humanity: An International Journal of Human Rights, Humanitarianism, and Development* 3 (1): 35–63.

Feldman, Allen. 1991. *Formations of Violence: The Narrative of the Body and Political Terror in Northern Ireland*. Chicago: University of Chicago Press.

Feldman, Gregory. 2011. *The Migration Apparatus: Security, Labor and Policy Making in the European Union*.

Feldman, Ilana. 2015. *Police Encounters: Security and Surveillance in Gaza under Egyptian Rule*. Stanford: Stanford University Press.

Feldman, Ilana, and Miriam Ticktin. 2010. *In the Name of Humanity: The Government of Threat and Care*. Durham, NC: Duke University Press.

Feldman, Keith P. 2011. "Empire's Verticality: The Af/Pak Frontier, Visual Culture, and Racialization from Above." *Comparative American Studies* 9 (4): 325–41.

Ferguson, James. 2006. *Global Shadows: Africa in the Neoliberal World Order*. Durham, NC: Duke University Press.

———. 2015. *Give a Man a Fish: Reflections on the New Politics of Distribution*. Durham, NC: Duke University Press.

Ferim, Valery. 2013. "African Solutions to African Problems: The Fault Line in Conflict Resolution in Africa." In *The African Union Ten Years After: Solving African Problems with Pan-Africanism and the African Renaissance*, ed. M. Muchie, P. Lukhele-Olorunju, and O. Akpor. Pretoria: Africa Institute of South Africa.

Fernando, Mayanthi. 2014. "Ethnography and the Politics of Silence." *Cultural Dynamics* 26: 235–44.

———. 2014. *The Republic Unsettled: Muslim French and the Contradictions of Secularism*. Durham, NC: Duke University Press.

Fisher, Jonathan. 2013. " 'Some More Reliable than Others': Image Management, Donor Perceptions and the Global War on Terror in East African Diplomacy." *Journal of Modern African Studies* 51 (1): 1–31.

Forte, Maximilian C. 2012. *Slouching towards Sirte: NATO's War on Libya and Africa*. Montreal: Baraka Books.

Foucault, Michel. 1979. *Discipline and Punish: The Birth of the Prison*. New York: Vintage Books.

Gathara, Patrick. 2017. "The Guns of October: How the Invasion of Somalia Changed Kenya." *The Elephant*. https://www.theelephant.info/.

———. 2018. "Five Years after the Westgate Mall Attack, a Culture of Silence Still Haunts Kenya." *Washington Post*, 27 September 2018.

Gelot, Linnéa, and Adam Sandor. 2019. "African Security and Global Militarism." *Conflict, Security & Development* 19 (6): 521–42.

Getachew, Adom. 2019. *Worldmaking after Empire: The Rise and Fall of Self-Determination*. Princeton, NJ: Princeton University Press.

Ghosh, Sahana. 2019. " 'Everything Must Match': Detection, Deception, and Migrant Illegality in the India-Bangladesh Borderlands." *American Anthropologist* 121 (4): 870–83.

———. 2023. *A Thousand Tiny Cuts: Mobility and Security across the Bangladesh–India Borderlands*. Berkeley: University of California Press.

Gidron, Yotam. 2020. *Israel in Africa: Security, Migration, Interstate Politics*. London: Bloomsbury Publishing.

Gifford, Paul. 2009. *Christianity, Politics, and Public Life in Kenya*. London: Hurst & Co.

Gill, Lesley. 2004. *The School of the Americas: Military Training and Political Violence in the Americas*. Durham, NC: Duke University Press.

Gilmore, Ruth Wilson. 2007. *Golden Gulag: Prisons, Surplus, and Opposition in Globalizing California*. Berkeley: University of California Press.

Gimode, Edwin A. 2007. "The Role of the Police in Kenya's Democratisation Process." In *Kenya: The Struggle for Democracy*, ed. Godwin Rapando Murunga and Shadrack Wanjala Nasong'o. Dakar: CODESRIA.

Gitau, Judy. 2016. *Civil–Military Relations in an Era of Violent Extremism: Policy Options for the Kenya Defence Forces*. Nairobi: CHRIPS, Centre for Human Rights and Policy Studies.

Glassman, Jonathan. 2011. *War of Words, War of Stones: Racial Thought and Violence in Colonial Zanzibar*. Bloomington: Indiana University Press.

Gluck, Zoltan. 2017. "Security Urbanism and the Counterterror State in Kenya." *Anthropological Theory* 17 (3): 297–321.

Goldberg, David Theo. 2009. "Racial Comparisons, Relational Racisms: Some Thoughts on Method." *Ethnic and Racial Studies* 32 (7): 1271–82.

———. 2016. "Militarizing Race." *Social Text* 34 (4) (129): 19–40.

Gona, George. 2008. "Changing Political Faces on Kenya's Coast, 1992–2007." *Journal of Eastern African Studies* 2 (2): 242–53.

Gonzalez, Vernadette Vicuna. 2013. *Securing Paradise: Tourism and Militarism in Hawai'i and the Philippines*. Durham, NC: Duke University Press.

Gordon, Avery F. 2008. *Ghostly Matters: Haunting and the Sociological Imagination*. Minneapolis: University of Minnesota Press.

Gould, Lauren, and Jolle Demmers. 2018. "An Assemblage Approach to Liquid Warfare: AFRICOM and the ' Hunt ' for Joseph Kony." *Security Dialogue* 49 (5): 364–81.

Gqola, Pumla Dineo. 2009. " 'The Difficult Task of Normalizing Freedom': Spectacular Masculinities, Ndebele's Literary/Cultural Commentary and Post-Apartheid Life." *English in Africa* 36 (1): 61–76.

Graham, Stephen. 2010. *Cities under Siege: The New Military Urbanism*. New York: Verso.

Greenburg, Jennifer. 2023. *At War with Women: Military Humanitarianism and Imperial Feminism in an Era of Permanent War*. Ithaca, NY: Cornell University Press.

Gregory, Derek. 2004. *The Colonial Present: Afghanistan, Palestine, Iraq*. Hoboken, NJ: Wiley-Blackwell.

———. 2006. "The Black Flag: Guantánamo Bay and the Space of Exception." *Human Geography* 88 (4): 405–27.

———. 2017. "Dirty Dancing." In *Life in the Age of Drone Warfare 2*, ed. Lisa Parks and Caren Kaplan. Durham, NC: Duke University Press.

Grewal, Inderpal. 1996. *Home and Harem: Nation, Gender, Empire, and the Cultures of Travel*. Durham, NC: Duke University Press.

———. 2005. *Transnational America: Feminisms, Diasporas, Neoliberalisms*. Durham, NC: Duke University Press.

———. 2017. *Saving the Security State: Exceptional Citizens in Twenty-First Century America*. Durham, NC: Duke University Press.

Grewal, Inderpal, and Caren Kaplan, eds. 1994. *Scattered Hegemonies: Postmodernity and Transnational:Feminist Practices*. Minneapolis: University of Minnesota Press.

Grewal, Zareena. 2013. *Islam Is a Foreign Country: American Muslims and the Global Crisis of Authority*. New York: NYU Press.

Gross-Wyrtzen, Leslie. 2022. " 'There Is No Race Here': On Blackness, Slavery, and Disavowal in North Africa and North African Studies." *Journal of North African Studies* 28 (3): 1–31.

Grovogui, Siba N. 2001. "Come to Africa: A Hermeneutics of Race in International Theory." *Alternatives: Global, Local, Political* 26 (4): 425–48.

———. 2006. *Beyond Eurocentrism and Anarchy: Memories of International Order and Institutions.* London: Palgrave Macmillan.

Gubara, Dahlia E. M. 2018. "Revisiting Race and Slavery through ʿAbd al-Rahman al-Jabarti's ʿAjaʾIb al-Athar." *Comparative Studies of South Asia, Africa and the Middle East* 38 (2): 230–45.

Gusterson, Hugh. 2016. *Drone: Remote Controlled Warfare.* Cambridge, MA: MIT Press.

Haki Africa. 2016. "What Do We Tell the Families? Killings and Disappearances in the Coastal Region of Kenya 2012–2016." Mombasa: Haki Africa.

Hall, Stuart. 1990. "Cultural Identity and Diaspora." In *Identity: Community, Culture, Difference,* ed. Jonathan Rutherford. London: Lawrence & Wishart, 222–37.

———.1996. *Stuart Hall: Critical Dialogues in Cultural Studies.* Abingdon, UK: Routledge.

Hanieh, Adam. 2018. *Money, Markets, and Monarchies: The Gulf Cooperation Council and the Political Economy of the Contemporary Middle East.* Cambridge, UK: Cambridge University Press.

Harker, Christopher. 2009. "Spacing Palestine through the Home." *Transactions of the Institute of British Geographers* 34 (3): 320–32.

Haugerud, Angelique. 1995. *The Culture of Politics in Modern Kenya.* Cambridge, UK: Cambridge University Press.

Hecht, Gabrielle. 2011. *Entangled Geographies: Empire and Technopolitics in the Global Cold War.* Cambridge, MA: MIT Press.

Henry, Marsha G. 2017. "Problematizing Military Masculinity, Intersectionality and Male Vulnerability in Feminist Critical Military Studies." *Critical Military Studies* 3 (2): 182–99.

Heredia, Marta Iñiguez de, and Zubairu Wai, eds. 2019. *Recentering Africa in International Relations: Beyond Lack, Peripherality, and Failure.* London: Palgrave Macmillan.

Hermez, Sami. 2017. *War Is Coming: Between Past and Future Violence in Lebanon.* Philadelphia: University of Pennsylvania Press.

Hesse, Barnor. 2007. "Racialized Modernity: An Analytics of White Mythologies." *Ethnic and Racial Studies* 30 (4): 643–63.

Higate, Paul. 2012. "Martial Races and Enforcement Masculinities of the Global South: Weaponising Fijian, Chilean, and Salvadoran Postcoloniality in the Mercenary Sector." *Globalizations* 9 (1): 35–52.

Higate, Paul, and Marsha Henry. 2010. "Space, Performance and Everyday Security in the Peacekeeping Context." *International Peacekeeping* 17 (1): 32–48.

Hillewaert, Sarah. 2019. *Morality at the Margins: Youth, Language, and Islam in Coastal Kenya.* New York: Fordham University Press.

Hirsch, Susan B. 2007. *In the Moment of Greatest Calamity: Terrorism, Grief, and a Victim's Quest for Justice.* Princeton, NJ: Princeton University Press.

Hirschkind, Charles. 2006. *The Ethical Soundscape: Cassette Sermons and Islamic Counterpublics.* New York Columbia University Press.

Hirschkind, Charles, and Saba Mahmood. 2002. "Feminism, the Taliban, and Politics of Counter-Insurgency." *Anthropological Quarterly* 75 (2): 339–54.

Ho, Engseng. 2004. "Empire through Diasporic Eyes: A View from the Other Boat." *Comparative Studies in Society and History* 46 (02): 210–46.

———. 2006. *The Graves of Tarim: Genealogy and Mobility across the Indian Ocean.* Berkeley: University of California Press.

Hochberg, Gil Z. 2015. *Visual Occupations: Violence and Visibility in a Conflict Zone.* Durham, NC: Duke University Press.

Hoffman, Danny. 2011. *War Machines: Young Men and Violence in Sierra Leone and Liberia.* Durham, NC: Duke University Press.

———. 2019. "Geometry after the Circle: Security Interventions in the Urban Gray Zone." *Current Anthropology* 60 (19): 98–107.

Hofmeyr, Isabel. 2012. "The Complicating Sea: The Indian Ocean as Method." *Comparative Studies of South Asia, Africa and the Middle East* 32 (3): 584–90.

Hönke, Jana, and Markus-Michael Müller. 2016. "The Global Making of Policing." In *The Global Making of Policing,* ed. Jana Hönke and Markus-Michael Müller. Abingdon, UK: Routledge, 1–19.

hooks, bell. 1990. *Yearning: Race, Gender, and Cultural Politics.* Boston: South End Press.

Horne, Gerald. 2009. *Mau Mau in Harlem? The U.S. and the Liberation of Kenya.* London: Palgrave Macmillan.

Huckerby, Jayne C., and Margaret L. Satterthwaite. 2013. "Introduction: A Gender and Human Rights Approach to Counter-Terrorism." In *Gender, National Security, and Counter-Terrorism: Human Rights Perspectives,* ed. Jane Huckerby and Margaret Satterwaite. Abingdon, UK: Routledge.

Human Rights Watch. 2014. "Kenya: End Abusive Roundups." New York: Human Rights Watch.

Hundle, Anneeth Kaur. 2019. "Insecurities of Expulsion: Emergent Citizenship Formations and Political Practices in Postcolonial Uganda." *Comparative Studies in South Asia, Africa and the Middle East* 39 (1): 8–23.

———. Forthcoming. *Insecurities of Expulsion: Race, Violence, Citizenship and Afro-Asian Entanglements in Transregional Uganda.* Durham, NC: Duke University Press.

Hunt, Krista. 2006. " 'Embedded Feminism' and the War on Terror." In *(En)Gendering the War on Terror: War Stories and Camouflaged Politics,* ed. Kim Rygiel and Krista Hunt. Farnham, UK: Ashgate.

Hyndman, Jennifer. 2004. "Mind the Gap: Bridging Feminist and Political Geography through Geopolitics." *Political Geography* 23 (3): 307–22.

Ihmoud, Sarah. 2019. "Murabata: The Politics of Staying in Place." *Feminist Studies* 45 (2): 512–40.

Ihmoud, Sarah, and Shanya Cordis. 2022. "A Poetics of Living Rebellion: Sociocultural Anthropology in 2021." *American Anthropologist* 124 (4): 813–29.

Ijomah, B. I. C. 1974. "The African Military Interventions: A Prelude to Military High Command." *Ufahamu: A Journal of African Studies* 5 (2): 51–80.

International Crisis Group. 2021. "Overkill: Reforming the Legal Basis for the U.S. War on Terror." New York: International Crisis Group.

Jackson, Will. 2011. "White Man's Country: Kenya Colony and the Making of a Myth." *Journal of Eastern African Studies* 5 (2): 344–68.

Jacobs, David, and Thomas Isbell. 2018. "Seven Years in, Slimmer Majority of Kenyans See Military Action in Somalia as Necessary." Afrobarometer Dispatch No. 241. https://www.afrobarometer.org.

Jaji, Rosemary. 2009. "Masculinity on Unstable Ground: Young Refugee Men in Nairobi, Kenya." *Journal of Refugee Studies* 22 (2): 177–94.

James, Erica Caple. 2010. *Democratic Insecurities: Violence, Trauma, and Intervention in Haiti*. Berkeley: University of California Press.

Jeganathan, Pradeep. 2004. "Checkpoint: Anthropology, Identity, and the State." In *Anthropology in the Margins of the State*, ed. Deborah Poole and Veena Das, 67–80. Santa Fe, NM: SAR Press.

Jones, Branwen Gruffydd. 2014. "'Good Governance' and 'State Failure': The Pseudo-Science of Statesmen in Our Times." In *Race and Racism in International Relations: Confronting the Global Colour Line*, ed. Alexander Anievas, Nivi Manchanda, and Robbie Shilliam. Abingdon, UK: Routledge.

Junaid, Mohamad. 2019. "Counter-Maps of the Ordinary: Occupation, Subjectivity, and Walking under Curfew in Kashmir." *Identities* 27 (3): 302–20.

Kaba, Mariame. 2021. *We Do This 'Til We Free Us: Abolitionist Organizing and Transforming Justice*. Chicago: Haymarket Books.

Kamau, Wanjiru Carolyne. 2006. "Kenya & the War on Terrorism." *Review of African Political Economy* 33 (107): 133–41.

Kamola, Isaac A. 2019. *Making the World Global: US Universities and the Production of the Global Imaginary*. Durham, NC: Duke University Press.

Kantai, Parselelo. 2013. "The Rise of Somali Capital." Chimurenga. https://chimurengachronic.co.za/.

Kapadia, Ronak K. 2019. *Insurgent Aesthetics: Security and the Queer Life of the Forever War*. Durham, NC: Duke University Press.

Kaplan, Caren. 2018. *Aerial Aftermaths: Wartime from Above*. Durham, NC: Duke University Press.

Kasfir, Sidney L. 2004. "Tourist Aesthetics in the Global Flow: Orientalism and 'Warrior Theatre' on the Swahili Coast." *Visual Anthropology* 17 (3–4): 319–43.

Kassem, Ramzi. 2013. "Gendered Erasures in the Global 'War on Terror': An Unmasked Interrogation." In *Gender, National Security, and Counter-Terrorism: Human Rights Perspectives*, ed. Jane Huckerby and Margaret Sattherwaite. Abingdon, UK: Routledge.

Katz, Cindi. 2005. "Lost and Found: The Imagined Geographies of American Studies." *Prospects* 30 (October): 17–25.

Kelley, Robin D. G. 2002. *Freedom Dreams: The Black Radical Imagination*. Boston: Beacon Press.

Kennedy, Dane. 1987. *Islands of White: Settler Society and Culture in Kenya and Southern Rhodesia*. Durham, NC: Duke University Press.

Kenya National Commission on Human Rights (NCHR). 2015. "The Error of Fighting Terror with Terror: Preliminary Report of KNCHR Investigations on Human Rights Abuses in the Ongoing Crackdown against Terrorism." Nairobi: Kenya National Commission on Human Rights.

Khalili, Laleh. 2011. "Gendered Practices of Counterinsurgency." *Review of International Studies* 37 (4): 1471–91.

———. 2012. *Time in the Shadows: Confinement in Counterinsurgencies*. Stanford: Stanford University Press.

Khan, Iftikhar A. 2023. "NADRA to Undertake Kenya's National Identity Management Project." *Dawn*, 16 May 2023.

Khayyat, Munira. 2022. *A Landscape of War: Ecologies of Resistance and Survival in South Lebanon*. Berkeley: University of California Press.

Kilcullen, David. 2006. "Twenty-Eight Articles." *Military Review* 86 (3): 103–8.

Kimari, Wangui. 2019. "The Story of a Pump: Life, Death and Afterlives within an Urban Planning of 'Divide and Rule' in Nairobi, Kenya." *Urban Geography* 42 (2): 141–60.

———. 2020. "War-Talk: An Urban Youth Language of Siege in Nairobi." *Journal of Eastern African Studies* 14 (4): 707–23.

Kimari, Wangui, and Henrik Ernstson. 2020. "Imperial Remains and Imperial Invitations: Centering Race within the Contemporary Large-Scale Infrastructures of East Africa." *Antipode* 52 (3): 825–46.

Kimathi, Al-Amin, and Alan Butt, eds. 2007. *Horn of Terror: Report of US-Led Mass Extraordinary Renditions from Kenya to Somalia, Ethiopia, and Guantanamo Bay, January–June*. Nairobi: Muslim Human Rights Forum.

Kindy, Hyder. 1972. *Life and Politics in Mombasa*. Nairobi: East African Publishing House.

Kioko, Ben. 2003. "The Right of Intervention under the African Union's Constitutive Act: From Non-Interference to Non-Intervention." *International Review of the Red Cross* 85 (December): 807–26.

Kramer, Paul A. 2006. *The Blood of Government: Race, Empire, the United States, and the Philippines*. Chapel Hill: University of North Carolina Press.

———. 2018. "How Not to Write a History of U.S. Empire." *Diplomatic History* 42 (5): 911–31.

Kresse, Kai. 2007. *Philosophising in Mombasa: Knowledge, Islam and Intellectual Practice on the Swahili Coast*. Edinburgh: Edinburgh University Press for the International African Institute.

———. 2009. "Muslim Politics in Postcolonial Kenya: Negotiating Knowledge on the Double-Periphery." *Journal of the Royal Anthropological Institute* 15: S76–S94.

———. 2013. "'On the Skills to Navigate the World, and Religion, for Coastal Muslims in Kenya.'" In *Articulating Islam: Anthropological Approaches to Muslim Worlds*, ed. Magnus Marsden and Konstantinos Retsikas. New York: Springer, 77–99.

———. 2016. "Kenya Twendapi?: Re-Reading Abdilatif Abdalla's Pamphlet Fifty Years after Independence." *Africa* 86 (1): 1–32.

Kumar, Deepa. 2017. "National Security Culture: Gender, Race, and Class in the Production of Imperial Citizenship." *International Journal of Communication* 11: 2154–77.

———. 2018. "See Something, Say Something: Security Rituals, Affect, and US Nationalism from the Cold War to the War on Terror." *Public Culture* 30 (1): 143–71.

Kundnani, Arun. 2014. *The Muslims Are Coming: Islamophobia, Extremism, and the Domestic War on Terror*. New York: Verso.

———. 2017. "Islamophobia as Ideology of US Empire." In *What Is Islamophobia*, ed. Narzanin Massoumi, Tom Mills, and David Miller. London: Pluto Press, 35–48.

Kuus, Merje. 2009. "Cosmopolitan Militarism? Spaces of NATO Expansion." *Environment and Planning A* 41 (3): 545–62.

Laurendeau, Jason. 2008. "'Gendered Risk Regimes': A Theoretical Consideration of Edgework and Gender." *Sociology of Sport Journal* 25: 293–309.

Lee, Christopher J. 2005. "The 'Native' Undefined: Colonial Categories, Anglo-African Status and the Politics of Kinship in British Central Africa, 1929–38." *Journal of African History* 46 (3): 455–78.

Lee, Christopher J., ed. 2010. *Making a World after Empire: The Bandung Moment and Its Political Afterlives*. Athens, OH: Ohio University Press.

Lewis, Joanna. 2000. *Empire State-Building: War & Welfare in Kenya, 1925–52*. Columbus: Ohio State University Press.

Li, Darryl. 2011. "A Universal Enemy? Foreign Fighters and Legal Regimes of Exclusion and Exemption Under the 'Global War on Terror.'" *Columbia Human Rights Law Review* 41: 355–428.

———. 2012. "Taking the Place of Martyrs: Afghans and Arabs under the Banner of Islam." *Arab Studies Journal* 20 (1): 12–39.

———. 2015. "Offshoring the Army: Migrant Workers and the US Military." *UCLA Law Review* 62.

———. 2018. "From Exception to Empire: Sovereignty, Carceral Circulation, and the 'Global War on Terror.'" In *Ethnographies of U.S. Empire*, ed. Carol McGranahan and John Collins. Durham, NC: Duke University Press, 456–75.

———. 2020. *The Universal Enemy: Jihad, Empire, and the Challenge of Solidarity*. Stanford: Stanford University Press.

———. 2022. "Captive Passages: Geographies of Blackness in Guantánamo Memoirs." *Transforming Anthropology* 30 (1): 20–33.

Lind, Jeremy, Patrick Mutahi, and Marjoke Oosterom. 2015. "Tangled Ties: Al-Shabaab and Political Volatility in Kenya." IDS Evidence Report No. 150. Institute for Development Studies, University of Susssex, Brighton, UK.

Lipsitz, George. 1998. *The Possessive Investment in Whiteness: How White People Profit from Identity Politics*. Philadelphia: Temple University Press.

Lonsdale, John M., and E. S. Atieno Odhiambo. 2003. *Mau Mau & Nationhood: Arms, Authority & Narration*. Athens, OH: Ohio University Press.

Lori, Noora. 2019. *Offshore Citizens: Permanent Temporary Status in the Gulf*. Cambridge, UK: Cambridge University Press.

Lowe, Lisa. 2015. *The Intimacies of Four Continents*. Durham, NC: Duke University Press.

Lubin, Alex. 2021. *Never-Ending War on Terror*. Berkeley: University of California Press.

Lubkemann, Stephen C. 2019. *Culture in Chaos: An Anthropology of the Social Condition in War*. Chicago: University of Chicago Press.

Luongo, Katherine. 2006. "If You Can't Beat Them, Join Them : Government Cleansings of Witches and Mau Mau in 1950s Kenya." *History in Africa* 33: 451–71.

Lutz, Catherine. 2001. *Homefront: A Military City and the American Twentieth Century*. Boston: Beacon Press.

———. 2006. "Empire Is in the Details." *American Ethnologist* 33 (4): 593–611.

———. 2009. "Bases, Empire, and Global Response." In *The Bases of Empire: The Global Struggle against U.S. Military Posts*, ed. Catherine Lutz. New York: NYU Press, 1–46.

———. 2009. "The Military Normal: Feeling at Home with Counterinsurgency in the United States." In Network of Concerned Anthropologists, *The Counter-Counterinsurgency Manual: Or, Notes on Demilitarizing American Society*. Chicago: Prickly Paradigm Press, 23–37.

———. 2011. "A Military History of the American Suburbs, the Discipline of Economics, and All Things Ordinary." *Antipode* 43 (3): 901–6.

Macdonald, Ayang. 2023. "Kenya Seeks NADRA Collaboration, Expertise on Digital ID Project." *Biometric Update,* 16 May 2023.

Macharia, Keguro. 2011. "War as 'Viagla.'" 21October.

———. 2016. "On Being Area-Studied: A Litany of Complaint." *GLQ: A Journal of Lesbian and Gay Studies* 22 (2): 183–90.

———. 2019. *Frottage: Frictions of Intimacy across the Black Diaspora*. Vol. 11. New York: NYU Press.

Machold, Rhys. 2018. "Reconsidering the Laboratory Thesis: Palestine/Israel and the Geopolitics of Representation." *Political Geography* 65: 88–97.

———. 2022. "India's Counterinsurgency Knowledge: Theorizing Global Position in Wars on Terror." *Small Wars & Insurgencies* 33 (4–5): 796–818.

Mackie, Vera. 2012. "The 'Afghan Girls': Media Representations and Frames of War." *Continuum: Journal of Media & Cultural Studies* 26: 115–31.

Mahajan, Nidhi. 2021. "Notes on an Archipelagic Ethnography: Ships, Seas, and Islands of Relation in the Indian Ocean." *Island Studies Journal* 16 (1): 9–22.

Mahmood, Saba. 2005. *The Politics of Piety: The Islamic Revival and the Feminist Subject*. Princeton, NJ: Princeton University Press.

———. 2015. *Religious Difference in a Secular Age: A Minority Report*. Princeton, NJ: Princeton University Press.

Maira, Sunaina. 2009. *Missing: Youth, Citizenship, and Empire after 9/11*. Durham, NC: Duke UniversityPress.

———. 2016. *The 9/11 Generation: Youth, Rights, and Solidarity in the War on Terror*. New York: NYU Press.

Makinda, S. M. 1983. "From Quiet Diplomacy to Cold War Politics: Kenya's Foreign Policy." *Third World Quarterly* 5 (2): 300–319.

Malkki, Liisa H. 1992. "National Geographic: The Rooting of Peoples and the Territorialization of National Identity among Scholars and Refugees." *Cultural Anthropology* 7 (1): 24–44.

Mama, Amina. 1998. "Khaki in the Family: Ender Discourses and Militarism in Nigeria." *African Studies Review* 41 (2): 1–17.

———. 2014. "Beyond Survival: Militarism, Equity and Women's Security." In *Development and Equity: An Interdisciplinary Exploration by Ten Scholars from Africa, Asia, and Latin America*, ed. Lina Johnson and Ton Dietz. Boston: Brill, 41–68.

Mama, Amina, and Margo Okazawa-Rey. 2012. "Militarism, Conflict and Women's Activism in the Global Era: Challenges and Prospects for Women in Three West African Contexts." *Feminist Review* 101: 97–123.

Mamdani, Mahmood. 1996. *Citizen and Subject: Contemporary Africa and the Legacy of Late Colonialism*. Princeton, NJ: Princeton University Press.

———. 2001. "Beyond Settler and Native as Political Identities : Overcoming the Political Legacy of Colonialism." *Comparative Studies in Society and History* 43: 651–64.

———. 2004. *Good Muslim, Bad Muslim: America, the Cold War, and the Roots of Terror*. Kampala: Fountain Publishers.

———. 2010. "Responsibility to Protect or Right to Punish?" *Journal of Intervention and Statebuilding* 4 (1): 53–67.

———. 2012. *Define and Rule: Native as Political Identity*. Cambridge, MA: Harvard University Press.

———. 2018. "Introduction: Trans-African Slaveries Thinking Historically." *Comparative Studies of South Asia, Africa and the Middle East* 38 (2): 185–210.

Man, Simeon. 2018. *Soldiering through Empire: Race and the Making of the Decolonizing Pacific*. Berkeley: University of California Press.

Markle, Seth M. 2013. "Brother Malcom, Comrade Babu: Black Internationalism and the Politics of Friendship." *Biography* 36 (3): 540–67.

Marsden, Magnus. 2009. "Talking the Talk: Debating Debate in Northern Afghanistan." *Anthropology Today* 25 (2): 20–24.

Martin, Lauren L., and Matthew L. Mitchelson. 2009. "Geographies of Detention and Imprisonment: Interrogating Spatial Practices of Confinement, Discipline, Law, and State Power." *Geography Compass* 3 (1): 459–77.

Martin, Phyllis M. 1991. "Colonialism, Youth and Football in French Equatorial Africa." *International Journal of the History of Sport* 8 (1): 56–71.

Maruska, Jennifer. 2009. "When Are States Hypermasculine?" In *Gender and International Security: Feminist Perspectives*, ed. Laura Sjoberg, 235–55. Abingdon, UK: Routledge.

Masco, Joseph. 2014. *The Theater of Operations: National Security Affect from the Cold War to the War on Terror*. Durham, NC: Duke University Press.

Mawiyoo, Ngwatilo. 2015. "You Are All Terrorists: The 'Sanitization' of a Nairobi Suburb." *Creative Time Reports*. https://creativetimereports.org/.

Mazrui, Alamin M., and Ibrahim Noor Shariff. 1994. *The Swahili: Idiom and Identity of an African People*. Trenton, NJ: Africa World Press.

Mazrui, Ali. 1963. "On Heroes and Uhuru-Worship." *Transition* 11: 23–28.

———. 1992. "Afrabia: Africa and the Arabs in the New World Order." *Ufahamu: A Journal of African Studies* 20 (3).

———. 1993. "The Black Intifada? Religion and Rage at the Kenyan Coast." *Journal of Asian and African Affairs* 4 (no. 2).

Mbembe, Achille. 2000. "At the Edge of the World: Boundaries, Territoriality, and Sovereignty in Africa." *Public Culture* 12 (1): 259–84.

———. 2002. "African Modes of Self-Writing." *Public Culture* 14 (1): 239–73.

———. 2017. *Critique of Black Reason*. Durham, NC: Duke University Press.

McClintock, Anne. 1995. *Imperial Leather: Race, Gender and Sexuality in the Colonial Contest*. Abingdon, UK: Routledge.

———. 2009. "Paranoid Empire: Specters from Guantanamo and Abu Ghraib." *Small Axe: A Caribbean Journal of Criticism* 13 (1): 50–74.

McEvoy, Claire. 2013. "Shifting Priorities: Kenya's Changing Approach to Peacebuilding and Peacemaking." Oslo: Norwegian Peacebuilding Resource Centre.

McFadden, Patricia. 2008. "Interrogating Americana: An African Feminist Critique." In *Feminism and War: Confronting US Imperialism*, ed. Robin L. Riley, Chandra Talpade Mohanty, and Minnie Bruce Pratt. New York: Zed Books, 56–67.

———. 2008. "Plunder as Statecraft: Militarism and Resistance in Neo-Colonial Africa." In *Security Disarmed: Critical Perspectives on Gender, Race, and Militarization*, 136–56. New Brunswick, NJ: Rutgers University Press.

McGranahan, Carole, and John F. Collins. 2018. "Introduction: Ethnography and U.S. Empire." In *Ethnographies of U.S. Empire*, ed. Carol McGranahan and John F. Collins. Durham, NC: Duke University Press.

McIntosh, Janet. 2009. *The Edge of Islam: Power, Personhood, and Ethnoreligious Boundaries on the Kenya Coast*. Durham, NC: Duke University Press.

———. 2016. *Unsettled: Denial and Belonging among White Kenyans*. Durham, NC: Duke University Press.

Mesok, Elizabeth. 2015. "Affective Technologies of War: US Female Counterinsurgents and the Performance of Gendered Labor." *Radical History Review* 2015 (123): 60–86.

———. 2022. "Beyond Instrumentalisation: Gender and Agency in the Prevention of Extreme Violence in Kenya." *Critical Studies on Terrorism* (15): 1–22.

Metcalf, Thomas R. 2007. *Imperial Connections: India in the Indian Ocean Arena, 1860–1920*. Berkeley: University of California Press.

Migue, Col. Pius, and Lt. Col. Oscar Oluoch. 2014. *Operation Linda Nchi: Kenya's Military Experience in Somalia*. Nairobi: Ministry of Defense.

Miles, Steven. 2006. *Oath Betrayed: Torture, Medical Complicity, and the War on Terror*. New York: Random House.

Mines, Keith. 2023. "Haiti Needs a Political Dialogue alongside the Multinational Security Mission." Blog post. *United States Institute of Peace*, 5 October 2023.

Minter, William. 2008. *Apartheid's Contras: An Inquiry into the Roots of War in Angola and Mozambique*. Charleston, SC: BookSurge Publishing.

Mirzoeff, Nicholas. 2011. *The Right to Look: A Counterhistory of Visuality*. Durham, NC: Duke University Press.

Mitchell, Sean T. 2010. "Paranoid Styles of Nationalism after the Cold War: Notes from an Invasion of the Amazon." In *Anthropology and Global Counterinsurgency*, ed. John D. Kelly, Beatrice Jauregui, Sean T. Mitchell, and Jeremy Walton. Chicago: University of Chicago Press, 89–104.

———. 2018. "Empire as Accusation, Denial, and Structure: The Social Life of U.S. Power at Brazil's Spaceport." In *Ethnographies of U.S. Empire*, ed. Carol McGranahan and John F. Collins, 369–87. Durham, NC: Duke University Press.

Miyonga, Rose. 2023. " 'We Kept Them to Remember': Tin Trunk Archives and the Emotional History of the Mau Mau War." *History Workshop Journal* 96: 96–114.

Mkandawire, Thandika. 2004. "Disempowering New Democracies and the Persistence of Poverty." In *Globalisation, Poverty and Conflict: A Critical "Development" Reader*, ed. M. Spoor. New York: Springer, 117–53.

Mogire, Edward, and Kennedy Mkutu Agade. 2011. "Counter-Terrorism in Kenya." *Journal of Contemporary African Studies* 29 (4): 473–91.

Molony, Thomas. 2018. "Social Media Warfare and Kenya's Conflict with Al Shabaab in Somalia: A Right to Know?" *African Affairs* 118 (471): 328–51.

Moody, Jessica. 2022. "How Rwanda Became Africa's Policeman." Blog post. *Foreign Policy*, 21 November.

Moore, Adam. 2019. *Empire's Labor: The Global Army That Supports US Wars*. Ithaca, NY: Cornell University Press.

Moore, Adam, and James Walker. 2016. "Tracing the US Military's Presence in Africa." *Geopolitics* 21 (3): 686–716.

Morton, Stephen. 2012. "Reading Kenya's Colonial State of Emergency after Agamben." In *Agamben and Colonialism*, ed. Simone Bignall and Marcelo Svirsky. Edinburgh: Edinburgh University Press.

Moyd, Michelle R. 2014. *Violent Intermediaries: African Soldiers, Conquest, and Everyday Colonialism in German East Africa*. Athens, OH: Ohio University Press.

Moyn, Samuel. 2022. *Humane: How the United States Abandoned Peace and Reinvented War*. London: Verso Books.

Mudimbe, V. Y. 1988. *The Invention of Africa: Gnosis, Philosophy, and the Order of Knowledge*. Bloomington: Indiana University Press.

Müller, Markus-Michael. 2016. "Entangled Pacifications: Peacekeeping, Counterinsurgency and Policing in Port-Au-Prince and Rio de Janeiro 1." In *The Global Making of Policing*, ed. Jana Hönke and Markus-Michael Müller. Abingdon, UK: Routledge, 77–95.

Mungai, Christine. 2021. "The Whiteness Conference." *Adi Magazine* (Winter).

Muriithi, B. M. J. "Stop Targeting Somalis, Says Raila," *Daily Nation*, 12 April 2014.

Murungi, Curtis. 2013. *The Letter and the Spirit: Politics, Intimacy, and Middle Class Constitution-Making in Kenya*. PhD diss., Stanford University.

Musila, Grace. 2009. "Phallocracies and Gynocratic Transgressions: Gender, State Power and Kenyan Public Life." *Africa Insight* 39 (1): 39–57.

———. 2012. "Violent Masculinities and the Phallocratic Aesthetics of Power in Kenya." In *The New Violent Cartography: Geo-Analysis after the Aesthetic Turn*, ed. Sam Okoth Opondo and Michael J. Shapiro. Abingdon, UK: Routledge, 151–70.

———. 2015. *A Death Retold in Truth and Rumour: Kenya, Britain and the Julie Ward Murder*. Suffolk, UK: James Currey.

Mutunga, Willy, ed. 1999. *Constitution-Making from the Middle: Civil Society and Transition Politics in Kenya, 1992–1997*. Nairobi: SAREAT.

Mwakimako, Hassan. 2007. "Christian-Muslim Relations in Kenya: A Catalogue of Events and Meanings." *Islam and Christian-Muslim Relations* 18 (2): 287–307.

Mwakimako, Hassan, and Justin Willis. 2014. "Islam, Politics and Violence on the Kenyan Coast." Observatoire des enjeux politiques et sécuritaires dans la Corne de l'Afrique 27.

Nagl, John. 2007. *The U.S. Army/Marine Counterinsurgency Field Manual*. Chicago: University of Chicago Press.

N'Diaye, Boubacar. 2002. "How Not to Institutionalize Civilian Control: Kenya's Coup Prevention Strategies, 1964–1997." *Armed Forces & Society* 28 (4): 619–40.

Ndzovu, Hassan. 2014. *Muslims in Kenyan Politics: Political Involvement, Marginalization, and Minority Status*. Evanston, IL: Northwestern University Press.

Neocleous, Mark. 2011. "The Police of Civilization: The War on Terror as Civilizing Offensive." *International Political Sociology* 5: 144–59.

———. 2014. *War Power, Police Power*. Edinburgh: Edinburgh University Press.

———. 2021. *A Critical Theory of Police Power: The Fabrication of the Social Order*. London: Verso Books.

Nesiah, Vasuki. 2013. "Feminism as Counter-Terrorism: The Seduction of Power." In *Gender, National Security, and Counter-Terrorism: Human Rights Perspectives*, ed. Jane Huckerby and Margaret Satterthwaite. Abingdon, UK: Routledge, 127–51.

———. 2020. "An Un-American Story of the American Empire: Small Places, From the Mississippi to the Indian Ocean." *UCLA Law Review* 67: 1450.

News24. 2017. "Forgetting Westgate: How Kenya Erases Terrorism." 9 September 2017.

Ngũgĩ wa Thiong'o. 1972. *Homecoming: Essays on Africa and Carribean Literature*. Bloomington: Indiana University Press.

———. 1986. "The Writer in a Neocolonial State." *Black Scholar* 17 (4): 2–10.

———. 1993. *Moving the Centre: The Struggle for Cultural Freedoms*. Suffolk, UK: James Currey.

———. 2009. *Something Torn and New: An African Renaissance*. New York: Basic Books.

———. 2016. "Abdilatif Abdalla and the Voice of Prophecy." In *Abdilatif Abdalla: Poet in Politics*, ed. Kai Kresse and Rose Marie Beck. Dar es Salaam: Mkuni na Nyota.

———. 2018. *Wrestling with the Devil: A Prison Memoir*. New York: New Press.

Ng'weno, Bettina, and L. Obura Aloo. 2019. "Irony of Citizenship: Descent, National Belonging, and Constitutions in the Postcolonial African State." *Law and Society Review* 53 (1): 141–72.

Niang, Amy. 2018. *The Postcolonial African State in Transition: Stateness and Modes of Sovereignty*. Lanham, MD: Rowman & Littlefield.

———. 2022. "Coups, Insurgency, and Imperialism in Africa." Blog post. *Review of African Political Economy Blog*, 8 March 2022.

Njoya, Wandia. 2018. "Invisible Citizens: Branding Kenya for Foreign Investors and Tourists." *The Elephant* (16 August). https://www.theelephant.info.

———. 2021. "A Class That Dare Not Speak Its Name: BBI and the Tyranny of the New Kenyan Middle Class." *The Elephant*. https://www.theelephant.info.

Nkrumah, Kwame. 1965. *Neo-Colonialism: The Last Stage of Imperialism*. New York: International Publishers.

Nyabola, Nanjala. 2014. "The Politics of Identity and Belonging in Kenya," *Al-Jazeera*, 23 June.

Nyerere, Julius K. 1969. "Stability and Change in Africa." *Mbioni: The Monthly Newsletter of Kivukoni College* 5 (10–11): 3–31.

Okech, Awino. 2018. "Boundary Anxieties and Infrastructures of Violence: Somali Identity in Post-Westgate Kenya." *Third World Thematics: A TWQ Journal* 3 (2): 293–309.

Olaloku-Teriba, Annie. 2018. "Afro-Pessimism and the (Un)Logic of Anti-Blackness." *Historical Materialism* 26 (2): 96–122.

Olivier, Djems. 2021. "The Political Anatomy of Haiti's Armed Gangs." *NACLA* (2 April).

Oloka-Onyango, J. 1990. "Police Powers, Human Rights and the State in Kenya and Uganda: A Comparative Analysis." *Third World Legal Studies* 1: 1–36.

Olsen, Gorm Rye. 2018. "The October 2011 Kenyan Invasion of Somalia: Fighting al-Shabaab or Defending Institutional Interests?" *Journal of Contemporary African Studies* 36 (1): 39–53.

Ombati, Cyrus. 2023. "Kenya Prepares Elite Paramilitary Units for Haiti Mission." *The Star* (3 October).

Ombati, Mokua. 2015. "Feminine Masculinities in the Military: The Case of Female Combatants in the Kenya Defence Forces' Operation in Somalia." *African Security Review* 24 (4): 403–13.

Omeje, Kenneth. 2008. "The War on Terror and the Crisis of Postcoloniality in Africa." *African Journal of International Affairs* 11 (2): 89–114.

Omeje, Kenneth, and John Mwangi Githigaro. 2012. "The Challenges of State Policing in Kenya." *Peace & Conflict Review* 7 (1): 1–8.

Omi, Michael, and Howard Winant. 1994. *Racial Formation in the United States.* Abingdon, UK: Routledge.

Ong, Aihwa. 1999. *Flexible Citizenship: The Cultural Logics of Transnationality.* Durham, NC: Duke University Press.

———.2011. "Introduction: Worlding Cities, or the Art of Being Global." In *Worlding Cities: Asian Experiments and the Art of Being Global.* Hoboken, NJ: John Wiley & Sons.

Open Society Foundations and Muhuri. 2013. "We Are Tired of Taking You to the Court: Human Rights Abuses by Kenya's Anti-Terrorism Police Unit."

Osborne, Myles. 2020. "'Mau Mau Are Angels . . . Sent by Haile Selassie': A Kenyan War in Jamaica." *Comparative Studies in Society and History* 62 (4): 714–44.

Osella, Filippo. 2012. "Malabar Secrets: South Indian Muslim Men's (Homo)Sociality across the Indian Ocean." *Asian Studies Review* 36 (4): 531–49.

Ossome, Lyn. 2018. *Gender, Ethnicity, and Violence in Kenya's Transition to Democracy: States of Violence.* London: Lexington Books.

Otuki, Neville. 2017. "Nairobi leads EA Arms Race with Sh96 Billion Military Budget." *Business Daily Africa* (25 April).

Padmore, George. 1953. "Behind the Mau Mau." *Phylon (1940–1956)* 14 (4): 355–72.

Paine, Robert. 1969. "In Search of Friendship: An Exploratory Analysis in 'Middle-Class' Culture." *Man* 4 (4): 505–24.

Parks, Lisa, and Caren Kaplan. 2017. "Introduction." In *Life in the Age of Drone Warfare,* ed. Caren Kaplan and Lisa Parks. Durham, NC: Duke University Press.

Pedraza, Diana Pardo, Xan Sarah Chacko, Jennifer Terry, and Astrida Neimanis. 2023. "Introduction: Domestication of War." *Catalyst: Feminism, Theory, Technoscience* 9 (1).

Peterson, Kristin. 2014. *Speculative Markets: Drug Circuits and Derivative Life in Nigeria*. Durham, NC: Duke University Press.

Pfingst, Annie, and Wangui Kimari. 2021. "Carcerality and the Legacies of Settler Colonial Punishment in Nairobi." *Punishment & Society* 23 (5): 697–722.

Pierre, Jemima. 2013. *The Predicament of Blackness: Postcolonial Ghana and the Politics of Race*. Chicago: University of Chicago Press.

———. 2023. "Haiti as Empire's Laboratory:" *NACLA Report on the Americas* 55 (3): 244–50.

Powell, Eve Troutt. 2003. *A Different Shade of Colonialism: Egypt, Great Britain, and the Mastery of the Sudan*. Berkeley: University of California Press.

Prashad, Vijay. 2007. *The Darker Nations: A People's History of the Third World*. New York: New Press.

Pratt, Nicola. 2020. *Embodying Geopolitics: Generations of Women's Activism in Egypt, Jordan, and Lebanon*. 1st ed. Berkeley: University of California Press.

Presley, Cora Ann. 1988. "The Mau Mau Rebellion, Kikuyu Women, and Social Change." *Canadian Journal of African Studies* 22 (3): 502–27.

Prestholdt, Jeremy. 2008. *Domesticating the World: African Consumerism and the Genealogies of Globalization*. Berkeley: University of California Press.

———. 2009. "Phantom of the Forever War: Fazul Abdullah Muhammad and the Terrorist Imaginary." *Public Culture* 21 (3): 451–64.

———. 2010. "Superpower Osama." In *Making a World after Empire: The Bandung Moment and Its Political Afterlives*, ed. Christopher J. Lee. Athens, OH: Ohio University Press, 315–50.

———.2011. "Kenya, the United States, and Counterterrorism." *Africa Today* 57 (4): 2–27.

———. 2013. "Fighting Phantoms: The United States and Counterterrorism in Eastern Africa." In *Lessons and Legacies of the War on Terror: From Moral Panic to Permanent War*, ed. Gershon Shafir, Everarde Meade, and William J. Aceves. Abingdon, UK: Routledge, 127–56.

———. 2014. "Politics of the Soil: Separatism, Autochthony, and Decolonization at the Kenyan Coast." *Journal of African History* 55: 249–70.

———. 2019. *Icons of Dissent: The Global Resonance of Che, Marley, Tupac and Bin Laden*. Oxford, UK: Oxford University Press.

Privacy International. 2017. "Track, Capture, Kill: Inside Communications Surveillance and Counterterrorism in Kenya."

Puar, Jasbir K. 2007. *Terrorist Assemblages: Homonationalism in Queer Times*. Durham, NC: Duke University Press.

Purdeková, Andrea. 2022. "Memory as Vulnerability: Reinhabiting Sites of Violence and the Politics of Triumphalist Amnesia in Kenya's War on Terror." *Security Dialogue* 53 (5): 385–401.

Qureshi, Asim. 2010. "'War on Terror': The African Front." *Critical Studies on Terrorism* 3 (1): 49–61.

Rabasa, A. 2009. *Radical Islam in East Africa*. Arlington, VA: RAND Corporation.

Rana, Junaid. 2011. *Terrifying Muslims: Race and Labor in the South Asian Diaspora.* Durham, NC: Duke University Press.

———. 2016. "The Racial Infrastructure of the Terror-Industrial Complex." *Social Text* 34 (4) (129): 111–38.

Rancière, Jacques. 1999. *Disagreement: Politics and Philosophy.* Minneapolis: University of Minnesota Press.

Rashid, Maria. 2020. *Dying to Serve: Militarism, Affect, and the Politics of Sacrifice in the Pakistan Army.* Stanford: Stanford University Press.

Rawlence, Ben. 2016. *City of Thorns: Nine Lives in the World's Largest Refugee Camp.* London: Picador.

Razack, Sherene H. 2004. *Dark Threats, White Knights: The Somalia Affair, Peacekeeping, and the New Imperialism.* Toronto: University of Toronto Press.

Razavi, Negar. 2022. "Navigating the 'Middle East' in Washington: Diasporic Experts and the Power of Multiplicitous Diplomacy." *Social Text* 40 (3) (152): 105–23.

Renda, Mary A. 2001. *Taking Haiti: Military Occupation and the Culture of US Imperialism, 1915–1940.* Chapel Hill: University of North Carolina Press.

Ricardo, C., and G. Barker. 2006. "Young Men and the Construction of Masculinity in Sub-Saharan Africa: Implications for HIV/AIDS, Conflict, and Violence." In *The Other Half of Gender: Men'sIssues in Development*, ed. M.vC. Correia and I. Bannon. Washington, DC: World Bank, 159–93.

Rinelli, Lorenzo, and Sam Okoth Opondo. 2013. "Affective Economies: Eastleigh's Metalogistics, Urban Anxieties and the Mapping of Diasporic City Life." *African and Black Diaspora* 6 (2): 236–50.

Rizvi, Mubbashir. 2019. *The Ethics of Staying: Social Movements and Land Rights Politics in Pakistan.* Stanford: Stanford University Press.

Robinson, Cabeiri deBergh. 2013. *Body of Victim, Body of Warrior: Refugee Families and the Making of Kashmiri Jihadists.* Berkeley: University of California Press.

Robinson, Cedric J. 1983. *Black Marxism: The Making of the Black Radical Tradition.* Chapel Hill: University of North Carolina Press.

Rodney, Walter. 1972. *How Europe Underdeveloped Africa.* Washington, DC: Howard University Press.

Rofel, Lisa. 2002. "Modernity's Masculine Fantasies." In *Critically Modern: Alternatives, Alterities, Anthropologies*, ed. Bruce M. Knauft. Bloomington: Indiana University Press.

Rofel, Lisa, and Carlos Rojas. 2022. *New World Orderings: China and the Global South.* Durham, NC: Duke University Press.

Rutazibwa, Olivia Umurerwa. 2014. "Studying Agaciro: Moving beyond Wilsonian Interventionist Knowledge Production on Rwanda." *Journal of Intervention and Statebuilding* 8 (4): 291–302.

Ruteere, Mutuma, and Marie Emmanuelle Pommerolle. 2003. "Democratizing Security or Decentralizing Repression? The Ambiguities of Community Policing in Kenya." *African Affairs* 102 (August): 587–604.

Sabaratnam, Meera. 2013. "Avatars of Eurocentrism in the Critique of the Liberal Peace." *Security Dialogue* 44 (3): 259–78.

Sahle, Eunice N. 2012. "Fanon and Geographies of Political Violence in the Context of Democracy in Kenya." *Black Scholar* 42 (3–4): 45–57.

Said, Edward. 1978. *Orientalism*. New York: Pantheon Books.

Saleh, Zainab. 2021. *Return to Ruin: Iraqi Narratives of Exile and Nostalgia*. Stanford: Stanford University Press.

Salem, Sara. 2019. "Haunted Histories: Nasserism and the Promises of the Past." *Middle East Critique* 28 (3): 261–77.

Salim, A. I. 1970. "The Movement of 'Mwambao' or Coast Autonomy in Kenya 1956–1963." *Hadith* 2.

Samudzi, Zoé. 2022. "Journey from the 'Center of the World': On U.S. Exceptionalism and Disgust." *The Funambulist*, 13 April 2022.

Santoru, Marina E. 1996. "The Colonial Idea of Women and Direct Intervention : The Mau Mau Case." *African Affairs* 95 (379): 253–67.

Scahill, Jeremy. 2013. *Dirty Wars: The World Is a Battlefield*. New York: Nation Books.

———. 2014. "The CIA's Secret Sites in Somalia." *The Nation* (10 December).

Schatzberg, Michael G., ed. 1987. *The Political Economy of Kenya*. SAIS Study on Africa. New York: Praeger.

Schields, Chelsea. 2023. *Offshore Attachments: Oil and Intimacy in the Caribbean*. Berkeley: University of California Press.

Schiller, Nina Glick. 1997. "Cultural Politics and the Politics of Culture." *Identities: Global Studies in Culture and Power* 4 (1): 1–7.

Schmidt, Elizabeth. 2018. *Foreign Intervention in Africa after the Cold War: Sovereignty, Responsibility, and the War on Terror*. Athens, OH: Ohio University Press.

Schrader, Stuart. 2019. *Badges without Borders: How Global Counterinsurgency Transformed American Policing*. Berkeley: University of California Press.

Scott, David. 2017. "Preface: Friendship as an Art of Living." *Small Axe: A Caribbean Journal of Criticism* 21 (3): vii–x.

Segell, Glen. 2023. "Including Africa Threat Analysis in Force Design 2030." *Journal of Advanced Military Studies* 14 (1): 183–200.

Seesemann, Rüdiger. 2007. "Kenyan Muslims, the Aftermath of 9/11, and the 'War on Terror.'" In *Islam and Muslim Politics in Africa*, ed. Benjamin F Soares and Rene Otayek. London: Palgrave.

Shabibi, Namir. 2020. "'Revealed: The CIA and MI6's Secret War in Kenya.'" *Daily Maverick* (28 August).

Shadle, Brett L. 2015. *The Souls of White Folk: White Settlers in Kenya, 1900s–1920s*. Manchester, UK: Manchester University Press.

Shalhoub-Kevorkian, Nadera. 2015. *Security Theology, Surveillance and the Politics of Fear*. Cambridge, UK: Cambridge University Press.

Sharp, Joanne P. 1996. "Hegemony, Popular Culture and Geopolitics: The Reader's Digest and the Construction of Danger." *Political Geography* 15 (6–7): 557–70.

———. 2011. "Subaltern Geopolitics." *Geoforum* 42 (3): 271–73.

Sheikh, Salah Abdi. 2007. Blood on the Runway: The Wagalla Massacre of 1984. Nairobi: Northern Publishing House.

Shilliam, R. 2008. "What the Haitian Revolution Might Tell Us about Development, Security, and the Politics of Race." *Comparative Studies in Society and History* 50 (3): 778–808.

———. 2021. *Decolonizing Politics: An Introduction.* Hoboken, NJ: John Wiley & Sons.

Shivji, Issa. 2003. "Law's Empire and Empire's Lawlessness: Beyond the Anglo-American Law." *Law, Social Justice and Global Development* (1).

Shohat, Ella. 1992. "Notes on the 'Post-Colonial.'" *Social Text* 31/32: 99–113.

Siegel, James. 1998. *A New Criminal Type in Jakarta: Counter-Revolution Today.* Durham, NC: Duke University Press.

Singh, Nikhil Pal. 2017. *Race and America's Long War.* Berkeley: University of California Press.

Sivanandan, A. 1991. "A Black Perspective on the War." *Race & Class* 32 (4): 83–88.

Smart, Devin. 2018. "'Safariland': Tourism, Development and the Marketing of Kenya in the Post-Colonial World." *African Studies Review* 61 (2): 134–57.

Smith, Christen A. 2016. "Facing the Dragon: Black Mothering, Sequelae, and Gendered Necropolitics in the Americas." *Transforming Anthropology* 24 (1): 31–48.

Smith, Malinda S. 2015. "Africa, 9/11, and the Temporality and Spatiality of Race and Terror." In *At the Limits of Justice: Women of Colour on Terror,* ed. Sherene H. Razack and Suvendrini Perera, 380–405. Toronto: University of Toronto Press.

Smith, Sara. 2020. *Intimate Geopolitics: Love, Territory, and the Future on India's Northern Threshold.* New Brunswick, NJ: Rutgers University Press.

Ṣóyẹmí, Ẹniọlá Ànúolúwapọ. 2023. "Making Crisis Inevitable: The Effects of U.S. Counterterrorism Training and Spending in Somalia." Providence, RI: Costs of War Project, Brown University.

Sparke, Matthew. 2005. *In the Space of Theory: Postfoundational Geographies of the Nation-State.* Minneapolis: University of Minnesota Press.

Springer, Simon. 2009. "Culture of Violence or Violent Orientalism? Neoliberalisation and Imagining the 'Savage Other' in Post-Transitional Cambodia." *Transactions of the Institute of British Geographers* 34 (3): 305–19.

———. 2011. "Violence Sits in Places? Cultural Practice, Neoliberal Rationalism, and Virulent Imaginative Geographies." *Political Geography* 30 (2): 90–98.

Srinivas, Smriti, Bettina Ng'weno, and Neelima Jeychandran. 2020. *Reimagining Indian Ocean Worlds.* Abingdon, UK: Routledge.

Stalcup, Meg. 2013. "Interpol and the Emergence of Global Policing." In *Policing and ContemporaryGovernance: The Anthropology of Police in Practice,* ed. William Garriott. London: Palgrave Macmillan, 231–62.

Stephens, Michelle Ann. 2005. *Black Empire: The Masculine Global Imaginary of Caribbean Intellectuals in the United States, 1914–1962.* Durham, NC: Duke University Press.

Stoler, Ann Laura. 2006. *Haunted by Empire: Geographies of Intimacy in North American History.* Durham, NC: Duke University Press.

———. 2013. *Imperial Debris: On Ruins and Ruination.* Durham, NC: Duke University Press.

———. 2016. *Duress: Imperial Durabilities in Our Times.* Durham, NC: Duke University Press.

Stoler, Ann Laura, Carole McGranahan, and Peter Perdue, eds. 2007. *Imperial Formations.* Santa Fe, NM: SAR Press.

Stubbs, Thomas. 2015. "Ethnopolitics and the Military in Kenya." In *Forging Military Identity in Culturally Pluralistic Societies: Quasi-Ethnicity,* ed. Daniel Zirker. Lanham, MD: Lexington Books, 69–88.

Tageldin, Shaden M. 2014. "The Place of Africa, in Theory: Pan-Africanism, Postcolonialism, Beyond." *Journal of Historical Sociology* 27 (3): 302–23.

Tahir, Madiha. 2017. "The Containment Zone." In *Life in the Age of Drone Warfare,* ed. Lisa Parks and Caren Kaplan. Durham, NC: Duke University Press.

———. 2019. "Violence Work and the Police Order." *Public Culture* 31 (3): 409–18.

———. 2021. "The Distributed Empire of the War on Terror." *Boston Review* (10 September).

Tate, Winifred. 2007. *Counting the Dead: The Politics of Human Rights Activism in Colombia.* Berkeley: University of California Press.

———. 2015. *Drugs, Thugs, and Diplomats: U.S. Policymaking in Colombia.* Stanford: Stanford University Press.

Taussig, Michael. 1999. *Defacement: Public Secrecy and the Labor of the Negative.* Stanford: Stanford University Press.

Terry, Jennifer. 2017. *Attachments to War: Biomedical Logics and Violence in the Twenty-First Century.* Durham, NC: Duke University Press.

Thiranagama, Sharika. 2013. *In My Mother's House: Civil War in Sri Lanka.* Philadelphia: University of Pennsylvania Press.

Thiranagama, Sharika, and Tobias Kelly. 2010. "Introduction: Specters of Treason." In *Traitors: Suspicion, Intimacy, and the Ethics of State-Building.* Philadelphia: University of Pennsylvania Press.

Thomas, Deborah A. 2011. *Exceptional Violence: Embodied Citizenship in Transnational Jamaica.* Durham, NC: Duke University Press.

———. 2019. *Political Life in the Wake of the Plantation: Sovereignty, Witnessing, Repair.* Durham, NC: Duke University Press.

———. 2022. "Can Black Lives Matter in a Black Country?" *Social Text* 40 (3): 17–35.

Thornton, Christy. 2021. *Revolution in Development: Mexico and the Governance of the Global Economy.* Berkeley: University of California Press.

Throup, David. 1992. "Crime, Politics and the Police in Colonial Kenya, 1939–1963." In *Policing and Decolonisaton: Politics, Nationalism, and the Police, 1917–65,* ed. David M. Anderson and David Killingray. Manchester, UK: Manchester University Press, 127–57.

———. 2012. "Kenya's Intervention in Somalia." *Center for Strategic and International Studies* 16 (2).

Tibbetts, Alexandra. 1994. "Mamas Fighting for Freedom in Kenya." *Africa Today* 41 (4): 27–48.

Ticktin, Miriam. 2011. *Casualties of Care: Immigration and the Politics of Humanitarianism in France*. Berkeley: University of California Press.

Tolan-Szkilnik, Paraska. 2023. *Maghreb Noir: The Militant-Artists of North Africa and the Struggle for a Pan-African, Postcolonial Future*. Stanford: Stanford University Press.

Tounsel, Christopher. 2021. *Chosen Peoples: Christianity and Political Imagination in South Sudan*. Durham, NC: Duke University Press.

Trouillot, M. R. 1995. *Silencing the Past: Power and the Production of History*. Boston: Beacon Press.

———. 2003. *Global Transformations: Anthropology and the Modern World*. New York: Palgrave Macmillan.

Tudor, Margot. 2023. *Blue Helmet Bureaucrats: United Nations Peacekeeping and the Reinvention of Colonialism, 1945–1971*. Cambridge, UK: Cambridge University Press.

Turse, Nick. 2012. *The Changing Face of Empire: Special Ops, Drones, Spies, Proxy Fighters, Secret Bases, and Cyberwarfare*. Chicago: Haymarket Books.

———. 2015. *Tomorrow's Battlefield: U.S. Proxy Wars and Secret Ops in Africa*. Chicago: Haymarket Books.

———. 2018. "The U.S. Military Says It Has a 'Light Footprint' in Africa." *The Intercept* (1 December).

United Nations. 2022. "Security Council Extends Mandate of United Nations Integrated Office in Haiti for One Year, Unanimously Adopting Resolution 2645." UN Security Council 9095th meeting (15 July).

Usiskin, Clara. 2019. *America's Covert War in East Africa: Surveillance, Rendition, Assassination*. London: Hurst & Co.

Vine, David. 2015. *Base Nation: How US Military Bases Abroad Harm America and the World*. New York: Metropolitan Books.

Virilio, Paul. 1989. *War and Cinema: The Logistics of Perception*. London: Verso.

Visweswaran, Kamala. 2012. "Occupier/Occupied." *Identities* 19 (4): 440–51.

Vitalis, Robert. 2013. "The Midnight Ride of Kwame Nkrumah and Other Fables of Bandung (Ban-Doong)." *Humanity: An International Journal of Human Rights, Humanitarianism, and Development* 4 (2): 261–88.

———. 2015. *White World Order, Black Power Politics*. Ithaca, NY: Cornell University Press.

Von Eschen, Penny M. 2014. *Race against Empire: Black Americans and Anticolonialism, 1937–1957*. Ithaca, NY: Cornell University Press.

Vora, Neha. 2018. *Teach for Arabia: American Universities, Liberalism, and Transnational Qatar*. Stanford: Stanford University Press.

Waal, Alex de. 2015. *The Real Politics of the Horn of Africa: Money, War and the Business of Power*. Malden, MA: Polity.

Wai, Zubairu. 2012. "Neo-Patrimonialism and the Discourse of State Failure in Africa." *Review of African Political Economy* 39 (131): 27–43.

Waller, Richard. 2006. "Rebellious Youth in Colonial Africa." *Journal of African History* 47 (1): 77–92.

Walley, Christine J. 2003. "Our Ancestors Used to Bury Their 'Development' in the Ground: Modernity and the Meanings of Development within a Tanzanian Marine Park." *Anthropological Quarterly* 76 (1): 33–54.

Wanyeki, L. Muthoni. 2020. "Foreign Policy and Regional Relations." In *The Oxford Handbook of Kenyan Politics*, ed. Nic Cheeseman, Karuti Kanyinga, and Gabrielle Lynch. Oxford, UK: Oxford University Press.

Ware, Rudolph T. 2014. *The Walking Qur'an: Islamic Education, Embodied Knowledge, and History in WestAfrica*. Illustrated edition. Chapel Hill: University of North Carolina Press.

Watts, Michael. 1996. "Islamic Modernities? Citizenship, Civil Society, and Islamism in a Nigerian City." *Public Culture* 8 (2): 251–89.

wa Wanjiru, K. 2010. "Abdilatif Abdalla: My Poems Gave Me Company." *Pambazuka News* 500 (14 October).

Wedeen, Lisa. 1999. *Ambiguities of Domination: Politics, Rhetoric, and Symbols in Contemporary Syria*. Chicago: University of Chicago Press.

Weheliye, Alexander G. 2014. *Habeas Viscus: Racializing Assemblages, Biopolitics, and Black Feminist Theories of the Human*. Durham, NC: Duke University Press.

Weiss, Brad. 2004. *Producing African Futures: Ritual and Reproduction in a Neoliberal Age*. Boston: Brill.

Weitzberg, Keren. 2017. *We Do Not Have Borders: Greater Somalia and the Predicaments of Belonging in Kenya*. Athens, OH: Ohio University Press.

——. 2020. "Biometrics, Race Making, and White Exceptionalism: The Controversy over Universal Fingerprinting in Kenya." *Journal of African History* 61 (1): 23–43.

Weizman, Eyal. 2006. "Walking through Walls: Soldiers as Architects in the Israeli-Palestinian Conflict." *Radical Philosophy* 136: 8–22.

Westerlund, David, and Eva Rosander. 1997. *African Islam and Islam in Africa: Encounters between Sufis and Islamists*. Athens, OH: Ohio University Press.

Wexler, Laura. 2000. *Tender Violence: Domestic Visions in an Age of U.S. Imperialism*. Chapel Hill: University of North Carolina Press.

Weyani Media. 2019. "We Harvest the Present from the Future We Planted Yesterday." *Weyani Media* (25 October).

Whelan, Teresa. 2006. "Africa's Ungoverned Space." *Verão* 114 (3): 61–73.

White, Luise. 1990. "Separating the Men from the Boys: Constructions of Gender, Sexuality, and Terrorism in Central Kenya, 1939–1950." *International Journal of African Historical Studies* 23 (1): 1–25.

Whittaker, Hannah. 2014. *Insurgency and Counterinsurgency in Kenya: A Social History of the Shifta Conflict, c. 1963–1968*. Boston: Brill.

Wilder, Gary. 2015. *Freedom Time: Negritude, Decolonization, and the Future of the World*. Chicago: University of Chicago Press.

Williams, Paul D. 2018. "Joining AMISOM: Why Six African States Contributed Troops to the African Union Mission in Somalia." *Journal of Eastern African Studies* 12 (1): 172–92.

——. 2018. *Fighting for Peace in Somalia: A History and Analysis of the African Union Mission (AMISOM), 2007–2017*. Oxford, UK: Oxford University Press.

Willis, Justin, and Ngala Chome. 2014. "Marginalization and Political Participation on the Kenya Coast: The 2013 Elections." *Journal of Eastern African Studies* 8 (00): 115–34.

Willis, Justin, and George Gona. 2013. "Pwani C Kenya? Memory, Documents and Secessionist Politics in Coastal Kenya." *African Affairs* 112 (446): 48–71.

Wilson, Amrit. 2013. *Threat of Liberation: Imperialism and Revolution in Zanzibar*. New York: Pluto Press.

Wondemagegnehu, Dawit Yohannes, and Daniel Gebreegziabher Kebede. 2017. "AMISOM: Charting a New Course for African Union Peace Missions." *African Security Review* 26 (2): 199–219.

Yonucu, Deniz. 2022. *Police, Provocation, Politics: Counterinsurgency in Istanbul*. Ithaca, NY: Cornell University Press.

Young, Alden, and Keren Weitzberg. 2021. "Globalizing Racism and De-Provincializing Muslim Africa." *Modern Intellectual History* (May): 1–22.

Yusuf, Mohammed. 2016. "How Kenya's Al-Shabaab Amnesty Is a Loaded Gun." *New Humanitarian* (31 August).

Zeleke, Elleni Centime. 2019. *Ethiopia in Theory: Revolution and Knowledge Production, 1964–2016*. Boston: Brill.

Zeleza, Paul Tiyambe. 2005. "Rewriting the African Diaspora: Beyond The Black Atlantic." *African Affairs* 104 (414): 35–68.

Zhan, Mei. 2009. *Other-Worldly: Making Chinese Medicine through Transnational Frames*. Durham, NC: Duke University Press.

Zia, Ather. 2019. *Resisting Disappearance: Military Occupation and Women's Activism in Kashmir*. Seattle: University of Washington Press.

Zilberg, Elana. 2011. *Space of Detention: The Making of a Transnational Gang Crisis between Los Angeles and San Salvador*. Durham, NC: Duke University Press.

Zulaika, Joseba, and William A. Douglas. 1996. *Terror and Taboo: The Follies, Fables, and Faces of Terrorism*. Abingdon, UK: Routledge.

INDEX

Note: Page numbers in *italics* indicate figures.

Abdalla, Abdilatif, v, 98, 139–40, *141*

abduction. *See* kidnapping

Abrahamsen, Rita, 42–43

activism: acceptable forms of, 79, 90, 91, 105; anti-terror laws and, 3; association with terrorism, 95, 101; defining, 90–91; by families, 102–3, 109–10, 126–27, 128, 130; police scrutiny and, 24, 86–87, 94, 95, 117

activists, 20, 22, 76, 100, 161–62; arrest/detention of, 24, 95–96, 168n18, 176n96; opaque police power and, 27, 83–84, 85, 90–92, 94, 106–7; public secrets and, 91–92. *See also* Abdalla, Abdilatif; human rights organizations; Mazrui, Alamin; Ngũgĩ wa Thiong'o

Adebajo, Adekeye, 12

Adesanmi, Pius, 184n96

Afghanistan, 144; US involvement in, 4, 10, 11, 54, 66, 99, 162, 168n6

Africa: anthropological focus in, 138–39; colonial inheritances of, 37, 54, 65, 72 (*see also* colonialism); early postindependence era and, 8–9; exceptionalism in, 51–52; foreign aid and, 44, 60, 67, 88, 122, 125–26, 148; gendered evaluations of, 48; as gray zone, 4; great power rivalry lens and, 8, 11, 25; Haiti and, 157, 158, 161; independence anxieties and, 38; indigenous vs. foreign Islam in, 18, 59, 66–67, 187n32; interventionism as world relation in, 14, 28, 40, 49, 157, 158; Muslim demographics of, 18; native capacity to govern and, 17, 48; as unstable, 7, 12, 16, 17, 35, 37, 88, 118; as US military laboratory, 12, 87, 159, 169n13 (*see also* AFRICOM); as victim, 49; as in the world, 8–9, 18–19, 41, 174n69. *See also* East Africa; Organization of African Unity; Pan-Africanism; race; racialization; war on terror, African responsibility in; *individual countries*

Africanness, 18, 49, 52, 59, 67, 176n96

"African solutions to African problems," 17, 28, 36, 49, 160, 184n96

African Union, the (AU): calls for Ethiopia to withdraw from Somalia, 182n67; depoliticization of intervention and, 35; framing in international community, 174n69; intervention in Somalia, 49 (*see also* AMISOM); security architecture of, 41, 44; the UN and, 182n59. *See also* Organization of African Union

African Union Transition Mission in Somalia (ATMIS), 44

AFRICOM (US Africa Command): base and detention site locations, 10–11, *11*, 26, 172n42; gray-zone operations of, 87–88; military partnerships and, 42, 88, 172n42

Aguilar, Mario, 198n16
Ahmed, Sharif Sheikh, 40
aid, foreign, 67, 88; security-related, 44, 60, 142, 148 (see also CVE). See also donors
Akyeampong, Emmanuel, 176n96
Al-Bulushi, Yousuf, 185n2
Al-Busaid dynasty, 63–64
Algeria, 13, 37, 114
Allen, Lori, 143
Al-Qaeda: alleged connections to, 1, 42, 117; effect on tourism, 60; US embassy bombings, 3, 7, 58. See also 9/11
Al-Shabaab, 126, 154, 155; allegations of ties to, 105, 117, 128; AMISOM materiel in hands of, 43; calls for dissolution of Somalia and, 52; calls to join, 135; defeat of ICU and, 42; Eastleigh raid for suspected links, 19–20, 89, 102, 111; effect on tourism, 60, 76; fictionalized, 119, 121; military propaganda of role against, 32; as morally evil, 30; ongoing combat against, 44, 135, 148, 149; questioning war against, 32; recruitment by, 58, 135, 150, 151; rise of, 3, 58; Somali police trained to counter, 12; spread of, 43, 76; stereotypes of, 54; 2011 invasion of Somalia and, 5, 40, 135; war opposition as support for, 30; youth traveling to join, 122, 134, 135, 144, 145. See also Eye in the Sky (Hood); Mission to Rescue (Foxton Media); rehabilitation; Somalia
Al-Shabaab, attacks by: El Adde, 34; Garissa University, 44, 93, 103, 112, 134; Manda Bay, 55–56; Mandera, 101–2; Paradise Hotel bombing, 67, 100; rise in, 15–16, 101–2; tourist kidnappings, 40, 185n6; Westgate Mall, 19, 29–31, 56, 100–101, 128, 179n8
AMISOM, 14, 43–44, 50, 51, 174n66, 183n78. See also African Union, the
Anderson, David, 38, 39
Angola, 11, 13, 160

Annan, Kofi, 13
anticolonialism, 63, 64, 102, 161–62, 172n37; the colonial intelligence apparatus and, 137; colonialism as provoking, 36–37, 114; domesticity and, 124–25, 139; post-World War II increase in, 147; worldmaking and, 9. See also Land and Freedom Army
Anti-Terror Police Unit (ATPU), 83–85, 169n10; disappearances and, 3–4, 136; home raids by, 81; human rights organizations and, 1, 91–94; kidnappings, 83, 84, 85; military uniforms of, 81; murder of Aboud Rogo and, 94, 103, 135, 150; plain-clothes death squads, 3, 83–84; US funding/training of, 3, 81, 83, 104, 135–36. See also extrajudicial killings
Arab ethnicity: Arabness and, 62, 67; Arab supremacy and, 64, 65, 176n92; within colonial racial systems, 18, 64, 65, 187n41; foreignness and, 59–60, 62, 66–67, 100; Kenyan elite Arabocentrism, 63–64; Omani rule and, 63; racialization as/of, 21, 26, 58, 59; transnationalism and, 62
Aretxaga, Begona, 94
arrests: of Abdilatif Abdalla, 98; of activists, 95, 168n18; arbitrary, 3, 76, 98, 104; for asking questions, 110, 130; border operations and, 2; of IPK leadership, 99–100; legislation regarding, 100–101; of Alamin Mazrui, 140; military involvement in, 32; of Aboud Rogo, 200n57; the Shifta War and, 20, 38; threat of, 75, 114, 135, 149, 152; threat of death and, 81; unknown authorization of, 92, 93, 96, 109, 130–31, 138. See also ATPU; disappearance, enforced
arrests, mass, 7, 38, 57, 58, 85, 101; Eastleigh raid and, 19–20, 89, 102, 111; the Kampala bombings and, 95; the Masjid Musa raid and, 85, 135, 151, 155
Asad, Talal, 33

Asians, 18, 62–63, 65, 176n94, 189n84

Atieno Odhiambo, E. S., 97

ATPU (Anti-Terror Police Unit), 83–85, 169n10; disappearances and, 3–4, 136; home raids by, 81; human rights organizations and, 1, 91–94; kidnappings, 83, 84, 85; military uniforms of, 81; murder of Aboud Rogo and, 94, 103, 135, 150; plain-clothes death squads, 3, 83–84; US funding/training of, 3, 81, 83, 104, 135–36. *See also* extrajudicial killings

AU (African Union, the), 174n69, 182n59, 182n67; depoliticization of intervention and, 35; intervention in Somalia, 49 (*see also* AMISOM); security architecture of, 41, 44. *See also* Organization of African Unity

Austin, Lloyd, 160, 161

Babu, Abdulrahman, 139

Bachmann, Jan, 169n13

Bakari, Mohamed, 98, 193n64, 193n73

Balala, Khalid, 99, 100, 150, 193n74

Bardawil, Fadi, 172n39, 174n68

Beckerleg, Susan, 199n42

Beckett, Greg, 93

Bell, Sandra, 139

belonging: benefits of, 20, 63; beyond borders, 38; civilization and, 13, 15, 161, 173n61; to the civilized world, 13; debates of, 38, 65, 148; fractured, 62; the home and, 113; new modes of, 27, 115; policy need for, 76; repoliticized, 18. *See also* citizenship; foreignness; indigeneity

Benjamin, Walter, 94, 192n41

Bhungalia, Lisa, 82, 88, 106, 112

Bishara, Amahl, 197nn82–83

Blackness: colonial-era mappings of, 17; difference within, 62; incorporation into empire, 49–51; modern construction of, 35; as monolithic, 176n96; as native, 73; as threat to order, 50–51;

as unstable category, 18–19, 28, 158, 184n97. *See also* race

Blunt, Robert, 180n26

borders: connections across, 18; Kenya–Uganda, 83; mobility across, 2; as suspect space, 18. *See also* worldmaking

borders, Kenya–Somalia: concern with Eritrea and, 42; detainees and, 1–2, 22, 168n6; justification for 2011 invasion of Somalia, 5, 40, 174n70; the Shifta War and, 35, 38, 177n104, 181n47; US interest in, 8; Wajir and, 39

Brand Kenya, 14, 26, 59, 60, 67, 68, 72, 74

Brickell, Katherine, 112

Brown, Katherine E., 196n56

Browne, Simone, 192

Bruner, Edward M., 71

Burton, Orisanmi, 141–42, 170n19, 202n15

Bush, George W., ix–x, 8, 148

Butler, Judith, 143–44

capitalism, racial, 16, 62, 67, 75, 185n2, 192n55

care: expectation of, 149; friendship as, 28, 137, 138, 155, 199n29; gendered, 29, 53–54; Muslim moral economies of, 95, 116, 130, 131, 132–33; work of, 54, 141–42

Central Intelligence Agency (CIA): coups backed by, 41; MYSTIC monitoring program, 90, 138; paramilitary training by, 5–6, 89, 126, 159, 169n10; secret prisons run by, 102–3; warlords backed by, 42. *See also* United States, the

Chome, Ngala, 65

Christianity: alliance with Muslim leaders, 22; American influence on, 22; Christians and Muslims in nonprofit work, 77; domination of Kenyan politics and, 22, 38, 65, 80; economic power in Kenya and, 65; influx on the coast, 58, 65, 187n29; as Kenyan majority, 19, 22, 38, 65, 80, 187nn29–30; morality of, 30; white, 16

CIA (Central Intelligence Agency): coups backed by, 41; MYSTIC monitoring program, 90, 138; paramilitary training by, 5–6, 89, 126, 159, 169n10; secret prisons run by, 102–3; warlords backed by, 42. *See also* United States, the

citizenship: conditional, 60; gendered, 102, 127; "good" or "bad," 22, 58–59, 77–78, 86; identification documents and, 1, 21, 58, 95, 97, 189n84, 192nn54–55; understandings of, 21–22, 148. *See also* belonging

civilization: belonging vs. exclusion, 13, 15, 161, 173n61; racialization of, 16

civil society, 21, 154; CVE workshops and, 77, 79, 82, 123, 125; heightened surveillance in, 60, 75; inclusion and, 76, 77

class, economic, 180n26, 188n43; difference and, 64; middle, 21, 26, 65, 120, 121, 145; state power and, 65; upper, 65; upper-middle, 116

Cold War, the, 8, 11, 13, 17, 41–42

Coleman, Simon, 139

colonialism: alterity and, 17; cartography and, 172n45; civilizational discourse and, 68, 69, 176n92; client states as form of, 41; "culture talk" of, 170n25; foreignness and, 26, 58, 59, 62, 65–66; gender and, 15, 27, 48, 71, 116, 124–25; geographic imaginaries of, 18; indirect rule and, 64, 76; land dispossession and, 68–69; legitimacy and, 97, 170n25 (*see also* anticolonialism); logics of, 21, 59, 67, 96; as military rule, 36–37; Omani rule as, 63–64; order and, 71, 86, 97; paternalism and, 37, 54; provoking anticolonialism, 36–37, 114; racialization of international knowledge and, 16; state of emergency under, 38, 70, 97–98, 147; symbolic victory over, 17; treatment of northeast Kenya in, 39; whiteness and, 26, 59, 60, 67, 68–69,

74–75, 192n54. *See also* neocolonialism; postcolonialism

colonialism, continuity of, 20, 25, 70, 79, 96; nostalgia and, 26, 59, 60, 71–72, 74–75

colonialism, counterinsurgency tactics of, 25, 35, 65, 86; collective punishment and, 20, 181n48; divide and rule tactics, 37–38; intelligence apparatus of, 137, 139–40, 199n33; social engineering and, 27, 116, 123, 124–25; state of emergency and, 38, 69–70, 97–98, 147–48

colonialism, racial systems of, 21, 54, 65–66, 157; Arabs within, 18, 64, 65, 187n41; Asians within, 18, 63; coastal Kenya and, 58; divide and rule and, 37–38; minorities within the colonized and, 18, 63; modes of control and, 116; natives/nonnatives and, 18, 62–63, 67–68, 73, 176n94, 187n41; spatial dimension of, 185n3; territory and, 62–63; tourism and, 71; war on terror reinscribing, 26

colonialism, violence and, 72, 74, 113, 157, 199n29; paramilitary units under, 38; policing within, 38, 96, 97–98

conspiracy theories, 27, 85–86, 94, 106

countering violent extremism (CVE), 102, 115–16, 123, 148; family life/parenting and, 122; foreign aid and, 60, 79, 82, 125–26, 148, 185n7; in Mombasa, 60, 77, 79, 125; in Nairobi, 122, 125

counterinsurgency: AMISOM and, 43; broad impact of, 147, 162; divide and rule and, 77, 202n15; doctrines of, 27, 111, 123, 170n19, 183n70; fragmentation and, 77, 142; the Global South's role in, 3; the home and, 113, 115, 123; laboratories for, 162, 169n13, 190n12; as necessary, 39, 53; in non-war spaces, 86, 169n13; public secrets and, 91–92; the Shifta War as, 20, 25, 35, 38–39; transmission of strategies for, 159;

women's gendered labor and, 54, 115–16, 122–24, 125, 126. *See also* colonialism, counter-insurgency tactics of; CVE; detention/arrest; policing; war on terror, the

counterterrorism, 149; abuses of, 90, 95–96, 122 (*see also* arrests, mass; disappearance, enforced; extrajudicial killings; policing, house raids and); AMISOM and, 43; challenging policies of, 21, 128, 129; containing populations and, 80; East African apparatus of, 8, 24, 95–96, 96; framing of the Muslim "community" and, 115; global apparatus of, 130; intent to contain populations and, 80 (*see also* Kenyan Muslims, as suspect population; violent extremism); as opaque, 12, 24, 86, 88, 95–96, 106, 109–10; pressure to embrace, 8; resistance to as suspicious, 91–92, 128; special police training and, 4, 12, 169n16 (*see also* ATPU); transnationality as suspect and, 2, 66, 116–17, 130, 195n32, 197nn82–83; US funding for, 5; US reliance on partner forces, 85–86, 88 (*see also* AFRICOM). *See also* CVE; geopolitics, as everyday reality; homeplace, the; informants; Kenya, security partnerships of; terrorism

coups, 6, 41, 47

criminalization, 199n29; of care, 95; of dissent, 86–87, 96–97; of the IPK, 96–97; of Kenyan Muslims as a whole, 7, 19, 22, 61, 97, 100, 126; of Kenyan Somalis, 20–21; of NGOs, 105; of young Muslim men, 28, 135, 137, 142, 144, 146, 155

crisis: democracy and, 6; in Haiti, 201n6; International Crisis Group, 42, 87; military deployment in, 41; of the youth, 144. *See also* Kenya, 2007 presidential elections in

cultural politics, 25, 32, 35–36, 40, 45–46, 55

CVE (countering violent extremism), 102, 115–16, 123, 148; family life/parenting and, 122; foreign aid and, 60, 79, 82, 125–26, 148, 185n7; in Mombasa, 60, 77, 79, 125; in Nairobi, 122, 125

Dar es Salaam, 139; US embassy bombings in, 3, 7. *See also* Tanzania

decolonization: decentering the West and, 172n39, 174n69; Kenyan independence and, 38, 177n104; pluralization and, 8; tourism and, 74–75

democracy: crisis and, 6; definition of, 6, 150; emergence from colonialism and, 37; Kenya as, 5–6, 140; promotion of, 5, 49, 105, 174n69; tensions of equality and, 22. *See also* liberalism

detention: AFRICOM sites and, 10, *11*; conventional warfare and, 147; counterinsurgency and, 147; rehabilitation as basis for, 148–49; UN support for indefinite, 149; US role in, 24, 96. *See also* arrests; disappearance, enforced; renditions

detention of activists, 83, 95, 102, 109–10, 116–17, 126–28, 129–32, 168n18; Al-Amin Kimathi, 24, 95–96

development: assistance for, 5; gender and, 115; military defense of, 42, 174n70; promotion of, 105; soft power and, 122; state promises of, 39; underdevelopment, 37; UN operations and, 173n56; US in Haiti, 202n12. *See also* foreign aid

difference, 18, 158, 170n25; articulation of, 7, 77; the coast and, 26, 59, 64, 67, 176n92; doctrinal, 65, 66, 193n71; flattened, 62; gendered, 53; heightened, 64; manipulation of, 193n71; political change and, 49; understanding/managing, 76; as unstable category, 61–62. *See also* racialization dignity, 72–73, 199n29

dignity, war on terror assaulting, 4, 7; cumulative effects of, 82, 146; standing against, 62, 113, 116, 132–33, 143, 202n15

disappearance, enforced, 5, 73, 104, 114, 145–46; geopolitics and, 27; prior to the 2007 elections, 3; questioning, 91, 92, 93; reporting, 128; rise in, 3–4, 58, 84–85, 135, 136; the RRT and, 89; spectral violence and, 85–86, 89; spousal trauma and, 127–28; supporting tourism and, 76; surveillance and, 90, 138; tracking, 95, 101, 102–3, 130–31. See also arrest; detention; renditions

dispossession, 16, 68, 69, 71, 80

dissent, repression of, 5, 86–87, 96–97, 98, 124, 145

divide and rule, 37, 50–51, 77, 100, 200n46

Djibouti, 10, 40, 43, 160

donors: activism and, 91; to the African Union, 43; civil society programming and, 76, 79, 82, 125; criminalization of dissent and, 105; human rights training and, ix; Kenya's donor-partners, 6, 104, 105, 146; minimal scrutiny of paramilitary action, 6. See also foreign aid

drones, 111, 113, 137, 194n17, 198n6; dramatized use, 115, 118, 119, 121; use in Somalia, 4, 10, 87

drug trafficking/use, 42, 144–45, 199n42

East Africa, 6; categorizations of Islam in, 66–67, 122, 155; counterterror apparatus in, 8, 95–96, 106; increase in home raids in, 111; Muslims in, 7–8, 111, 122, 172n37 (see also Kenyan Muslims); Omani effect on, 63–64; precolonial coastal divisions in, 63; as relational space, 16, 21; as theater of operations, 10; treatment of female detainees in, 168n6; US embassy bombings in, 3, 7, 58; waning US hegemony in, 171n30; war on terror in, 4,

7–8, 10, 12, 24 (see also AFRICOM). See also Africa; colonialism; tourism; individual countries

Eastleigh raid, 19–20, 89, 102, 111

economy, global, 44, 60, 73, 116

economy, Kenyan: Christian power within, 65; COVID and, 12–13; as EAC leader, 46; economic development, 71, 174n70; foreign investment and, 72, 174n70; marginalization within, 39, 99, 135, 144, 154; need for credit, 12, 173n55; pressure placed on, 8, 12–13, 171n28, 173n55. See also development; tourism

Edwards, Erica, 49, 50–51, 177n109

empire: AFRICOM as facilitating, 10; anti-imperialism and, 12, 42, 139, 158, 161–62 (see also Land and Freedom Army); consequences of questioning, 105; containment and, 21; cultural imperialism, 173n61; as diffuse/elastic, 8, 10, 12, 88, 91, 104–6, 107; financial, 12–13; formations of, 8, 25, 45, 86, 158, 178n117; imagined geographies of, 24; intimacy with, 44, 106–7; maintenance of, 56, 82; need for gendered roles, 125; race and, 9, 16, 49, 50–51, 175n82 (see also racialization); right to violence and, 118–21, 143–44; romanticized encounters with, 9, 115, 118–22, 119, 122, 128; sensorial life of, 19; threat to, 9, 50–51, 161; the US and, 8, 88, 159, 160, 168n8, 171n30. See also colonialism; entanglement; homeplace as site of geopolitical concern; interventionism; policing; power

Enloe, Cynthia, 53, 183n89

entanglement, 28, 178n117; diverting attention from, 56, 66, 74; in the drug trade, 199n42; of gender and geopolitics, 115, 124; imperceptible, 45; imperial, 6, 14, 21, 55–56, 85, 124, 158, 159; increasing, 85; political and economic, 44; of war-making and race-making, 7, 9, 28, 45, 158; in white supremacy, 26, 60, 74. *See also* home-place as site of geopolitical concern; interventionism

epistemology: Euro-American, 176n96; frames of, 143–44; geographic, 62; phantom, 86, 106; pluriversal, 158; whiteness as tool of, 16–17

equality: gender and, 53–54, 122–23; as idea, 17; legal, 22, 76–77; performance of, 160; as stated commitment, 21; struggle for, 49–50

Ethiopia: military budget/size, 15, 175n73; new alliances post-9/11, 42; renditions to, 3, 95–96; Somalia Front-line States Summit and, 40

Ethiopia, invasion of Somalia (2006) and: AMISOM and, 43, 174n66; calls to withdraw, 182n67; as ICU action, 42; refugees from, 1–3; renditions and, 2–3; United Nations backing of, 43; US backing of, 1, 42–43

ethnicity: colonial categories of, 62, 63, 67–68, 97, 176n94; constitutional rights and, 189n84; within Kenyan Muslims, 19, 65, 193n71; maintaining divisions of, 65, 180n26; political alliances and, 98; precolonial categories of, 176n92; tensions of, 5, 174n70, 176n85; war and, 13, 176n85. *See also* Kenya, ethnic Somalis in; race

ethnography, 21, 26, 27, 55–56, 107, 115, 117, 143. See also *individual narratives*

Euro-American military, fictional, 115, 118–22, *119*, *122*, 128

Euro-Americans: as donors, 6; notions of Blackness and, 176n96; as policymakers, 12, 15; as saviors, 158; as security partners, 6, 88, 105, 109, 159; as tourists, 67, 71, 76; travel advisories issued by, 60, 73

exceptionalism: Black, 50–51; Kenyan, 7, 13, 17, 26, 51–52, 161; US, 12

extrajudicial killings, 73, 76, 89, 127, 149; house raids and, 81, 111, 114; human

rights organizations questioning, 91, 92, 93, 94; prior to the war on terror, 85; rise in, 58, 81, 101, 135. *See also* Rogo, Aboud; violence

extremism, 27, 42, 142, 148, 154. *See also* CVE; terrorism; violent extremism

Eye in the Sky (Hood), 115, 118–22, *119*, *122*, 128, 196n44

Fanon, Frantz, 72, 114, 142, 185n3

FBI (Federal Bureau of Investigation), 2, 7, 58, 131–32, 172n37

Feldman, Gregory, xi

femininity: defying stereotypes of, 102, 125, 127; home and, 102, 111, 112; militarized, 53–54, 120, 121, 184n107; monitoring children and, 27, 102, 111, 116, 132, 196n56 (*see also* CVE); security feminists and, 120, 121; varying treatment of, 125, 168n6; and winning the family unit, 115

Ferguson, James, 173n61

foreign aid, 67, 88; security-related, 44, 60, 142, 148 (*see also* CVE). *See also* donors

foreignness: Arab and Swahili Muslims and, 26, 58, 59–60, 63–64, 67; colonial categories of, 26, 58, 59, 62, 65–66; as demonized, 73; as discursive strategy, 66; Islam and, 18, 59, 66–67, 187n32; Kenyan Somalis and, 26, 59, 77; of Muslim terrorists, 17, 58, 66, 73; repoliticized, 18. *See also* belonging

Foucault, Michel, 147

Foxton Media: *Mission to Rescue*, 25, 36, 52–53, 55–56

friendship: in anthropology, 138–39, 198n16; ethnography and, 143; as reciprocal care, 28, 137, 138, 155, 199n29; remaking the self and, 28, 137, 142; as resistance, 134, 139–41, 146, 156, 199n33; strains on, 136; young Muslim men and, 28, 135, 152–54, 155–56

Gaddafi, Muammar, 41

Gathara, Patrick, 31, 74, 179n8

gender: colonial control and, 27, 48, 68, 71; differential effect of the war on terror and, 120, 127–28; (re)fashioning of, 125, 183n89; hierarchy and, 33; militarism and, 25, 28, 35, 53–54, 123, 137, 142, 154; reform and, 148. *See also* femininity; homeplace, the; masculinity; paternalism

General Service Unit (GSU)/Rapid Response Team (RRT), 89, 126, 169n10

geographies: colonial-era mappings of Islam and, 17, 65–66; conceptualizations of difference and, 18, 59, 61–62, 63, 66; distinctions of, 17–18, 39, 62, 64, 65, 159; of empire, 4, 24, 173n45, 185n3; enlivened, 24, 107; of expanded policing, 4, 111, 114, 132, 190n12 (*see also* policing, house raids and); imaginaries of, 18, 24, 26, 59, 118, 120; navigating policed landscapes and, 27, 86, 87, 94, 103, 130, 133; prejudice and, 66; racialization and, 60, 65–66, 79–80, 88, 185n3; of relation, 16, 17–18, 62, 65, 176n96, 178n117; shape-shifting, 3, 27, 87, 107; shifting, 87, 107, 162; urban, 27, 81, 86, 88, 103, 107 (*see also* gray zones; urban spaces)

geopolitics: affective, 15, 60, 73, 124, 125, 126, 175n74; analysis of, 8; economic, 60, 73; Ethiopian concerns of, 42; expanded concept of, 15, 45, 53; gender and, 15, 25, 35–36, 53, 115; landscape of, 5, 25, 171n30; obscured involvement in, 27, 53, 85–86; of the present, 8, 24–25; of race, 15–19, 21, 49, 60; sites of, 27, 110, 112, 115, 117–18, 130, 175n74 (*see also* homeplace as site of geopolitical concern); US positioning and, 160, 171n30. *See also* AFRICOM

geopolitics, as everyday reality, 25, 27, 86, 87, 103, 106; exchange of information and, 110, 115, 130; as surveillance

awareness, 136. *See also* war on terror, the, the embodied dimensions of

Getachew, Adom, 9, 172n39

Gilmore, Ruth Wilson, 172n38

Glassman, Jonathan, 63–64, 176n92

Global South, the: foreign credit and, 12; gender essentialization of, 126; postindependence in, 9; racialization of, 88, 126; role in entangled pacifications, 3, 96, 159; state relationships within, 45, 158, 159, 161; as US military laboratory, 87, 159, 169n13. See also *individual countries*

Gordon, Avery, 114, 175n83

Gqola, Pumla Dineo, 54

gray zones, 4, 87–90, 106, 152

Great Britain. *See* colonialism; United Kingdom, the

Greenburg, Jennifer, 115, 125, 184n107

Grovogui, Siba, 16, 174n69

GSU (General Service Unit)/Rapid Response Team (RRT), 89, 126, 169n10

Haiti: Kenyan intervention in, 9, 28, 157, 158, 159–60, 161–62, 201n7; revolution and, 9, 157, 161; US intervention in, 160, 201nn6–7, 202n12

Haki Africa, 92–94; disappeared persons and, 84–85, 92, 93; legal activity and, 92; Majengo police raid and, 101–2; as tied to Al-Shabaab, 105

heroism: search for national, 33, 34, 48, 180n26; security, 30, 31, 32, 34, 45

hierarchies, 21, 61–62. *See also* race, hierarchy and

Hoffman, Danny, 87, 182n70

homeplace, the, 111–12, 125; belonging and, 27, 110, 114–15, 116, 117, 130, 132–33; as place of geopolitical knowledge, 115, 130; politics of warning and, 117; as thoroughfare, 113, 116; violence as haunting, 114. *See also* policing, house raids and

homeplace as site of geopolitical concern, 112, 124, 129, 130, 132; fictionalized, 115,

117–18, 119, 121. *See also* policing, house raids and

Hood, Gavin: *Eye in the Sky*, 115, 118–22, *119*, *122*, 128

hooks, bell, 113, 133

human rights: abuses of, 2, 76, 77, 84, 90, 95 (*see also* Leahy Law, the); depoliticization of, 90; Kenyan Human Rights Commission, 85; as lens, 22

human rights organizations, 90–96, 101; condemnation of Kenyan actions, 19–20; documentation of abuses, 2, 76, 77, 84, 90; funding and, 91; international, 19, 76, 95–96, 117; International Center for Transitional Justice, ix, x–xi; Kenyan National Human Rights Commission, 103–4; Muslim Human Rights Forum, 22; Muslims for Human Rights, 77, 79, 94–95, 100, 105; trust in the security apparatus and, 77, 79. *See also* Haki Africa

ICC (International Criminal Court), 5, 174n70

ICU (Islamic Courts Union), 1, 2, 3, 42, 168n6. *See also* Somalia

identification documents: biometric, 89–90; colonial (kipande), 97, 192nn54–55; constitutional right to, 189n84; difficulty obtaining, 21, 58, 95; seizure of, 1

identities: cultural, 16, 66; culture talk and, 66, 170n25; debated, 38; linked to territory, 62; mistaken, 81, 89; political, 16, 48, 66, 99, 135, 170n25; religious, 66, 193n65, 193n71 (*see also* Christianity; Kenyan Muslims); transnational, 64. *See also* ethnicity; race; racialization

ideology: alliances of, 98; conflicting, 157–58; of the homeplace, 117–18; Islamist, 42, 186n9, 193n65; of militarism and war-making, 33, 53, 55; of order, 97, 137; political, 80–81, 150, 193n65; in rehabilitation programs, 146–47, 148; whiteness as, 70, 187n43

Ihmoud, Sarah, 186n12

Indian Ocean: Kenya's strategic position on, 8; transregional connections of, 18, 58, 62, 66–67, 116

indigeneity, 26, 58, 59, 65, 66–67, 187n32. *See also* belonging

inequality, 17, 36, 58, 72, 73, 161

informants: CVE training and, 77; erosion of bonds and, 138, 145, 146; fictionalized, 119; history in Kenya, 137; recruitment of, 83, 149, 151, 156

instability: anxieties of, 67; Haiti and, 160, 202n12; Kenyan law and, 179n15; solutions to, 12, 35, 42, 44, 88, 169n13; stereotypes of, 7, 16, 35, 88

intelligence, 103, 149; British, 105–6; colonial apparatus of, 97–98, 137, 139–40, 199n33; deficits in, 125, 146; fictionalized, 118; hidden insurgent assumptions of, 112, 130; National Intelligence Service, 101, 137, 197n80; US, 105–6, 160, 172n37, 182n64 (*see also* CIA). *See also* informants; surveillance

International Center for Transitional Justice, ix, x–xi

International Criminal Court (ICC), 5, 174n70

International Crisis Group, 42, 87

interventionism: critical theory of, 14, 174n68; expanding, 14; as gendered, 25, 45–54; in Haiti, 9, 28, 157, 159–60, 161–62, 201nn6–7; legitimating, 16, 28, 40–45, 54, 157–58, 170n19, 182n59; as moral act, 40, 41, 52; norms and politics of, 14; Pan-African rhetoric and, 9, 28, 157–58, 161; privileging of, 25; public anxiety and, 32–33; as relationship to the wider world, 28, 35, 41–42; reluctance toward, 35, 40–41; the "responsibility to protect" and, 35, 44; subtle, 26; US, 12, 26, 160, 201n6; US avoidance of, 12, 88, 160 (*see also* AFRICOM). *See also* AMISOM; Ethiopia, invasion of Somalia (2006) and; militarism

Iraq, 4, 10, 54, 66, 144, 162, 168n6

Islam: burial customs of, 94–95; colonial-
era mappings of, 17, 65–66; converts
to, 118, 128; foreign/Arab vs. local, 18,
59, 65–67; heightened political presence of, 99; individual understanding
of, 150; as irrational, 146; political
culture hostility to, 22, 148, 186n9 (*see
also* Islamic Party of Kenya); restoring
order and, 145, 199n42; self-appointed
experts on, 66; transnationalism
and, 62, 99; as violent, 13, 14, 17, 118
(*see also* violent extremism); war
on terror as war on, 7, 61. *See also*
Kenyan Muslims; mosques; Muslims;
radicalism

Islamic Courts Union (ICU), 1, 3, 42. *See
also* Somalia

Islamic Party of Kenya (IPK), 96,
98–100, 193n71, 193n74, 193nn64–65,
200n57

Israel: biometric technology and, 89–90;
Kenya's security partnership with, 89,
136, 169n10, 191n25; Paradise Hotel
ownership and, 67, 100; settler colonialism in, 113, 186n12, 197nn82–83

Jackson, Will, 71–72

Juma, Monica, 52, 56

Junaid, Mohamad, 103

Kalenjin people, ix, 37

Kamau, Wanjiru, 171n28

Kampala: Al-Shabaab attack in, 24, 83, 95,
102, 109, 110, 168n18; arrest of activist
relatives in, 110, 130; arrest of activists
in, 24, 95, 168n18; Luzira Prison in, 95,
117, 126–27, 129, 132, 192n49. *See also*
Uganda

KANU (Kenya African National Union),
98, 100

Kapadia, Ronak, 19, 172n45

Kaplan, Caren, 172n45

Kassem, Ramzi, 127–28

Katitu, Christopher, 44–45, 56

Katumanga, Masumbayi, 37

KDF (Kenya Defense Forces), 54, 104,
169n16, 173n56; citizen support of,
31, 36; conflicting framing in
Westgate attack, 30, 31; constitutional
deployment within Kenya, 179n15;
critique/ridicule of, 14–15, 45–46,
55; El Adde attack and, 34; internal
deployment and, 32; KDF Queens,
54; Kenya Defense Forces Day, 31, 55;
masculinity and, 35–36, 45–49, 53,
54, 55; propaganda for, 25, 36, 52–53,
55–56; public visibility of, 34, 46;
recruitment of Kenyan Muslims, 135;
secrecy on casualties, 55; service in
Somalia and, 44–45; state spending
on, 15, 43, 175n73; symbolism of, 25,
30, 46–47, 47, 48, 73; willingness to
deploy, 36

Kelley, Robin D. G., 141

Kennedy, Dane, 188n43

Kenya: critique of as terrorist sympathiz-
ing, 101, 128; independence of, 20,
31, 35, 38, 39, 64; international image
and, 5, 13–14, 15, 25, 36, 55–56, 73, 104
(*see also* Brand Kenya); intervention in Haiti, 9, 28, 157, 158, 159–60,
161–62, 201n7; as key US ally, 5, 8,
104, 109–10, 159; land ownership in,
58, 65, 68–69, 71, 74; as leader, 7, 17,
53, 158, 201n7; military spending of,
13, 15, 175n73; as moral force, 14, 15,
30, 52; as needing intervention, 120;
Prevention of Terrorism Act, 100–101;
security architecture of, 5; Security
Laws Amendment Act (2014), 101;
the Shifta War and, 20, 25, 35, 38–39;
states of emergency in, 20, 38–39,
70, 97–98, 147; 2010 constitution, 6,

32, 76, 179n15, 189n84; the UN and, 14, 45, 51–52, 157, 173n56; use of Pan-African language, 9, 28, 157, 161; US military bases in, 10–11, *11*, 55 (*see also* AFRICOM); US security assistance and, 5, 8; view of place on world stage, 48, 52, 158; *Wanted* billboards in, 19, 134–35, 144, 145. *See also* Islamic Party of Kenya; Kenyatta, Jomo; Kenyatta, Uhuru; Moi, Daniel Arap; security apparatus, Kenyan

Kenya, cities of: Lamu, 60, 99, 103, 108, 116, 185n6; Malindi, 60, 94, 99, 153; Mandera, 92, 101–2; Wajir, 10, 32, 39, 104. *See also* Mombasa; Nairobi

Kenya, coast of: as Al-Shabaab recruitment area, 58, 60; failed autonomy of, 59, 64, 65, 80; influx of Christians in, 58, 65, 187n29; and Kenya as place-in-the-world, 59; land ownership in, 58, 65, 71, 80; Muslims as foreigners and, 58, 59; negotiated power relations and, 61, 81–82; as Oriental, 26, 59–60, 67; police cooperation and, 77–79; questioned indigeneity and, 26, 58, 59, 65, 66–67, 187n32; race and, 26, 63–67; security raids in, 58, 67; siege anxiety in, 81–82; as site of extremism, 154; tourism and, 26, 58, 59–60, 67, 75, 76, 80, 199n42. *See also* Kenyan Muslims; Mombasa; tourism

Kenya, economy of: Christian power within, 65; COVID and, 12–13; as EAC leader, 46; economic development, 71, 174n70; foreign investment and, 72, 174n70; marginalization within, 39, 99, 135, 144, 154; need for credit, 12, 173n55; pressure placed on, 8, 12–13, 171n28, 173n55. *See also* development; tourism

Kenya, elites of: Arabocentrism and, 63–64; aspirational whiteness and, 70; fetishization of order and, 86, 97; Kenya's leadership against terror and, 6–7; Kenya's public image and, 13–14, 60, 72, 142 (*see also* Brand Kenya); as maintaining colonial power relations, 60, 180n26; as masculinist world, 10; neocolonial tourism and, 74; normalization of militarism and, 9; treatment of soldiers and, 44–45

Kenya, ethnic Somalis in, 26; collective punishment of, 20–21, 35, 38, 39; colonial categorization of, 18, 26, 37, 59, 63; as foreigners, 18, 26, 59, 77, 176n93, 177n104, 189n84; history of vilification of, 20, 35, 39, 177n104 (*see also* Shifta War, the); independence-era anxieties, 65; recruited to fight in Somalia, 135; as terror threat, 29, 35, 66–67, 77, 89, 118 (*see also* Eastleigh raid). *See also* Kenya, coast of; Kenyan Muslims

Kenya, security partnerships of, 3, 8, 42, 80, 87, 89, 103; Euro-American, 6, 88, 105, 109, 159; Israel, 89, 136, 169n10, 191n25; public critique of, 122, 135; US, 8, 104, 109–10, 159 (*see also* AFRICOM)

Kenya, 2007 presidential elections in, 13, 46, 72, 88, 157; anti-Muslim actions before, 3; International Criminal Court (ICC) investigations, 5, 174n70; violence and, ix, 5, 13, 72, 85, 157, 175n70

Kenya, 2011 invasion of Somalia and, 5, 30, 39–40, 177n70; AMISOM and, 43; effects of extended deployment, 44–45; international law and, 40, 182n69; as new interventionism, 14–15; questioning repercussions of, 135

Kenya African National Union (KANU), 98, 100

Kenya Defense Forces (KDF), 54, 104, 169n16, 173n56; citizen support of, 31, 36; conflicting framing in Westgate attack, 30, 31; constitutional deployment within Kenya, 179n15; critique/ridicule of, 14–15, 45–46, 55; El Adde attack and, 34; internal deployment and, 32; KDF Queens, 54; Kenya Defense Forces Day, 31, 55; masculinity and, 35–36, 45–49, 53, 54, 55; propaganda for, 25, 36, 52–53, 55–56; public visibility of, 34, 46; recruitment of Kenyan Muslims, 135; secrecy on casualties, 55; service in Somalia and, 44–45; state spending on, 15, 43, 175n73; symbolism of, 25, 30, 46–47, 47, 48, 73; willingness to deploy, 36

Kenyan Muslims, 6, 19, 77, 112–13, 115, 136, 148; actions against before 2007 presidential elections, 3; activism associated with terrorism, 95; anticipation of violence and, 106–7; appointments under Daniel Arap Moi, 22; coded as foreign, 17; good/bad Muslims and, 66, 120; as minority demographic, 65, 95, 187nn29–30; Mombasa demographics of, 65; Muslims for Human Rights, 77, 79, 94–95, 100, 105; political culture hostility to, 22, 148, 186n9 (see also Islamic Party of Kenya); political inclusion and, 6, 22, 76, 99; racial/ethnic distinctions within, 19, 65; racialization of, 19, 26, 29, 58, 59, 116, 120, 121; as unified community, 19, 65; US in Kenyan affairs and, 109–10; view of war on terror as war on Islam and Muslims, 7, 61, 66, 80, 186n9. See also Kenya, coast of; Mombasa

Kenyan Muslims, as suspect population: difficulty obtaining identification documents and, 21, 58, 95; Masjid Musa police raid and, 84–85, 135, 150–51, 155; police abuse/harassment and, 3, 57–58, 61, 76, 82, 85, 106–7, 146 (see also arrests, mass; ATPU; policing, house raids and); political organization as suspect, 96–97, 98 (see also Islamic Party of Kenya); public speech/critique and, 22, 75–76, 79, 81, 93–95, 107, 145, 150; questioned indigeneity of, 26, 58, 59, 65, 66–67, 187n32; stereotyped as terrorists, 19, 22, 73, 76, 118, 119, 121, 126 (see also CVE). See also abduction; paranoia; renditions; surveillance; violent extremism

Kenyan Muslims, marginalization of, 7, 80, 125–26; Al-Shabaab recruitment and, 135; difficulty obtaining identification and, 21, 58, 95; dismissal of, 77, 79; drug trade associated with, 145; economic, 39, 99, 135, 144, 154; failure to condemn, 146; political inclusion to combat, 6; the Shifta War and, 38–39. See also Islamic Party of Kenya; policing, house raids and

Kenyan Muslims (young men): criminalization of, 28, 135, 137, 142, 144, 146, 155; feelings of siege, 81–82; making sense of the world, 137, 150, 155–56; as manipulated/vulnerable, 28, 137, 146; psychological effect of disappeared peers, 135; reform and, 28, 137, 147, 148 (see also rehabilitation); stereotypes of, 6, 28, 133, 136, 137, 142–43, 152, 154–55. See also friendship

Kenyan Muslims (young men), targeted by police, 84, 135, 147, 148; effect of arrest/imprisonment on social status, 153–54; police killings of, 111, 135; police roundups and, 57–58, 101, 126, 135–36; Wanted billboard and, 134–35, 144, 145. See also arrests, mass; CVE; disappearance, enforced; rehabilitation

Kenyatta, Jomo, 33, 56, 59, 71, 74, 139–40; the Shifta War and, 20, 25, 35, 38–39

Kenyatta, Uhuru, 14, 29; Africa–Caribbean Community Summit and, 158; hidden insurgents concept and, 112–13; increase in police forces under, 5; masculinity and, 46–48, 47; rise in Al-Shabaab attacks and, 30–31; Security Laws Amendment Act (2014) and, 101; tourism and, 73

Khalili, Laleh, 112, 120, 123, 147, 159, 170n19

Khayyat, Munira, 114

Kibaki, Mwai, 40, 72

kidnapping, 40, 185n6; colonial power and, 36; state-sponsored, 2, 81, 84, 89, 91, 127–28, 131 (see also renditions)

Kikuyu people, ix, 33, 70, 71, 97, 180nn26–27

Kilcullen, David, 115

Kimani, Martin, 157, 158

Kimari, Wangui, 81, 88–89

Kimathi, Al-Amin, 22, 23, 95–96

kipande, 97, 192nn54–55. See also identification documents

Kirshenblatt-Gimblett, Barbara, 71

knowledge: dangerous, 94; dismissal of, 79, 82; embodied formations of, 25, 94, 106 (see also war on terror, embodied dimensions of); gendered, 124; professionalization of, 87, 90; racialization of, 16; subjugated/subaltern, 61, 82, 130, 145, 162; as suspect, 92; of the war on terror's infrastructure, 96; worldmaking and, 61

knowledge, everyday geopolitical, 106, 138, 141; navigating policed landscapes and, 27, 86, 87, 94, 103, 130, 133; secrecy and, 91–92, 145; sharing of, 110, 115, 130

Kramer, Paul, 173n48, 175n82

bin Laden, Osama, 80, 113, 118

Lamu, 60, 99, 103, 108, 116, 185n6

Land and Freedom Army (Mau Mau), 133; as anticolonial symbol, 9, 180n27; collective punishment and, 20; colonial ban on, 33; colonial counterinsurgency and, 35; colonial framing of, 69–70; colonial police and military powers against, 38, 86; colonial state of emergency and, 97–98; conflicting sentiments about, 33, 180n26; female membership in, 125

Leahy Law, the, 89, 159, 191n23

legal system: acquittal and rearrest of activists, 131–32; activists' navigation of, 109, 110, 128, 129; advocacy seen as terrorism link, 105; antiterror legislation, 3, 97, 100–101, 150, 171n28; circumvention of, 89, 159, 168n3; colonial, 62, 64, 68, 69; expanded police powers and, 3, 85, 100; frustrations with, 102; Islamic, 1, 3, 42, 94; the Leahy Law and, 89, 159, 191n23; postponed court dates and, 92; terror suspects' lack of access to, 90. See also criminalization

legitimacy: of imperialism, 16, 97, 118; of police as protection, 79; of racialized law, 62, 176n94; of representation, 96–97, 98; of violence, 30, 33, 79, 118, 121, 168n8

legitimacy of militarism/war-making, 6, 28, 43, 49, 89–90, 137, 170n19; legality and, 5, 182n69

Li, Darryl, 13, 66, 185n110, 195n32

liberalism: feminism and, 126; governance and, 6, 149; intervention as modernity and, 49; intervention as obligation and, 41–42, 170n19; legality of war and, 5, 182n69; racial, 17, 49–51; rehabilitation and, 147; war/police distinction and, 169n14. See also democracy

Libya, 13, 41, 168n4, 174n69, 182n60

Lubin, Alex, 169n8

Luo people, ix, 186n27

Lutz, Catherine, 32–33

Macharia, Keguro, 46, 176n96

Machold, Rhys, 190n12

Mahmood, Saba, 22

Maira, Sunaina, 138

Malcolm X, 139

Malindi, 60, 94, 99, 153

Mama, Amina, 33, 36–37

Mamdani, Mahmood: Cold War
    Africa and, 11; "culture talk" and, 66,
    170n25; "define and rule" and, 76;
    "subject races" and, 18, 62–63, 67–68,
    187n41

manhood. See masculinity

masculinity, 10, 141, 153, 185n110; Uhuru
    Kenyatta and, 46–48, 47; making of,
    155–56, 199n32; militarism and, 35–36,
    45–49, 53, 54, 183n89, 184n107; pater-
    nalism and, 15, 29, 37, 40, 52, 161; per-
    formance of, 25, 48; questioned, 14–15,
    25, 45–46; the war on terror and, 15, 25,
    45–46, 48–49, 53, 55, 183n89

Masjid Musa: raid and mass arrests,
    84–85, 135, 150–51, 155. See also Rogo,
    Aboud

Mau Mau. See Land and Freedom Army

Mayers Ranch, 71–72. See also tourism

Mazrui, Alamin, 71, 140

Mazrui, Ali, 80, 100

McClintock, Ann, 48

McFadden, Patricia, 37

media, global, 6, 13, 29, 76, 137–38, 144,
    159. See also Eye in the Sky (Hood)

media, Kenyan: Christian majority sensi-
    bility and, 19; coverage of surveillance,
    90, 137–38; the ICU and, 42; lauding of
    military and, 29–30, 31–32; mytholo-
    gizing masterminds, 117; perpetuat-
    ing Muslim stereotypes and, 67, 142,
    154–55; security as responsibility and,
    40, 145; shaping response to events, 30,
    56, 89, 144, 145; transnational Muslim
    militancy and, 67, 100. See also Mission
    to Rescue (Foxton Media)

media, social: critique of tourism indus-
    try on, 74; deleting, 151–52; document-
    ing prayer on, 108; Kenyan opinion of
    Somalis on, 52; public opinion of the
    military on, 29, 34, 55; questioning the
    security state on, 134–35; seeking dis-
    appeared people on, 131

Mesok, Elizabeth, 126

Mijikenda people, 100, 186n26

militarism: colonial, 36–37; as deviant,
    49; everyday experience of, 25; Uhuru
    Kenyatta and, 46–47, 47; legitimacy of,
    6, 43, 49, 137, 170n19; liberalism and,
    41–42; masculinity and, 35–36, 45–49,
    53, 54, 183n89, 184n107; as moral, 40;
    normalization of, 36–47, 47; overt, 26;
    public support for, 46; as subtle, 26,
    33, 34, 35, 111; as symbolic victory over
    colonial legacies, 17

military, Kenyan. See KDF

Mission to Rescue (Foxton Media), 25, 36,
    52–53, 55–56

Mitchell, Sean T., 106

Mogadishu, 1, 2, 24, 40, 52, 102–3. See also
    Somalia

Mohamud, Hassan Sheikh, 40

Moi, Daniel Arap: conflicting interests of,
    193n73; creation of special police units,
    98, 198n8; IPK and, 98–100; Muslim
    appointments under, 22

Mombasa: Al-Shabaab recruitment in,
    135, 144; CVE programs in, 60, 77, 79,
    125; danger of public critique in, 75–76,
    79, 93–94, 107, 145, 150; importance of
    port of, 65, 144; IPK support in, 99;
    Majengo neighborhood, 81, 84, 101,
    135, 149–50; Muslim demographics
    of, 21, 65; Old Town, 58, 59, 75–76, 81,
    152; Paradise Hotel bombing, 67, 100;
    popularity of Osama bin Laden in, 80;
    protests in, 94, 150; Sakina mosque,
    146; security operations in, 32, 58, 67;
    security-related infrastructure in, 58,

88–89; stereotypes of, 59–60, 67, 76, 102; tourist killings in, 76; 2015 police raid in, 57–58, 61, 82; US base in, 10. *See also* Haki Africa

Mombasa, police security operations in: colonial, 97; home raids, 81, 111, 126; mosque raids, 84–85, 101–2, 135, 150–51, 155; nighttime checkpoints and, 152; post-Paradise Hotel bombing, 67; rehabilitation programs and, 146–47, 148–49; roundups of young men, 57–58; threat of, 75, 103; *Wanted* billboard, 134–35, 144, 145

morality: Christian, 30; intervention and, 35, 40–45, 52, 174n68; Islamic, 95, 145; Kenya as force of, 14, 15, 30, 52; panics of, 98; racialization of, 16; rehabilitation and, 148; suspicions about, 18; violence to, 72

mosques: imams as informants in, 146; as places of radicalization, 112–13; raids of, 84–85, 101–2, 135, 150–51, 155; social media in, 108; surveillance of, 81, 153. *See also* Islam

Mozambique, 11, 14

Mungai, Christine, 16–17, 75

Museveni, Yoweri, 14, 40, 45, 48

Musila, Grace, 48, 68, 183n86, 184n91

Muslims: "culture talk" and, 66, 171n25; demographics in Africa, 18; good/bad, 66, 120; mobility of as threat, 2, 66, 130; stereotypes of women's agency and, 126; terrorist stereotype and, 6, 14, 17, 22, 29, 73 (see also *Eye in the Sky* (Hood); *Mission to Rescue* (Foxton Media)). *See also* Islam

Muslims, Kenyan, 6, 19, 77, 112–13, 115, 136, 148; activism associated with terrorism, 95; anticipation of violence and, 106–7; anti-Muslim actions before 2007 presidential elections, 3; appointments under Daniel Arap Moi, 22; coded as foreign, 17; good/bad Muslims and, 66,

120; as minority demographic, 65, 95, 187nn29–30; Mombasa demographics of, 65; Muslims for Human Rights (MUHURI), 77, 79, 94–95, 100, 105; political culture hostility to, 22, 148, 186n9 (*see also* Islamic Party of Kenya); political inclusion and, 6, 22, 76, 99; racial/ethnic distinctions within, 19, 65; racialization as Arab/Swahili, 26, 58, 59; racialization of, 19, 29, 116, 120, 121; as unified community, 19, 65; US in Kenyan affairs and, 109–10; war on terror as war on Islam and Muslims and, 7, 61, 66, 80, 186n9. *See also* Kenya, ethnic Somalis in; Kenya, marginalization of Muslim minority in; Mombasa

Muslims, Kenyan (as suspect population): difficulty obtaining identification documents and, 21, 58, 95; Masjid Musa police raid and, 84–85, 135, 150–51, 155; police abuse/harassment, 3, 57–58, 61, 76, 82, 85, 106–7, 146 (*see also* arrests, mass; ATPU; policing, house raids and); political organization as suspect, 96–97, 98 (*see also* Islamic Party of Kenya); public speech/critique and, 22, 75–76, 79, 81, 93–95, 107, 145, 150; questioned indigeneity of, 26, 58, 59, 65, 66–67, 187n32; stereotyped as terrorists, 19, 22, 73, 76, 118, 119, 121, 126 (*see also* CVE). *See also* abduction; paranoia; renditions; surveillance; violent extremism

Muslims, Kenyan (marginalization of), 7, 80, 125–26; Al-Shabaab recruitment and, 135; difficulty obtaining identification and, 21, 58, 95; dismissal of, 77, 79; drug trade seen as, 145; economic, 39, 99, 135, 144, 154; failure to condemn, 146; political inclusion to combat, 6; the Shifta War and, 38–39. *See also* Islamic Party of Kenya; policing, house raids and

Muslims, Kenyan (young men): criminalization of, 28, 135, 137, 142, 144, 146, 155; feelings of siege, 81–82; making sense of the world, 137, 150, 155–56; as manipulated/vulnerable, 28, 137, 146; psychological effect of disappeared peers, 135; reform and, 28, 137, 147, 148 (*see also* rehabilitation); stereotypes of, 6, 28, 133, 136, 137, 142–43, 152, 154–55. *See also* friendship

Muslims, Kenyan (young men, targeted by police), 84, 135, 147, 148; effect of arrest/imprisonment on social status, 153–54; police killings of, 111, 135; police roundups and, 57–58, 101, 126, 135–36; *Wanted* billboard and, 134–35, 144, 145. *See also* arrests, mass; CVE; disappearance, enforced; rehabilitation

Muslims, Swahili, 19, 57–58, 61, 82

Muslims for Human Rights (MUHURI), 77, 79, 94–95, 100, 105

Mutua, Makau, 52, 56

Mwakimako, Hassan, 95

Mwangi, Boniface, *78*, 79

Nairobi: Al-Qaeda attacks in, 3, 7, 58; Al-Shabaab attacks in, 19, 29–31, 56, 100–101, 128, 179n8; CVE in, 122, 125; detention in, 1–2, 22, 102; Eastleigh neighborhood, 19, 89, 102, 103, 111, 118, 130, 195n40; police support in, 79; security-related infrastructure in, 88–89; support for military in, 34; transport to Mogadishu from, 22–24, *23*, 102–3; transport to Uganda from, 83; UN counterterrorism conference in, 52. See also *Eye in the Sky* (Hood)

Nairobi, police security actions in, 83, 97, 109, 126, 130–31, 152; Eastleigh raid, 19–20, 89, 102, 111

Nasir, Abdillahi, 64

National Intelligence Service (NIS), 101, 137, 197n80

nationalism: accusations of subversion and, 41, 172n37, 181n47, 199n33; anticolonial, 48, 63, 64, 147, 172n37, 199n33; decolonization and, 38, 63, 64, 177n104; methodological, 14, 190n5; the military and, 31, 34, 46, 48, 52, 55, 180n27; Pan-African, 41; paternalism and, 52; rehabilitation programs and, 147; transnationalism and, 173n48

nationalism, Kenyan: decolonization and, 38, 48, 63, 177n104, 180n27; interventionism and, 52; the soldier-hero and, 31–32, 34, 46–47, 55, 180n27; subversion against, 181n47

nation-state, the: Africa as other and, 16; belonging beyond, 38, 61; enforcement of, 38; gendered interactions of, 14–15, 45–46, 54, 55; new, 58; reifying, 66; thinking beyond, 62, 75, 177n104. *See also* Brand Kenya

Ndzovu, Hassan, 64, 187n30

neocolonialism, 41, 74–75, 189n90. *See also* colonialism, continuity of

Nesiah, Vasuki, 171n30

networks: of detention, 192n49; of empire, 10, 12, 88; of informants, 137; of kinship, 116; of nonprofits, 77; of police power, 86; social, 117, 130–31; of suspected terror, 19, 43, 89, 115; of US counterterror operations, 10, 12, 26

NGOs (nongovernmental organizations): CVE and, 122; informants within, 146; Kenya Muslim Youth Alliance, 77; NGO Coordination Board, 105. *See also* Haki Africa

Ngũgĩ wa Thiong'o, 9; in exile, 140, 161; friendship with Abdilatif Abdalla, 140, *141*; the Haitian revolution and, 161; psychological terror and, 70; questioning the security apparatus and, 91, 98, 198n8; whiteness and, 69, 70

9/11: aftermath of 1998 embassy bombings and, 7; alliances prompted by, 14, 42, 159; imperial warfare and, 14, 112;

initiating a surveillance generation, 138; initiating war-making as worldmaking, 10; Osama bin Laden iconography and, 80; Yoweri Museveni and, 14; "radical" Islamic threat and, 7, 13; US terrorism law after, 100. *See also* counterterrorism; interventionism; soft power; United States, the; war on terror, the

Njoya, Wandiya, 70, 72–73, 74–75

Nkrumah, Kwame, 9, 41

nongovernmental organizations (NGOs): CVE and, 122; informants within, 146; Kenya Muslim Youth Alliance, 77; NGO Coordination Board, 105. *See also* Haki Africa

Nyabola, Nanjala, 20

Nyerere, Julius, 8, 9

OAU (Organization of African Unity), 35, 40–41. *See also* African Union, the

Obama, Barack, 49, 50, 108

Odinga, Raila, 20, 30, 150

Ogada, Mordecai, 74, 75

Okazawa-Rey, Margo, 33

Olaloku-Teriba, Annie, 176n96

Oman, 63–64

Omi, Michael, 62

Onyango-Obbo, Charles, 46

order: Blackness as threat to, 50–51; colonial ideology of, 71, 86, 96, 97, 137; global, 9; Kenyan elites and, 86, 97; policing and, 86, 91, 97, 169n13

Organization of African Unity (OAU), 35, 40–41. *See also* African Union, the

Orientalism, 26, 59, 60, 67, 118, 120, 170n25

other, the, 15–16, 18. *See also* race; racialization

Owuor, Yvonne Adhiambo, 31

Padmore, George, 68

Paine, Robert, 138

Palestinians, 113, 114, 181n48, 197n83

Pan-Africanism: legitimating foreign intervention, 9, 28, 157–58, 161; reproducing racialized power formations, 9

paramilitary units: Rapid Response Team/ General Service Unit (GSU), 89, 101, 104, 126, 169n10; use in the Shifta War, 20, 38; US-trained, 5–6, 89, 126, 159, 169n10

paranoia: activists and, 86, 93–94, 105–6, 107; presidential–military relations and, 47; social, 110–11, 115, 117, 127, 129, 138; young Muslim men and, 28, 137, 138, 151–52, 156

paternalism, 15, 29, 37, 40, 52, 161; feminized, 54

pathologization: of African security forces, 12; of anticolonial insurgency, 69, 200n51; of colonial populations, 200n51; of "extremism," 21, 61, 81, 142, 154; of the Kenyan coast, 80, 81; of lived experience, 61, 79, 143, 154

performance: of care work, 54; geopolitical, 15, 25, 28, 53; of masculinity, 35–36, 48; of racial equality, 160; of security, 21; of sovereignty, 35, 54

peripheries, 8, 13, 14, 39, 159, 171n30, 178n117

Peterson, Kristin, 86, 164

Pierre, Jemima, 17, 67–68, 176n85

police: as agents of abuse, 27, 77, 85, 98, 127 (*see also* disappearance, enforced; extrajudicial killings; policing, house raids and); coastal cooperation campaign, 77–79, *78*; conflicting framing in Westgate attack, 29–30; demands for identification, 57–58; election violence by, 85; increase under Uhuru Kenyatta, 5; mosque raids by, 84–85, 101–2, 135, 150–51, 155; plain-clothes, 30, 83, 104, 131; public trust and, 77–79, *78*, 125; questioned effectiveness in Haiti, 159; resistance to, 57–58, 61; special units under Daniel Arap Moi, 98, 198n8; spectral violence of, 27, 85; use of military tactics, 27; US training of special units, 12, 26, 81, 86, 87, 89. *See also* ATPU; paramilitary units policing: amorphous, 89, 152, 182n70; colonial roots of, 97, 98, 137; consent to, 125; geographies of, 4; investment in, 88; IPK strike and, 99–100; justifying, 58, 73; new modes of, 26; normalization of, 77, 79; opacity of, 27, 85, 86, 91, 94, 102–3; order and, 86, 91, 97; population-centered, 27, 111, 148 (*see also* Kenyan Muslims, as suspect population; violent extremism); stabilization as, 169n13; supranational actors and, 27, 85, 89–90, 92; technologies of, 4; threats of, 75; understandings of citizenship and, 21–22. *See also* ATPU; CVE; disappearance, enforced; extrajudicial killings; security

policing, house raids and: confrontation by inhabitants, 108; Eastleigh and, 19, 89, 102, 111; enduring effects of, 113, 114, 127, 132; extrajudicial killings and, 81, 111, 114; as intrusion on the feminine, 27, 111, 127; as intrusion on the private, 27, 111; Majengo and, 101; as state terror, 126

policy, 18, 145; foreign, 14–15, 43, 48–49, 160; gendered language of, 115–16, 122–23; land, 71

policymakers: African security forces and, 12, 35, 43; American dependence on Africa and, 160; Kenyan lobbying of, 188n74; normalizing obfuscating language, 4, 59; racialization of Africa and, 15–16; soft power and, 122; speculation and, 106; the "violent extremist" category and, 148

policymakers, Kenyan: African/Arab Islam distinction and, 65; Al-Shabaab and, 44, 58, 76, 150; homogenizing of Muslims and, 59, 154; inclusion rhetoric and, 76; mythologizing of masterminds, 116–17; western legacy and, 72–73

Polisi Ni Rafiki (the police are our friends), *78*, 79

political economy, 13, 15, 17, 28, 33

politics: Christian domination of, 22, 38, 65, 80; of concealment, 159; creating categories and, 148; cultural analysis of, 79; depoliticization, 6, 35, 38, 90; elites of, 9, 97, 142, 154; frustration and, 79, 80, 84, 99, 135, 146, 150, 154; identities and, 16, 48, 66, 99, 135, 170n25; ideology of, 80–81, 150, 193n65; landscape of, 101, 115, 117–18; masculinity and, 15, 35–36, 45–49; Muslim inclusion and, 6, 22, 76, 99; political consciousness, 7, 61, 82; political culture, 22, 148, 186n9; political potential, 143, 144; political violence, 80–81, 175n76; reform and, 98; of standing one's ground, 61, 79, 129, 150; of staying in place, 186n12; of warning, 115, 117, 195n29. *See also* anticolonialism; Brand Kenya; geopolitics; interventionism; Islamic Party of Kenya

postcolonialism, 14, 16, 20, 21, 27, 48, 52, 59; enduring presence of colonialism in, 60, 70, 72–73, 74, 79–80, 96, 117, 159; racialization and, 63; scholarship of, 112

post-traumatic stress disorder (PTSD), 44–45, 149

power: collecting information on, 91; decentering, 158; dispersal of, 88; embodied knowledge and, 94; imperial, 9, 10, 94, 104, 107 (*see also* colonialism); institutions of, 81; operations of, 82, 144; phantom, 3, 24, 27, 85–86, 93, 94, 106; relations of, 10, 27, 56, 60, 81, 111–12, 115; soft, 60, 111, 115, 122 (*see also* CVE); specific workings of, 86; state, 5, 48, 65 (*see also* ATPU; Kenya Defense Forces; policing). *See also* masculinity; militarism; surveillance

preemption, 120, 137, 148, 169n13. *See also* risk

Prestholdt, Jeremy, 80–81, 99

private, the: friendship as, 136–37; the
    home as, 27, 111, 112, 113, 117, 121, 125
PTSD (post-traumatic stress disorder),
    44–45, 149

race: as contingent/unstable, 16, 19, 28,
    61–63, 161; as geographic difference,
    18, 67; identity and, 17, 19; imbrication
    with religion, 17; imperialism and, 16,
    176n82; indigeneity and, 26; logics of,
    60; maintaining divisions of, 65; other-
    ing and, 15–16, 18; overlap with space,
    63–65 (see also Kenya, coast of); pro-
    cesses of, 176n96, 185n2; racial liberal-
    ism, 17, 49–51; refashioned/reproduced
    through warfare, 17, 25, 35, 49; signifi-
    cations of, 73; Zanzibari intellectuals
    on, 64. See also Blackness; ethnicity;
    Pan-Africanism
race, hierarchy and, 18, 33, 49, 50, 61–62,
    176n85; colonial, 16–17, 65, 69–70, 74
    (see also colonialism, racial systems
    of); global systems of, 62, 75; and
    Islam as alien, 65; overcoming, 49;
    performances of equality and, 160;
    reinforcement of, 50; reproduction of,
    9; tourism and, 74
race-making, 7, 35, 49, 158, 160
racial capitalism, 16, 62, 67, 75, 185n2,
    192n55
racialization: of Africa, 4, 17, 49, 54, 118;
    as/of Arabs, 21, 26, 58, 59, 62, 63; as
    Asian, 63; of capacity to govern, 17, 48;
    experiences of, 19; of the global order,
    9, 16, 45, 49, 62, 75, 176n85; hierarchies
    and, 16–17, 49, 62, 74, 75, 176n85; his-
    tories of, 59; humanity and, 184n97; of
    international knowledge, 16; within
    Kenyan Muslims, 19; multiple orders
    of, 62, 63; of Muslim mobility, 66,
    73, 116; of Muslim women, 126; pre-
    colonial, 63–64; processes of, 63, 73,
    176n96, 185n2; reform and, 148; of
    risk, 60, 67; as/of Somalis, 21, 29, 35,

53, 56, 63, 77; subordination and, 62,
    68; of surveillance, 28, 120; of suspi-
    cion, 22, 77, 115, 121; as Swahili, 21, 26,
    58, 59; of threat, 17, 28, 29, 35, 88, 102,
    154; of urban spaces, 88; of violence,
    16, 60. See also Blackness; colonial-
    ism, racial systems of; rehabilitation;
    whiteness
racism: attempts to counter, 129; defini-
    tion of, 172n38; imperialism/colonial-
    ism and, 16, 69–70, 157; symbolic
    victory over, 17; in the US, 49, 50–51,
    161. See also colonialism, racial sys-
    tems of
radicalization: as everyday concern, 144;
    familial responsibility and, 112–13;
    mothers' insights on, 124; as nonna-
    tive, 58, 66–67; perceived sources of,
    112–13, 151; rehabilitation and, 134; state
    discourse of, 75–76
Rancière, Jacques, 91
Rapid Response Team (RRT)/General
    Service Unit (GSU), 89, 126, 169n10
Razack, Sherene, 52
reform: land policy and, 71; political,
    98; security sector, 88; young Muslim
    men and, 28, 137, 147, 148 (see also
    rehabilitation)
refugees, 13; Somali, 52, 89, 111, 135; tor-
    ture of, 2, 168n6
rehabilitation, 28; as basis for prison sys-
    tems, 147; colonial, 70, 147; as homog-
    enizing, 154; recidivism prevention
    and, 146–47; as required, 152; skepti-
    cism of, 148–49
renditions: community news of,
    130; definition of, 168n3; gen-
    dered impacts of, 127, 168n6; to
    Guantanamo, 83; Kampala attacks
    and, 83, 95; to Mogadishu, 103;
    paramilitary units and, 5; 2007
    Kenya–Somalia border action and,
    2, 95, 168n6. See also disappearance,
    enforced; kidnapping

resistance: anticolonial, 37, 38, 69, 72, 97, 137, 139–40, 147; to antiterror laws, 100; to domestication and brokenness, 202n15; friendship as, 138; liberal feminist conceptualization of, 126; security risk assessment and, 86; to structural power, 134. *See also* Land and Freedom Army (Mau Mau)

Rice, Condoleeza, 49, 50

rights activists, 21, 76, 83–84, 90, 100, 117, 129; Muslim Human Rights Forum, 22–24, 24. *See also* Haki Africa; human rights organizations

risk: anticipation of, 24, 27, 87, 103–4, 148; assessment of, 87, 103; distribution to US-trained African forces, 4, 106; negotiation of, 82; perceived, 44, 86, 89, 123; racialization of, 60, 67; travel advisories and, 60. *See also* preemption

Rogo, Aboud, 94–95, 103, 135, 136, 149–50, 192n45, 200n57

RRT (Rapid Response Team)/General Service Unit (GSU), 89, 126, 169n10

Ruto, William, 14, 48–49

Rwanda, 13, 14, 37, 41

Said, Edward, 59

Saleh, Zainab, 159

Samatar, Abdi, 182n67

Saudi Arabia, 100, 110, 174n69

Scott, David, 139

secrecy, 55, 85, 90, 91–92, 102–3, 107, 137–38, 139

security: cultural politics of, 36; as frame, 22, 143–44, 146; good/bad citizenship and, 22, 77–78; ICU as providing, 42; imperative of, 22, 76–77; Kenya's special responsibility to, 15; Kenya's unilateral action on, 43; language of, 40; logics of, 44; militarization as fundamental to, 33, 39, 40; performance of, 21; personal calculations of, 27, 103,

117; questioning of, 145; as racializing, 21; regimes of, 21; suspicious behavior and, 91–92, 94, 125, 149; tourism and, 60, 67; understanding of citizenship and, 21–22; US assistance for, 5. *See also* CVE; policing; preemption; war on terror, the

security, Kenya's partnerships in, 3, 8, 42, 80, 87, 89, 103; Euro-American, 6, 88, 105, 109, 159; Israel, 89, 136, 169n10, 191n25; public critique of, 122, 135; US, 8, 104, 109–10, 159 (*see also* AFRICOM)

security apparatus, Kenyan, 135, 149, 191n25; colonial roots of, 38; doubts as to effectiveness, 101–2; as gendered, 29, 45–46; identification documents and, 57–58; lack of information and, 102; material infrastructure of, 88–89; National Intelligence Service, 101, 137, 197n80; propaganda for, 25, 36, 52–53, 55–56; protection from, 149; public trust in, 77–79, 78, 125; risk assessment and, 103; US relationship with, 104. *See also* ATPU; paramilitary units; police; surveillance

security experts, 19, 59, 111, 145, 154

security forces, 12, 182n70; AFRICOM reliance on in Africa, 88; deployment tied to aid, 88; Eastleigh Raid and, 19–20, 89, 102, 111; the Leahy Law and, 89, 159, 191n23; raids in Mombasa, 57, 58; reform and, 88; reframing of, 12, 25, 35; Westgate Mall attack and, 29–30. *See also* AMISOM; RRT

security state, the, 22, 25, 92, 102

Shabibi, Namir, 169n10

Shalhoub-Kevorkian, Nadera, 113

Sharif, Abubaker, 135, 136

Shariff, Ibrahim Noor, 71

Shifta War, the, 20, 25, 35, 38–39

Shohat, Ella, 9

Singh, Nikhil Pal, 49, 184n97

slavery, 9, 63, 139, 157, 160, 161, 176n96
Smith, Malinda, 168n6
social media: critique of tourism industry on, 74; deleting, 151–52; documenting prayer on, 108; Kenyan opinion of Somalis on, 52; public opinion of the military on, 29, 34, 55; questioning the security state on, 134–35; seeking disappeared people on, 131
soft power, 60, 111, 115, 122. *See also* CVE
solidarities: overlooked, 139; Pan-African, 28, 157; race and, 160–61; in relations to power, 7, 61, 139, 140–41, 146, 155, 161; severing, 161, 162; South–South, 9
Somalia: AMISOM and, 14, 43–44, 174n66; calls for dissolution of, 52; care work in, 54; CIA-backed warlords in, 42; drone warfare in, 4, 10, 87; El Adde attack in, 34; Islamic Courts Union, 1, 3, 42; Mogadishu, 1, 2, 24, 40, 52, 102–3; northeastern Kenya's relationship to, 38; as place of war, 26; refugees in Kenya, 52, 111; Somalia Front-line States Summit, 40; support for Kenyan action in, 34; US withdrawal from, 8. *See also* Al-Shabaab; Kenya, ethnic Somalis in
Somalia, Ethiopian invasion of (2006): AMISOM and, 43, 174n66; as antiterror action, 42; refugees from, 1–3; renditions and, 2–3; United Nations backing of, 43; US backing of, 1, 42–43
Somalia, Kenyan invasion of (2011), 5, 30, 39–40, 177n70; AMISOM and, 43; effects of extended deployment, 44–45; international law and, 40, 182n69; as new interventionism, 14–15; questioning repercussions of, 135
South Africa, 13, 109
special operations forces, 87, 159, 169n13; *Mission to Rescue* (Foxton Media) and, 25, 36, 52–53, 55–56

spectacle, 4, 21, 46, 55, 97, 102, 106–7, 117
Springer, Simon, 66
stability: international, 52; Kenya as beacon of, 14, 26, 49, 60, 73; need for, 19, 52; Somalia and, 1, 42, 44, 52; and white comfort, 26, 60, 71, 74
Stoler, Ann, xii, 158–59, 178n117
subaltern populations: empire's relations with, 56; knowledge of, 82, 130; resistance and, 141; romanticizing of, 9
Sudan, 13, 99, 100, 186n27
Supreme Council of Kenyan Muslims (SUPKEM), 98, 193n63
surveillance: of activists, 86; aerial, 113, 118, 119, 120; civil society as space of, 60, 198n6; colonial, 199n33; of the home, 113, 114, 119; justifying, 58; Kenyan history of, 137; of Kenyan Muslims as a whole, 19; MYSTIC monitoring program, 90, 138; new modes of, 26, 113, 118 (*see also* drones); opacity of, 24; and personal security, 103, 117; protection from effects, 144; provoking resistance, 146; racialized, 28; rehabilitation and, 148, 149; risk assessment and, 87, 103; of telecommunications, 90, 101, 137–38, 197n80; of 2007 Kenyan returnees, 3; US-supplied, 42, 55. *See also* informants
surveillance, awareness of, 136, 138, 143, 153, 155; anxiety prompted by, 79, 129, 148, 149, 156. *See also* paranoia
Suttner, Raymond, 54
Swahilis, 19, 66, 185n6; as foreign, 26, 58, 59; as indigenous, 65; racialization and, 21, 26, 58, 59; Swahili language, 176n92

Tahir, Madiha, 12, 88
Tanzania, 1, 100; Dar es Salaam, 3, 7, 139. *See also* Nyere, Julius
Tate, Winifred, 90
Taussig, Michael, 91–92

terrorism: as amorphous, 87, 89, 152, 183n70; antiterrorism legislation, 3, 97, 100–101, 150, 171n28; as barbaric, 33; Kenya as front line against, 5; Muslim activism tied to, 95, 101, 128; psychological, 70; rhetoric of, 126; risk of tied to aid, 44, 169n16; state, 20, 103, 126 (*see also* disappearance, enforced; extrajudicial killings; policing); threat of, 16; US, 11. *See also* Al-Shabaab; counterterrorism; Kenyan Muslims, as suspect population; radicalization; rehabilitation; violent extremism

terrorists: fear of, 60; as hiding within civilian space, 112–13; Mau Mau as, 20, 97; potential suspects, 27; as threat to tourism, 73

terrorists, stereotypes of, 6, 14, 73, 120, 143; as foreign, 17, 58, 66; social and kinship ties and, 90–91; as "violent extremists," 28, 42, 137, 142, 148, 154; *Wanted* billboard and, 144

terror suspects: believed diffuse networks of, 89; detention of, 1–2, 24; legal cases against, 90 (*see also* detention of activists); military involved in arresting/detaining, 32; military tactics to track, 27, 90, 106, *119*, 138 (*see also* surveillance); political identity and, 135; social ties and, 90–91, 134–35. *See also* policing, house raids and

Thiranagama, Sharika, 142–43

torture: at Abu Ghraib, 144; colonial-era, 36; of detained refugees, 2, 168n6; intercepted content and, 90, 138; laws against, 168n3; under Daniel Arap Moi, 98; of Mombasa residents, 81; of Wajir residents, 39

tourism: branding whiteness and, 74; Brand Kenya and, 14, 26, 59, 60, 67, 68, 72, 74; coastal reliance on, 58, 75, 76, 80, 199n42; the coast as Oriental and, 26, 59–60, 67; colonial nostalgia and, 26, 59, 60, 71–72, 74–75, 186n6; Jomo Kenyatta

presidency and, 71; land ownership and, 58; Mayers Ranch and, 71–72; as mode of power, 67; travel advisories and, 60, 73–74, 76, 171n28; whiteness and, 59, 60, 67, 68, 71, 73, 74–75

transnationality: crime and, 89–90; familial/domestic, 116; feminism and, 27, 112; of governance, 5; imaginaries of, 99; of Muslim militancy, 67; of Muslim mobility, 2, 62, 66, 116, 130, 195n32; nationalism and, 173n48; racialization and, 62; solidarity and, 7, 162. *See also* interventionism

trauma: house raids and, 113, 114, 127, 132; imprisonment and, 149, 152; the Mau Mau legacy and, 180n26; post-traumatic stress disorder, 36, 44–45; 2007 election violence and, 72

Trouillot, Michel Rolph, 61, 81, 167n13

Uganda: AFRICOM and alliances, 42; Al-Shabaab bombings in, 24, 83, 95, 102, 109, 110, 168n18; AMISOM and, 14, 43, 174n66; arrest of Al-Amin Kimathi in, 95; critique of Kenya by, 45, 46, 48; military spending of, 13, 15; Yoweri Museveni and, 14, 40, 45, 48; rendition to, 83, 95, 109. *See also* Kampala

Uganda, imprisonment in, 24, 95, 117, 132, 192n49; Luzira prison, 95, 117, 126–27, 129, 132, 192n49

United Kingdom, the, 99, 171n28; activists from, 168n18; as authorizing police action, 83, 85, 104, 191n24; government representatives of, 85; MI6, 89, 105; security personnel from, 83, 89, 102, 104, 105 (see also *Eye in the Sky* (Hood)); training/funding special police units, 81, 83, 135–36, 169n10; travel advisories and, 76. *See also* colonialism

United Muslims of Africa (UMA), 100

United Nations, the: the African Union and, 174n69, 182n59; AMISOM and, 43; Charter Article 51 of, 40, 182n69;

intervention in Haiti and, 157, 201n7; Kenya as hub for, 8; Kenya's bid for Security Council seat in, 51–52; legitimation of Ethiopian invasion of Somalia, 42–43; peacekeeping missions, 14, 45, 52, 173n56; and realities of security actions, 43, 149; "responsibility to protect" doctrine and, 35, 41; Security Council of, 42–43, 52, 157, 182n59, 192n45; support of indefinite detention, 149

United States, the: access to Kenyan military facilities, 8 (*see also* AFRICOM); Africa as gray zone and, 4; "African solutions to African problems" and, 28, 160; AMISOM and, 43, 44; as authorizing police action, 85, 92, 96, 104, 109, 136, 191n24; backing of Ethiopian invasion of Somalia, 42–43; Brand Kenya support from, 72; counterinsurgency thinking of, 86, 172n37; Department of Defense of, 5, 55, 105, 190n16, 202n12; dissociation from violence, 16, 160, 172n42; drone use and, 10, 54–55, 93; embassy bombings in East Africa, 3, 7, 58; embassy presence in Kenya, 5, 7, 58, 96, 104, 129; empire and, 8, 88, 159, 160, 168n8, 171n30; FBI, 2, 7, 58, 131–32, 172n37; funding from, 12, 44, 81, 83, 104, 160, 185n7, 190n16, 202n12 (*see also* Leahy Law, the); hunt for Osama bin Laden and, 113, 118; ICU and, 42; interrogation of terror suspects, 83; and local/foreign Muslim distinction, 66; National Security Agency of, 90, 137–38; partner forces in general, 12, 86, 87–88, 159, 160, 161; partnership with Kenya, 8, 104, 109–10 (*see also* ATPU); Patriot Act, 100, 171n28; pitfalls of centering on, 8, 12, 173n48; race and racism in, 49; role in detentions, 24, 96; security assistance from, 5, 8, 169n16; State Department of, 41, 104, 181n23, 185n7,

202n12; terror infrastructure of, 11; training of African forces, 4, 27, 44 (*see also* ATPU); travel advisories issued, 76; unchecked power of, 80; waning hegemony of, 25. *See also* CIA

urban spaces: colonial policing in, 97; geographies of, 27, 81, 86, 88, 103, 107; material ruin of, 88; military tactics in, 87; police as infrastructure of, 88–89; racialization of, 88; risk assessment and, 86; war on terror reshaping, 106–7

US Africa Command (AFRICOM): base and detention sites of, 10–11, *11*, 26, 55–56, 172n42; creation of, ix–x; gray-zone operations of, 87–88; military partnerships and, 42, 88, 172n42

violence: Africa as plagued by, 7, 12, 15–16, 26; anticipation of, 106–7; anti-Somali, 20; asphyxiatory, 82; colonial, 64, 67, 72, 74; distributed capacity for, 12, 16; as haunting, 114; imperial, 20; IPK strike and, 99–100; legitimate/illegitimate, 30, 33, 53, 69, 79, 118, 121; making sense of, 136; matrix of, 87; Muslim stereotypes and, 17, 19, 59 (*see also* Kenya, coast of; Kenyan Muslims, as suspect population); papered over, 64; political, 80–81, 175n76; public demonstrations and, 150; racial, 67; racialized, 9; resistance to, 72 (*see also* Land and Freedom Army); spikes in, 75, 76; as state prerogative, 91, 114; stereotypes of African security forces and, 35, 88; structural, 169n15; supranational actors and, 27; threat of, 10; tourism and, 67; 2007 presidential elections and, 5, 13, 72, 85, 157, 175n70; Wajir security operation and, 39; white supremacy and, 72–73, 74. *See also* Ethiopia, invasion of Somalia; extrajudicial killings; policing; policing, house raids and; terrorism; warfare; war on terror, the violence, colonialism and, 72, 74, 96, 113, 157, 199n29; as post-colonial inheritance, 35, 38, 39

violent extremism: CVE and, 60, 77, 102, 115–16, 122, 123, 148; as excuse for surveillance and policing, 58; police as extremists, 126; political alliances to fight, 42; rehabilitation and, 28, 137, 148, 154; rhetoric of, 21, 126, 154; stereotypes and, 60, 73, 126, 142, 148, 154–55 (*see also* Kenyan Muslims (young men), targeted by police)

visuality, 118, 119, 120, 172n45

Wajir, 10, 32, 39, 104

war: as civilized violence, 33; as diffuse, 3; endless, 7, 9, 24, 44, 172n45; intelligence as weapon of, 137–38; as making/unmaking, 142–43; masculinity and, 35–36, 183n89, 184n107; as necessary evil, 53; questioning, 32, 56; racial liberalism as cover for, 49–51; reality of, 5, 34, 36, 125; sites experienced as war zones, 4, 27, 81, 113; strategized in the civilian realm, 112; support for, 33, 34, 144; as unmaking worlds, 15, 27, 36, 169n15. *See also* violence

war-making: AMISOM as apparatus for, 43; conventional use of detention in, 147; as cultural field, 13; domestic, 142; imperial, 12, 14, 45, 112, 121; intertwined with race-making, 49, 158, 160–61; legitimation of, 48; masculinity and, 35–36, 45–49, 53, 54, 183n89; popular consent and, 56, 125, 144; refashioned/reproduced race and, 17. *See also* counterinsurgency; gray zones

war on terror, the: accountability and, 85; Africanization of, 40; alliances in, 5, 48–49, 91, 96 (*see also* security, Kenya's partnerships in); beginnings in East Africa, 7–8; citizenship and, 21–22, 26, 59; as civilizational project, 13, 33;

consequences for Muslims globally, 7, 155; critical reflection on, 130, 155; as form of police action, 4, 27, 85, 86; gender and, 115–16, 123–25, 127, 129, 132, 137; the home and, 115, 118–21 (*see also* policing, house raids and); infrastructure of, 96, 110; the Kenyan military and, 25, 30–32, 36, 48–49, 53; Kenya's place in the world and, 6–7, 17; motivations for, 80; Muslim mobility and, 2, 66, 116, 130, 195n32, 197nn82–83; visuality and, 118, 119, 120, 172n45; war rooms of, 118, 121. *See also* gray zones; policing; surveillance

war on terror, African responsibility in, 14, 15, 17, 40, 88; as Kenya's war, 14, 31, 32–33, 34, 40, 53, 55 (see also *Mission to Rescue* (Foxton Media)); logics of, 32; masculinity and, 15, 25, 45–46, 48–49, 53, 55; meaningful participation and, 13; and military solutions to political problems, 5; national consciousness and, 31; political and economic interests of, 80; popular support for, 7, 25, 31–32, 34, 36, 55, 56 (*see also* soft power); "rehabilitation" and, 149, 155; reshaping public attitudes and, 111–12; secrecy and, 91–92, 107; subaltern knowledge and, 130; surveillance and, 137, 146; as war on Islam and Muslims, 7, 61, 66, 80; as worldmaking, 10

war on terror, as expanding/elastic, 12, 87–88, 107, 110, 115, 121, 137, 168n8. *See also* policing, house raids and

war on terror, embodied dimensions of, 19, 21–24, 155–56; activism and, 90–91; anxiety and, 79, 103, 129, 148, 149, 156 (*see also* paranoia); collective support and, 126–27; disorientation and, 130; gendered labor and, 123–24; navigating policed landscapes and, 27, 86, 87, 94, 103, 130, 133; physical/emotional stress, 108–9, 128–30, 132; stereotypes of young Muslim men and, 6, 137, 143, 155; travel restrictions and, 109, 110, 132. *See also* geopolitics, as everyday reality; homeplace, the; rehabilitation

war on terror, the: as long war, 19–21

Weitzberg, Keren, 20–21, 38, 176n93, 177n104, 181n42

Westgate Mall attack, 19, 29–31, 56, 100–101, 128, 179n8

Wexler, Laura, 121

Whitaker, Hannah, 39, 181n48

White, Luise, 124–25

whiteness: as claim to civilization, 68; as claim to modernity, 49, 68, 70; colonial, 26, 59, 60, 67, 68, 69; colonial policing and, 97; as constructed, 68, 69; and racialized hierarchies, 16–17, 49, 69, 70, 192n54; tourism and, 59, 60, 68, 71, 74, 75

white supremacy: colonial rhetoric and, 68, 69, 70, 187n43; enduring, 16, 26; histories of, 59; logics of, 72; media and, 118; symbolic victory over, 17; tourism and, 72, 74–75; violence and, 72–73, 74; white saviorism, 49

Winant, Howard, 62

worldmaking: conflicting nature of, 9–10, 172n39; creating public consent and, 56; defining, 9–10; expanding war on terror and, 10–15, 35–36 (*see also* Kenya, security partnerships of; masculinity); the home and, 28,

132–33; imperialism as, 172n39; interrelation beyond borders and, 7, 61, 158; knowledge-making as, 61, 92 (*see also* geopolitics, as everyday reality); labor of, 73 (*see also* tourism: colonial nostalgia and); lifeworlds and, 21, 26, 86, 107, 161 (*see also* homeplace, the; urban spaces); mapping power and, 10–15 (*see also* geopolitics; power); new modes of, 28, 73, 80, 82, 107, 115 (*see also* friendship); as ongoing process, 10, 25, 36, 59, 75 (*see also* race; racialization); the past and, 162; as productive of other worlds, 36; reconstituting the global order and, 9; through interventionism, 36; transnational solidarity and, 7, 162; urban spaces and, 86. *See also* interventionism

worldmaking, remaking and, 7, 24, 25, 56; anticolonialism and, 9; ongoing processes of, 10; personal security and, 27. *See also* friendship

Yemen, 10, 54, 55

Zanzibar: Abdulrahman Babu and, 139; intellectual culture of, 64, 176n92, 186n22; international film festival of, 53; as part of a coastal state, 64–65, 186n26

Zeleza, Paul, 176n96

Printed and bound by CPI Group (UK) Ltd, Croydon, CR0 4YY

24/11/2024

14598081-0002